NON-STATE ACTORS, SOFT LAW AND PROTECTIVE REGIMES

By offering critical perspectives of normative developments within international law, this volume unites academics from various disciplines to address concerns regarding the interpretation and application of international law in context. The authors present common challenges within international criminal law, human rights, environmental law and trade law, and point to unintended risks and consequences, in particular for vulnerable interests, such as women and the environment. Omissions within normative or institutional frameworks are highlighted. Further, the importance of addressing accountability of state and non-state actors for violations or regressions of minimum protection guarantees is underscored. Overall, it advocates harmonization over fragmentation, pursuant to the aspiration of asserting the interests of our collective humanity, without necessarily advocating an international constitutional order.

CECILIA M. BAILLIET is a professor at the Faculty of Law, University of Oslo, where she is also Deputy Director of the Department of Public and International Law and Director of the Master's Program in Public International Law. Her fields of research include international public law, human rights, refugee law and counter-terrorism.

NON-STATE ACTORS, SOFT LAW AND PROTECTIVE REGIMES: FROM THE MARGINS

Edited by

CECILIA M. BAILLIET

CAMBRIDGE
UNIVERSITY PRESS

CAMBRIDGE
UNIVERSITY PRESS

32 Avenue of the Americas, New York NY 10013-2473, USA

Cambridge University Press is part of the University of Cambridge.

It furthers the University's mission by disseminating knowledge in the pursuit of education, learning and research at the highest international levels of excellence.

www.cambridge.org
Information on this title: www.cambridge.org/9781107021853

First published 2012
First paperback edition 2014

A catalogue record for this publication is available from the British Library

Library of Congress Cataloguing in Publication data

Non-state actors, soft law, and protective regimes : from the margins / [edited by] Cecilia M. Bailliet.
p. cm.
ISBN 978-1-107-02185-3 (Hardback)
1. International law. 2. Soft law. I. Bailliet, Cecilia.
KZ1293.N66 2012
341.2–dc23
2012017171

ISBN 978-1-107-02185-3 Hardback

For Marianne, with whom I share a renewed appreciation of sisterhood due to our parallel experience of motherhood.

and

For Julian, who used to fall asleep to my stories of superheroes and is now trying to save the planet by harnessing the sun.

In honour of our mother, Esther, proceeds of this volume will be donated to a charity supporting education for girls.

CONTENTS

NOTES ON CONTRIBUTORS

SUMUDU ATAPATTU is the Associate Director of the Global Legal Studies Center and Senior Lecturer at University of Wisconsin Law School. She teaches international environmental law, and is author of *Emerging Principles on International Environmental Law* (2006). Dr Atapattu holds an LLM (public international law) and a Ph.D. (international environmental law) from the University of Cambridge (UK); and is an attorney-at-law of the Supreme Court of Sri Lanka. She is also the Lead Counsel for Poverty and Human Rights at the Center for International Sustainable Development Law in Montreal, Canada. Before moving to the US, she was an associate professor at the Faculty of Law, University of Colombo and a consultant to the Law & Society Trust, Colombo.

CECILIA M. BAILLIET Professor, Deputy Director of the Department of Public and International Law, and Director of the Master's Program in Public International Law at the University of Oslo. She has a doctoral degree in law from the University of Oslo and a combined JD/MA (honours) degree from the George Washington University Law School & Elliott School of International Affairs. She has served as consultant to national and international organizations, and her research has been the basis for the creation of guidelines in various institutions. Her research addresses the vulnerability of humanity, examining the cross-fields of international public law, human rights, women's law, refugee law, humanitarian law and counter-terrorism. Among her publications are: *Security: A Multidisciplinary Normative Approach* (2009) and *Cosmopolitan Justice and Its Discontents* (co-edited with Katja Franko Aas, 2011).

KARIMA BENNOUNE is a professor of law and Arthur L. Dickson Scholar at the Rutgers School of Law, Newark (USA). She is a former legal adviser for Amnesty International, and a former member of the Board of Directors of Amnesty International – USA. Bennoune served as a Center for Women's Global Leadership delegate to the NGO Forum at the Fourth World

Conference on Women in Beijing. Her article, 'Terror/Torture' (*Berkeley Journal of International Law* (2008)), was designated one of the top-ten global security law review articles of 2008 by Oxford University Press. In 2011, she won the Chancellor's Distinguished Research Award at Rutgers University, Newark (USA). She is currently writing a book about Muslim opponents of fundamentalism.

REBECCA M. BRATSPIES is a professor of law at the CUNY School of Law, New York City, where she teaches international law, environmental law, administrative law and property. She has published widely on regulation of genetically modified organisms, and on the intersection of human rights and environmental regulation. Her recent work focuses on how the role of legal systems can promote sustainability. She is a research scholar with the Center for Progressive Reform, an appointed member of the ABA Standing Committee on Environmental Law, and a vice-chair of the ABA Section on Energy, Environment and Resources. She holds a BA in Biology from Wesleyan University and a JD *cum laude* from the University of Pennsylvania.

CHRISTINE BYRON joined Cardiff Law School in September 2008 and teaches public international law, human rights law and criminal law at an undergraduate level and international humanitarian law at a postgraduate level. Prior to joining Cardiff, she worked as a lecturer in law at the University of Manchester. She is a graduate in law from Newcastle University and received her LLM and Ph.D. from the University of Liverpool. After completing her master's degree, she spent six months working as a law clerk at the International Criminal Tribunal for the former Yugoslavia, before commencing her doctorate. Her monograph on war crimes and crimes against humanity in the Rome Statute of the International Criminal Court, which is based on her doctoral thesis of the same name, has recently been published. She has been involved in the training of humanitarian workers and military lawyers, both in this country and abroad, for several years.

HILARY CHARLESWORTH is an Australian Research Council Laureate Fellow and Distinguished Professor of International Law and Human Rights at the Australian National University, Canberra. She has written extensively on feminist analysis of international law, including with Christine Chinkin *The Boundaries of International Law: A Feminist Analysis* (2000). Together with Christine Chinkin, she was awarded the Goler T. Butcher Medal of the American Society of International Law in 2006 for her contribution to the development of international human rights law. She is judge ad hoc in the ICJ in the *Whaling in Antarctica* case.

ANNE HELLUM is a lawyer and anthropologist who received a Doctor Juris degree from the University of Oslo. She is Professor at the Department of Public and International Law at the University of Oslo and Director of the Institute of Women's Law, Child Law Discrimination and Equality Law. Her research cuts across human rights law, discrimination law and anthropology of law. She has written extensively on the relationship between women's human rights and legal pluralism in Zimbabwe, South Africa, Pakistan and Norway. Her most recent publications are: *Human Rights, Gendered Realities and Plural Legalities* (with Julie Stewart, Amy Tsanga *et al.*, 2007); *Discrimination and Equality Law* (with Kirsten Ketscher, 2008); and *From Transnational Relations to Transnational Laws: Northern European Laws at the Crossroads* (with Shaheen S. Ali and Anne Griffiths, 2010). She is the recipient of a research grant from the Norwegian Research Council's Global Partner programme where she directs the project Gender, Human Rights and Water Governance, a comparative research on the human right to water in South Africa, Malawi, Zimbabwe and Kenya.

EDDA KRISTJÁNSDÓTTIR received her law degree from the New York University School of Law in 1998. She clerked at the International Court of Justice and subsequently worked as legal counsel at the Permanent Court of Arbitration, for, among others, the Eritrea–Ethiopia Claims Commission. Since 2005, she has worked at the University of Amsterdam Department of International Law, developing and managing the Oxford University Press online database International Law in Domestic Courts, and teaching public international law and dispute resolution. Ms Kristjánsdóttir is a member of the International Law Association's Committee on Reparations for Victims of Armed Conflict.

CATHARINE A. MACKINNON, the Elizabeth A. Long Professor of Law and long-term James Barr Ames Visiting Professor of Law at Harvard Law School, specializes in sex equality issues under international and constitutional law. She pioneered the legal claim for sexual harassment and, with Andrea Dworkin, created ordinances recognizing pornography as a civil rights violation. Representing Bosnian women survivors of Serbian genocidal sexual atrocities, Professor MacKinnon won with co-counsel a damage award of $745 million in August 2000 in *Kadić* v. *Karadžić*, which first recognized rape as an act of genocide. In addition to scholarly works that include: *Sex Equality* (2001), *Toward a Feminist Theory of the State* (1989), *Only Words* (1993), *Women's Lives, Men's Laws* (2005) and *Are Women Human?* (2006), she has published widely in journals and the popular press. Professor MacKinnon holds a BA from Smith College, a JD from Yale Law School, and a Ph.D. in political science from Yale. She has taught at Yale, Chicago, Harvard, Osgoode Hall, Stanford, Basel and Columbia, among others, and spent a year at the Institute for Advanced Study at Stanford. Professor MacKinnon practises and consults nationally and internationally, and works with Equality Now, an NGO promoting international sex equality rights for women, and the Coalition for Trafficking in Women. She has served as Special Gender Adviser to the Prosecutor of the International Criminal Court since November 2008.

FIONNUALA NÍ AOLÁIN is concurrently the Dorsey and Whitney Chair in Law at the University of Minnesota Law School and a professor of law at the University of Ulster's Transitional Justice Institute in Belfast, Northern Ireland. She is co-founder and Associate Director of the Institute. She has previously been Fellow at the Institute of Advanced Studies Hebrew University (Jerusalem) (2011–12); Visiting Scholar at Harvard Law School (1993–94); Associate-in-Law at Columbia Law School (1994–6); Visiting Professor at the School of International and Public Affairs, Columbia University (1996–2000); Associate Professor of Law at the Hebrew University in Jerusalem, Israel (1997–9); and Visiting Fellow at Princeton University (2001–2). She has published extensively in the fields of emergency powers, conflict regulation, transitional justice and sex-based violence in times of war.

HARI M. OSOFSKY is an associate professor with tenure and the 2011 Lampert Fesler Research Fellow at the University of Minnesota Law School. She is also the Associate Director of Law, Geography & Environment of the Consortium on Law and Values in Health, Environment & the Life Sciences and an affiliated faculty member in geography and conservation biology at the University of Minnesota. Osofsky has published a co-edited book on climate change litigation (Cambridge University Press, 2009), and has received peer recognition from both legal and geography scholars for her recent articles.

BEATE SJÅFJELL, Professor dr. juris at the University of Oslo, Faculty of Law, is the author of *Towards a Sustainable European Company Law: A Normative Analysis of the Objectives of EU Law, with the Takeover Directive as a Test Case* (2009). Beate is the project leader for the research project 'Sustainable Companies', and head of the Company Law Research Group at the Faculty of Law in Oslo. Beate has written a number of papers on EU company and securities law and the integration of sustainable development, including: 'Political Path Dependency in Practice: The Takeover Directive' (*Yearbook of European Law* (2008)); 'Internalizing Externalities in EU Law: Why Neither Corporate Governance nor Corporate Social Responsibility Provides the Answers' (*George Washington International Law Review* (2010)).

ACKNOWLEDGEMENTS

This book originated from the conference 'Creation of International Law: An Exploration of Normative Innovation, Contextual Application and Interpretation in a Time of Flux', hosted by the Department of Public and International Law of the University of Oslo, 6–7 August 2010. This venue brought together scholars from different sub-fields of international law. For several, it was the first time they had met each other. The presentation of research across disciplines proved stimulating and challenging, as we identified common concerns. We sought to promote the establishment of new cross-field networks and exchange of ideas, commencing with publication of this volume.

I wish to extend my warmest thanks to Professor Aslak Syse, Director of the Department of Public and International Law, Professor Ole Kristian Fauchald, Head of the Research Group on the Internationalization of Law, and Øyvind Henden, Administrative Head of Department, for understanding the importance of the conference and offering their generous support. We acknowledge the kind, practical assistance provided by Elisabeth Wenger-Hagene and Linn Bævre to the participants at the conference. The authors are indebted to the scholars who graciously offered commentary on initial drafts of the chapters, including Andreas Føllesdal, Ole Kristian Fauchald, Nobuo Hayashi, Simon O'Connor, Malcolm Langford, Christoffer Eriksen and Christina Voigt.

I also wish to extend appreciation to the commissioning editor at Cambridge University Press, Finola O'Sullivan for enabling this volume to come to fruition.

1

Introduction

CECILIA M. BAILLIET

International law has undergone tremendous evolution in recent years. The establishment of subsystems such as: international human rights, humanitarian law, international criminal law, trade law, and environmental law spawned a diversity of specialized institutions, tribunals, committees, normative frameworks, and dispute resolution mechanisms.[1] These include procedures for pursuing claims, assigning accountability for violations, and providing reparation for victims. Positive perspectives on the proliferation of regimes argue that this reflects the maturation of international law. One may consider the view of Bruno Simma:

> Each regime has thus established its separate epistemic communities of lawyers working in the field, institutions developing and applying the law, and courts and tribunals enforcing it ... The formation of specific methods of interpretation or enforcement is inherent in the set-up of such regimes, and the expertise that lawyers will accumulate by working within them, as well as bodies of case law of the various courts and tribunals mandated to interpret and enforce these regimes, will contribute to a growing and ever more dense corpus of law which responds to the needs of the specific regime. In a positive light, these sub-systems of international law, more densely integrated and more technically coherent, may show the way forward for general international law, as both laboratories and boosters for further progressive development at the global level.[2]

[1] See generally, Peter Malanczuk, *Akehurst's Modern Introduction to International Law* (7th edn., New York: Routledge, 1997), 7–8, addressing the vast expansion of areas of transnational concern.

[2] Bruno Simma, 'Universality of International Law from the Perspective of a Practitioner', *European Journal of International Law*, 20 (April 2009), 265, arguing that proliferation of tribunals and fragmentation have not prevented the development of coherent international law. See also Thomas M. Franck, *Fairness in International Law and Institutions* (New York: Oxford University Press, 1995).

In contrast, critical approaches reflect upon the emergence of stratified networks and conferences among expert scholars and government officials as possibly weakening the unity of the field.[3] The creation of internal orders may result in limited opportunities for critical review of normative or theoretical interpretation as external opinion may not be solicited or considered relevant. As an example, the majority of legal literature within the field of human rights is largely positive in orientation.[4] There is a revolving door between scholars and members of the UN human rights machinery (as well as close linkages to non-governmental organizations (NGOs)) which has benefits and drawbacks. Critical perspectives are more likely to come from fields external to law, such as anthropology and sociology.[5]

Furthermore, each subsystem functions autonomously, blocking reference to input from other subsystems.[6] Within humanitarian law, some scholars have effectively erected barriers to perspectives from human rights law. They dispute human rights experts' technical mastery of the concepts of international humanitarian law apply (e.g. "direct

[3] On fragmentation, see International Law Commission/Martii Koskenniemi, *Fragmentation of International Law: Difficulties Arising from the Diversification and Expansion of International Law*, A/CN.4/L.682 (April 13, 2006). See also Christoffer C. Eriksen and Marius Emberland, *The New International Law: An Anthology* (Leiden and Boston, MA: Martinus Nijhoff, 2010), addressing polycentric "decision-making structures and fragmented spheres of law."

[4] For a critical legal article, see Oona Hathaway, 'Why Do Nations Join Human Rights Treaties?', *Journal of Conflict Resolution*, 51(4) (2007), 588. See also: Beth Simmons, *Mobilizing for Human Rights: International Law in Domestic Politics* (New York: Cambridge University Press, 2009), presenting an alternative view; Elizabeth Bartholet, 'International Adoption: Thoughts on the Human Rights Issues', *Buffalo Human Rights Law Review*, 13 (2007), 151, criticizing UN and human rights NGOs. A forthcoming publication which promises critical perspectives is Frederic Megret and Philip Alston, *The United Nations and Human Rights: A Critical Appraisal* (New York and Oxford: Oxford University Press, 2011).

[5] See for example: Costas Douzinas, *Human Rights and Empire* (Routledge, 2007); Richard Ashby Wilson and Jon P. Mitchell, *Human Rights in Global Perspective* (London: Routledge, 2003); Anne Hellum, Shaheen Sardar Ali, and Anne Griffiths (eds.), *From Transnational Relations to Transnational Law: Northern European Laws at the Crossroads* (Farnham: Ashgate, 2011).

[6] Franceso Francioni, 'International Human Rights in an Environmental Horizon', *European Journal of International Law*, 21(1) (2010), 41, lamenting the reluctance of human rights courts to move beyond the "individualistic perspective" in order to address environmental claims in a meaningful way. See also Petros C. Mavroiodis, 'No Outsourcing of Law? WTO as Practiced by WTO Courts', *American Journal of International Law*, 102(3) (July 2008), 421, discussing the neglect of the World Trade Organization (WTO) adjudicating bodies of non-WTO sources.

participation in hostilities") and question their familiarity with combat operations.[7] This reflects a possible fear that human rights considerations will irreparably dilute international humanitarian law.[8] There is also concern regarding potential risks of political/power dilemmas behind normative development, given that government officials pursue state imperatives to advance the national interest above broader objectives in their contributions to the technical advancement of law.[9]

[7] See Michael N. Schmitt 'Military Necessity and Humanity in International Humanitarian Law: Preserving the Delicate Balance', *Virginia Journal of International Law*, 50 (2010), 796–839. The counter-perspective is supported within public international law and human rights tribunals and committees: see International Court of Justice (ICJ), *Legal Consequences of the Construction of a Wall in the Occupied Palestinian Territory*, Advisory Opinion, 2004 ICJ Reports (July 9, 2004), at paras. 106–13, confirming the relevance of human rights law in situations of occupation. See also: ICJ, *Armed Activities on the Territory of the Congo* (*Democratic Republic of the Congo* v. *Uganda*), ICJ Reports (December 19, 2005), para. 216; UN Human Rights Committee, General Comment No. 31, CCPr//C/21/Rev.1/Add.13 (May 26, 2004), at para. 11, noting the complementary nature of human rights and humanitarian norms in situations of armed conflict; European Court of Human Rights, *Isayeva, Yusupova and Bazayeva* v. *Russia* (December 19, 2002), and *Cyprus* v. *Turkey* (10 May 2001). See also Marco Sassòli and Laura Loson, 'The Legal Relationship Between International Humanitarian Law and Human Rights Law Where It Matters: Admissible Killing and Internment of Fighters in Non-International Armed Conflict', *International Review of the Red Cross*, 90(871) (September 2008), calling for choice of law based on specific applicability to the situation (available online at: www.icrc.org/eng/resources/documents/article/review/review-871-p599.htm; last accessed February 15, 2012).

[8] An additional point of concern is that the relationship between conservative international humanitarian law (IHL) scholars and the International Committee of the Red Cross (ICRC) appears strained at times, with the former alleging that that latter lacks sufficient expertise within the field or is inappropriately responding to pressures from human rights NGOs or other actors. See W. Hays Parks, Part IX of the ICRC, '"Direct participation in Hostilities" Study: No Mandate, No Expertise, and Legally Incorrect', *New York University Journal of International Law and Politics*, 42(3) (spring 2010), 770 (available online at: www.law.nyu.edu/ecm_dlv4/groups/public/@nyu_law_website__journals__journal_of_international_law_and_politics/documents/documents/ecm_pro_065930.pdf; last accessed February 15, 2012).

[9] For a specific example, see the Program on Humanitarian Policy and Conflict Research at Harvard University (HPCR) Manual on Air and Missile Warfare completed by academic and government experts (available online at: www.ihlresearch.org/amw). The experts originated from Australia, Belgium, Germany, Sweden, the United States, Switzerland, the UK, Norway, and Canada. Slaughter would highlight the state's interest as being defined by the individuals and groups within it. Anne-Marie Slaughter, 'International Law in a World of Liberal States', *European Journal of International Law*, 6 (1995), 503, 505. See also: Anne-Marie Slaughter and David Zaring, 'Networking Goes International: An Update', *Annual Review of Law and Social Science*, 2 (2005), 211, 215; Sean Kanuck, 'Pragmatic Law for International Security', in Cecilia M. Bailliet (ed.), *Security: A Multidisciplinary Normative Approach* (Leiden and Boston, MA: Martinus Nijhoff,

In contrast, at the regional level, the Inter-American Human Rights Court has proved more open to referring to norms from other regimes.[10] Linked to this counter-trend is a growing literature in which human rights scholars examine the failure of international organizations engaged in development work to incorporate human rights perspectives within their operations and/or policies.[11]

Hence, the unfolding of fragmentation is complex and riddled with contradictions, progression, and retrogression. Paul Schiff Berman concludes:

> Instead of bemoaning either the 'fragmentation' of law or the messiness of jurisdictional overlaps, we should accept them as a necessary consequence of the fact that communities cannot be hermetically sealed off from each other. Moreover, we can go further and consider the possibility that this jurisdictional messiness might, in the end, provide important systemic benefits by fostering dialogue among multiple constituencies, authorities, levels of government, and non-state communities. In addition, jurisdictional redundancy allows alternative ports of entry for strategic actors who might otherwise be silenced.[12]

The chapters within this book cross disciplinary boundaries. They advocate harmonization over fragmentation pursuant to the aspiration of asserting the interests of our collective humanity without necessarily advocating an international constitutional order. In the spirit of global legal pluralism they call for communication among multiple legalities – finding common concerns among the different orders, while respecting

2009), at 350 and 360, explaining that government practitioners "are literally paid to seek the greatest economic, political, or military advantage for their respective countries" and "government practitioners strive to resolve specific issues and manage risks within the purview of their public mandates, particular departments or agencies, and terms of office."

10 Lucas Lixinski, 'Treaty Interpretation by the Inter-American Court of Human Rights: Expansionism at the Service of the Unity of International Law', *European Journal of International Law*, 21(3) (2010), 585–604.

11 See: Mac Darrow and Louise Arbour, 'The Pillar of Glass: Human Rights in the Development Operations of the United Nations', *American Journal of International Law*, 103(3) (July 2009), 446; Galit A. Sarfaty, 'Why Culture Matters in International Institutions: The Marginality of Human Rights at the World Bank', *American Journal of International Law*, 103(4) (October 2009), 647; Guglielmo Verdirame, *The UN and Human Rights: Guarding the Guardians* (New York: Cambridge University Press, 2010), assessing UN humanitarian operations and their compliance with human rights law.

12 Paul Schiff Berman, 'Federalism and International Law through the Lens of Legal Pluralism', *Missouri Law Review*, 73 (Fall 2008), 1151.

internal perspectives.[13] Hence, this book may be characterized as a product of the post-fragmentation period, in which scholars seek to redirect attention towards articulating the necessary components to realize the universal aspirations articulated in the UN Charter preamble of attaining "the equal rights of men and women and of nations large and small . . . to promote social progress and better standards of life in larger freedom."[14] It is suggested that the construction of instrumental architecture to pursue a global humanitarian imperative is contingent on the recognition of the interdependence and interrelatedness of norms and interests across and between sub-fields, improving the participation and inclusion of vulnerable groups and individuals, and

[13] See Emmanuel Melissaris, *Ubiquitous Law: Legal Theory and the Space for Legal Pluralism* (Farnham: Ashgate, 2009). William Twining defining legal pluralism, comments that it "primarily articulates detachment from legal centralism revolving around state law, criticism of the exclusiveness of state law, decentralization of court-centered judicial studies, exploration of non-state legal orders, unveiling of informal socio-legal practices, and an understanding of law as a multi-centered field that deals with the convergence of norms, localities, states, global sites, and practices. Scholarship of legal pluralism has underscored the ways in which various identities and traditions have decentralized state law and offered non-state legal orders" ('Normative and Legal Pluralism: A Global Perspective', *Duke Journal of Comparative and International Law*, 20 (spring 2010), 473). See also: Paul Schiff Berman, 'From International Law to Law and Globalization', *Columbia Journal of Transnational Law*, 43 (2005), 485; Andreas Fischer-Lescano and Gunther Teubner, 'Regime-Collisions: The Vain Search for Legal Unity in the Fragmentation of Global Law', *Michigan Journal of International Law*, 25 (2004), 999; William W. Burke-White, 'International Legal Pluralism', *Michigan Journal of International Law*, 25 (2004), 963; Paul Schiff Berman, 'The New Legal Pluralism', *Annual Review of Law and Social Science*, 5 (2009), 225; Nico Krisch, 'The Pluralism of Global Administrative Law', *European Journal of International Law*, 17 (2006), 247; David Kennedy, 'The Mystery of Global Governance' *Ohio Northern University Law Review*, 34 (2008), 827; Brian Z. Tamanaha, 'Understanding Legal Pluralism: Past to Present, Local to Global', *Sydney Law Review*, 30 (2008), 375. As noted by Gráinne de Búrca: "Pluralist approaches to the international legal order claim to preserve space for contestation, resistance, and innovation, and to encourage tolerance and mutual accommodation in pursuit of accountability" ('The European Court of Justice and the International Legal Order after *Kadi*', *Harvard International Law Journal*, 50 (winter 2010), 1).

[14] See: A. A. Cancado Trindade, *International Law for Humankind: Toward a New Jus Gentium* (Leiden and Boston, MA: Martinus Nijhoff, 2010); Raphael Domingo, *The New Global Law* (New York: Cambridge University Press, 2010). On improving human well-being and agency, see: Amaryta Sen, 'Democracy as a Universal Value', *Journal of Democracy*, 10(3) (1999), 3. On the concept of global justice, see: Thomas Pogge and Darrel Mollendorf, *Global Justice: Seminal Essays* (St. Paul, MN: Paragon, 2008); and Boaventura de Sousa Santos, *Toward a New Legal Common Sense* (London: Butterworths, 2002), on the emancipative potential of law.

addressing the accountability of state and non-state actors for violations or regressions of minimum protection guarantees.

This book may also be considered post-Westphalian, as it seeks to move beyond the focus of the international legal system upon states as primary subjects.[15] At present nearly all sub-fields of international law underscore the importance of non-state actors and sub-state actors in contemporary normative evolution, interpretation, and enforcement.[16] International lawmaking is increasingly characterized by a transnational legal process of evolvement, in which civil society and others contribute to the articulation of recognition of legal rights at national, regional, and international levels.[17] The authors pursue a call for "consciousness raising" by identifying gaps and conundrums presented by omissions within normative or institutional frameworks to address vulnerable interests, including women, children, and the environment. Several

[15] See: Antonio Cassese, *International Law* (2nd edn., Oxford: Oxford University Press, 2005), 3–6; Malcolm Shaw, *International Law* (6th edn., New York: Cambridge University Press, 2008), 43–9; Anthony Carty, *Philosophy of International Law* (Edinburgh: Edinburgh University Press, 2007).

[16] See: Anne Peters, Lucy Koechlin, Till Förster, and Gretta Fenner Zinkernagel (eds.), *Non-State Actors as Standard Setters* (Cambridge: Cambridge University Press, 2009); Steve Charnovitz, 'The Relevance of Non-State Actors to International Law', in Rüdiger Wolfrum and Volker Röben (eds.), *Developments of International Law in Treaty Making* (Berlin and New York: Springer, 2005), 544–8; Andrew Clapham, *Human Rights Obligations of Non-State Actors* (Oxford: Oxford University Press, 2006); Philip Alston, *Non-State Actors and Human Rights* (Oxford: Oxford University Press, 2005); Anne-Marie Slaughter, 'The Real New World Order', *Foreign Affairs*, 76(5) (Sept.–Oct. 1997), 183–97; Philippe Sands, 'Turtles and Torturers: The Transformation of International Law', *New York University Journal of International Law and Policy*, 33 (2001), 527, 529–30; Peter J. Spiro, 'Non-State Actors in Global Politics', *American Journal of International Law*, 92(4) (1998), 808.

[17] See, for example, Philip C. Jessup: "All law which regulates actions and events that transcend national frontiers. Both public and private international law are included, as are other rules which do not wholly fit into such standard categories" (*Transnational Law* (New Haven, CT: Yale University Press, 1956), 3). Also: Harold Hongju Koh, 'Why Do Nations Obey International Law?', *Yale Law Journal*, 106 (1997), 2599, discussing transnational legal process; Thomas Risse, Stephen C. Ropp, and Kathryn Sikkink, *The Power of Human Rights: International Norms and Domestic Change* (Cambridge: Cambridge University Press, 1999), addressing transnational human rights networks; Mireille Delmas-Marty, *Ordering Pluralism. A Conceptual Framework for Understanding the Transnational Legal World* (Oxford: Hart, 2009); Anne Hellum, Shaheen Sardar Ali, and Anne Griffiths (eds.), *From Transnational Relations to Transnational Law* (Farnham: Ashgate, 2011); Malcolm Langford (ed.), *Social Rights Jurisprudence: Emerging Trends in International and Comparative Law* (New York: Cambridge University Press, 2008), describing the acknowledgement of justiciability of social rights within national, regional, and international jurisdictions.

chapters highlight the importance of giving voice to victims and affected parties, such as via participation in design of substantive and reparative norms. Also included within this volume is a reflection upon the contribution of feminist approaches to international law, as well as the pursuit of sustainable development.[18] The authors were invited to discuss to what extent non-state actors (such as multinational companies or NGOs) promote the creation of new (quasi-legal) norms and why regulation is difficult by institutions at different levels.

Overview of the chapters

Part I tackles the silence of victims within international criminal law brought about by normative and institutional gaps. It opens with Catharine MacKinnon's chapter, in which she attributes gender as having transformed international law, altering doctrines relating to state vs. private actors, jurisdiction, and sovereignty via NGO identification of everyday sexual atrocities. Nevertheless, she asserts that the international legal literature ignores the innovation linked to penalization of gender crimes. To the extent recognition is given, it is largely within the context of international criminal law. She highlights the existence of a "very real norm of nonobservance of the prohibition of gender crimes." Everyday gender crimes remain subject to denial and victims are silenced. MacKinnon underlines the fact that nations are not the principal actors in either disobeying or enforcing obedience to laws against gender crime. She poses the question as to whether rape should be recognized as a separate international crime on its own terms. MacKinnon identifies everyday gender crimes as "the longest-running siege of crimes against humanity in the history of the world" and that "sexually violated women and international jurisdiction belong together." Sadly, it is claimed that women attain more rights the further away from home they get.[19]

[18] On feminism and international law, see Hilary Charlesworth and Christine Chinkin, *The Boundaries of International Law: A Feminist Analysis* (New York: Juris, 2000); Doris Buss and Ambreena Manji, *International Law: Modern Feminist Approaches* (Oxford: Hart, 2005). On sustainable development, see Christina Voigt, *Sustainable Development as a Principle of International Law: Resolving Conflicts Between Climate Measures and WTO Law* (Leiden and Boston, MA: Martinus Nijhoff, 2009); see generally Patricia Birnie, Alan Boyle, and Catherine Redgwell, *International Law and The Environment* (3rd edn., Oxford: Oxford University Press, 2009).

[19] See also Rosa-Linda Fregoso and Cynthia Bejarano (eds.), *Terrorizing Women: Feminicide in the Americas* (Durham, NC: Duke University Press, 2010), addressing the national-state's failure to protect women from violence, and the pursuit of transnational remedies.

In Chapter 3, Christine Byron analyzes the situation of the female child within the situation of armed conflict. She studies the overlooked issue of sexual abuse of female children by the same forces they have been recruited to (rather than enemy forces). The chapter seeks to dismantle the legal cloak of invisibility around the victims by discussing to what extent sexual abuse would constitute a crime against humanity or a war crime. She also addresses the failure of the International Criminal Court (ICC) to prosecute commanders for rape and the sexual enslavement of girls. Byron examines the *nullem crimen* principles and indicates the devastating possibility that girls may give evidence as to their child-soldier experience, but not address rape they have endured. In conclusion, she calls for the girl child soldier to be heard, adding: "If the Office of the Prosecutor feels that such prosecutions cannot succeed currently, then the Rome Statute needs to be amended."

Fionnuala Ní Aoláin in Chapter 4 provides a critical review of the lack of transformative impact of UN Security Council Resolutions 1325, 1820, 1888, and 1889 on the situation of women in conflict and post-conflict situations. She identifies a situation of fragmentation and characterizes the UN Security Council as further compounding the stratification of norms that women receive in post-conflict and conflict settings. Aoláin describes "An ongoing pattern of international lawmaking for and about women has been consistent marginalization of those issues women identify as affecting them most. Lawmaking does not undo marginalization; it may serve to compound certain exclusions and inequalities." She notes the tendency of the international community to issue soft law pertaining to women in conflict, rendering enforcement possibilities weak. In addition, possibilities are limited for women's enjoyment of agency, autonomy, and the pursuit of cross-issue coalitions to build power and influence. She underscores that "Women are the group most historically marginalized and excluded from the peacemaking and peace-building process across all jurisdictions and conflicts," and this is unfortunately not remedied by the elaboration of new norms.

In Chapter 5, Edda Kristjánsdóttir examines victim reparations at the ICC and the issue of complementarity. She highlights dilemmas such as what constitutes an adequate national procedure, whether the choice of reparation reflects the wishes of victims, and how the reparations provisions of the Rome Statute are being incorporated into domestic procedures. The chapter scrutinizes protection gaps between the international and national levels of criminal justice, and seeks to highlight the importance of re-examining the normative framework from the perspective of upholding the primacy of the interests and needs of the victims for whom the institutions were established in the first place.

Part II presents international human rights law and addresses dilemmas relating to the emergence of non-state actors as violators and enforcers of human rights and the need for accountability measures applicable to civil society. It opens with Cecilia M. Bailliet's chapter, in which she queries what is to become of the human rights international order within an age of neo-medievalism. Bailliet contends that human rights must be released from their tie to sovereignty and be reinterpreted via recognition of the individual's fundamental obligations towards self, family, community, state, and humanity. She describes the escalation of a phenomenon of failing or failed states, as well as a counter-trend of authoritarianism, and reviews the main legitimacy challenges facing the international human rights system.

She also identifies a challenge presented by cultural differentiation which requires restoration of the balance between rights and duties. She further notes that "the emphasis of the international human rights community on rights, often to the exclusion of duties, may well be one of the factors behind widespread rejection/marginalization of human rights within Africa, the Middle East, and Asia. Several regimes and social actors view NGOs with accompanying individual-focused human rights policies as sources of instability and antagonism, actually challenging the larger communitarian or collective interest . . . Should human rights institutions and NGOs take into account duties in conjunction with rights, they may well find increased spaces for dialogue with societal and state actors, thereby setting a foundation for increased legitimacy." Bailliet characterizes the emergence of new soft law addressing due diligence obligations of transnational companies as an example of a creative, new protection approach, but indicates concern for weakness regarding accountability. Her conclusion calls for a transnational flexible approach towards the articulation and implementation of duties depending on the context of application and guaranteeing the participation of individuals and vulnerable groups.

In Chapter 7, Karima Bennoune addresses the issue of diversity of NGOs, examining the dynamic between women's human rights NGOs and "mainstream" human rights actors. She describes trends towards viewing NGOs within a unitary paradigm: as a homogeneous group, as the saviors of international law dilemmas; or alternatively as unaccountable, political actors. She underscores how NGOs shape international adjudication by bringing cases, drafting *amici*, providing information, making statements, and verifying and sometimes enforcing state compliance within international law. Most importantly, she lauds NGOs for setting agendas and prioritizing international law debates. Within human rights, she notes that NGOs have an important role, given the limited enforcement capacity of the legal system, the under-resourcing of the UN human rights machinery, and the nature of the human rights project. She assesses NGO dynamics within the definition of torture and the attitude of NGOs towards fundamentalist non-state actors in the context of the war on terror. Bennoune suggests that "we need to contemplate how to confront situations when differences in the stances of NGOs instead cause problems for women's human rights advocacy, and arguably shape international law process and discourse in ways that are harmful to women's human rights or are at odds with the views of women's human rights defenders (who may of course themselves have diverse positions)."

Chapter 8 discusses transnational legal dilemmas involving women's access to justice as exemplified by a case study of the Pakistani-Norwegian migrant community in Oslo. Anne Hellum reviews Norway's response to the CEDAW (Convention on the Elimination of All Forms of Discrimination against Women) Committee's conclusions addressing concern for the availability of legal remedies for migrant women. She then presents the experience of a Pakistani women's organization and its coordination with NGOs to navigate a range of institutions, including Norwegian courts and imams, and norms, inter alia Norwegian law, Islamic law, and international human rights. She explains how the informal justice spaces provided by non-state entities promote pluralism, choice, and recognition to women who have been marginalized by state law, as well as religious and customary legal orders. Hellum also assesses the complex relationship between the right to legal information, choice, and autonomy in the context of transnational identity. She notes "For people living transnational lives, neither international nor national laws are the sole mechanisms for regulating their affairs." Her chapter seeks to demonstrate how "a grounded, pluralist, and relational women's law approach" can support migrant women's access to justice.

Part III presents tensions pertaining to sovereignty and normative implementation within international environmental law. It opens with Hari M. Osofsky's chapter, which takes note of the participation of NGOs, corporations, cities and states in forums addressing climate change. There they create transnational agreements and try to influence the primary dialogue among nation-states. Nevertheless, she points out the exclusion of these from the main negotiating table, relegating them to indirect participation. Osofsky proposes that although the agreements among sub-state entities are nonbinding as a formal international legal matter, they contain more substantive commitments than the nation-state submissions pursuant to the Copenhagen Accord. The chapter explores the conceptual implications of a juxtaposition of the limited formal progress at a national level with significant sub-national efforts. Osofsky queries "current international legal efforts should focus primarily on achieving better agreements in negotiations among nation-state parties, or whether more inclusive conceptions of international law creation which shift that focus somewhat might actually serve as a tool in solving this problem [of climate change]." She pursues a "permeable model of the nation state," treating transnational agreements among sub-national governmental entities as constituting a more meaningful part of the creation of the international law of climate change. Osofsky discusses the transnational climate change agreements made among cities, states, and provinces and the complexity of incorporating those agreements into international treaty-making.

In Chapter 10, Sumudu Atapattu evaluates the value of soft law instruments within international environmental law. She underlines that although soft law has traditionally been perceived as the regimes of NGOs, within environmental law it is actually states that promote it. Atapattu notes: "Sometimes it is useful to think of hard law–soft law phenomenon as a continuum rather than a dichotomy and complementing rather than competing with each other." She describes how although states formerly did not pay attention to soft law, they now pay meticulous attention to the drafting language and have even begun to enter reservations to these soft law instruments. She reviews the identification of important principles relating to sustainable development, as well as common but differentiated responsibilities, and the precautionary principle. Atapattu attributes soft law to developing entire fields of law, such as climate change, biodiversity, and desertification. She articulates the conceptual innovations provided by the germination of soft law: "While it is not the instrument itself that creates law, rather subsequent state practice; what shapes such state practice is the soft law instrument." Nevertheless, Atapattu provides a realistic conclusion which reminds us of the importance of maintaining an instrumental focus to assure effective implementation of protection norms.

Atapattu relates to this discussion by addressing the phenomenon of shifting conceptions of what is law by reflecting upon the increased influence of soft law within international environmental law.[20]

Chapter 11 addresses the conundrum presented by the fact that "both environmental and trade values are repeatedly asserted to be at the core of international law and international civil society" and challenges the "putative relationship between global trade and environmental protection embodied by the environmental Kuznets curve hypothesis." Rebecca Bratspies underlines the importance of considering the developing world's experience with Northern colonialism, environmental exploitation, protectionism, and overconsumption. She suggests that these experiences must be part of any genuine conversation about sustainability, trade and environmental protection "if only because drawing the boundaries between trade policy and environmental decision-making implicates state sovereignty. Ignoring or denying this context gives rise to the suspicion that sustainability discourse is just another way for developed countries to exert power over developing countries."

Bratspies highlights that the core of this concern is the critical question of who shapes a state's sustainability policies: the state through its regulatory powers, or the collection of individual and systemic choices we call "the market"? Bratspies studies the situation of national shrimp farmers pursuing sustainable technologies who are priced out of the global market. She underscores that it is the global market that sets the condition for farming, *not* the farmers or the community. Bratspies is cautious about soft law: "It remains to be seen whether self-regulation and environmental safeguards through voluntary codes of practice can be an effective form of governance in the absence of binding legal obligations, or a state entity tasked with enforcing the rules."

In Chapter 12, Beate Sjåfjell demonstrates how the principle of sustainable development can be enforced by EU law upon member states enacting company law. She examines the normative language within the Lisbon Treaty and further examines the duties of EU institutions, including those of the European Council, Commission, Parliament and Court

[20] See Alan Boyle, 'Soft Law in International Law-Making', in Malcolm D. Evans, *International Law* (2nd edn., Oxford: Oxford University Press, 2006), 141; see also Gregory C. Shaffer and Mark A. Pollack, 'Hard vs. Soft Law: Alternatives, Complements, and Antagonists in International Governance', *Minnesota Law Review*, 94(3) (2010), 706.

of Justice: (a) a duty to stay within the framework of general objectives; (b) a duty to seek a balance between the general objectives; (c) a general duty to act; and (d) a duty to undertake specific action under certain circumstances. She further reviews indirect legal implications of the EU member states and *de lege ferenda* regional general principle of sustainable development. Sjåfjell supports Bratspies by calling for the elaboration of EU accountability standards to enforce sustainable development. She argues that EU law not only contains a legal basis to integrate environmental protection requirements in all areas where necessary, but also sets out a duty for the EU institutions to do so and for the Member States to support such efforts.

This volume seeks to highlight challenges relating to the contemporary international and transnational evolution of law, giving voice to actors previously ignored and reevaluating subsystem sources, institutions, and frameworks. For several of the scholars, this book is their first opportunity to present their work together, as they normally publish within their specific sub-field of expertise. The cross-disciplinary exposure to research issues and approaches is intended to reveal common dilemmas and concerns. The authors within this collection seek to inspire academics and practitioners to pursue similar comparative reflection and promote contemporary international lawmaking in a spirit of cooperation towards improvement of the universal human condition and habitat.

The conclusion is written by Hilary Charlesworth.

PART I

Protection gaps within international criminal law

2

Creating international law: gender as new paradigm

CATHARINE A. MACKINNON

Gender as reality, analysis, and rubric has created some of the fastest and most far-reaching transformations in international law in our time. Gender crimes in particular present a striking trajectory of innovation on the international legal scene, going from virtual non-recognition to accepted institutionalization in under thirty years – by any legal measure, the speed of light. The reality in which this normative evolution is grounded has been one of atrocity: atrocities that have become more visible as women have spoken out, often through non-governmental organizations (NGOs), atrocities that have filled evolving functions in conflicts as dynamics among men have impelled their varied instrumentalization.

The feature that perhaps most distinguishes these developments, in contrast to others that have stimulated international legal innovation, is how utterly familiar the acts are. Sexual atrocities are normal in everyday life, occur in peace as well as in war, and are by no means confined to official actors or to conflict that is recognized as organized. In one form or another, gender crimes are illegal in every legal system in the world. Yet they are breaking paths in international law, a development that mainstream international legal literature has largely ignored. Analysis of how and why this change is occurring shows one way law is created internationally.

As a conceptual innovation, the fundamental idea of gender crime originated in the early 1970s with the creation of sexual harassment law.[1] What had always been classified as a socially ungrounded sex

The assistance and collegiality of Lisa Cardyn and Taylor Landis is gratefully acknowledged.

[1] See Catharine A. MacKinnon, *Sexual Harassment of Working Women: A Case of Sex Discrimination* (New Haven, CT: Yale University Press, 1979).

crime – rape[2] – was first understood as occurring because of the social status location and power differential of the parties in the gendered domain. Substantively, in sexual harassment law, rape was first legally recognized as based in gender inequality, hence a violation of human and civil rights and a form of sex discrimination. The fundamental idea that originated here is that sex crimes are gender based – that is, they happen because of the social meaning of sex: being a woman or a man in society. Crimes that happen because of gendered roles, meanings, stereotypes, and scripts socially assigned to groups on the basis of their sex were understood as criminal forms of sex discrimination: crimes of sex inequality. This idea was conceived, and law created accordingly, because women listened to women and believed them and took what they were saying seriously. Nothing more, nothing less.

Among other things, this legal conceptual resituation of these facts meant that, although individuals victimized by these atrocities are at times violated alone and in isolation and one at a time, the violation itself is intrinsically collective and group based, not individual. Everyone who is raped is harmed personally, but rape itself is theorized as an attack on a woman because she is a member of the group 'women', defined as such and targeted as such for this specific violation. What had been thought of as a crime without social particularity, what had been considered a crime with an individual victim, when understood as a gender-biased violation, became reconfigured as a crime against a group that is inflicted on one of its members. Rape understood as a gender crime became seen as an attack on women as such, often including their racial and ethnic particularities, that was inflicted through the rape of each woman.

The innovation termed 'sexual harassment' has been widely accepted in national systems around the world, often, although not always, as sex discrimination.[3] Its underlying realization – that sexual aggression is gender based – has also been embraced and extended to many sex-based abuses and given international normative dimension by the Committee on the Elimination of Discrimination against Women in its General Recommendation 19 in 1992,[4] becoming stronger in operation when

[2] See, e.g., *Williams* v. *Saxbe*, 413 F Supp. 654 (DC Cir. 1976); *Barnes* v. *Costle*, 561 F 2d 983 (DC Cir. 1977); *Meritor Savings Bank, FSB* v. *Vinson*, 477 US 57 (1986).

[3] For examples of both, see generally Catharine A. MacKinnon and Reva B. Siegel (eds.), *Directions in Sexual Harassment Law* (New Haven, CT: Yale University Press, 2004).

[4] See Convention on the Elimination of All Forms of Discrimination against Women, New York, 18 December 1979, in force 3 September 1981, GA Res. 34/180, UN GAOR, 34th Sess.,

many nations adopted the Optional Protocol.[5] The central insight was developed through regional systems in a series of human rights cases in Europe, many on torture,[6] and through instruments and cases in Latin America,[7] especially concrete and detailed in the Convention of Belém do Pará,[8] and recently articulated in provisions of the African Protocol.[9] On facts of gender crime, state responsibility for inaction has expanded from state actors to non-state actors in the human rights setting.[10] During this same period, from the late 1980s to the early 2000s, attention to facts of gender crime, seldom so-called, migrated back into the international criminal justice system through ad hoc tribunals. In the process, criminal responsibility, including for acts of less-than-official actors, also became more readily attributable to superiors.[11]

Supp. No. 45, UN Doc. A/34/46; Committee on the Elimination of Discrimination against Women, General Recommendation No. 19, UN Doc. A/47/38 (1 February 1992), para. 7.

5 Optional Protocol to the Convention on the Elimination of all Forms of Discrimination against Women, New York, 6 October 1999, in force 22 December 2000, GA Res. 4, UN GAOR, 54th Sess., Supp. No. 49, UN Doc. A/RES/54/4.

6 See *Suheyla Aydin* v. *Turkey*, 25 ECHR 251 (1997); *Akkoç* v. *Turkey*, 34 ECHR 51 (2000). For later developments, see *M. C.* v. *Bulgaria*, 15 ECHR 627 (2003) (on rape), and *Opuz* v. *Turkey*, Appl. No. 33401/02, Judgment, ECHR (2009) (on domestic violence).

7 See, e.g., *Maria da Penha Maia Fernandes* v. *Brazil*, Case 12.051, 2001 IACHR, Rep. No. 54/01, OEA/Ser.L/V/II.111 doc. 20 rev., at 704 (16 April 2001).

8 Organization of American States, Inter-American Convention on the Prevention, Punishment and Eradication of Violence against Women (Convention of Belém do Pará), Belém do Pará, 6 June 1994, in force 3 May 1995, 33 ILM 1534 (1994).

9 See especially Protocol to the African Charter on Human and Peoples' Rights on the Rights of Women in Africa, Maputo, 11 July 2003, in force 25 November 2005, Arts. 1(j), 3(4), 4(2), 5(d), 11(3), 22(b), 23(b) (online at: www.achpr.org/english/_info/women_en.html).

10 This has been a gradual development through case law on the human rights side. See *M. C.* v. *Bulgaria*; *Opuz* v. *Turkey*; *González et al.* ('*Cotton Field*') v. *Mexico*, 2009 IACHR, Judgment (16 November 2009) (Preliminary Objection, Merits, Reparations, and Costs). *Opuz* is especially stunning in holding Turkey responsible for a batterer killing his mother-in-law.

11 See *Prosecutor* v. *Bagosora*, Case No. ICTR-98-41-T, Judgment and Sentence (18 December 2008) (holding Bagosora, a military officer, liable for command responsibility at trial for sexual atrocities by forces including unofficial ones); *Prosecutor* v. *Semanza*, Case No. ICTR-97-20-T, Judgment and Sentence, para. 479 (15 May 2003) (finding Semanza criminally responsible under Arts. 6(1) and 6(3) for rape in a situation where he 'addressed a crowd and ... encouraged them to rape Tutsi women before killing them. Immediately thereafter, one of the men from the crowd had non-consensual sexual intercourse with Victim A[.]'). *Prosecutor* v. *Akayesu*, Case No. ICTR-96-4-T, Judgment (2 September 1998); *Prosecutor* v. *Kunarac*, Case No. IT-96-23 and IT-96-23/1-A, Appeals Judgment (12 June 2002). See also *Prosecutor* v. *Gacumbtsi*, Case No. ICTR-2001-64-T, Judgment, para. 328 (17 June 2004) (holding defendant liable under Art. 6(1) for verbally 'instigating the rape of Tutsi women and girls' who 'were raped by young men who, being in the neigbourhood, heard the bourgmestre's [Gacumbtsi] instigation').

The International Criminal Tribunal for Rwanda (ICTR) gave depth and dimension to the pursuit of gender crimes, implicitly if powerfully in the Akayesu[12] case and those following its definition of rape,[13] as the International Criminal Tribunal for the former Yugoslavia (ICTY) developed tools for individual liability for collective criminality.[14] The concept of gender crime has tacitly influenced other international rubrics, such as the international definition of trafficking codified in the Palermo Protocol,[15] often the more so when the sex and the equality do not appear as such on the page. And gender crime has taken explicit form in its highest expression to date across the Rome Statute of the International Criminal Court (ICC), superimposed on international humanitarian law and embodied in the charging practices of its Prosecutor.[16]

Gender crime thus evolved from tears in the eyes of women confiding in women to international norm to international crime in a few short years through interaction of theory with practice, civil with criminal approaches, and domestic with international responses. Domestic and international human rights and civil rights structures cognized acts of violence against women as gendered, as criminal law on the international

[12] *Prosecutor* v. *Akayesu*, para. 688 (defining 'rape as a physical invasion of a sexual nature, committed on a person under circumstances which are coercive. Sexual violence, which includes rape, is considered to be any act of a sexual nature which is committed on a person under circumstances which are coercive.').

[13] For discussion, see Catharine A. MacKinnon, 'Defining Rape Internationally: A Comment on *Akayesu*', in *Are Women Human? And Other International Dialogues* (Cambridge, MA: Harvard University Press, 2007), 237–46.

[14] See Patricia Viseur Sellers, 'Individual(s') Liability for Collective Sexual Violence', in Karen Knop (ed.), *Gender and Human Rights* (Oxford: Oxford University Press, 2004), 153–94. The ICTY brought few cases principally for rape, *Prosecutor* v. *Kunarac* being exceptional.

[15] Protocol to Prevent, Suppress and Punish Trafficking in Persons, Especially Women and Children, Supplementing the United Nations Convention Against Transnational Organized Crime, GA Res. 25 (II), Art. 3(a), at 54–55, UN Doc. A/55/383 (2 November 2000) (including 'the abuse of power or of a position of vulnerability' as part of the definition of trafficking, going to sexual exploitation).

[16] Rome Statute of the International Criminal Court, Arts. 7(1)(g) and 7(1)(h), Rome, 17 July 1998, in force 1 July 2002, 2187 UNTS 90 (enumerating as crimes against humanity, '[r]ape, sexual slavery, enforced prostitution, forced pregnancy, enforced sterilization, or any other form of sexual violence of comparable gravity[]' and '[p] ersecution', respectively); Art. 8(e)(vi) (establishing as war crimes 'rape, sexual slavery, enforced prostitution, forced pregnancy, as defined in article 7, paragraph 2 (f), enforced sterilization, and any other form of sexual violence also constituting a serious violation of article 3 common to the four Geneva Conventions').

level incorporated gender analysis – explicitly seen as effectuating human rights through criminal law – into its treatment of sex crimes. International criminal and humanitarian law began paying more attention than it ever had to rape in conflict under the aegis of the concept of gender crime, giving new life and muscular practice to long-existing but little-used prohibitions,[17] creating something that had not been there before. The international community embraced the understanding that sexual assaults against women and girls are based on the sex of the victim or the perpetrator or both – that is, it grasped the gendered inequality of their relation in this criminal act in social context – as reflected in the magisterial and conceptually cogent report of the Secretary-General in 2006.[18]

Until the Rome Statute, on the criminal side of international law these developments reflected an *analysis of* laws whose elements remained legally defined in other terms. And that approach remains a fertile possibility. But then, in the Rome Statute, a basis in gender became an element of a crime in positive international law for the first time in its definition of persecution as a crime against humanity.[19] Gender crime is also referenced explicitly throughout this multilateral treaty from its description of the crimes to how their victims and witnesses are to be treated procedurally.[20] In other words, gender evolved beyond a norm or

[17] See, e.g., Hugo Grotius, *The Rights of War and Peace, in Three Books*, Jean Barbeyrac (ed. and trans.), reprint edn., 3 vols. (Clark, NJ: Lawbook Exchange, 2004), vol. III, 572–3; Francis Lieber, 'Instructions for the Government of Armies of the United States in the Field' (The Lieber Code), US War Department General Orders No. 100, § 2, Arts. 37 and 47 (24 April 1863), in Dietrich Schindler and Jiri Toman (eds.), *The Laws of Armed Conflicts: A Collection of Conventions, Resolutions and Other Documents* (4th edn., Leiden and Boston, MA: Martinus Nijhoff, 2004), 3, 8–9; Protocol Additional to the Geneva Conventions of 12 August 1949, And Relating to the Protection of Victims of International Armed Conflicts (Protocol I), Art. 76, Geneva, 8 June 1977, in force 7 December 1978, 1125 UNTS 3; Geneva Convention Relative to the Protection of Civilian Persons in Time of War (Fourth Geneva Convention), Art. 3, Geneva, 12 August 1949, in force 21 October 1950, 6 UST 3516, 75 UNTS 287.

[18] *In-depth Study on All Forms of Violence Against Women: Report of the Secretary-General*, UN Doc. A/61/122/Add.1 (6 July 2006).

[19] Rome Statute, Art. 7(1)(h) ('Persecution against any identifiable group or collectivity on political, racial, national, ethnic, cultural, religious, gender as defined in paragraph 3, or other grounds that are universally recognized as impermissible under international law, in connection with any act referred to in this paragraph or any crime within the jurisdiction of the Court[.]').

[20] For the ICC's procedures on victims and witnesses, see Rome Statute, Art. 43(6) (providing that '[t]he Registrar shall set up a Victims and Witnesses Unit within the Registry. This Unit shall provide, in consultation with the Office of the Prosecutor,

analytic overlay into a feature of positive international law. All the sex crimes under the Rome Statute's prohibitions – including 'rape, sexual slavery, enforced prostitution, forced pregnancy, enforced sterilization or any other form of sexual violence of comparable gravity'[21] as well as trafficking in persons as a form of enslavement[22] – make up this category termed 'gender crime', this innovation. Men and boys who are subjected to sexual atrocities and other forms of gender-based aggression are, of course, covered as such along with women and girls. Regrettably, in my view, 'gender' does not explicitly cover gays and lesbians as such,[23] but they are covered as women and men, and crimes of discrimination against them are often, even almost always, highly gendered.

Like many things in life, the term for this development is better in French – *les crimes à caractère sexiste* – but unlike many things expressed in French, this one is also more politically direct. To do something about such crimes, internationally and otherwise, in the words of the ICC's first Prosecutor Luis Moreno-Ocampo, marks a 'new era'.[24]

The most striking quality of the pursuit of these crimes by the ICC has been their variable centrality to every prosecution so far. Each case shows how sexual abuse is a specific tool of each conflict, exposing the particular work it does in each setting. Lubanga allegedly made boys into rapists and girls into sex slaves in order to make them into child soldiers he could command and use at will. In a signal example of gender mainstreaming, the Prosecutor argued that being taught to rape, as well

protective measures and security arrangements, counselling and other appropriate assistance for witnesses, victims who appear before the Court, and others who are at risk on account of testimony given by such witnesses. The Unit shall include staff with expertise in trauma, including trauma related to crimes of sexual violence.'); *ibid.*, Art. 68 (discussing '[p]rotection of the victims and witnesses and their participation in the proceedings' and describing, *inter alia*, Court policies for cases 'where the crime involves sexual or gender violence' and 'special means' that 'shall be implemented in the case of a victim of sexual violence').

21 *Ibid.*, Art. 7(1)(g).

22 *Ibid.*, Art. 7(2)(c) (defining enslavement).

23 *Ibid.*, Art. 7(3) ('For the purpose of this Statute, it is understood that the term 'gender' refers to the two sexes, male and female, within the context of society. The term 'gender' does not indicate any meaning different from the above.'). Various observers indicate the intention of this addition to exclude coverage of atrocities committed on the basis of homosexuality. See Valerie Oosterveld, 'The Definition of Gender in the Rome Statute of the International Criminal Court: A Step Forward or Back for International Criminal Justice', *Harvard Human Rights Journal*, 18 (2005), 55–84.

24 Luis Moreno-Ocampo, Prosecutor of the International Criminal Court, Prosecutor's Statement on Review Conference in Uganda 3 (31 May 2010) (available online at: www.icc-cpi.int/nr/exeres/2386f5cb-b2a5-45dc-b66f-17e762f77b1f.htm).

as being raped, harmed the children who were forced to become soldiers.[25] Bemba and Katanga were charged with sending their forces to rape en masse as retaliation for prior attacks, for resources or political power.[26] Bemba's troops were said to rape men in authority to destroy their capacity to lead, as well as women to instill terror for political control and to shatter community cohesion, eliminating the possibility of support for forces seen politically as the enemy.[27] The arrest warrant of President Al Bashir of Sudan accuses him of using rape in his genocide, no doubt because it is effective in destroying the peoples of the South, and because the evidence it leaves is quieter than death, or so he thinks.[28] For decades, Joseph Kony has, according to the ICC's first charges, violated the humanity of his (perhaps) sixty wives and the whole schools he abducts and parcels out to his henchmen,[29] very

[25] *Prosecutor* v. *Lubanga*, ICC-01/04–1/06, Opening Statement by the Prosecutor (26 January 2009).

[26] See *Prosecutor* v. *Bemba*, ICC-01/05–1/08, Opening Statement by the Prosecutor (22 November 2010), 3 (noting that '[w]omen were raped systematically to assert dominance and to shatter resistance. Men were raped in public to destroy their authority, their capacity to lead'); *Prosecutor* v. *Katanga*, ICC-01/04–01/07, Decision on the Confirmation of Charges (30 September 2008), para. 443 (concluding that there was 'sufficient evidence to establish substantial grounds to believe that rape was a common practice following an attack and that combatants who forced women to engage in sexual intercourse intended to commit such acts by force or threat of force').

[27] See *Prosecutor* v. *Bemba*, Opening Statement by the Prosecutor.

[28] *Prosecutor* v. *Al Bashir*, ICC-02/05-01/09-3, Second Decision on the Prosecution's Application for a Warrant of Arrest (12 July 2010), para. 30 ('The Chamber is therefore satisfied that there are reasonable grounds to believe that acts of rape, torture and forcible displacement were committed against members of the targeted ethnic groups. Accordingly, the Chamber finds that there are reasonable grounds to believe that the material element of the crime of genocide by causing serious bodily or mental harm . . . is fulfilled').

[29] For a brief overview covering decades of such violence, see, e.g., Marc Lacey, 'A Mother's Bitter Choice: Telling Kidnappers No', *New York Times*, 25 January 2003 (describing the aftermath of Kony's famous 1996 abduction of 139 girls from a Catholic boarding school in northern Uganda); Human Rights Watch, 'CAR/DR Congo: LRA Conducts Massive Abduction Campaign', 11 August 2010 (describing how '[t]he LRA assigns abducted girls to commanders for sex or as servants. Refusing sexual relations often results in death'), available online at: www.hrw.org/en/news/2010/08/11/cardr-congo-lra-conducts-massive-abduction-campaign; and Human Rights Watch, *'As if We Weren't Human': Discrimination and Violence against Women with Disabilities in Northern Uganda* (New York: Human Rights Watch, 2010) (describing the lasting harm of the LRA's (Ugandan rebel Lord's Resistance Army) decades-long assault on the women of Uganda), available online at: www.hrw.org/en/reports/2010/08/26/if-we-weren-t-human. See also *Prosecutor* v. *Kony*, ICC-02/04-01/05-53, Warrant of Arrest for Joseph Kony (8 July 2005) (as amended 27 September 2005), para. 16 (in which Pre-Trial Chamber II notes, *inter alia*, 'that the

possibly because he wants this many girls to be at his disposal and for his use as 'wives', and because he wants the power of a cult leader, for which he needs conflict to continue. Maybe some Hutu *génocidaires* who fled Rwanda into Congo continue to rape in order to have something to bargain away for permission to return home.[30] Weaponized rape proves to be a highly flexible tactic for multiple criminal strategies.

In addition to subordinating women, which rape always does, these cases provide glimpses into what work the rape is doing in conflicts among men. Rape in war furthers war aims. Genocidal rape destroys peoples. When sexual abuse is a crime against humanity, it often seems to be an end in itself. These rapes are committed in order to commit them, much like they are committed every day of the week in every part of the world, only more intensively so and often with more explicit organization. Rapes that are crimes against humanity are greater in frequency if not necessarily more intense in their brutality. (Those who describe rapes in conflict as unusually brutal are apparently unacquainted with the brutality of many rapes outside recognized zones of conflict.) But it is no accident that gender was first recognized as an express element in an international crime under the rubric of crimes against humanity, where the future of conflict lies. Campaigns of crimes against humanity are the messiest of the 'new wars',[31] organized principally along social–hierarchical lines, of which gender is one, often combined with ethnicity or religion or politics, rather than being organized according to neat military hierarchies that fit the 'old war' model. Where reality is headed, it is right that international law would head there too, with gender as the leading edge.

Gender crimes, in other words, are prominent in ICC prosecutions because they are prominent in the contexts being prosecuted. This only becomes remarkable against the backdrop of the prior and still largely

evidence submitted . . . suggests that JOSEPH KONY raped REDACTED and induced the commission of the crime of rape', as bases for the rape and sexual enslavement charges in Counts 1–3 of the Warrant, among other charges).

30 For example, the Democratic Forces for the Liberation of Rwanda (Les Forces démocratiques de libération du Rwanda, or FDLR) are widely known to have left Rwanda following the conflict and moved to Congo where they continue to perpetuate violence, including gender atrocities. For further discussion of this concept, see generally Human Rights Watch, *'You Will Be Punished': Attacks on Civilians in Eastern Congo* (13 December 2009), available online at: www.hrw.org/en/reports/2009/12/14/you-will-be-punished?print

31 See Mary Kaldor, *New and Old Wars: Organized Violence in a Global Era* (Stanford, CA: Stanford University Press, 1999).

existing norms that deny their existence, ignore them, shame their victims, define their injuries in legally unprovable or empirically unrealistic ways, and erect barriers that play on rape myths in the guise of procedure. Since these crimes essentially have never been taken seriously before, domestically or internationally, rubrics such as fair trial and right of confrontation, for just two examples, have never been shaped with these possible prosecutions and their dynamics in mind, as if the rapes actually happen. It is as if there is a tacit agreement underlying law enforcement to look the other way as women and children and sometimes men are sexually violated: to minimize, trivialize, denigrate, shame, and silence the victims, to destroy their credibility legally and socially and further shatter their psyches and dignity, so these abuses can continue unredressed and unimpeded. This is what impunity looks like. It is how gender crimes are standardly treated every day of the week in every corner of the world. The more power the accused has, the more this dynamic operates. The Rome Statute, and the body of the ICC's first cases under it, says to the world that here, at least, this deal is off.

What light does the literature on the creation, force, and development of international law shed on these issues? The interesting answer, I think, is none. Much of that literature is engaged with questions that have no relevance to these developments. For example, they do not illuminate or even ask the canonical question, 'why is international law obeyed', so central to this literature, because in this area, it is not. Of gender crimes, one could not observe, with the sainted Lou Henkin, 'that *almost all nations observe almost all principles of international law and almost all of their obligations almost all of the time*.'[32] The more salient question is why laws against gender crimes are not obeyed, domestically or internationally. Further, nations are not the principal actors in either disobeying laws against gender crimes or, here, in enforcing obedience to them. This throws into relief the fact that sexually violated women, that is most women, including those raped in war, have been in this respect living on the other side of Henkin's 'almost all' hedge almost all the time. Their reality has not, in the past, significantly distinguished between national and international law. And it is not only the absence of enforcement, but also a very real norm of nonobservance of the prohibition of gender crimes, of nonenforcement virtually as a matter of policy, that stands out.

[32] Louis Henkin, *How Nations Behave: Law and Foreign Policy* (2nd edn., New York: Columbia University Press, 1979), 47 (emphasis in original).

For gender crimes, why nations obey international laws is the wrong question all the way from its unit of analysis to its presumptions and observations of reality. The question here becomes not only why many men disobey almost all laws against sexual assault almost all the time, but further why, given this, they even have them. If most international and national laws are mostly obeyed, why are those against gender crimes mostly not? Why, in more pointed terms, do men, in their gendered capacities, first create and then routinely ignore laws against sexual abuse both within and across state lines? And what light, if any, does pursuit of this question shed on why nations – meaning in essence men organized into states – obey the laws they do obey, including when they are not enforced by force, which after all is the reason the question is being asked in the international context in the first place. And then why, given this context so overwhelmingly to the contrary, has it become possible for the ICC to strike out such an exceptional path?

In a gendered perspective – applying gender analysis, which is not a description of demography or a two-part finger-pointing head-counting exercise – the answer may be that, as to gender crimes, men tend to reflexively create, obey, and enforce on other men those rules that respect and enhance their power as men, according to norms that, in the sense of preserving male dominance over women and other men, they see as being in their interest. Exceptions to this generalization are still just that: exceptions. Rules that serve this end, they will obey and see to be legitimate. Thomas Franck is thus on the right track in speaking of the power of legitimacy among nations,[33] but in omitting gender, he cannot answer his own questions. The same difficulty besets his definition of legitimacy as 'factors that affect our willingness to comply voluntarily with commands'.[34] This 'our' is a bit gender neutral. Not asking about gender means not asking why women obey laws, which overwhelmingly they do, even more than men do, although they have typically had virtually no voice in their creation. Perhaps the answer is that women are kept in line by a perfect combination of force with socialization – which strongly bears upon the question the realists and the idealists fight over in international relations. One would think it would interest them.

Assuming Franck's 'voluntarily' means without immediate physical force, his definition of the legitimate could apply to intimidation or to

[33] See Thomas M. Franck, *The Power of Legitimacy among Nations* (New York: Oxford University Press, 1990).

[34] *Ibid.*, 150.

socialization, which an unequal social context corrupts. In a gendered perspective, legitimacy concerns the conditions under which men think it is right to accede to other men's power. The truth is, committing gender crimes has seldom before taken away men's sense that other men rightly exercised power over them. In a real way, these crimes have conferred that legitimacy more than they have undermined it. If this is right, men have known all along that the laws against what are in reality gender crimes have never been the real rules. The real rules are that men with power can commit these crimes, and will respect certain other men committing them, and may even respect other men because they commit them, in part because that is how masculinity is defined, and in part so they can commit them themselves if they want to, or know they can.

On this reading of how male power is organized in this sphere, the laws against sexual violation have functioned fundamentally as window-dressing. Perhaps these rules serve a function wholly apart from inducing compliance: to legitimize an unequal social order by distracting from the real impunity for violations that everyone knows will go unpunished. In this light, the distinctive contribution of the international arena, particularly the Rome Statute, has been to treat them like other legal prohibitions. Rule of law arrives. The aim of the Rome Statute in this respect is ultimately to delegitimize these crimes as a means of attaining and exercising power.

Given the magnitude of these legal developments, with the evolving prominence of the instrumentalization of the crimes themselves, the extent to which mainstream literature in international law[35] has largely gone right along in the absence of any deep engagement with its gendered dynamics, indeed ignored gender as a factor in international relations altogether, is striking. Even as the actors on the real world stage embrace and develop the concept and highlight its realities, this literature keeps on asking the same questions and debating the same answers on the same theoretical terms, turning a blind eye to what these challenging developments and innovations expose and demand and imply and promise. The field's static typologies, descriptive at best, neither

[35] Literature on this topic prominently includes Henkin, *How Nations Behave*; Abram Chayes and Antonia Handler Chayes, *The New Sovereignty: Compliance with International Regulatory Agreements* (Cambridge, MA: Harvard University Press, 1995); Thomas M. Franck, *Fairness in International Law and Institutions* (New York: Oxford University Press, 1995). The themes, and his own view, are cogently presented in Harold Hongju Koh, 'Review Essay: Why Do Nations Obey International Law?', *Yale Law Journal*, 106 (1997), 2599–659.

predicted nor usefully describe these changes, far less do they trace their trajectory or grasp their significance or portent.

Missing, among other things, is any conception that studying the behavior of nations, including compliance with law or not, is studying male behavior, behavior that is gendered to its core. In this connection, it is stunning to encounter Hannah Arendt discussing Kant on 'radical evil' as a phenomenon 'about whose nature so little is known',[36] and lovely Carlos Nino asking 'how shall we live with evil?'[37] in the context of accountability for past atrocities. When the social reference point is not the Holocaust as it has ordinarily been understood, or *terrorismo del estado*, or the Cold War, but intimacy, its crimes cannot be dismissed as blank 'evil', nor are they past. They are accounted for, and confronted, as the highly explicable gendered actions of men with whom their victims are all too familiar in everyday life into the present moment. Women, who are not baffled moralists, know a lot about this phenomenon (perhaps Arendt did but did not see what she knew as knowledge), living with it every day as they do. Perhaps we have reached a turning point in the relative invisibility of this analysis, one developed by women survivors, NGO organizers, advocates, jurists, and scholars.

Some truly interesting and potentially consequential questions that arise around gender crime that this literature is useless in illuminating concern, for one, the relation of sexual atrocities to existing international legal rubrics. Rape, for example, is now a recognized instrument of war, genocide, torture, and terrorism, and a common crime against humanity. It is integral to human trafficking, slavery, and forced marriage. Should it continue to be flushed out everywhere it rears its ugly head, or should it be recognized as a separate international crime on its own terms, and if so, structured how? Arguably rape violates customary international law.[38] What is at stake in the

[36] Hannah Arendt, *The Human Condition* (Chicago: University of Chicago Press, 1958), 241.

[37] Carlos Santiago Nino, *Radical Evil on Trial* (New Haven, CT: Yale University Press, 1996), vii.

[38] As rape in some form is a crime everywhere, domestically and internationally, even if its prohibition is largely ineffective, inquiry into this question would develop the literature on customary international law at a crucial tension within it. No universally accepted definition of customary international law exists, but a basic introduction can be found at *Restatement of the Law Third, the Foreign Relations Law of the United States* (St. Paul, MN: American Law Institute, 1987), §102(2) (stating that '[c]ustomary international law results from a general and consistent practice of states followed by them from a sense of legal obligation,' noting that such state practice 'can be general even if it is not universally followed' and that 'it must appear that the states follow the practice from a sense of legal obligation . . . a practice that is generally followed but which states feel legally free to disregard does not contribute to customary law'). Scholars discuss the process of development of custom for purposes of customary international law extensively, see, e.g., Anthony A. D'Amato, *The Concept of Custom in International Law* (Ithaca, NY: Cornell University Press, 1971), 32, 62, but

question of whether it should be a separate international crime? It has developed exponentially in its multiple sites so far. What difference would it make if it was carved out separately? No existing international literature I know provides a grip on this question, leaving the silver lining of freedom to develop our own approaches to its evolution, strategic and principled.

because they generally ignore gender crime, do not interrogate the relationship between a formal prohibition and its actual use with the clarity that would come from this particular context. Examples of legal authorities opining on the question of rape as a violation of customary international law can be found in Eritrea Ethiopia Claims Commission (EECC), Partial Award: Central Front Eritrea's Claims 2, 4, 6, 7, 8 and 22, The Hague, 28 April 2004, paras. 37–8, available online at: www.pca-cpa.org/showfile.asp?fil_id=662, and EECC, Partial Award: Central Front Ethiopia's Claim 2, The Hague, 28 April 2004, para. 35 (both based on agreement of parties to arbitration that rape of civilians in conflict between them violates customary international law under relevant articles of Geneva Conventions); *Prosecutor* v. *Furundzija*, Case No. IT-95–17/1, Judgment (ICTY 10 December 1998), paras. 165, 168 (discussing customary international humanitarian law as including rape as torture or as an outrage on personal dignity); *Prosecutor* v. *Kunarac*, Judgment (ICTY 22 February 2001), paras. 406, 408, 436; *Prosecutor* v. *Musema*, Case No. ICTR-96-13-A, Judgment and Sentence (ICTR 27 January 2000), paras. 285–7; *Prosecutor* v. *Akayesu*, paras. 585, 599, 608; and *Doe I* v. *Unocal Corp.*, 395 F 3d 932, 945 (9th Cir. 2002). See also International Committee of the Red Cross, Customary International Humanitarian Law (March 2005), Rule 93, available online at: www.icrc.org/ihl.nsf/FULL/612?OpenDocument; Human Rights Watch, *Targeting the Anuak: Human Rights Violations and Crimes against Humanity in Ethiopia's Gambella Region* (New York: Human Rights Watch, 2005), 56–7; UN Commission on Human Rights, Contemporary Forms of Slavery: Systematic Rape, Sexual Slavery and Slavery-like Practices During Armed Conflict, Final Report Submitted by Ms. Gay J. McDougall, Special Rapporteur, UN Doc. E/CN.4/Sub.2/1998/13 (22 June 1998), para. 36, available online at: www.unhchr.ch/Huridocda/Huridoca.nsf/0/3d25270b5fa3ea998025665f0032f220?Opendocument. For some relevant discussion by legal scholars, see Christine M. Chinkin, 'Women's International Tribunal on Japanese Military Sexual Slavery', *American Journal of International Law*, 95 (2001), 338; Rosalind Dixon, 'Rape as a Crime in International Humanitarian Law: Where to From Here?', *European Journal of International Law*, 13 (2002), 697–8, 719; Jordan J. Paust, 'Above the Law: Unlawful Executive Authorizations Regarding Detainee Treatment, Secret Renditions, Domestic Spying, and Claims to Unchecked Executive Power', *Utah Law Review*, 2 (2007), 407–8; Patricia Viseur Sellers, 'Sexual Violence and Peremptory Norms: The Legal Value of Rape', *Case Western Reserve Journal of International Law*, 34 (2002), 297–8, 302; Kelly D. Askin, 'Prosecuting Wartime Rape and Other Gender-Related Crimes Under International Law: Extraordinary Advances, Enduring Obstacles', *Berkeley Journal of International Law*, 21 (2003), 300. For discussion of the legal status of rape in conflict under the even more demanding international norm of *jus cogens*, see David S. Mitchell, 'The Prohibition of Rape in International Humanitarian Law as a Norm of Jus Cogens: Clarifying the Doctrine', *Duke Journal of Comparative and International Law*, 15 (2005), 226; Dean Adams, 'The Prohibition of Widespread Rape as a Jus Cogens', *San Diego International Law Journal*, 6 (2005), 362, 397. Much of the literature on rape as a violation of customary international law relies on its recognition as a form of torture. As rape is also a gender crime, it is also a form of sex discrimination, around which international consensus is building as a violation of customary international law as well.

The innovative creation of the law of gender crime in substance has also opened procedural possibilities that this literature also gets nowhere near, including the possibility to undo, get around, neutralize, or change the many obstacles, devices, traditions, and norms that have long operated in law to ensure that sexual assault as an everyday matter is never stopped. These doctrines appear gender neutral but ensure that the legal system will never respond to the victims' experience in substance, whatever the law seems to criminalize on its face. Gender crime, as it evolves as a matter of substantive law, is altering major technical rubrics such as state vs. private actor, challenging some accepted doctrines of jurisdiction and sovereignty, resisting many traditional cultural practices, and walking right across the line between war and peace. These abstractions may appear empty and neutral, their corresponding legal doctrines fair and principled, but in this setting, they have been anything but.

In this context, the international arena, the ICC in particular, opens a specific opportunity. Sexually violated women and international jurisdiction belong together, I think, not only because both are denigrated for not resorting to force in that neither has an army at its command. Most women and children are most violated at home, or close to home in the localities that form the states that have been the traditional units of international law. The men at home are the least likely to do anything about these violations because that is where they are most likely to do it themselves, so where they are most likely to identify with others who do it there. As a result, the further away from home women go, the experience has been, the more rights they get. Distance appears to attenuate the male bond, making it more likely that women's violations will be recognized as real.[39] This is both why women are inherently not a national group but a transnational one, and why gender crimes have been most powerfully recognized in international law first.

With this trans-historical and trans-cultural reality of gender crime is also highlighted the darker fact that, as of yet, there is no 'post-conflict' for gender crimes. The daily campaign of violence against women, well documented as a worldwide war on women – with substantial variation but also substantially invariant impunity – is the longest-running siege of crimes against humanity in the history of the world. The conflict goes on, its weapons forged daily, lying around to be seized for accelerated

[39] This argument is made more fully in Catharine A. MacKinnon, 'Introduction: Women's Status, Men's States', in *Are Women Human?*, 1–17.

deployment in every conflict among men in which they become convenient, with no embargo imaginable and no disarmament treaties in sight. A gender perspective thus raises, along with the question of what kind of justice we envision and negotiate, the question of what peace means.

In pursuing the gender crimes the Rome Statute defines, wherever they happen of concern to the international community, arises the possibility of developing grounded procedures and reality-based substantive doctrines that respond to the practical imperatives for their effective prosecution. Focus on those most responsible can include the rapists themselves (usually the so-called 'little fish') when they are most responsible, as well as those who deploy and permit them, sustaining the Nuremberg principle from the top down as well as from the bottom up. Positive complementarity[40] could become a well-traveled two-way street between the national and the international, including always crucial NGOs. The opportunity is open for the ICC and other international institutions to know what women know: there will be no meaningful collective security in a world of gender injustice. By setting an example, supporting institution-building, and through cooperation, the response of the public order to gender crime can be transformed in and outside recognized zones of conflict, in war and in so-called peace. Neither utopian nor apologetic,[41] this work for real change provides an effective paradigm for international law's creative development.

[40] This ICC standard could be seen as one form of Harold Koh's 'transnational legal process,' through which international and domestic become interpenetrated, an accessible discussion of which can be found at Harold Hongju Koh, 'Jefferson Memorial Lecture: Transnational Legal Process After September 11th', *Berkeley Journal of International Law*, 22 (2004), 337–54.

[41] Martti Koskenneimi, *From Apology to Utopia: The Structure of International Legal Argument* (rev. edn., New York: Cambridge University Press, 2005) is in reference.

3

Legal redress for children on the front line: the invisibility of the female child

CHRISTINE BYRON

1 Introduction

The problem of the use of child soldiers is now well known and, indeed, their use in armed conflicts has not decreased in recent years, with an estimated 250,000 soldiers currently less than 18 years old.[1] Technological advances such as 'automatic weapons and lightweight arms have increased the desirability and utility of child soldiers'.[2] Children make obedient and cheap soldiers, yet those who survive such employment 'are often physically injured and psychologically scarred, having lost years of schooling and socialization'.[3]

This chapter, however, will not concentrate on the problem of legal redress for the use of child soldiers per se, but on ensuring legal redress, in terms of criminal prosecution for those who sexually abuse the female child on the front line with their forces. This problem is often overlooked as it is commonly thought that the main threat of sexual violence to women in armed conflict is from male combatants of the opposing armed forces. Legal redress for this abuse has been prosecuted in recent years by the International Criminal Tribunal for Rwanda (ICTR) and the International Criminal Tribunal for the former Yugoslavia (ICTY) as both a crime against humanity and a war crime.[4] Jurisdiction over such

[1] Report of the Special Representative of the Secretary-General for Children and Armed Conflict, 17 August 2006, A/61/275, para. 11. See generally, M. Happold, *Child Soldiers in International Law* (Manchester: Manchester University Press, 2005).

[2] *Ibid.*

[3] 'Children and Armed Conflict: Report of the Secretary-General', 19 July 2000, A/55/163-S/2000/712, para. 38.

[4] See such cases as: *Akayesu*, Trial Chamber Judgment, 2 September 1998, Case No. ICTR-96-4-T, paras. 692–7; *Furundžija*, Trial Chamber Judgment, 10 December 1988, Case No. IT-95-17/1-T, paras. 269 and 275; *Kunarać et al.*, Trial Chamber Judgment, 22 February 2001, Case No. IT-96-23-T, paras. 883, 886 and 888.

crimes is also included in the Rome Statute of the International Criminal Court (ICC).[5] However, female child soldiers and 'camp followers' are uniquely vulnerable to sexual abuse by their own forces. This chapter will consider the problems in legal redress for the total experience of the female child on the front line, which often includes sexual violence in addition to (or instead of) a combat role. This issue has to be dealt with at the intersection between three types of law: international humanitarian law, human rights law and international criminal law.

The expression 'child soldiers' will be used to mean those children and young people under 15 years of age who engage directly in hostilities. International humanitarian law (IHL) only prohibits the use of child soldiers under the age of 15 and merely exhorts state parties in recruiting among those between 15 and 17 to 'endeavour to give priority to those who are oldest'[6] and the Rome Statute only provides jurisdiction over those conscripting, enlisting or using in hostilities, children under 15.[7] Children and young women, who despite these provisions become involved in an armed conflict, are very vulnerable to sexual abuse from male combatants in the same armed force and also deserve to see the perpetrators of such abuse prosecuted.[8] Indeed, Alfredson comments that '[many] sexually exploited child soldiers take on active combat roles' and gives examples of children in conflicts in Colombia, Sierra Leone and Uganda who have suffered sexual abuse while fulfilling military roles.[9]

[5] See, Articles 7(1)(g) and 8(2)(b)(xxii) and (e)(vi), Rome Statute of the International Criminal Court, Rome, 17 July 1998, in force 1 July 2002, 2187 UNTS 3; (1998) 37 ILM 999. Note that the trial of *Jean-Pierre Bemba Gombo*, ICC-01-05/01-08, which commenced 22 November 2010, includes charges of rape as a war crime and as a crime against humanity. See Chapter 2, this book, for a discussion of the development of sexual assault and rape as an international crime and the approach of the Prosecutor of the ICC.

[6] Article 77(2), Protocol Additional to the Geneva Conventions of 12 August 1949, and Relating to the Protection of Victims of International Armed Conflicts (Protocol I), 8 June 1977, in force 7 December 1978, 1125 UNTS 3; (1977) 16 ILM 1391; UKTS (1999) 29. Note that while Additional Protocol II prohibits the use of child soldiers in stronger language in Article 4(3) it does not include the exhortation with respect to the 15–17-year-olds.

[7] Article 8(2) (b) (xxvi) and 8(2) (e) (vii) of the Rome Statute.

[8] The human rights law protections for under 18-year-olds will not be discussed here as this essay is primarily concentrating on how international criminal law can be used to prosecute for war crimes and therefore uses the IHL concept of children as being under 15.

[9] L. Alfredson, Coalition to Stop the Use of Child Soldiers, 'Sexual Exploitation of Child Soldiers: An Exploration and Analysis of Global Dimensions and Trends', January 2001, available online at: www.reliefweb.int/rw/lib.nsf/db900SID/LGEL-5RPBPA?OpenDocument (last accessed 25 August 2011).

The term 'child camp followers' will be used to refer to those under 15 years old who accompany the armed forces in a non-combatant role, such as a cook, cleaner or as a 'wife' or 'girlfriend' of the soldiers.[10] The expressions 'wife' and 'girlfriend' in inverted commas are used to denote the type of situation referred to by McDougall, who commented with respect to the Lord's Resistance Army in Uganda that girls as young as 12 have been given to the commanders as wives in sham marriages and that '[e]ach soldier may have several such wives, and many of the children have become pregnant and have contracted sexual diseases'.[11] Despite such reports, only seven years ago the problem of female child soldiers was ignored by a UN disarmament and demobilisation programme in the Democratic Republic of the Congo; a former demobilisation officer commenting that they 'did not touch the issue of the girl soldiers, but wrongly took them as the dependants of combatants ...[at the time] it was not seen as a serious issue'.[12]

2 Crimes against humanity

In order for crimes against humanity to be considered at all, there must first be a widespread or systematic attack against a civilian population of which the sexual abuse of the children or young people formed a part, or that the sexual abuse of children was itself so widespread or systematic that it satisfied this criteria.[13] Assuming that this is the case, with respect to the camp followers, whose duties are as 'wives' or 'girlfriends' coupled with domestic duties such as cooking and cleaning, it is clear that such girls would be considered civilians and therefore sexual abuse against them could be charged as a crime against humanity.

[10] The age of 15 has been chosen, as this chapter is primarily concentrating on the abuse of children, although many comments on the treatment of child camp followers would be relevant to older camp followers.

[11] G. McDougall, Special Rapporteur, Sub-Commission on Prevention of Discrimination and Protection of Minorities, 'Contemporary Forms of Slavery: Systematic Rape, Sexual Slavery and Slavery-Like Practices During Armed Conflict', Update to Final Report, UN Doc. E/CN.4/Sub.2/2000/21, 6 June 2000, para. 13.

[12] K. Glassborow, 'Plight of Girl Soldiers "Overlooked"', Institute for Peace and War Reporting, 8 November 2006, available online at: www.iwpr.net/ru/print/node/12996 (last accessed 25 August 2011).

[13] For a discussion of the meaning of this expression, see C. Byron, *War Crimes and Crimes against Humanity in the Rome Statute of the Criminal Court*, (Manchester: Manchester University Press, 2009), 191–202.

Under the Rome Statute of the ICC, offences such as Article 7(1) (g) particularly rape, sexual slavery and sexual violence, would seem appropriate charges for those who have sexually abused camp followers. However, the approach of the Appeals Chamber in the Special Court for Sierra Leone in the case of *Brima, Kamara and Kanu*, in which they found that forced marriage was different from sexual slavery and could be charged as a separate crime against humanity under 'other inhumane acts', is to be commended.[14]

The Appeal Chamber defined forced marriage, in the context of the Sierra Leone conflict as 'a situation in which the perpetrator through his words or conduct … compels a person by force, threat of force, or coercion to serve as a conjugal partner, resulting in severe suffering, or physical, mental or psychological injury to the victim'.[15] The judgment confirms that forced marriage was of a similar gravity to other crimes against humanity 'including enslavement, imprisonment, torture, rape, sexual slavery and sexual violence'.[16] This approach acknowledges the experience of the female child in a prosecution that recognises her particular suffering and is an approach which could and should be taken in appropriate cases by the Office of the Prosecutor at the ICC.

A consideration of charges of crimes against humanity for the sexual abuse of child soldiers causes problems because crimes against humanity must be committed as part of an attack against a 'civilian population' and arguably child soldiers are no longer civilians. Assuming that there is a widespread or systematic attack against civilians, Wells comments that even if children who participate in combat lose their civilian status 'their initial abduction and forced recruitment can, and should be characterized as … an attack on a civilian population'.[17] If the child

[14] *Prosecutor* v. *Brima, Kamara and Kanu*, Appeal Chamber Judgment, 22 February 2008, SCSL-2004-16-A, para. 195. See discussion in M. Frulli, 'Advancing International Criminal Law: The Special Court for Sierra Leone Recognizes Forced Marriage as a "New" Crime Against Humanity', *Journal of International Criminal Justice*, 6 (2008), 1033–42.

[15] *Prosecutor* v. *Brima, Kamara and Kanu*, Appeal Chamber Judgment, 22 February 2008, SCSL-2004-16-A, para. 196.

[16] *Ibid.*, para. 200. These findings of the Appeal Chamber in *Brima et al.* were approved and followed in *Prosecutor* v. *Sesay, Kallon and Gbao*, Appeal Chamber Judgment, 26 October 2009, SCSL-04-15-A.

[17] S. Wells, 'Crimes against Child Soldiers in Armed Conflict Situations: Application and Limits of International Humanitarian Law', *Tulane Journal of International and Comparative Law*, 12 (2004), 287–306, at 300. See also S. O'Connor, 'at the point of recruitment or initial use the child cannot be a member of an armed force or armed groups and are certainly persons, before recruitment or use, that *are* taking no active part

soldiers were abducted and forcibly recruited in such a manner (it should be remembered that some child soldiers are 'volunteers'),[18] then, depending on the circumstances, this could amount to enslavement, imprisonment or more likely be subsumed under 'other inhumane acts'.[19]

Despite this being a possible way to charge a perpetrator of sexual violence against children with *some* crimes against humanity in *some* circumstances, it is not alone an ideal solution. Such a charge would not reflect the total experience of the female child. Can child soldiers be brought within the definition of civilian for the purposes of crimes against humanity? The jurisprudence from the ICTY and ICTR is instructive in this regard. The ICTY Appeal Chamber in the *Blaškić* case required that the victim of an individual crime against humanity be a civilian and emphasised that '[i]f he is indeed a member of an armed organization, the fact that he is not armed or in combat at the time of the commission of crimes, does not accord him civilian status'.[20] If the ICC were to follow this approach, a perpetrator of sexual violence against child soldiers could not be prosecuted for a crime against humanity.

The approach that the ICC will take to the expression 'civilian population' is still unclear and the definition of a 'civilian population' was not addressed in the Elements of Crimes. Robinson states that the Preparatory Commission felt that this complex and still evolving notion was better left to resolution in case law, but agreed that it was a 'flexible test'.[21] However,

in hostilities', in 'Why a Child Is Not a Soldier', in C. Eboe-Osuji (ed.), *Protecting Humanity: Essays in International Law and Policy in Honour of Navanethem Pillay* (Leiden, Boston MA: Martinus Nijhoff, 2010), 237–73 at 250; original emphasis.

[18] See A. Abbott, 'Child Soldiers – The Use of Children as Instruments of War', *Suffolk Transnational Law Review*, 23 (2000), 499–573, at 510–11 and 516, on why some children enlist voluntarily.

[19] See Article 7(1)(c), (e) and (k) of the Rome Statute. Note that the Elements of Article 7 (c) require that 'The perpetrator exercised any or all of the powers attaching to the right of ownership over one or more persons, such as by purchasing, selling, lending or bartering such a person or persons, or by imposing on them a similar deprivation of liberty', Elements of Crimes, Assembly of State Parties to the Rome Statute of the International Criminal Court, Official Records, First Session, ICC-ASP/1/3, 3–10 September 2002; the Elements of Article 7(e) require that 'The perpetrator imprisoned one or more persons or otherwise severely deprived one or more persons of physical liberty.'

[20] *Blaškić*, Appeal Chamber Judgment, 29 July 2004, Case No. IT-95-14, para. 114.

[21] R. Lee (ed.), *The International Criminal Court: Elements of Crimes and Rules of Procedure and Evidence* (New York: Transitional, 2001), 78, and see H. von Hebel and D. Robinson, 'Crimes within the Jurisdiction of the Court', in R. Lee (ed.), *The International Criminal Court: The Making of the Rome Statute: Issues, Negotiations, Results* (The Hague: Kluwer 1999), 79–126, at 97, fn. 54.

it seems unlikely that the ICC will be able to prosecute all or indeed any perpetrators of sexual abuse against child soldiers for such abuse as a crime against humanity. This makes it important to consider whether such abuse could amount to a war crime.

3 War crimes

3.1 International armed conflicts

With respect to international armed conflicts, it has always been considered that the IHL treaties only protect certain persons; that is, protected persons who find themselves 'in the hands of a party to the conflict or Occupying Power of which they are not nationals'.[22] While it is true that the *Tadić* Appeal Judgment held that 'in modern inter-ethnic armed conflicts such as that in the former Yugoslavia, new States are often created during the conflict and ethnicity rather than nationality may become the grounds for allegiance';[23] this is still predicated upon the victim being in the hands of the enemy and so does not assist with the question of whether it can be a war crime to sexually abuse your own national child soldiers and camp followers. As Wells comments, the experiences of child soldiers suggests that 'from the perspective of child combatants in modern armed conflicts, distinctions between enemy and friendly forces may no longer be so distinct'.[24]

Nevertheless, Additional Protocol I includes in Article 77 'Protection of Children', provisions which undeniably bind a party to deal with its own children in a particular way, including the requirement that the parties to a conflict 'take all feasible measures in order that children who have not attained the age of fifteen years do not take a direct part in hostilities'. The use of child soldiers is, of course, now accepted as a war

[22] Article 4, Geneva Convention Relative to the Protection of Civilian Persons in Time of War of August 12, 1949, in force 21 October 1950, 75 UNTS 287; UKTS (1958) 39. A similar requirement of protection relying upon being in enemy hands is contained in Article 5, Geneva Convention for the Amelioration of the Condition of the Wounded and Sick in Armed Forces in the Field of August 12, 1949, in force 21 October 1950, 75 UNTS 31; UKTS (1958) 39; Article 16, Geneva Convention for the Amelioration of the Condition of Wounded, Sick and Shipwrecked Members of Armed Forces at Sea of August 12, 1949, in force 21 October 1950, 75 UNTS 85; UKTS (1958) 39 and Article 4, Geneva Convention Relative to the Treatment of Prisoners of War of August 12, 1949, in force 21 October 1950, 75 UNTS 135; UKTS (1958) 39.

[23] *Prosecutor* v. *Tadić*, Appeal Chamber Judgment, Case No. IT-94-1-A, 15 July 1999, para. 166.

[24] Wells, 'Crimes against Child Soldiers', 302.

crime, whether we accept the *Hinga Norman* Decision in the Appeals Chamber of the Special Court for Sierra Leone, that it was criminalised under customary international law by 1996, or simply accept that the law crystallised in 1998 with the inclusion of this crime in the Rome Statute.[25]

However, Article 77 of Additional Protocol I did not simply constrain states with respect to their use of their children as soldiers but also stated in paragraph 1 that '[c]hildren shall be the object of special respect and shall be protected against *any form of indecent assault*'.[26] Article 76(1) on the protection of women is even more emphatic in this regard, stating that '[w]omen shall be the object of special respect and *shall be protected in particular against rape, forced prostitution and any other form of indecent assault*'.[27] These Articles are both in Chapter II of Section III,[28] entitled 'Measures in Favour of Women and Children', and the International Committee of the Red Cross (ICRC) commentary states that '[t]he rule applies quite generally and therefore covers all women who are in the territory of Parties involved in the conflict'.[29] There is no minimum age on this Article, so it is clear that international humanitarian law prohibits the rape, forced prostitution or any other sexual assault of female child soldiers and camp followers by their own forces.

It is submitted that this total prohibition of sexual violence against women, including the female child, at all times and in all places during an international armed conflict represents customary international law. This argument can be sustained as the prohibition of sexual violence against all persons in the territory of the parties to the conflict is confirmed by Article 75 of Additional Protocol I. Article 75 on fundamental guarantees, which is generally accepted as representing customary international law,[30]

[25] See *Prosecutor* v. *Norman*, Appeal Decision on the preliminary motion based on lack of jurisdiction (child recruitment), 13 May 2004, SCSL-2004-14-AR72(E), para. 53 and Article 8(2)(b)(xxvi) of the Rome Statute.

[26] Author's emphasis. [27] Author's emphasis.

[28] Section III is unpromisingly entitled 'Treatment of Persons in the Power of a Party to the Conflict'.

[29] Y. Sandoz, C. Swinarski and B. Zimmermann (eds.), *Commentary on the Additional Protocols of 8 June 1977 to the Geneva Conventions of 12 August 1949* (Geneva: ICRC and Martinus Nijhoff, 1987), 892.

[30] See for example comments of M. Matheson and B. Carnahan, 'Customary Law and Additional Protocol I to the Geneva Conventions for Protection of War Victims: Future Directions in Light of the US decision Not to Ratify', *American Society International Law Proceedings*, 81 (1987), 26–43, at 31 and 37 respectively. See also J. Henckaerts and L. Doswald-Beck, *Customary International Humanitarian Law*, 2 vols. (Cambridge: Cambridge University Press 2005) vol. 1, Rules 90 and 93, 315–19 and 323–7.

states that acts 'prohibited *at any time and in any place* whatsoever' include 'outrages upon personal dignity, in particular humiliating and degrading treatment, enforced prostitution and any form of indecent assault'.[31]

Therefore, both treaty and customary international humanitarian law prohibit sexual abuse of child soldiers and camp followers by their own forces. However, the real question is whether sexual abuse of child soldiers and camp followers by their own forces has been criminalised under international law and whether the individuals carrying out such abuse could be prosecuted before an international court such as the ICC. The Appeal Chamber in *Tadić* suggested that factors to look for, when considering whether a violation of IHL would entail individual criminal responsibility under international law, include 'State practice indicating an intention to criminalise the prohibition, including statements by government officials and international organisations, as well as punishment of violations by national courts and military tribunals'.[32]

Clearly there is no evidence of states treating intra-forces sexual abuse as an international criminal offence, but it is submitted that it would be open for the ICC to prosecute perpetrators of such abuse on two grounds. First, a notable absence from the chapeau of Article 8(2) (b) ('[o]ther serious violations of the laws and customs applicable in international armed conflict') is any reference to protected persons. This suggests that, contrary to the grave breach offences, protected person status under the Geneva Conventions is not a requirement for the victims of Article 8(2) (b), and indeed the Elements of Crimes for this section make no reference to protected person status.[33] Many of the Elements of Article 8(2) (b) require either that the victim is a civilian or that the victim is in the power of an adverse party; for example the Elements for the war crime of mutilation require that any persons mutilated 'were in

[31] Article 75(2)(b) of Additional Protocol I; author's emphasis.

[32] *Prosecutor* v. *Tadić*, Appeal Chamber Decision on the Defence Motion for Interlocutory Appeal on Jurisdiction, Case No. IT-94-1-AR72, Appeal Chamber, 2 October 1995, para. 128. Note that there is evidence of states prosecuting service personnel who sexually assault other service personnel on the same side, but only as an ordinary criminal offence: for example the recent British Courts Martial Appeal Court decision in *R* v. *Stables* [2010] EWCA Crim 2405, in which the conviction of a medical assistant, in the Royal Navy, for assault by penetration was quashed.

[33] See W. Schabas, *An Introduction to the International Criminal Court* (2nd edn, Cambridge: Cambridge University Press, 2001), 123. The Elements for the grave breach provisions all require that '[s]uch person or persons were protected under one or more of the Geneva Conventions of 1949'.

the power of an adverse party'.[34] However, neither the Elements of the war crime of outrages upon personal dignity, under Article 8(2) (b) (xxi), nor the Elements of the war crime of rape, sexual slavery, enforced prostitution, enforced pregnancy, enforced sterilisation and sexual violence under Article 8(2) (b) (xxii) have any restrictive requirements in respect of the victims. This suggests that these Articles may have been intended to apply to all victims of sexual abuse within the territory of the states parties, or at least that the ICC could find that the Articles do so apply.

While the chapeau of Article 8(2) (b) also notes that the Court will have jurisdiction over war crimes 'in particular when committed as part of a plan or policy or as part of a large scale commission of such crimes', it is still arguable that the Court could take jurisdiction over lesser-scale war crimes if the offences include sexual violence against children. This is based upon the importance of the sexual integrity of children and the grave and long-lasting consequences of such abuse for the victims involved, not least damage to sexual organs, sexually transmitted diseases, pregnancy and birth without medical assistance and forced abortions.[35]

Second, in a prosecution before the ICC an individual accused of sexual abuse of child soldiers or camp followers in his own forces may well argue that this is a new crime and so offends against the principle of *nullum crimen sine lege*, which is enshrined in the Rome Statute in Article 22. The *nullum crimen* issue was raised in the Special Court for Sierra Leone in the *Hinga Norman* Decision by the Appeal Chamber on the question of whether the use of child soldiers was criminalised in 1996, the time-frame in the indictment.[36] The prosecution had submitted that '[t]he principle of *nullum criminen sine lege* should not be rigidly applied to an act universally regarded as abhorrent. The question is whether it was foreseeable and accessible to a possible perpetrator that the conduct was punishable.'[37] While the Appeal Chamber did not explicitly state whether they agreed with the Prosecutor, their reference to the ICTY Decision in *Hadžihasanović* that 'it must be foreseeable and

[34] Elements of Crime for Article 8(2) (b) (x), 25.

[35] For a more in-depth discussion of the harm caused by sexual abuse, see J. Gilbertson, 'Little Girls Lost: Can the International Community Protect Girl Soldiers?', *University of La Verne Law Review*, 29 (2008), 219–44, at 224–7.

[36] *Prosecutor* v. *Norman*, Appeal Decision on the preliminary motion based on lack of jurisdiction (child recruitment), 13 May 2004, SCSL-2004-14-AR72(E).

[37] *Ibid.*, para. 2(d).

accessible to a possible perpetrator that his concrete conduct was punishable',[38] echoes the comments of the prosecution and suggests that they interpreted the law similarly.[39] However, it must be noted that former Judge Shahabuddeen of the International Court of Justice and the ICTY has supported Justice Robertson's dissent in this case, where he stated that 'it is precisely when the acts are abhorrent and deeply shocking that the principle of legality must be most stringently applied to ensure that a defendant is not convicted . . . of a non-existent crime'.[40]

Greenwood's interpretation of *nullum crimen* is that the principle is not infringed 'where the conduct in question would universally be acknowledged as wrongful and there was doubt only in respect of whether it constituted a crime under a particular system of law'.[41] This approach is also taken by Van Schaak, commenting that tribunals 'will even cite particular domestic law as a source of advance notice that certain conduct is prohibited'.[42] In a reference to the *Delalić et al.* case she comments that in that case the ICTY reasoned that 'the prohibition in domestic law of the predicate act provides sufficient notice of the wrongfulness and criminality of the underlying conduct, even when the act is prosecuted under an unprecedented international law analog that requires a showing of additional elements such as the existence of an armed conflict'.[43] She finishes by arguing that 'the characterization of the crime prosecuted as an international crime is of no moment when a defendant had notice that the underlying conduct was proscribed by domestic law'.[44]

[38] ICTY, Decision on Joint Challenge to Jurisdiction, *Prosecutor* v. *Hadžihasanović, Alagić and Kubura*, Case No. IT-01-47-PT, T. Ch. II, 12 November 2002, para. 62.

[39] *Prosecutor* v. *Norman*, Appeal Decision, on the preliminary motion based on lack of jurisdiction (child recruitment), 13 May 2004, SCSL-2004-14-AR72(E), para. 25.

[40] *Ibid.*, Dissenting Opinion of Justice Robertson, para. 12 and see M. Shahabuddeen, 'Does the Principle of Legality Stand in the Way of Progressive Development of Law?', *Journal of International Criminal Justice*, 2 (2004), 1007–17, at 1010.

[41] C. Greenwood, 'International Humanitarian Law and the *Tadić* Case', *European Journal of International Law*, 7 (1996), 265–83, esp. at 281.

[42] B. Van Schaak, '*Crimen sine lege*: Judicial Lawmaking at the Intersection of Law And Morals', *Georgetown Law Journal*, 97 (2008), 119–92, at 168, referring to *Prosecutor* v. *Milutinović et al.*, Appeal Chamber Decision on Dragolub Ojdanić's Motion Challenging Jurisdiction: Joint Criminal Enterprise, 21 May 2003, IT-99-37-AR72, paras. 40–1.

[43] Van Schaak, '*Crimen sine lege*', referring to *Prosecutor* v. *Delalić et al.*, Trial Chamber Judgment, 16 Nov 1998, Case No. IT-96-21-T, para. 312.

[44] *Ibid.*, 169. A similar approach is taken by B. Juratowitch, 'Retroactive Criminal Liability and International Human Rights Law', *British Yearbook of International Law*, 74 (2004), 337–62, at 361–2.

The European Court of Human Rights has also taken a flexible approach to this issue in the case of *CR* v. *United Kingdom*, relating to the scope of Article 7 of the European Convention of Human Rights which states that 'no one shall be held guilty of any criminal offence on account of any act or omission which did not constitute a criminal offence under national or international law at the time when it was committed'.[45] The Court held that 'Article 7 ... of the Convention cannot be read as outlawing the gradual clarification of the rules of criminal liability through judicial interpretation from case to case, provided that the resultant development is *consistent with the essence of the offence and could reasonably be foreseen*'.[46] This case related to the removal of the former immunity for husbands in the crime of rape when the victim was their wife. The Court seemed particularly persuaded in this case by the fact that this was not a new criminal offence, but rather the extension of the current offence by the deletion of immunity for certain perpetrators (that is, husbands).[47]

The two lines of argument above would support the prosecution of individuals who sexually abuse female child soldiers or camp followers. First, child sexual abuse is considered unlawful in practically all countries and so the defendants could be prosecuted in their own domestic systems if the domestic criminal justice system was working properly. Second, it is acknowledged that it is a criminal offence *under international law* to sexually abuse children in occupied territory, children who are prisoners of war and children who are interned for reasons related to the conflict.[48] It is submitted that the former immunity (if it can be called that) under international law for those who commit sexual abuse of children within the same force should be removed, allowing prosecution before the ICC.

Nevertheless, it may still be difficult to overcome the *nullum crimen sine lege* argument, especially before the ICC. Article 22 of the Rome Statute requires that 'the definition of a crime shall be strictly construed and shall not be extended by analogy' and that '[i]n case of ambiguity, the definition shall be interpreted in favour of the person being investigated, prosecuted or convicted'.[49] Van Schaak expresses concern over this

[45] *CR* v. *United Kingdom*, European Court of Human Rights Judgment, 22 November 1995, Application No. 20190/92, para. 34.

[46] *Ibid.* Author's emphasis. [47] *Ibid.*, paras. 41–2.

[48] For example see Articles 13 and 14 of Geneva Convention III; Articles 27 and 37 of Geneva Convention IV and Article 75(2) of Additional Protocol I.

[49] Article 22(2) of the Rome Statute of the ICC.

'robust' provision, but Meron expresses the view that Article 21 of the Statute on applicable law 'opens the door widely to additional sources of international law, including custom as well as "general principles", stating that he believes 'it will be especially important for the ICC to draw on the practices and jurisprudence of other international criminal courts in matters of procedure, customary law, interpretation of relevant treaties'.[50] The approach the ICC will take to these issues is yet to be seen.

3.2 *Non-international armed conflicts*

Legal redress for war crimes committed against child soldiers and camp followers in a non-international armed conflict raises issues other than those discussed above. The main obstruction to the prosecution of sexual violence against child soldiers is that under Common Article 3 IHL only protects '[p]ersons taking no active part in the hostilities, including members of armed forces who have laid down their arms and those placed hors de combat by sickness, wounds, detention or any other cause'. Additional Protocol II states that it develops and supplements Article 3 'without modifying its conditions of application' equally is clearly only intended to protect those not taking part in the hostilities.[51]

It is clear that Common Article 3 of the Geneva Conventions and Article 4 'Fundamental guarantees' of Additional Protocol II proscribe sexual abuse of camp followers. Common Article 3 prohibits 'cruel treatment' and 'outrages upon personal dignity, in particular humiliating and degrading treatment'. Indeed, the Appeal Chamber of the Special Court for Sierra Leone opined in the *Hinga Norman* jurisdiction decision that these Common Article 3 prohibitions include 'the treatment of child soldiers in the course of their recruitment'.[52] Additional Protocol II, Article 4 also prohibits 'rape, enforced prostitution and any form of

50 'The Principle of Legality in International Criminal Law', *American Society of International Law Proceedings*, 103 (2009), 101–12; B. Van Schaak, '*Crimen sine lege*', at 103; and Meron, 'Principle of Legality', at 109.

51 Article 1 of the Protocol Additional to the Geneva Conventions of 12 August 1949, and Relating to the Protection of Victims of Non-International Armed Conflicts (Protocol II), 8 June 1977, in force 7 December 1978, 1125 UNTS 609; (1977) 16 ILM 1442; UKTS (1999) 30.

52 *Prosecutor* v. *Norman*, Appeal Decision on the preliminary motion based on lack of jurisdiction (child recruitment), 13 May 2004, SCSL-2004-14-AR72(E), para. 28; and see O'Connor, 'Why a Child Is Not a Soldier', 249–50.

indecent assault'. Both Articles apply to civilians or those who have ceased to take a direct part in hostilities. On the issue of whether there can be criminal responsibility for their breach, since the *Tadić* Interlocutory Appeal Decision that 'customary international law imposes criminal liability for serious violations of common Article 3, as supplemented by other general principles and rules on the protection of victims of internal armed conflict, and for breaching certain fundamental principles and rules regarding means and methods of combat in civil strife', it has been accepted that serious breaches of Common Article 3 and much of Additional Protocol II entail individual criminal responsibility.[53]

This, however, leaves the problem of whether war crimes can be committed in a non-international armed conflict against child soldiers. The answer could lie in whether they are taking an 'active' or 'direct' part in hostilities, such individuals not coming under the protection of Common Article 3 or Additional Protocol II respectively. The ICRC has recently issued guidance on the notion of 'direct participation in hostilities' and while some of its guidance is controversial, it may help to decide whether child soldiers may be protected under Common Article 3 or Additional Protocol II.[54] First, those whose continuous function is to engage in hostilities are considered members of the organised fighting forces of a non-state party and so are not civilians protected under the conventions.[55] Therefore, it is arguable that those child soldiers whose main function is to fight the enemy will not be protected.

Nevertheless, the concept of a child having a continuous combatant function is strongly contested by O'Connor, who argues that while an adult could be conscripted or enlisted and so effectively become a combatant, a

[53] *Prosecutor* v. *Tadić*, Appeal Chamber Decision on the Defence Motion for Interlocutory Appeal on Jurisdiction, Case No. IT-94-1-AR72, A. Ch., 2 October 1995, para. 134. Note that the Judgment of the ICTR Trial Chamber in *Akayesu*, stated that the fundamental guarantees of Article 4, Additional Protocol II, are recognised as part of customary international law and concluded that 'it is clear that the authors of such egregious violations must incur individual criminal responsibility for their deeds' (*Prosecutor* v. *Akayesu*, ICTR Trial Chamber Judgment, ICTR-96-4-T, T. Ch. I, 2 September 1998, paras. 16–17).

[54] ICRC (N. Melzer, legal adviser ICRC), *Interpretive Guidance on the Notion of Direct Participation in Hostilities under International Humanitarian Law* (Switzerland: ICRC, 2009). See D. Akande, 'Clearing the Fog of War? The ICRC's Interpretive Guidance on Direct Part in Hostilities', *International and Comparative Law Quarterly*, 59 (2010), 180–92.

[55] ICRC, *Interpretive Guidance*, 33–4.

child could not.[56] He reasons that, as there is no prohibition under international law against civilian participation in hostilities per se, an adult could be a combatant.[57] However, as there is an international law prohibition against child participation in hostilities, he argues that a child is not permitted to 'fulfil any function synonymous with that of the soldier and thus the term "child soldier" becomes conceivably erroneous and potentially wrong as a matter of law'.[58] Although, this approach would assist in the prosecution of those who abuse child soldiers in a non-international armed conflict, it is questionable whether this argument can be maintained. Article 77(3) in Additional Protocol I, deals with the exceptional situation in which children under 15 take part in an armed conflict and provides that they should continue to have the benefits of Article 77 'whether or not they are prisoners of war'.[59] Although, this provision applies to international armed conflicts, nevertheless, it clearly envisages circumstances in which children could become combatants.[60]

What of camp followers who are also used to carry ammunition or spy on the enemy, or even occasionally fight? What is their status? According to the ICRC guidance, such children would be protected unless they take a direct part in hostilities which requires three cumulative criteria:

1. the act must be likely to adversely affect the military operations or military capacity of a party to an armed conflict or, alternatively, to inflict death, injury, or destruction on persons or objects protected against direct attack (threshold of harm);
2. there must be a direct causal link between the act and the harm likely to result either from that act, or from a coordinated military operation of which that act constitutes an integral part (direct causation);
3. the act must be specifically designed to directly cause the required threshold of harm in support of a party to the conflict and to the detriment of another (belligerent nexus).[61]

[56] O'Connor, 'Why a Child Is Not a Soldier', 261–2. [57] *Ibid.*, 261.
[58] *Ibid.*, 262. [59] O'Connor mentions this provision (*ibid.*, 243).
[60] O'Connor's argument is that this Article was based on the idea that some children may voluntarily join an armed uprising and that 'the law has developed to the point where such voluntarism is impermissible' (*ibid.*). While I would not disagree with this latter statement, it does not seem to me that Additional Protocol I intended that forcibly recruited children should be denied POW status – and so did envisage the concept of 'child soldiers' more generally.
[61] ICRC, *Interpretive Guidance*, 46.

The guidance suggests that merely carrying weapons or equipment would not amount to a direct causal link unless carried as integral part of a specific operation;[62] so child porters would not lose their protection if they were just responsible for carrying weapons and ammunition when the group moved to another area. With respect to belligerent nexus, the guidance comments that this is generally not influenced by factors such as 'personal distress or preferences, or by the mental ability or willingness of persons to assume responsibility for their conduct. Accordingly, *even civilians forced to directly participate in hostilities or children below the lawful recruitment age may lose protection* against direct attack.'[63]

Therefore, it seems that if child soldiers can be said to have a continuous combat function, they are not protected by Common Article 3 and Additional Protocol II at all and so are not protected at any time by their provisions relating to protection from sexual abuse, in addition to their being a lawful target for enemy combatants at all times. With respect to camp followers, who only occasionally engage in hostilities, they would lose their protection under the conventions when they did so and at that time become lawful targets for enemy combatants. However, at the time they were being sexually abused they would clearly not be taking a direct part in hostilities and so abuse of them would still breach Common Article 3 and Additional Protocol II, as they would retain their civilian status.

The forgoing arguments on the liability for sexual abuse of child soldiers and camp followers in a non-international armed conflict are based upon the assumption that in internal conflicts there are no obstacles to prosecutions for war crimes for the sexual abuse of children in the same armed group as the abusers. The clearest case of international criminal liability for, *inter alia*, abusing people of their own ethnicity in a non-international armed conflict is the case of *Limaj, Bala and Musliu* before the Trial Chamber of the ICTY.[64] They were members of the Kosovo Liberation Army and indicted with crimes against both Serbian civilians and 'Kosovo Albanian civilians *who were perceived as Serbian collaborators*'.[65] It is submitted that this indictment was merely descriptive of the context in which war crimes were alleged in that context and does not purport to set out a rule that civilians in the armed

[62] *Ibid.*, 53. [63] *Ibid.*, 60; author's emphasis.

[64] *Prosecutor* v. *Limaj, Bala and Musliu*, Trial Chamber Judgment, Case No. IT-03-66-T, Trial Chamber II, 30 November 2005.

[65] *Ibid.*, para. 1; author's emphasis.

camp of the abusers cannot be protected by Common Article 3 or Additional Protocol II. Furthermore, children in many non-international armed conflicts are kidnapped and forced into service for armed groups. Coomaraswamy, in her *amicus curiae* brief for the ICC in the case of *Lubanga*, referred to a child who was kidnapped on her way home from school by an armed group and forced to act as a domestic aide while being sexually abused and was also later forced to help carry out attacks on villages.[66] It would be perverse to suggest that this child could not be protected by Common Article 3 because, with little choice in the matter, she was in the same armed camp as her abusers.[67]

Therefore, it is submitted that in an *international* armed conflict, those who sexually abuse either child soldiers or camp followers can be individually criminally responsible for such abuse; but it would seem from the discussion above that in a *non-international* armed conflict only those who abuse camp followers or children without a continuous combat function could have individual criminal liability. This suggests that in a non-international armed conflict a soldier can sexually abuse child soldiers in his unit with impunity under international law. It is submitted that this is not in fact the case, or at the least, should not be the case before the ICC.

The Interlocutory Decision of the Appeals Chamber in *Tadić* considered the dichotomy between international and non-international armed conflicts. Albeit in the context of use of weapons, the now well-known statement that '[what] is inhumane, and consequently proscribed, in international wars, cannot but be inhumane and inadmissible in civil strife',[68] seems appropriate here when considering the sexual abuse of vulnerable children and young people. The Appeals Chamber recognised the increased suffering in non-international armed conflicts, that they had become 'more and more cruel and protracted', and acknowledged the impact on international law as a result of the rise of human rights,

[66] R. Coomaraswamy, UN Special Representative of the Secretary-General for Children and Armed Conflict, *amicus curiae* brief on the situation in the Democratic Republic of the Congo in the case of *Prosecutor* v. *Thomas Lubanga Dyilo*, 17 March 2008, available online at: www.un.org/children/conflict/_documents/AmicuscuriaeICCLubanga.pdf (last accessed 25 August 2011), para. 16.

[67] See also Wells, 'Crimes against Child Soldiers', and text accompanying n. 24 above, that 'from the perspective of child combatants in modern armed conflicts, distinctions between enemy and friendly forces may no longer be so distinct'.

[68] *Prosecutor* v. *Tadić*, Appeal Chamber Decision on the Defence Motion for Interlocutory Appeal on Jurisdiction, Case No. IT-94-1-AR72, A. Ch., 2 October 1995, para. 119.

stating that 'in the area of armed conflict the distinction between interstate wars and civil wars is losing its value as far as human beings are concerned'[69] and questioned why, among others abuses, rape, should only be prohibited in an international armed conflict.[70] The Chamber concluded that '[i]f international law ... must gradually turn to the protection of human beings, it is only natural that the aforementioned dichotomy should gradually lose its weight'. This approach considers international law as a whole when deciding upon the protection of individuals and shows the benefits of avoiding fragmentation in this body of law.

Therefore, in addition to the weighty reasons as to why female child soldiers should be protected from sexual abuse in non-international armed conflicts, can we go further and say that they *are* protected? Could the Office of the Prosecutor at the ICC bring a prosecution against a soldier for sexually abusing child soldiers within his unit in such a conflict? The Prosecutor could not use Article 8(2) (c), which is based on Common Article 3 as the Elements for each crime require that '[s]uch person or persons were either *hors de combat*, or were civilians, medical personnel, or religious personnel, taking no active part in the hostilities'. However, Article 8(2) (e) does not have such restrictions. Indeed, Article 8(2) (e) already breaks the mould of only protecting civilians in non-international armed conflicts by including Articles prohibiting the treacherous killing or wounding of a combatant and a declaration that no quarter will be given.[71]

Additionally, it may be seen that some offences are restricted to civilian victims by their nature, such as the war crime of attacking civilians under Article 8(2) (e) (i), and others require that the victim is in the hands of an adverse party, such as the war crime of mutilation or scientific experiments under Article 8(2) (e) (ix). However, the offence of rape, sexual slavery, enforced prostitution, enforced pregnancy, enforced sterilisation and sexual violence under Article 8(2) (e) (vi) has no such restrictions. Therefore, it is submitted that the Office of the Prosecutor should where appropriate charge those responsible for the sexual abuse of child soldiers and camp followers under this Article. The abusers of camp followers could also be charged under the appropriate provisions of Article 8(2) (c) as they would be considered civilians.

[69] *Ibid.*, para. 97. [70] *Ibid.*

[71] Article 8(2) (e) (ix) and (x) of the Rome Statute.

4 Command responsibility

Proving command responsibility for the abuse of child soldiers and camp followers will not be easy. The sexual abuse and forced marriage is unlikely to be ordered and it will be necessary to prove that the commander 'knew or, owing to the circumstances at the time, should have known that the forces were committing or about to commit such crimes'.[72] SaCouto and Cleary have commented on this problem with respect to sexual violence more generally.[73] They state that 'while the ad hoc tribunals have used circumstantial or pattern evidence to establish that an accused ordered certain crimes, a review of sexual violence and gender-based cases before these tribunals indicates that they appear more reluctant to do so in these types of cases'.[74]

SaCouto and Cleary compare the *Galić* case with the *Kajelijeli* case.[75] In the former, the ICTY Trial Chamber accepted that the 'striking similarity' of the crimes over a long period by soldiers under the control of the accused allowed them to conclude that the acts were not 'sporadic acts' of individual soldiers but instead 'must have emanated from a higher authority or at least had its approval'.[76] However, in the *Kajelijeli* case, which concerned rape and sexual violence, the ICTR declined to take a similar approach. SaCouto and Cleary comment on the 'credible evidence that soldiers under the effective control of the accused had committed a series of rapes and sexual assaults over a period of days', and the approach of the Trial Chamber to note that the Prosecution had failed to prove that the accused was physically present during any of the rapes or had 'issued a specific

[72] Article 28 of the Rome Statute sets out the 'should have known' standard for military commanders and the 'consciously disregarded information which clearly indicated' standard for non-military superiors.

[73] S. SaCouto and K. Cleary, 'Symposium: Prosecuting Sexual and Gender-Based Crimes before International/ized Criminal Courts: The Importance of Effective Investigation of Sexual Violence and Gender-Based Crimes at the International Criminal Court', *American University Journal of Gender, Social Policy and the Law*, 17 (2009), 337–59.

[74] *Ibid.*, 353–4.

[75] See *Prosecutor* v. *Galić*, ICTY Trial Chamber Judgment, 5 Dec. 2003, Case No. IT-98-29-T and *Prosecutor* v. *Kajelijeli*, ICTR Trial Judgment, 1 Dec. 2003, Case No. ICTR-98-44A-T, discussed in SaCouto and Cleary, 'Symposium', 354–5.

[76] *Prosecutor* v. *Galić*, ICTY Trial Chamber Judgment, 5 Dec 2003, Case No. IT-98-29-T, para. 741, approved on appeal, *Prosecutor* v. *Galić*, ICTY Appeal Chamber Judgment, 30 Nov. 2006, Case No. IT-98–98-29-A, paras. 177–178.

order to rape or sexually assault' the victims.[77] Disappointingly, the prosecution did not appeal this finding.[78]

Nevertheless, in the Appeals Chamber of the Special Court for Sierra Leone, in the case of *Sesay, Kallon and Gbao*, the Court approved the Trial Chamber's finding that Kallon had superior responsibility for the forced marriages carried out by his subordinates.[79] The Appeal Chamber stated that 'the Trial Chamber was correct in concluding that the commission of the crime was so widespread and obvious, that Kallon was on notice of the risk that similar crimes would be carried out by [the soldiers] over whom he exercised effective control'.[80] It is to be hoped that the ICC will take this more progressive approach with respect to war crimes and crimes against humanity against child soldiers and camp followers.

5 Conclusion

Throughout this chapter it has been argued that prosecutions following armed conflicts, in which child solders and camp followers have been used, should reflect the total experience of the female child, which often includes sexual abuse. As has been explained, prosecutions for crimes against humanity are not a complete answer. There may not be a widespread or systematic attack against a civilian population and such prosecutions probably will not be able to redress sexual violence against child combatants.

War crimes prosecutions for the sexual abuse of child soldiers would address these problems but a further obstacle to such prosecutions is that the Elements of Crime of the ICC require that each war crime is committed 'in the context of and associated with' an armed conflict.[81] This means that there must be a nexus between the crime itself and the armed conflict; a concept that was explained by the ICTY Appeal Chamber in *Tadić* where the Court held that 'in the context of an armed conflict' as meaning 'that the alleged crimes were closely related to the hostilities'.[82] The Appeal Chamber of the ICTY in *Kunarać* elaborated

[77] *Prosecutor* v. *Kajelijeli*, ICTR Trial Judgment, 1 Dec 2003, Case No. ICTR-98-44A-T, para. 681.
[78] *Prosecutor* v. *Kajelijeli*, ICTR Appeal Judgment, 23 May 2005, Case No. ICTR-98-44A-A.
[79] *Prosecutor* v. *Sesay, Kallon and Gbao*, SCSL Appeal Chamber Judgment, 26 October 2009, SCSL-04-15-A, paras. 856–61.
[80] *Ibid.*, para. 861.
[81] Elements of Crimes, 125–44.
[82] *Prosecutor* v. *Tadić*, Appeal Chamber Decision on the Defence Motion for Interlocutory Appeal on Jurisdiction, Case No. IT-94-1-AR72, Appeal Chamber, 2 October 1995, para. 70.

the concept of 'nexus' in a case involving sexual violence, holding that '[t]he armed conflict need not have been causal to the commission of the crime, but the existence of an armed conflict must, at a minimum, have played a substantial part in the perpetrator's ability to commit it, his decision to commit it, the manner in which it was committed or the purpose for which it was committed'.[83] Alfredson argues persuasively that sexual violence against children by armed groups is 'not merely a random and uncontrolled by-product of war' but is rather 'a systematic and strategic aspect of the war machine to which children are particularly vulnerable' and 'often occurs as part of a horrific strategy of maintaining both a child and adult labour force of recruits, and an exacting hierarchy of obedience and loyalty'.[84] Therefore, it is submitted that indeed there is normally a nexus between sexual abuse of child soldiers and camp followers and the armed conflict in which they are involved.

While it is true that the concept of criminal responsibility under international law for war crimes against an individual's own forces sounds novel, so did the concept of international law interfering with the way a State treated its own citizens, before the Second World War and the concept of crimes against humanity. It must also be noted that the war crime of enlisting, recruiting or using child soldiers already *does* bind both state and non-state actors with respect to the way they treat their 'own' children.

It has been argued throughout this chapter that the ICC can and should use its war crimes provisions to prosecute those who commit such acts. Regretfully this has not so far happened. For example, despite evidence from several NGOs that Thomas Lubanga Dyilo is responsible for other serious crimes and that his militia raped and sexually enslaved many girls,[85] he has only been charged with enlisting and conscripting children and using them to participate actively in hostilities.[86] This may

83 *Prosecutor* v. *Kunarać, Kovać and Vuković*, Appeal Chamber Judgment, Case No. IT-96-23 and IT-96-23/1-A, 12 June 2002, para. 58. For a discussion of the concept of nexus with an armed conflict before the ICC, see Byron, *War Crimes*, 14–16.

84 Alfredson, 'Sexual Exploitation of Child Soldiers'.

85 See discussion by SaCouto and Cleary, 'Symposium', 341, referencing Human Rights Watch comment 'DR Congo: ICC Charges Raise Concern', available online at www.hrw.org/en/news/2006/07/31/dr-congo-icc-charges-raise-concern (last accessed 25 August 2011) and Institute for War and Peace Reporting 'Plight of Girl Soldiers "Overlooked"', available online at: www.iwpr.net/ru/print/node/12996 (last accessed 25 August 2011).

86 Although see the arguments in Coomaraswamy's *amicus curiae*, n. 66 above, that 'use' of child soldiers should include 'any sexual acts perpetrated' as 'during war, the use of girl children in particular includes sexual violence' (para. 25).

be disappointing, but it is perhaps a reflection of the difficulties in taking the approach advocated in this chapter. Indeed, as it has been said, the *nullum crimen* principle set out in Article 22 of the Rome Statute is an exacting one and may be an insuperable obstacle to the strategy suggested here.

Nevertheless, such limited charges raise the spectre of young girls giving evidence that they were used as child soldiers but being told that their testimony as to sexual violence is not relevant to the charge and cannot be given. If the Office of the Prosecutor feels that such prosecutions cannot succeed currently, then the Rome Statute needs to be amended. A holistic view of the international law in this area, including both the international humanitarian law prohibition on sexual abuse of all women in the conflict area and the international human rights law requirement to protect the dignity and sexual autonomy of children, mandates such an approach.[87] Recognition that sexual abuse of such vulnerable young people, whether by state forces or non-state armed groups, is a war crime, will help to ensure that female children who have been abused in this way feel that the international community recognises the harm that has been done to them; that they are not invisible.

There is a common saying that 'children should be seen and not heard'. It is time that the plight of sexually abused female child soldiers and camp followers was both seen and heard.

[87] Articles 76 and 77 of Additional Protocol I discussed above, and see Article 34, Convention on the Rights of the Child, 20 November 1989, in force 2 September 1990, 1577 UNTS 3, 'States Parties undertake to protect the child from all forms of sexual exploitation and sexual abuse' and Article 39 of the Convention on the Rights of the Child which requires States Parties, following *inter alia*, abuse, inhuman and degrading treatment and armed conflicts 'to take all appropriate measures to promote [their] physical and psychological recovery'.

4

International law, gender regimes and fragmentation: 1325 and beyond

FIONNUALA NÍ AOLÁIN

The perceived or actual fragmentation of international law continues to preoccupy international scholars and practitioners. From treaty interpretation to judicial branch supremacy and onwards to governance theory, the form and effect of splintering international legal norms infuses debate and passion.[1] This chapter engages with this particular scholarly fixation by examining international lawmaking and enforcement in conflict and post-conflict settings. From a feminist perspective, do the presumed benefits of a unitary, cohesive system of international law really accrue to women? When fragmentation occurs and legal regimes multiply do women benefit? If so, how?

For those who wax lyrical about the potential benefits of fragmentation, asking the woman question yields some unexpected results. Disparate, non-binding legal norms, which overpopulate the responses to "women's issues," may not necessarily yield transformative results. Informality often equates with non-enforcement and uncertainty as to the nature of the legal obligations posed. It is not entirely clear that working within the highly masculine structures characterizing international lawmaking and international relations has been to women's advantage

The work for this chapter was completed while the author was a Fellow at the Institute for Advanced Studies at the Hebrew University in Jerusalem.

[1] See e.g. International Law Commission/Martii Koskenniemi, Fragmentation of International Law: Difficulties Arising from the Diversification and Expansion of International Law, A/CN.4/L.682, 13 April 2006; Gerhard Hafner, 'Pros and Cons Ensuing from Fragmentation of International Law', *Michigan Journal of International Law*, 25 (2004), 849; J. H. H. Weiler, 'The Interpretation of Treaties: A Re-examination Preface', *European Journal of International Law*, 21 (2010), 507; Martti Koskenniemi and Paivi Leino, 'Fragmentation of International Law? Postmodern Anxieties', *Leiden Journal of International Law*, 15 (2002), 553; Eyal Benvenisti and George W. Downs, 'The Empire's New Clothes: Political Economy and the Fragmentation of International Law', *Stanford Law Review*, 60 (2007), 595.

over the decades.[2] Feminist scholars have revealed the masculinity of the international legal order, showing how it produces hierarchy, exclusivity, and reproduces public–private dichotomies that rarely work to women's advantage. There is evident pessimism about the mainstream indifference to feminist interventions, and deepening unease that feminist scholarship will remain confined to backwater status.[3]

Hilary Charlesworth has deftly captured an almost entirely one-sided conversation between feminist international law scholars and the mainstream in which feminist theorizing and insight "is an optional extra, a decorative frill on the edge of the discipline".[4] With the concept of fragmentation to the fore this chapter explores what implications follow for women's legal protections and status given the increased regulatory presence of international law in conflict and post-conflict settings.[5] The chapter explores the tensions inherent in international lawmaking on issues that directly regulate women's lives in the fraught context of armed conflict and post-conflict sites. Section 1 explores the gendered dimensions of conflict, setting the stage for the analysis that follows. Section 2 follows with a general overview of recent institutional and normative developments designed to advance women's roles in conflict and post-conflict settings. Section 3 merges the analysis to assess how we are to understand and place the broader debates concerning fragmentation and legitimacy within these developments. Particular attention is paid to the enforcement of UNSC 1325 and its progeny.

Scripting women into the normative framework of war and peace regulation is a departure for which there are few antecedents. The regulation of armed conflict since the earliest inception of a distinct *law* of armed conflict has been a decidedly masculine affair. The historical accounts reveal that men made accommodations about the status of conflict and the behavior of combatants with other men.[6] Women occasionally made appearances,

[2] See Hilary Charlesworth and Susan Harris Rimmer, 'Feminist Internationalisms', *Australian Feminist Law Journal*, 32 (2010), 3.

[3] J. Ann Tickner, 'You May Never Understand: Prospects for Feminist Futures in International Relations', *Australian Feminist Law Journal*, 32 (2010), 9.

[4] Hilary Charlesworth, 'Talking to Ourselves: Feminist Scholarship in International Law?', in Sari Kovo and Zoe Peterson (eds.), *Feminist Perspectives on Contemporary International Law: Between Resistance and Compliance* (Oxford: Hart, 2011), 17.

[5] To some extent the chapter overlaps with Professor MacKinnon's contribution to this volume (Chapter 2), but is evidently far more pessimistic in outlook.

[6] See e.g. Françoise Krill, 'The Protection of Women in International Humanitarian Law', *International Review of the Red Cross*, 249 (1985), 337–63.

but despite these cameo roles the law of armed conflict "contains culturally specific male and female actors," playing out gender specific roles and stereotypes unrelentingly present in other arenas.[7] More international law does not, per se, undo the persistence of discrimination and the validation of a female point of view in the realization and enforcement of regulatory frameworks. It may result in little more than the cosmetic changing of desk chairs on a regulatory passageway doomed to failure.

1 Gendering conflict and its aftermath

Conflicts affect both men and women, but women face additional issues during and after wars that men do not, including, of course, pervasive sexual violence, forced impregnation, reproductive violence, sexually transmitted diseases, and forced abortion. Women and their children experience internal displacement and dominate the refugee populations across conflicts. Women are also differentially affected because of their role as the primary caretakers of the household and family. In this regard, traditional gender dichotomies may be further entrenched and exacerbated during times of extreme violence. Paradoxically and in parallel, the social upheaval created by armed conflict upends the social order in many societies, undoing rigid boundaries between public and private and paradoxically allowing women to augment their economic and social capital.[8] For example, during some conflicts in which aspects of a functioning state and economy continue to exist, women can take on roles as workers and laborers outside of the home. These opportunities would never transpire in 'normal' circumstances as conflict opens up intended and unintended spaces for empowerment "effecting structural and social transformations and producing new social, economic and political realities that redefine gender and caste hierarchies."[9]

Armed conflict has long been the site of international legal regulation, with humanitarian law ranking as one of the oldest sites of normative interstate action.[10] But, because armed confrontation between and

[7] Judith Gardam,'The Neglected Aspect of Women and Armed Conflict: Progressive Development of the Law', *Netherlands International Law Review*, 52 (2005), 197.

[8] See, generally, Fionnuala Ní Aoláin, Dina Haynes and Naomi Cahn, *On the Frontlines: Gender, War and the Post-Conflict Process* (Oxford: Oxford University Press, 2011).

[9] Veena Das, *Critical Events: An Anthropological Perspective on Contemporary India* (Oxford: Oxford University Press, 1997).

[10] Gary Solis, *The Law of Armed Conflict: International Humanitarian Law in War* (Cambridge: Cambridge University Press, 2010).

within states was carried out by male combatants, the laws of war were generally constructed from the vista of a soldier's need for ordered rules within which to wage war on behalf of the state. Consequently women's interests fared notoriously badly when accountability was sought for the behavior of combatants. Moreover, a particular notion of the female body and person as the subject in humanitarian law pervades its rules, with honor, virtue and vulnerability emerging as triumphant traits.[11] As Judith Gardham has pointed out, the essentialist subjectivity of women in war has been compounded by the fact that "[t]he feminist voice in International Humanitarian Law (IHL) . . . has always been relatively muted."[12]

A broad scholarly silence (with some notable exceptions) has long been the general rule. Yet, in recent years there has been an evident explosion of normative interest in, policy writing about and scholarly interface addressing the reality of sexual violence during war.[13] Such concentrated attention was clearly needed to redress a gaping normative and conceptual chasm. It has, as Professor MacKinnon outlines in this volume, given birth to a striking body of legal norms, in the newly emerging domain of international criminal law.[14] The greater expressiveness of international criminal norms towards sexual crimes experienced by women is not to be scoffed at. It marks a significant achievement of recognition for victims of sexual crimes and for the feminist advocates who have attained the articulation. However, the undulating focus on sexual violence as the primary focus of women's experience of and response to armed conflict has given some feminists reason to pause.

Significant augmentation of international humanitarian law and international criminal law means that there is no doubt as to the augmented responsibility for acts of violence directed at women during

[11] Judith G. Gardam and Michelle J. Jarvis, *Women, Armed Conflict and International Law* (Boston, MA: Brill, 2001), 95–112.

[12] See Judith Gardam, 'War, Law, Terror Nothing New for Women', *Australian Feminist Law Journal*, 32 (2010), 61.

[13] See e.g. Colleen Duggan, Claudia Paz y Paz Bailey and Julie Guillerot, 'Reparations for Sexual and Reproductive Violence: Prospects for Achieving Gender Justice in Guatemala and Peru', *International Journal of Transitional Justice*, 2 (2008), 192–213; Kelly Dawn Askin, 'The Quest for Post-Conflict Gender Justice', *Columbia Journal of Transnational Law*, 41 (2003), 509; Valerie Oosterveld, 'The Gender Jurisprudence of the Special Court for Sierra Leone: Progress in the Revolutionary Front Judgments', *Cornell International Law Journal*, 44 (2011), 49.

[14] See Chapter 2 in this volume.

armed conflict,[15] but practical and structural problems still persist. The trouble is, in part, linked to a structural propensity that has led feminists to focus on existing and inadequate rules protecting women at the expense of deep engagement with the broader system that regulates the resort to and engagement of force between and within states. A pragmatic story can be told that goes along the following lines: because of the visibility of sexual violence in conflict, the Former Yugoslavia being the prime example, sex-based violations became the rallying point to address the lacunae of legal remedies. What follows is a linear story in which feminist input helped shape the Statutes of the Ad Hoc Tribunals for the Former Yugoslavia and Rwanda. This input combined with strong NGO attention to the prosecution of sexual crimes, allied with gender-sensitive-mainstreaming policies established a gendered input to international criminal law. Following through to the sequential efforts to establish an international criminal court, a significant regulatory presence was established by feminist advocates. This produced a set of norms entrenched within the ICC Statute advancing protection for women where international criminal law jurisdiction can be established. A hopeful articulation of these developments points to the capacity of domestic legal systems to be recharged and responsive to international norm making, thereby producing a local–global interface to the benefit of women.

But, establishing rules about sexual violence is only one part of the regulatory dimensions emergent in conflict accountability and settlement. Criminal sanction and enforcement constitutes only a tiny sliver of the post-conflict context. Other key venues are the contexts in which conflicts are negotiated, paused and settled. A revitalized post-Cold War milieu allowed for greater attention to the vagrancies of conflict sequencing and endings. This created an expanded role for overarching international legal structures – namely peacemaking agreements and transitional structures. Both become particularly relevant to advance advocacy for women's experiences. It was abundantly clear that women were highly marginalized in these settings, their issues rarely addressed, and the "deals" were largely being done without them.[16] While women were missing from key roles

[15] See *Prosecutor* v. *Kunarac et al.*, No. IT-96-23 and IT-96-23/1-A (June 12, 2002); *Prosecutor* v. *Delalić et al.*, No. IT-96-21-A (Feb. 20, 2001); *Prosecutor* v. *Furundzija*, No. IT-95-17/1-T (Dec. 10, 1998); *Prosecutor* v. *Jean-Paul Akayesu*, No. ICTR 96-4-T (Sept. 2, 1998).

[16] See, generally, Nadera Shalhoub-Kevorkian, *Militarization and Violence against Women in Conflict Zones in the Middle East: A Palestinian Case Study* (Cambridge: Cambridge University Press, 2009).

in peace negotiations and government, they often dominated in civil society movements that created "safe" and neutral spaces in conflicted societies. In this latter role, women often provided the grassroots networking and social support structures relied upon by local and international elites to embed peace processes.[17] There emerged impassioned advocacy for women's inclusion in peace processes and garnering support for mainstreaming the issues of particular concern to women into the fulcrum of the 'deals' being made. Feminist advocacy, political opportunity and a willingness by states to cede declaratory space leads to the enactment of Security Council Resolutions 1325, 1820, 1888, and 1889.

2 Getting to 1325

Starting in October 2000, the United Nations Security Council adopted over a period of ten years four thematic resolutions on women, peace and security.[18] The adoption of Security Council resolutions is, in itself, a notable signal, given the legal and political status of normative pronouncements by that body. Resolution 1325 aims to centralize or 'mainstream' gender by encouraging member states and UN bodies to: fund gender-sensitive technical development and training; consider the different ways that conflict impacts women and girls; and strive to involve women in peace negotiations, policing, peacekeeping, and humanitarian operations.[19] The resolution emphasized the importance of involving women and girls in post conflict peace processes and "the urgent need to mainstream a gender perspective into peacekeeping

[17] Ní Aoláin *et al.*, *On the Frontlines.*

[18] These four thematic resolutions have provoked (in part) the emergence of governance feminism, describing what is considered as the establishment status of feminist ideas in the international mainstream. See, generally, Janet Halley *et al.*, 'From the International to the Local in Feminist Legal Responses to Rape, Prostitution/Sex Work, and Sex Trafficking: Four Studies in Contemporary Governance Feminism', *Harvard Journal of Gender and the Law*, 29 (2006), 335. While not directly responding to that assertion, this author remains unconvinced of the empirical assertions underpinning governance feminism claims, and its connection in a meaningful sense with the experiences of women in the contexts explored in this chapter.

[19] See SC Res. 1325, UN Doc. S/RES/1325 (Oct. 31, 2000); see also 'UN Peacekeeping, Gender, Peacekeeping and Peacebuilding' available at www.unac.org/peacekeeping/en/un-peacekeeping/fact-sheets/gender-peacekeeping-peacebuilding (last visited June 13, 2010); see also press release, 'Annan calls for greater focus on women in UN peace missions', UN doc. (Oct. 22, 2002).

operations." The implementation of 1325 has also involved UN member states (to varying uptake and degree) as they develop national action plans as a means to advance implementation of the resolution.[20]

Feminist responses to 1325 have been mixed. Some have lauded it as demonstrating a definitive shift in status for women in the war-and-peace matrix. Others have been more hesitant.[21] This analysis sites itself in the quizzical category. I suggest that the Security Council resolutions repeat patterns we have seen elsewhere in international lawmaking insofar as it affects women, and that the resolutions should be viewed in conjunction with broader normative developments.[22] In particular, for the purposes of this analysis, they should be viewed as part of an ever-fragmenting domain of international legal norms, and the fragmentation itself should be viewed as part of a wider enforcement problem for women. While some scholars embrace the "messiness" of law's fragmentation and the myriad of jurisdictional overlaps that result,[23] feminist scholarship can forensically tease out where the burden of disarray lies and whom specifically is more likely to be the subject of its negative effects.

On the positive side 1325 can be lauded for including women in the "peace and security" dimensions of international lawmaking. Security Council resolutions are not to be scoffed at, emerging from the highest pinnacle of the international lawmaking apex, and communicate an evident normative weight. Some initial skepticism has been replaced by greater feminist confidence that recent resolutions have "managed to build on the footholds created by the earlier resolutions and slowly strengthen the feminist content of the institutional agenda."[24] But, caution is, I suggest still warranted.

20 Aisling Swaine, 'Assessing the Potential of Action Plans to Advance Implementation of United Nations Security Council Resolution 1325 by Member States', *Yearbook of International Humanitarian Law*, 12 (2009), 403–33. In parallel in 2002, UNICEF published an evaluation of gender and conflict that was co-authored by Ellen Johnson Sirleaf, now the President of Liberia, which assessed the implementation of 1325. Two years later, in 2004, the US Department of Defense, the UN, and NATO each adopted policies addressing the trafficking of humans in and around military deployments.

21 Dianne Otto, 'The Exile of Inclusion: Reflecting on Gender Issues in International Law over the Last Decade', *Journal of International Law Melbourne*, 10(1) (2009), 11–26.

22 See e.g. Declaration on the Elimination of Violence Against Women, United Nations General Assembly, 20 December, 1993, A/RES/48/104

23 Paul Berman, 'Federalism and International Law through the Lens of Legal Pluralism', *Missouri Law Review*, 73 (2008), 1151.

24 Dianne Otto, 'Power and Danger: Feminist Engagement with International Law through the UN Security Council', *Australian Feminist Law Journal*, 32 (2010), 97.

An ongoing pattern of international lawmaking for and about women has been consistent marginalization of those issues women identify as affecting them most. Lawmaking does not undo marginalization, it may serve to compound certain exclusions and inequalities. Lawmaking may insidiously suggest that substantive change is being advanced, while in reality the act of making the law itself becomes the end point of political change, an exercise in somewhat cynical political manipulation. Some human rights scholars have documented a worrying pattern in state treaty creation and ratification suggesting that the process of making law may be viewed as the performative point for state action, and that states evidence no intention to perform the stated obligations of the treaty's obligations.[25] Similar concerns are relevant to our assessment of broader norm creation and expansion, including the adoption of Security Council resolutions.

Thus, for example, the Convention on the Elimination of All Forms of Discrimination against Women Convention came late in the human rights treaty game, arriving to an already fragmented human rights corpus. Peripheral status was evident when its oversight committee was initially located in Vienna (and not in the central UN hubs of New York and Geneva), regulating its membership and its issues to the margins of the human rights arena. Location has been remedied but structural barriers remain. The Convention is riddled with reservations, many undermining the "object and purpose" of the treaty itself, with little challenge offered by states. Until relatively recently there was no individual complaint mechanism to review direct complaints against states under the CEDAW Convention.[26] Whether the new complaint mechanism can address the systemic non-implementation of core aspects of the treaty remains an open question. In parallel, the mainstream human rights treaty bodies have generally avoided dealing with so-called 'women's issues'. Until relatively recently, reproductive rights were off the jurisprudential agenda of these bodies. The Council of Europe's implementation bodies (Commission and Court) largely

[25] Oona Hathaway, 'Why Do Nations Join Human Rights Treaties?', *Journal of Conflict Resolution*, 51 (2007), 588; Ryan Goodman and Derek Jinks 'Measuring the Effects of Human Rights Treaties', *European Journal of International Law*, 14 (2003), 171.

[26] The Optional Protocol (OP) was adopted on 6 October 1999. www2.ohchr.org/english/law/cedaw-one.htm. States that have become parties to the OP recognize the competence of the Committee on the Elimination of Discrimination Against Women to receive complaints from persons within their jurisdiction alleging violations of their rights under the Convention.

screened out cases involving reproductive rights or health through apparently neutral admissibility hurdles. Recent reproductive rights jurisprudence from the European Court of Human Rights evidences hesitancy, state deference and an unwillingness to address the endemic discriminations that underpin women's lived lives and reproductive choices.[27] Gender-neutral jurisprudence was a hallmark across human rights bodies, explaining in part the paucity of attention to sexual violence, and the persistent inability to address how experiences such as rape, sex-based harm, reproductive harms, forced prostitution and trafficking could 'fit' the treaty-based standards of torture, inhuman treatment, deprivation of liberty and violations of the right to life. 'Hard' legal norms of the human rights variety have generally been an exclusionary zone for women. The knock-on consequences have been significant in both normal and conflict zones of enforcement.

In the conflict regulation arena power and status dynamics are indisputably in evidence. Here, women invariably get the 'soft' end of legal norms and legal enforcement thereby making them potentially more vulnerable to the under-enforcement of legal norms.[28] This is evident in the post conflict terrain but in ways that are complex and difficult to address given the host of political, diplomatic and institutional structures designed to address and prevent conflict ignition.

UNSC 1325's conception links to a broader set of concerns related to the fragmentation of international law which is a relevant point of reflection for feminist scholars. For some, the growing proliferation of international regulatory institutions and overlapping jurisdictions following the end of the Cold War is a cause for optimism and celebration. I offer some words of gendered caution. Drawing on Benvenisti and Downs's analysis, we should remain aware that fragmentation "operates to sabotage the evolution of a more democratic and egalitarian international regulatory system."[29] A fragmented system is more difficult to reform. As feminist scholars have underscored, the complexity of multiple overlapping legal and policy regimes in conflict and post-conflict societies have made advocacy for, as well as representation and inclusion

[27] *A, B and C* v. *Ireland* (European Court of Human Rights) (2010), 2030.

[28] Fionnuala Ní Aoláin and Eilish Rooney, 'Underenforcement and Intersectionality: Gendered Aspects of Transition for Women', *International Journal of Transitional Justice*, 1 (2007), 338.

[29] Benvenisti and Downs, 'Empire's New Clothes'.

of women arduous.[30] In some respects the more rules added to the mix, the harder the overall task of enabling coherence. Fragmentation may precisely be in the interest of powerful states and even non-state actors because it enables them to maintain their domination of international systems or to move their claims to other fora when they are unable to get the results they desire in a particular legal arena. UNSC 1325 and its progeny may simply generate another dimension to facilitate "forum shopping" for states in respect of their legal obligations entrenching discrimination and inequality for women.

For feminists, as we evaluate the content, structure and influence of this series of Security Council resolutions we should take the challenge of fragmentation seriously. In this view, the enactment of 1325 and its progeny is a prime example of fragmented norm creation. The Security Council takes on a new regulatory arena (women and war) and offers significant rhetorical comfort, but in fact creates no oversight, implementation or benchmarking of the goals set out in the resolution. The resolutions are divorced from the treaty law that protects women's rights to non-discrimination and equality, in a manner that allows states to potentially eschew treaty obligation by reference to the mandates of post-conflict imperatives and process (with less oversight) facilitated by the security council resolutions. Much feminist activism is expended producing the desired outcome, but fundamentally it remains unclear if the delivery for women in terms of actual change to negotiated settlements and their gender-sensitive content is meaningful and transformative.

Fragmentation is not only evidenced in the multiplication of arenas where women's interests are singled out. It is an internal and replicating feature of these new genres of enforcements. Thus, 1325 has bred a progeny of subsequent resolutions. Resolution creation, not unlike law-making more generally becomes an end in itself. In June 2008, through Resolution 1820, the United Nations Security Council added to its corpus of activity around gender in conflict and post-conflict settings. Here it affirmed that rape should be treated as a war crime – but only after several countries questioned whether rape really was an appropriate topic for Security Council review.[31] Security Council Resolution 1820

[30] Ní Aoláin *et al.*, *On the Frontlines.*

[31] See SC Res. 1820, UN Doc. S/RES/1820 (June 19, 2008); see generally 'UN classifies rape a "war tactic"', BBC News, June 20, 2008, available at http://news.bbc.co.uk/2/hi/americas/7464462.stm

can be read in many ways, but one interpretation is that it stands as an acknowledgment to the failings of 1325, not least by giving it a preeminent legal status by placing the needs and issues that affect women as a matter affecting international peace and security. Other commentators have been more sanguine and pessimistic, noting that the scope of 1820 narrowed the issue of interest to the Security Council largely to one of concern with sexual harms. Any language of agency and autonomy was pushed aside in the process,[32] recreating in turn a patriarchal comfort zone in which protection of vulnerable (and weak) women becomes the imprimatur of the largely masculine political entity. Moreover, rather than enacting or revisiting multilateral agreements with real enforcement 'bite' the creation of micro-institutional interest points operates "to limit the opportunity of weaker actors to build the cross-issue coalitions that could potentially increase their bargaining power and influence."[33] Feminist scholars and activists have much to be wary of in this sizing down and containment exercise. What is also clear is that the ambiguous boundaries and the overlapping authorities created by fragmentation dramatically increase the transaction costs that international legal bodies (and activists) must incur when they engage with or seek to rationalize the legal order that emerges. The splintered character of the international women's movement (such as it is) evidenced by diverse interests, by North–South divides, and by the inevitability that intersectional interests will produce variable points of political interface – is further fractured in its political efforts by ever shifting forum creation and expansion.[34] While much remains uncertain as to the enforcement of the resolution, multiple mandates and multiple agency roles is a clear motif.

The Security Council further expanded its preoccupation with sexual violence in 2009 by the passage of resolution 1888, requiring that peacekeeping missions protect women and girls from the harms of sexual violence. In that same year, resolution 1889 addressed the obstacles to women's participation in peace processes and peace-building, calling for the UN Secretary-General to submit to the Security Council a set of indicators for use at the global level to track the implementation of

[32] Diane Otto, 'The Exile of Inclusion: Reflections on Gender Issues in International Law over the Last Decade', *Melbourne Journal of International Law*, 10 (2009), 11.

[33] Benvenisti and Downs, 'Empire's New Clothes', at 596.

[34] Some of these themes are echoed by Karima Bennoune's contribution to this volume (see Chapter 7).

SCR 1325. Many feminist critics are cynical and underwhelmed by the scope of the Security Council resolutions, noting the lack of any vision of gender equality premised on principles of equality of outcomes and autonomy for women. Moreover, in line with a broader fragmentation critique, the seeming inevitability or organic development of a fragmented set of norms, leaves powerful states from having to "assume responsibility for the shortcomings of a global legal system that they themselves have played a major role in creating."[35] On one reading, ongoing attention to women in the Security Council can be read as achievement on its own terms. What remains less evident is whether an ongoing set of further rarified resolutions does little more than clutter the political and legal landscape, but offers little by way of direct remedy for women in conflict and post-conflict settings.

The Security Council resolutions have not occurred in a norm-creation vacuum. In 2000, the United Nations proclaimed its Millennium Development Goals, which include gender equality as one of eight goals.[36] The Human Rights Council Resolution 5/1 recognizes the importance of gender integration and specifically mandates as a principle that the Universal Periodic Review "fully integrate a gender perspective" into all aspects of the review.[37] On September 15, 2009, the General Assembly announced a fundamental consolidation of all agencies and bodies tasked with women's issues broadly defined at the United Nations. It adopted a resolution on system-wide coherence where it recommended that there ought to be strengthening,[38] consistency, and impact of the United

[35] Benvenisti and Downs, 'Empire's New Clothes', at 600. They also note that powerful states pursue a number of "fragmentation strategies". These include: "(1) avoiding broad, integrative agreements in favor of a large number of narrow agreements that are functionally defined; (2) formulating agreements in the context of one-time or infrequently convened multilateral negotiations; (3) avoiding whenever possible the creation of a bureaucracy or judiciary with significant, independent policymaking authority and circumscribing such authority when its creation is unavoidable; and (4) creating or shifting to an alternative venue when the original one becomes too responsive to the interests of weaker states and their agents" (*ibid.*).

[36] See United Nations Millennium Declaration GA Res. 55/2, UN Doc. A/RES/55/2 (Sept. 18, 2000); World Bank, *Global Monitoring Report 2007* (2007), available at www-wds.worldbank.org/external/default/WDSContentServer/WDSP/IB/2007/04/11/000112742_20070411162802/Rendered/PDF/394730GMR02007.pdf. A broader critique is the extent to which the goals are linked to the neoliberal economic policies that trace to the "Washington Consensus" and have contributed considerably to the limitation of the capacities of states in the Global South and hence to the decline in their legitimacy.

[37] HRC Res. 5/1, para. k, UN Doc. HR/RES/5/1 (June 18, 2007).

[38] GA Res. 62/277, UN Doc. A/RES/62/ 277 (Oct. 7, 2008).

Nations institutional gender equality architecture by streamlining and combining existing gender institutions. The new unit is envisaged to bring together the Office of the Special Adviser on Gender Issues and Advancement of Women (OSAGI), the Division for the Advancement of Women (DAW), the UN Development Fund for Women (UNIFEM), and the International Institute for Research and Training for the Advancement of Women (INSTRAW). It is evident that an enhanced (or weakened) body will substantially impact on broader institutional initiatives to advance women's equality and to concentrate institutional international efforts to transform women's lives in post-conflict societies. These developments evidence much activity, but equally ferocious fragmentation of priorities across multiple actors, agencies, and institutions.

The proliferation of rules and institutions represents for some a concrete reality, and an unavoidable dimension of an ever-expanding international system. Increasing the body of norms, as well as the institutions that interpret them is viewed as advancing competition with legitimacy and diversity benefits.[39] Exalting the virtues of "the more the merrier," there is a sense in which new mechanisms can be seen as a positive assertion of the responsiveness of the legal imagination to social change.[40] Koskenniemi and Leino have posited that while universalism may be desirable, its advancements also "echo imperial concerns, and never more so than when they are spoken from high positions in institutions that administer flexible standards that leave the final decision always to those speakers themselves."[41] This imperial tendency is one that feminists instinctively recognize, and understand its patriarchal pitfalls.

In sum, there has been, on one view, an extraordinary amount of political and legal energy devoted to women in the preeminent international institutional settings. This flurry of 'soft' and 'hard' law at the international level can be interpreted in multiple ways. First, it is a promising advance, signaling the increased importance that key international organizations and states have given to realities experienced by

39 William Thomas Worster, 'Competition and Comity in the Fragmentation of International Law', *Brooklyn Journal of International Law*, 34 (2008), 119.

40 Jonathon Charney, 'The Impact on the International Legal System of the Growth of International Courts and Tribunals', *New York University Journal of International Law and Politics*, 31 (1999), 697.

41 Koskenniemi and Leino, 'Fragmentation of International Law?', at 578–9. See generally, Martti Koskenniemi, 'Legal Universalism: Between Morality and Power in a World of States', in S. Chen (ed.), *Law, Justice, and Power: Between Reason and Will* (Stanford, CA: Stanford University Press, 2004), 46.

women in war. In this regard, such positive legal and political developments having the capacity to aggregate the benefits of international presence for women should be welcomed. Second, and conversely, such international declarations and positions can be viewed critically. They represent part of a broader phenomenon, namely the way in which the term 'woman' or 'women' can be brought into play (as a legal or political matter) without actually doing any substantive work for the subjects thus conjectured. Merely tacking on gender mainstreaming to preconceived post-conflict priorities, plans, and programs will have little benefit for women and for the societies in which they live if the underlying post-conflict processes are flawed. I remain wary of the traction such new norms bring to peace treaty negotiations on the ground, and new empirical work analyzing the use of Resolution 1325 in peacemaking and peace-building processes shows that it is unclear whether women do better under the deals that result.[42]

3 Lawmaking, enforcement, and 1325

Women are the group most historically marginalized and excluded from the peacemaking and peace-building process across all jurisdictions and conflicts.[43] Peacemaking results in the creation of legal norms and they have both domestic and international effect. Women have had little input into and few gains from such processes to date. Harms to women in conflict have historically been resigned to a space outside the regulatory and enforcement framework of international humanitarian law. Despite decades of advocacy, only the narrow thread of penetrative sexual violence has made a substantial appearance on the regulatory landscape. Despite a flurry of new norms in the past two decades, little seems to have changed for women.

Without consistent attention, traditional gender dichotomies may be further entrenched and exacerbated during times of extreme violence and may be extended in the post-conflict phase. A challenge for feminists who venture into the war-and-peace arena is that while direct physical harm to women has captured some segment of the public and diplomatic imagination, unrelenting deep and entrenched discrimination

42 Christine Bell and Catherine O'Rourke, 'The Impact of UNSC Resolution 1325 on Peace Processes and Their Agreements', *International and Comparative Law Quarterly*, 59 (2011), 9–19.

43 *Ibid.*

lingers on the sidelines.[44] What becomes visible to regulation and what remains unaddressed poses both conceptual and practical dilemmas. An ongoing challenge remains persistent obstructions in redress for those harms that affect women most profoundly. Perhaps even more basically a willingness to hear what those harms constitute in various sites of conflict, and understand the variance between sites remains lacking. The constant tendency to assume a lumped and disaggregated mass of women's experiences across all conflicts is still the norm. An intense knowledge gap is evident, as is a lack of empirical data documenting what women experience in war. These knowledge gaps are combined with little meaningful capacity for women to articulate what they need and how they need it during times of war and its aftermath. The obstructions partly result from the selective visibility of women's issues and harms in the highest institutional arena of the United Nations and other decision-making entities. The selectivity links with the regulatory weight attached to certain issues and the obscurity of others.

Visibility thus comes in compromised form. When those issues that affect women differentially reach crisis proportions, and neatly coalesce with broader harms experienced by their communities as a whole, witness the emerging presence of international law. When the normality of endemic discrimination is mooted and seeks regulatory redress traction is invariably lost. And, so, without a really hard conversation prioritizing the need for comprehensive regulatory action across the totality of women's experiences in conflict we may in fact lose the capacity to address the driving social and legal structures that enable and undergrid harms to women.

We need to ask whether the production of a series of high-profile Security Council resolutions constitutes progress when states have avoided broad integrative agreements that would bind them to concrete outcomes, commitments and review. The resolutions come without a bureaucracy or judiciary having significant independent policymaking authority. National implementation plans, that are intended to evidence state action, may further fragment the enforcement landscape as states take radically different approaches to confronting the legacies of conflict for women. With no overarching body to review the adequacy of national action plans, and no integrative process to match them to the treaty obligations of states under the CEDAW Convention and other

44 Hilary Charlesworth, 'Saddam Hussein: My Part in his Downfall', *Wisconsin International Law Journal*, 23 (2005), 127.

relevant treaties such as the Covenant on Economic, Social and Cultural Rights, it remains unclear if norm expansion is a positive, neutral or negative progression for women. There is no evidence that the state-level responses will be enshrined in 'hard' domestic law. Rather, women find themselves (again) relegated to the mainstreaming policy domain that has proven woefully inadequate in other contexts to address deep-seated discrimination and exclusion. It is possible to interpret the resolutions as a form of forum shifting in which the driver states capitalize on the Security Council as a forum that could contain the interests of transnational interest groups and in parallel harness the political goodwill that accrues symbolically to presence on issues defending women's sexual integrity.

The paucity of attention to women's experiences of war makes any legal or political action highly attractive to policymakers and activists. Security Council resolutions hold particular sway, offering both political status and visibility but some wariness is warranted. Feminist scholars have offered a variety of views on the opportunities posed by the UNSC resolutions. In the skeptical tradition this chapter suggests that some attention is also warranted to the scattered landscape of international legal regulation for women, in which there is no evident hierarchy, a lack of substantive enforcement capacity, disjointed expertise, and ongoing norm splintering. This fragmentation may confound its critics and deliver, but some concern as to the value of the process and the construction of the edifice of enforcement may be equally necessary.

5

Who is most able and willing?

Complementarity and victim reparations at the International Criminal Court

EDDA KRISTJÁNSDÓTTIR

1 Introduction

In a quest for justice, Liberia has retained law firms to file civil damages claims against companies, governments, and international banks alleged to have aided and abetted Liberia's former President, Charles Taylor, while UN investigators search the world over for his hidden assets.[1] Mr Taylor is on trial before the Special Court for Sierra Leone – an international ad hoc criminal tribunal. If he could instead stand trial before the International Criminal Court (ICC), the world's only permanent international criminal tribunal and which has the power to order reparations to victims,[2] how might the suits and

This chapter builds on a paper originally presented at the seminar, the Joint Role of International and National Courts in Prosecuting Serious Crimes and Providing Reparations: The African Experience, organized by DOMAC, Redress and Denmark, co-sponsored by South-Africa, at the Kampala ICC Review Conference, 4 June 2010. The study forms part of the EU FP7-funded research project DOMAC (Impact of International Courts on Domestic Criminal Procedures in Mass Atrocity Cases), www.domac.is. The author thanks Doris Buss, André Nollkaemper, Birgit Schluetter, and participants at the Kampala seminar and the conference in Oslo that resulted in this volume for helpful comments on previous drafts.

[1] See Doreen Carvajal, 'The elusive fortune of Charles Taylor', *New York Times*, 31 May 2010, 1 (failure to find the money has left donor nations to cover Taylor's monthly $100,000 legal bills and the costs of his $20 million trial).

[2] See www.icc-cpi.int/Menus/ICC/Structure+of+the+Court/Victims ('For the first time in the history of humanity, an international court has the power to order an individual to pay reparation to another individual; it is also the first time that an international criminal court has had such power.') See also Christian Tomuschat, 'Reparation for Victims of Grave Human Rights Violations', *Tulane Journal of International and Comparative Law*, 10 (2002), 529, explaining the court's procedural uniqueness.

investigations by public and private actors differ?[3] The ICC has jurisdiction to prosecute private persons, not legal entities such as banks or corporations,[4] and its ability to admit a case is premised on a finding that the state which has jurisdiction over the case is not itself investigating or prosecuting the suspect, or, if it is investigating or prosecuting, is unable or unwilling to do so genuinely. This test has come to be referred to as the 'complementarity principle', or 'classical complementarity'.

For the sake of argument, if the Taylor trial could be held at the ICC, might Liberia's zealous pursuit of his assets affect the admissibility of the ICC case, since the ICC is not to proceed if the case is being genuinely 'investigated' by a state with jurisdiction over it?[5] Or would Liberia need to hold off on civil suits (even against banks and legal entities that the ICC could not itself go after) until the ICC had convicted and sentenced Taylor? The ICC can make an order directly against a convicted person specifying appropriate reparations to, or in respect of, 'victims',[6] but not to states – even if, as in the Taylor case, the accused is alleged to have had public taxes and proceeds from the country's mines and industry paid into his personal accounts.[7]

To take a different example: in 2000, civil domestic judgments were rendered in the United States against the former Bosnian Serb wartime

[3] Rule 105 of the Rules of Procedures and Evidence of the Special Court for Sierra Leone provides: '(B) Pursuant to the relevant national legislation, a victim or persons claiming through him may bring an action in a national court or other competent body to obtain compensation. (C) For the purposes of a claim . . . the judgment of the Special Court shall be final and binding as to the criminal responsibility of the convicted person for such injury' (see www.sc-sl.org, relative to essential court documents).

[4] But see Eva Dwertmann, *The Reparations System of the International Criminal Court: Its Implementation, Possibilities and Limitations* (Leiden and Boston, MA: Martinus Nijhoff, 2010), 57, noting the ICC's stated intent to prosecute corporate executives who knowingly trade with perpetrators of war crimes. See also Joanna Kyriakakis, 'Corporations and the International Criminal Court: The Complementarity Objection Stripped Bare', *Criminal Law Forum*, 19 (2008), 115; Beth Stephens, 'The Amorality of Profit: Transnational Corporations and Human Rights', *Berkeley Journal of International Law*, 20 (2002), 45.

[5] Rome Statute of the International Criminal Court, art. 17, www.icc-cpi.int (Legal Texts and Tools). See further section 2 below.

[6] *Ibid.*, art. 75(2). See also ICC Rules of Procedure and Evidence, ICC-ASP/1/3, Rule 85: '"Victims" may include organizations or institutions that have sustained direct harm to any of their property which is dedicated to religion, education, art or science or charitable purposes, and to their historic monuments, hospitals and other places and objects for humanitarian purposes' (www.icc-cpi.int).

[7] Carvajal, 'Elusive fortune'.

leader Radovan Karadžić,[8] who was captured eight years later and brought before the International Criminal Tribunal for Former Yugoslavia (ICTY) to stand trial. Unlike the ICC, the ICTY lacks jurisdiction to order reparations. If it had been possible to try Karadžić at the ICC instead, where victims are allowed to participate, how would the earlier domestic civil case affect the prosecution's options? Might a different group of victims be entitled to reparation for guilt found by the ICC than for the liability adjudicated by the US court, all to be settled out of the defendant's assets?

The present chapter explores the yet to be triggered reparations procedure of the ICC and its potential implications for the future of transnational public law litigation of the type exemplified by the Taylor and Karadžić cases. It asks how the ICC will balance its retributive and restorative mandates in practice and the role of the complementarity principle with respect to reparations. Should states wait with restitution efforts and do nothing for victims while the ICC tries the accused – a process which may take years and end in acquittal – because proactive transnational action for victims might interfere with the admissibility or outcome of a trial before the ICC? The chapter argues that, given sufficient political will, the complementarity concept and principled guidance from the ICC on reparations could be a catalyst for restorative justice – and even supply a missing link in the legal landscape of reparations for international law violations – by connecting legal reparation with means to enforce it. However, the chapter less sanguinely recognizes that no reparations are guaranteed by the ICC's legal framework with respect to reparations, a fact which blunts the impact the complementarity principle can have on the chances of redress at state level.

Section 2 briefly outlines the competence of the ICC with respect to reparations. Section 3 considers the competence of ICC member states with respect to reparations as they incorporate the reparations provisions of the Rome Statute into their domestic legal systems and

[8] A federal jury in New York returned a $745 million verdict against Karadžić in a civil case focusing on women who were raped during the war in the 1990s, *Kadić* v. *Karadžić*, 93 Civ. 1163 (SDNY 10 Aug. 2000), and $4.5 billion in damages to victims of rape, torture and genocide in *Doe I et al.* v. *Karadžić*, 93 Civ. 878 (PKL) (SDNY 25 Sept. 2000). See also 'Karadžić faces financial penalties', *International Herald Tribune*, 26 July 2008 (www.iht.com), recounting how Karadžić, after arrest, faced repossession of his property to pay for millions of dollars he was accused of embezzling from the Republika Srpska, in addition to the billions of dollars awarded to victims in 2000.

harmonize them with domestic procedural laws – procedures which may contain more or fewer options than the ICC's jurisdiction. Section 4 explores the complementarity principle and its meaning in the context of reparations. Section 5 concludes by suggesting issues on which the ICC could provide helpful guidance.

2 Competence of the ICC with respect to reparations

The word 'complementary' appears in the very first article of the Rome Statute establishing the ICC:

> An International Criminal Court ... is hereby established. It shall be a permanent institution and shall have the power to exercise its jurisdiction over persons for the most serious crimes of international concern, as referred to in this Statute, and shall be *complementary* to national *criminal* jurisdictions.[9]

This first provision already presents a puzzle. The whole institution of the ICC is to be complementary to national jurisdictions, which might suggest that the ICC reparations procedure, as part of that whole, is complementary to some national alternative. But article 1 specifically speaks of national 'criminal' jurisdictions, despite the fact that an order for reparations at the ICC can only be made after the end of the criminal proceedings (i.e. after conviction); is a victim-focused, not defendant-focused determination; and does not constitute a penalty.[10] Thus, the ICC reparation proceeding is in effect a finding of liability, which in some countries is handled through civil, not criminal, jurisdiction.[11] Would a legal system that does not happen to include liability to victims in its criminal procedures always have to be complemented by the ICC in situations of serious crimes of international concern? Or is article 1 not relevant at all to the ICC's restorative jurisdiction?

[9] Rome Statute, above n. 5, art. 1 (emphases added). Crimes under the ICC's jurisdiction are: genocide, crimes against humanity, war crimes, and the crime of aggression (*ibid.*, art. 5).

[10] ICC reparations orders are not penalties; they focus on the harm of victim, not the guilt of the perpetrator. See Dwertmann, *Reparations*, 42, 68–75 and 246.

[11] *Ibid.*, 72–3 ('In some jurisdictions, civil liability automatically follows the finding of criminal responsibility of a person ... In other legal systems, as a general rule, criminal courts do not recognize equating civil and criminal liability').

2.1 *A test of admissibility*

The way in which the complementarity principle works is explained in article 17 of the Rome Statute – 'Issues of admissibility' – which provides that a case shall be inadmissible where:

> 1. (a) The case is being investigated or prosecuted by a State which has jurisdiction over it, unless the State is unwilling or unable genuinely to carry out the investigation or prosecution;
>   (b) The case has been investigated by a State which has jurisdiction over it and the State has decided not to prosecute the person concerned, unless the decision resulted from the unwillingness or inability of the State genuinely to prosecute.[12]

Articles 1 and 17 speak only to the court's criminal jurisdiction and to the decision whether to prosecute, not whether to order reparations after conviction. That issue is addressed in article 75(1) of the statute, which provides that the court 'shall establish principles relating to reparations to, or in respect of, victims'. The rest of article 75 is couched in permissive language, i.e. 'may' – not 'shall'.[13] The court thus has the ability to order reparations, but it is unclear to what extent it is prepared to use it or how, as no case before it has yet reached the reparations stage. Suffice it to say that the 'stick' of classical complementarity – understood in the

[12] Rome Statute, above n. 5, art. 17(1).

[13] *Ibid.*, art. 75:

> 1. The Court *shall* establish principles relating to reparations to, or in respect of, victims, including restitution, compensation and rehabilitation. On this basis, in its decision the Court *may*, either upon request or on its own motion in exceptional circumstances, determine the scope and extent of any damage, loss and injury to, or in respect of, victims and will state the principles on which it is acting.
> 2. The Court *may* make an order directly against a convicted person specifying appropriate reparations to, or in respect of, victims, including restitution, compensation and rehabilitation. Where appropriate, the Court *may* order that the award for reparations be made through the Trust Fund provided for in article 79.
> 3. Before making an order under this article, the Court *may* invite and shall take account of representations from or on behalf of the convicted person, victims, other interested persons or interested States.
> 4. In exercising its power under this article, the Court *may*, after a person is convicted of a crime within the jurisdiction of the Court, determine whether, in order to give effect to an order which it may make under this article, it is necessary to seek measures under article 93, paragraph 1.
>
> (emphases added)

original sense as signaling to states that unless they take action to bring perpetrators to justice the ICC can do so – appears missing when it comes to reparations. There is no sense that states must do something for victims or else the court will step in. The ICC is, at this point in time at least, first and foremost a criminal court. It can only hold out a hope to victims that their tormentors will be convicted, and that then, and only then, it may (not shall) order reparations to be enforced by states or through the ICC Trust Fund for Victims (see below). The official ICC website, however, contains more encouraging language:

> The victim-based provisions within the Rome Statute provide victims with the opportunity to obtain, where appropriate, some form of reparation for their suffering. It is the balance between retributive and restorative justice that will enable the ICC, not only to bring criminals to justice but also to help the victims themselves obtain justice.[14]

In a similar vein, the website of the Trust Fund for Victims explains that 'the Rome Statute established a unique system in which the elements of retributive and restorative justice aim to be reconciled'.[15] This could be read to mean that the two aims are of equal weight, when in fact the latter is wholly dependent upon the former. The question of liability for reparations cannot be reached at the ICC if the criminal trial is conducted at national level (which is the officially preferred forum, given the primacy of domestic jurisdiction built into article 17), whether or not the state in question has any will or ability to secure reparation for the victims. If the state investigates or prosecutes competently and in good faith, the case remains inadmissible at the ICC and the reparations stage will not be reached at the ICC, even if no reparations are available at the domestic level. Moreover, since the ICC itself strictly speaking does not have to order reparations, as explained above, it is difficult to argue that a state's failure to do so means that its prosecution of the accused was not carried out 'genuinely'. If a case is admissible at the ICC and the court orders reparations, it does not necessarily have to conduct a claims process under its auspices.[16] The court is thus not required to do much,

[14] www.icc-cpi.int/Menus/ICC/Structure+of+the+Court/Victims

[15] www.trustfundforvictims.org/legal-basis. The present chapter is concerned only with 'legal' reparations, not the possibility of the Trust Fund for Victims to cooperate with the victim community under its 'second mandate' (see below n. 19 and accompanying text).

[16] See Fiona McKay, presentation in Report of DOMAC WP7 Workshop, 8 December 2008, at www.domac.is. For discussion, see Dwertmann, *Reparations*, 114.

although it is certainly 'able' to go further, and expectations are high. The opinions of the victims are relevant to the choice of action, and the court is obligated to ascertain their views.[17]

A different question could arise if the ICC has admitted a criminal case but the state nevertheless investigates genuinely with an eye to bringing or allowing civil claims against the accused (or his aiders and abettors) or creating an alternative forum for claims processing concurrently with the ICC prosecution. As the example of Liberia shows, this is not a far-fetched scenario. The defendant might then argue that the domestic investigations rendered the ICC case against him inadmissible under article 17. And, supposing that a national claims process presented a greater or speedier chance of redress for victims than their post-trial prospects at the ICC, should such options be postponed or abandoned because they might affect admissibility of the ICC case? If a state conducts a bona fide reconciliation and reparations process, say, out of assets handed over by the accused in exchange for a plea bargain acceptable to the victims, would the case thereby become admissible at the ICC (on grounds that this unduly shielded the accused)[18] – or could the domestic restorative aim and the wishes of the victims trump the retributive purpose of the ICC and the international fight against impunity? A hint of an answer may be found in the relationship between the court and its twin organ the Trust Fund for Victims.

2.2 *The Trust Fund for Victims*

Article 79 of the Rome Statute creates the Trust Fund for Victims, which serves a dual role: (1) 'Reparations: implementing Court-ordered reparations awards against a convicted person when directed by the Court to do so; and (2) General Assistance: using voluntary contributions from donors to provide victims and their families in situations where the Court is active with physical rehabilitation, material support, and/or psychological rehabilitation.'[19] The general assistance – or 'second mandate' – is funded exclusively by voluntary contributions and may be implemented during trial and before conviction, but only after the Trust Fund has notified the court of the necessity to assist victims, and as long

[17] Rome Statute, above n. 5, art. 75(3) ('Before making an order under this article, the Court may invite and shall take account of representations from or on behalf of the convicted person, victims, other interested persons or interested States').

[18] *Ibid.*, art. 17(2)(a). [19] www.trustfundforvictims.org/two-roles-tfv

as the court does not determine that the proposed activity or project would 'pre-determine any issue to be determined by the court, including the determination of jurisdiction pursuant to article 19, *admissibility pursuant to articles 17 and 18*, or violate the presumption of innocence pursuant to article 66, or be prejudicial to or inconsistent with the rights of the accused and a fair and impartial trial'.[20] This indicates that activities undertaken purely for the benefit of victims at state level could also be deemed to affect admissibility of the criminal case at the court.

2.3 *Available remedies*

Much political controversy surrounded the creation of the ICC, and it will inevitably continue to carry out its mandate in a highly charged political landscape. The ICC has jurisdiction to order not only compensation but also restitution and rehabilitation.[21] The primary remedy under international law is *restitutio in integrum*, but legal remedies do not address the situations that predate the violation of law.[22] The law can only blindly assume that people wish to be restored to the situation that existed before the legal violation took place; it does not address cultural stigma attached to victimhood or the prejudices or power imbalances that may have led to the violence in the first place. Court-ordered reparations by definition require a legal duty, whereas reparations made available in acknowledgment of a moral duty, e.g. by the executive in pursuit of transitional justice, have a far greater flexibility as to scope and modalities.

[20] Regulations of the Trust Fund for Victims, para. 50, ICC-ASP/4/Res.3, www.trustfundforvictims.org (emphasis added).

[21] Rome Statute, above n. 5, art. 75(1). It is worth noting that prosecution fulfills one type of reparation, namely satisfaction to victims in the form of seeing their tormentor brought to justice and having the ability to participate in the trial. See Articles on Responsibility of States for Internationally Wrongful Acts with commentaries, arts. 34 and 37, Yearbook of the International Law Commission, 2001, vol. II, Part II, and Basic Principles and Guidelines on the Right to a Remedy and Reparation for Victims of Gross Violations of International Human Rights Law and Serious Violations of International Humanitarian Law, UNGA Res. 60/147 (16 December 2005), available at www2.ohchr.org/english/law/remedy.htm, Principle IX.22(f) listing as satisfaction 'Judicial and administrative sanctions against persons liable for the violations'.

[22] See e.g. Declaration of International Law Principles on Reparation for Victims of Armed Conflict (Substantive Issues), International Law Association Committee on Reparation for Victims of Armed Conflict, art. 7, adopted 20 August 2010, ILA Resolution 2/2010, available at www.ila-hq.org; Articles on Responsibility of States for Internationally Wrongful Acts, above n. 21, art. 35.

Reparations, too often left until the end of a case or left out altogether, have a tendency to revolve around the very thing that caused the violation, such as disputes among different groups over who may live on what land. They may expose that those who were enriched by the violations are not always the villains but perhaps companies and countries that regard themselves as far removed from the violence. If and when the ICC readies itself to indicate who owns a plot of land, and who is entitled to social benefits or enjoys access to a cultural or natural resource at domestic level – in the context of a trial against an individual – it could see its fragile political support wane even further. The court has thus far taken a cautious approach to the restorative mandate. And so, it seems, have its member states.

3 Competence of states with respect to reparations

Nothing in the main reparations provision of the Rome Statute is to be interpreted as prejudicing the rights of victims under national or international law.[23] This means that 'even when a victim's claim for reparations filed with the court is turned down, this shall not be interpreted as implying a general statement on the victim's right to reparations under national and international law or have any impact on the victim's rights in other fora'.[24] Victims and disenfranchised groups in ICC situation states who do not trust their governments to have their best interests at heart may prefer to bring their cases to an international forum, but the ICC's restorative jurisdiction is clearly not designed as an exclusive recourse that ousts any other. The ICC's ability to avail victims is in many ways more procedurally limited than the competence of states.[25] Unlike the ICC, some domestic legal systems can hold corporations criminally liable, such as Australia, which incorporated the Rome Statute into a federal criminal law that does not distinguish between corporate and natural persons.[26] Variations on this theme are also found

[23] Rome Statute, above n. 5, art. 75(6). [24] Dwertmann, *Reparations*, 115–16.

[25] On states being able to go farther than the ICC in terms of the retributive mandate, see Harmen G. van der Wilt, 'Genocide, Complicity in Genocide and International v. Domestic Jurisdiction: Reflections on the van Anraat Case', *Journal of International Criminal Justice*, 4 (2006), 239.

[26] Australia's International Criminal Court Act 2002, No. 41, 2002, text available through ICC Legal Tools via www.icc-cpi.int

in the laws of Belgium, Canada, France, India, Japan, the Netherlands, Norway, the United Kingdom and United States.[27]

Some states may allow civil claims against acquitted criminal defendants, as was famously illustrated in the case of O. J. Simpson, where the victims' families in a double homicide case won a wrongful death lawsuit against the accused, although he had been acquitted of murder in the criminal trial. The Simpson case had a transnational effect, for instance inspiring families of bombing victims in Omagh, Northern Ireland, to win a landmark case against IRA dissidents in UK courts, where civil suits also have a lower threshold of proof than criminal cases.[28] The ICC cannot order reparations in cases where it has acquitted the accused.[29]

3.1 *Domestic implementation of the Rome Statute*

Despite the above-mentioned domestic opportunities to provide restorative justice for international crime victims, a survey of national acts implementing the Rome Statute reveals that, to the extent they address reparations at all, they tend not to go further than commitments to cooperate with the ICC and execute its orders. Some such statutes appear to have been based on the Commonwealth Model Law to Implement the Rome Statute,[30] which reflects the fact that the only way in

[27] Kyriakakis, 'Corporations and the International Criminal Court', at 147; and Anita Ramasastry and Robert C. Thomas, 'Commerce, Crime and Conflict: Legal Remedies for Private Sector Liability for Grave Breaches of International Law: A Survey of Sixteen Countries' (FAFO Institute of Applied International Studies, 2006), available at www.fafo.no/pub/rapp/536/536.pdf

[28] AP, 'IRA dissidents are found liable for Omagh bombing', *International Herald Tribune*, 9 June 2009, mentioning that the plaintiffs were prompted by the *Simpson* case to pursue a civil remedy.

[29] There can be no order for reparations if the accused is acquitted. See Dwertmann, *Reparations*, 69.

[30] Model Law to Implement the Rome Statute of the International Criminal Court and Report of the Commonwealth Expert Group on Implementing Legislation for the Rome Statute of the International Criminal Court (Commonwealth Secretariat, March 2005), section 88 'Enforcement of orders for victim reparation':

> (1) Where the ICC requests enforcement in accordance with article 109 of the Statute of an order requiring reparation made under article 75 of the Statute, the Minister shall give authority for the request to proceed, if he or she has reasonable grounds to believe that –
>
> (a) neither the conviction in respect of which the order was imposed nor the order requiring reparation is subject to further appeal; and

which the statute obligates member states to adapt domestic laws is indeed the requirement that they be capable of implementing the cooperation obligations in Part 9 ('international cooperation and judicial assistance').[31] Although there is no explicit requirement on states to harmonize their legislation with the remainder of the statute's provisions, it has been argued that 'Article 17 provides an incentive for States to enact implementing legislation which allows effective investigations and prosecutions at the domestic level',[32] and that the statute's preamble hints at such expectation when it states that 'it is the duty of every State to exercise its criminal jurisdiction over those responsible for international crimes' and 'the most serious crimes of concern to the international community as a whole must not go unpunished and that their effective prosecution must be ensured by taking measures at the national level and by enhancing international cooperation.'[33] The preamble, incidentally, does not mention reparations at all.

The issue of whether states do have procedures, or opt to amend existing procedures, for victims to claim reparations for harm caused by crimes within ICC jurisdiction touches on 'ability'. It harkens back to debates about the 'complementarity objection' that was used to justify omitting jurisdiction over corporate crimes from the Rome Statute. Jurisdiction over corporations, the argument went, would have meant that states which did not recognize corporate criminal responsibility would automatically be 'unable' genuinely to prosecute, while states that did have such jurisdiction could undertake investigation or prosecution and thereby stave off ICC prosecution.[34] Cassese and others have argued that legislative impediments such as amnesty laws do indeed render states genuinely unable to proceed, triggering complementary ICC jurisdiction.[35] Similar arguments could be made if states lack provisions for

(b) the order can be enforced in the manner provided in this section . . .

(6) The Minister shall consult with the ICC as to whether the funds realized through the enforcement of an order under this section should be transferred directly to specified victims or through the Victims Fund of the ICC.

31 See Alain Pellet, 'Entry into Force and Amendment of the Statute', in Cassese *et al.*, *International Criminal Law*, vol. 1, 145, 152–3.

32 Carsten Stahn, 'Complementarity: A Tale of Two Notions', *Criminal Law Forum*, 19 (2007), 87, 92.

33 Rome Statute, above n. 5, preamble; see Kyriakakis, 'Corporations and the International Criminal Court', at 130.

34 See Kyriakakis, 'Corporations and the International Criminal Court', at 117, discussing the negotiating history.

35 *Ibid.*, at 127, citing Cassese *et al.*, *International Criminal Law*, 352.

addressing gender crimes, a central tenet of the Rome Statute.[36] But the objection vis-à-vis corporate criminal responsibility did not result in broadening the ICC's jurisdiction beyond natural persons.

In addition to formal barriers in domestic laws and procedures (such as a lack of group or class actions procedures), the practical complexities of reparations claims for mass atrocities, and the challenges they pose for even the most robust legal systems, have led states on numerous occasions to 'outsource' or delegate some of the aspects of deciding them.[37] Such delegation to an external implementation mechanism should therefore not be seen as a sign of a state's 'inability' to provide reparations; indeed, the ICC may itself direct reparations orders to be handled by an international organization.[38] States have responded to mass claims in many different ways, such as through legislative solutions, like the German Foundation Law on World War II forced labor;[39] or by referring claims to international arbitration, such as the Iran–United States Claims Tribunal[40] and the Eritrea–Ethiopia Claims Commission.[41] Even though the ICC is primarily concerned with 'situation' states, the fact remains that few non-situation states have implemented special (mass) reparations procedures into their laws, and it would be unfair to hold situation states to a higher standard than states with stable justice systems. More fundamentally, however, the 'complementarity objection' does not really obtain in the context of reparations, as ICC-ordered reparations are not exclusive of other fora. At any rate, the different avenues that are in principle available to states to redress mass atrocities – legislative, administrative, etc. – would make it extremely difficult and counter-productive to evaluate states' genuine ability or willingness, as section 4 will discuss below.

To repeat: article 17 of the Rome Statute entails that there would be no case before the ICC if a state with jurisdiction had taken action to

[36] See Catharine MacKinnon, Chapter 2 in this volume, n. 16 and accompanying text: 'gender crime has taken explicit form in its highest expression to date across the Rome Statute'.

[37] Consider e.g. the Swiss banks class action in the United States, in which the federal district court seized of the settlement concerning assets that had lain dormant in bank accounts since the Holocaust delegated claims processing to different international bodies while keeping the case anchored in the domestic judicial system (www.swissbankclaims.org).

[38] Rules of Procedure and Evidence, above n. 6, Rule 98(4).

[39] Stiftung 'Erinnerung, Verantwortung, Zukunft' (www.stiftung-evz.de).

[40] See www.iusct.org

[41] See www.pca-cpa.org

investigate or prosecute and was able and willing to do so genuinely. Even if unable to prosecute, however, the state might have an interest in reclaiming misappropriated assets from the accused. It is likely to have more options than the ICC for pursuing aiders or abettors, corporate actors, banks, etc. In light of the primacy of domestic jurisdiction underlying the whole design of the ICC, it is therefore curious to note the 'top-down' manner in which the Rome Statute is being incorporated into domestic laws. Most member states merely commit to enforcing possible ICC reparation orders and to cooperate with the court – becoming in effect an enforcement arm of the international court. By comparison, transnational public law litigation has often been 'complementary' in nature, as the examples cited at the start of this chapter show, involving domestic courts and institutions interfacing with international organizations and arbitral tribunals to process and decide claims; human rights courts evaluating domestic reparations schemes; and domestic litigations[42] leading to internationally administered mass claims processes. Such practices have encouraged plaintiffs to use the specter of suing abroad as leverage to push for reparations at home.[43] Granted, this practice has been ad hoc, politically driven, fragmented, and far from universal, but it has shown just how much is possible once the decision has been made to do something.

Canada is a notable exception to the top-down approach. It has implemented the Rome Statute in its Crimes Against Humanity and War Crimes Act, which goes beyond merely committing to carry out ICC orders. The Act establishes the Crimes Against Humanity Fund, into which shall be paid moneys obtained through enforcement in Canada of ICC reparations orders, fines or forfeiture, and moneys from disposition of seized property derived as the result of the commission of a crime against humanity; and any donations to the fund. The Attorney General of Canada may make payments out of the fund to the ICC Trust Fund for Victims; victims of offences under the Act or the Rome Statute, and to the families of those victims; or otherwise as the Attorney General sees fit.[44] Canada is thus prepared to pay assets obtained through a criminal

[42] Notably under the US Alien Tort Statute, 28 USC §1350.

[43] See e.g. Isabel Kershner, 'Israeli advocacy group begins campaign to help Palestinians sue over settlements', *New York Times*, 30 January 2009 (www.nyt.com), quoting legal counsel of Israeli advocacy group for Palestinian land claims against Israel: 'if Israel does not compensate them . . . they will eventually turn to foreign courts.'

[44] Canada's Crimes Against Humanity and War Crimes Act (2000, c. 24), ss. 30–31, text available through ICC Legal Tools database, at www.icc-cpi.int

process directly to the victims of international crimes.[45] It can further accept donations and pay them to the victims, similar to what the ICC Trust Fund can do with funds from sources other than the convicted party ('second mandate' sources). And Canadian courts may themselves impose fines in relation to offences under the Act and award those to victims.

The ICC can only impose fines and order reparations after trial and conviction. If the defendant's assets have by then been moved or tapped for e.g. legal costs, or if the defendant is acquitted, states which waited for an order to enforce will have waited in vain instead of using the time during trial to pursue available avenues for victims. (Victims might be eligible for reparations regardless of the defendant's guilt or innocence.) If states wait for the ICC to take the lead on reparations (after trial, if at all), that could have a net cooling effect on reparations initiatives, rather than the court's having a catalytic effect on domestic redress. More clarity and coordination is therefore needed to ensure that willing states can proceed to do everything within their ability without violating due process rights of the accused or in any way frustrating the ICC's ability to fulfill both its mandates.

4 'The false precision of geometry'[46]

The word 'complementarity' means 'the state or quality of being complementary', i.e., 'completing', 'forming a complement', or 'offsetting mutual lacks'.[47] In geometry, two angles are said to be complementary if they add up to 90 degrees. When two areas (or sounds or colors) are in a complementary relationship, they do not overlap or act as substitutes for one another; they add up to form a whole. As has already been noted, the ICC does not have exclusive jurisdiction to order reparations for

[45] The French ICC implementation statute also provides that the national court can issue the compensation directly to the victim; text available through ICC Legal Tools database, at www.icc-cpi.int

[46] Phrase borrowed from Harold Hongju Koh, 'Transnational Public Law Litigation', *Yale Law Journal*, 100 (1991), 2347, 2381, writing in the context of class action suits in the US by victims of human rights violations.

[47] *American Heritage Dictionary*, 3rd edn. For discussion of whether the term relates only to admissibility or more broadly to relationships between the ICC and national jurisdictions, see Immi Tallgren, 'Completing the "International Criminal Order": The Rhetoric of International Repression and the Notion of Complementarity in the Draft Statute for an International Criminal Court', *Nordic Journal International Law*, 67 (1998), 197.

crimes within its jurisdiction. There is thus no 'either/or' determination to be made in terms of whether the court or any other forum can carry that function. A more relevant question to ask is what each side can do that the other cannot.

The 'classical complementarity' rule is relatively straight forward: the ICC cannot try crimes under its jurisdiction if a state with jurisdiction is investigating them or prosecuting (unless it is unable or unwilling to do so genuinely). This ability of the ICC to step into the shoes of the domestic jurisdiction presupposes a certain functional symmetry between the two levels. There has been much work and attention on ensuring compatibility of criminal procedures between international tribunals and member states, but when it comes to reparations, there simply is no natural overlap between the ICC and a 'typical' domestic equivalent. The ICC is unique at the international level in its ability to award reparations from individuals to individuals in a tort-like procedure tagged onto an international criminal court function. Even though 'national criminal laws have been regarded as the closest examples and role models for the possibility to award reparations before the ICC',[48] there is no common format shared by all the domestic legal systems of the world that could be held up as the court's mirror procedure.[49] Some legal systems allow civil parties to participate in criminal trials, while in others tort and criminal jurisdictions are entirely separate areas of law governed by different standards.[50] The ICC model is akin to those legal systems that couple penalization of crimes with what is in essence a private remedy,[51]

48 Dwertmann, *Reparations*, at 9.

49 See e.g. Beth Stephens, 'Conceptualizing Violence under International Law: Do Tort Remedies Fit the Crime?', *Albany Law Review*, 60 (1997), 579, 583.

50 See David D. Friedman, *Law's Order: What Economics Has to Do with Law and Why It Matters* (Princeton, NJ: Princeton University Press, 2000): 'fines under criminal law go to the government while damage payments under civil law go to the victim, the private party who is suing ... only the government can drop a criminal prosecution [while] a civil case ... can be settled out of court' (108–9).

51 Such combination of criminal and reparations proceedings seems to be gaining support at international and above-national level, see e.g. UN Economic and Social Council, Guidelines on Justice in Matters involving Child Victims and Witnesses of Crime, Res. 2005/20, art.36 E/2005/INF/2/Add.1 ('combined criminal and reparations proceedings should be encouraged'); European Council Framework Decision of 15 March 2001 on the standing of victims in criminal proceedings, art.9 (2001/220/JHA)('Each Member State shall ensure that victims of criminal acts are entitled to obtain a decision within reasonable time limits on compensation by the offender in the course of criminal proceedings, except where, in certain cases, national law provides for compensation to be awarded in another manner'). Dwertmann, *Reparations*, 15.

but in other instances, a comparison between the ICC and a domestic procedure would need to be drawn somewhere on a spectrum between criminal and tort procedures. Different national legal systems may allow class actions, *partie civile* procedures, private prosecutors, *actio popularis*, and so on, and there may be differences too in the overall purpose of reparations from system to system, ranging from punitive damages to strict liability for harm caused without fault.

Although article 1 of the Rome Statute clearly states that the ICC shall be complementary to national 'criminal' jurisdictions, its reparations determination is meant to be victim focused: the nature and amount of reparation orders is determined after conclusion of the criminal trial and is to depend on the harm suffered by the victims, not the extent of the defendant's guilt or wrongdoing.[52] Victims claiming reparations before the ICC may have no comparable 'judicial' avenue available at domestic level, depending on the legal system. However, the state may still be 'able' and 'willing' to handle the matter in a more traditional manner through its political branches and administrative mechanisms. The ICC, by ordering that assets seized from the defendant go directly to the victims, may in fact be at cross-purposes with a state which, had it been able to prosecute, would have collected the fine into the government treasury and offered redress to the victims as part of a transition to peace, such as through pensions, disability benefits, educational grants, symbolic, commemorative, or other measures. While the ICC is to encourage and defer to such local ownership of solutions, its sponsors may balk at reparations in certain countries being distributed through local personal status laws that do not recognize equal rights of men and women to own real property or inherit awards.[53]

By virtue of its design as a court for trying individual perpetrators, the ICC cannot order states to provide reparations, but it has to rely on states to implement its orders.[54] If the Rome Statute is construed narrowly, the ICC reparations procedure need not involve any kind of claims process at all – only the adoption of principles, which the court

[52] Rome Statute, above n. 5, art. 75(1); Rules of Procedure and Evidence, above n. 6, Rule 97(1): 'Assessment of Reparations': 'Taking into account the scope and extent of any damage, loss or injury, the Court may award reparations.'

[53] See e.g. Centre on Housing Rights and Evictions (COHRE), 'In Search of Equality, survey of law and practice related to women's inheritance rights in the Middle East and North Africa (MENA) region' (Geneva, Switzerland, October 2006), www.cohre.org

[54] Rome Statute, above n. 5, art. 75(2); Rules of Procedure and Evidence, above n. 6, Rules 218–19.

will reportedly develop jurisprudentially, on a case-by-case basis.[55] But it does have the ability, under its constituting instruments, to do more than that. Eventual claims for reparation before the ICC could be: (1) managed by the court's Registry (which even in a single case could prove a vast undertaking); (2) by the Trust Fund for Victims (which has regulations in place but would need staff and infrastructure reinforcements to implement them);[56] (3) assigned to external experts;[57] or (4) be channeled to a domestic process.[58] In light of the mass scope of the cases within its jurisdiction, it may be necessary to combine some or all of these options in any given situation. In fact, much about deciding and processing individual claims for mass atrocities that had seemed impossible in domestic law and impracticable under international law has actually been possible to achieve through complementary efforts of transnational litigation and 'mass claims processes'.

4.1 *Positive complementarity*

The ICC Prosecutor has famously indicated that the ultimate success of the court will be situations in which it need not step in and hold trials because it has helped national institutions to function adequately.[59] This approach has become known in ICC doctrine as 'positive complementarity', which takes the concept beyond the admissibility test in article 17 of the Rome Statute – the 'threat-based' method of 'foster [ing] compliance through a sophisticated system of carrots and sticks ("classical complementarity")'[60] – to that of a 'policy tool to maximize

[55] See Dwertmann, *Reparations*, 48 ff.

[56] Regulations of the Trust Fund for Victims, above n. 20. See also www.icc-cpi.int/Menus/ICC/Structure+of+the+Court/Victims/Reparation ('If the Court decides to order collective reparation, it may order that reparation to be made through the Victims' Fund and the reparation may then also be paid to an inter-governmental, international or national organisation').

[57] E.g. the International Organization for Migration, which has extensive experience with mass claims processes. See Norbert Wuehler and Heike Niebergall (eds.), *Property Restitution and Compensation: Practices and Experiences of Claims Programmes* (Geneva: International Organization for Migration, 2008), text available online through Google books.

[58] See McKay, presentation in Report of DOMAC WP7 Workshop.

[59] Statement by the Prosecutor (16 June 2003), available at www.icc-cpi.int

[60] Stahn, 'Complementarity', at 89.

the impact of the Court' through 'burden-sharing on the basis of the comparative advantages and assistance.'[61]

International claims practice and transnational litigation are in a sense examples of positive complementarity in action, allowing domestic courts to outsource decision-making to administrative bodies, tapping into expertise from non-law disciplines, and making use of modern technology, communications networks, international organizations, NGOs, crowd-sourcing, etc. No one expects the ICC to address every situation in-house; for example, the stated policy of the Trust Fund is to complement the work of existing programs, and mobilize others to address the needs of victims. And, to quote José E. Alvarez:

> We should not expect that the ICC's establishment will end attempts at hybrid international/national efforts (as has occurred with respect to Sierra Leone and was attempted in Cambodia), civil suits in national courts (such as the Karadzic litigation in the United States), novel proceedings (such as the Scottish trial in the Netherlands of the Lockerbie bombers), or interstate disputes involving crimes covered by the ICC Statute (such as Bosnia's case in the ICJ). All of these alternatives to the ICC will continue to be regarded as necessary in particular cases, depending on political circumstances.[62]

The reparations framework of the Rome Statute presents interesting opportunities – especially in light of the ways in which member states can implement it domestically. The examples of Canada and Australia show that the possibility already exists for a state to pursue reparations domestically and steer funds from locally convicted perpetrators (perhaps even corporations) into the ICC Trust Fund for Victims, thereby linking up with a potential for a mass claims facility at the international level.

4.2 *Mass claims*

The regulatory framework of the Trust Fund for Victims equips it to respond in a manner similar to that of a mass claims process. The term is generally used to refer to mechanisms such as arbitral tribunals,

[61] *Ibid.*, at 89 and 109. For argument that positive complementarity has a basis in the Rome Statute, see William W. Burke-White, 'Implementing A Policy of Positive Complementarity in the Rome System of Justice', *Criminal Law Forum*, 19 (2008), 59.

[62] 'The New Dispute Settlers: (Half) Truths and Consequences', *Texas International Law Journal*, 38 (2003), 405, 420. Erika de Wet, 'The Relationship between the International Criminal Court and Ad Hoc Criminal Tribunals: Competition or Symbiosis?', *Die Friedens-Warte*, 83 (2008), 4.

compensation and property claims commissions, and administrative claims programs established to decide claims for reparation 'when a large number of parties have suffered damages arising from the same diplomatic, historic or other event.'[63] Many of the methods and innovations used in international mass claims processes originate from domestic large-scale litigation practices, such as inferential statistical methods to calculate compensatory damages to a large group of victims.[64] The method of using statistics and other such methods in mass tort cases became a model for the United Nations Compensation Commission (UNCC), which further developed techniques for verifying and valuating claims on a mass scale that have since been used in a number of other international and national claims processes involving victims and survivors of widespread abuses.[65]

It is clear that the drafters of the Trust Fund regulations drew upon the experience accumulated in transnational litigation and mass claims processes; it can even refer cases to bodies that have expertise in such matters.[66] The fund's regulations authorize adoption of administrative procedures as necessary to implement the regulations, and the Trust Fund plays a key role in drafting implementation plans for eventual ICC-ordered reparations.[67] The regulations for instance expressly allow different classes and subclasses of claimants to be designated on the basis

[63] Howard M. Holtzmann, 'Mass Claims', para. 1, in R Wolfrum (gen. ed.), *Max-Planck Encyclopedia of Public International Law*, online edition (Oxford University Press), www.mpepil.com. Examples include the UNCC, the Commission for Real Property Claims of Displaced Persons and Refugees in Bosnia and Herzegovina (CRPC), and the German Forced Labour Compensation Programme for slave and forced labor during World War II.

[64] See *Hilao* v. *Estate of Marcos*, 103 F 3d 767 (9th Cir. 1996); annotated at ILDC 841 (US 1996).

[65] E.g. Holocaust-related claims program at the International Organization for Migration and elsewhere, and property claims processes arising out of the war in the Balkans in the 1990s. See Veijo Heiskanen, 'Virtue Out of Necessity: International Mass Claims and New Uses of Information Technology', in the International Bureau of the Permanent Court of Arbitration (ed.), *Redressing Injustices through Mass Claims Processes Innovative Responses to Unique Challenges* (Oxford: Oxford University Press, 2006); Howard M. Holtzmann and Edda Kristjánsdóttir (eds.), *International Mass Claims Processes: Legal and Practical Perspectives* (Oxford: Oxford University Press, 2007), section 5.06 on mass claims techniques; Wuehler and Niebergall, *Property Restitution and Compensation.*

[66] On the influence of mass claims processes in the Trust Fund Regulations, see Edda Kristjánsdóttir, 'International Mass Claims Processes and the ICC Trust Fund for Victims', in Carla Ferstman, Mariana Goetz and Alan Stephens (eds.), *Reparations for Victims of Genocide, War Crimes and Crimes against Humanity* (Leiden and Boston, MA: Martinus Nijhoff, 2009), 167.

[67] Regulations of the Trust Fund for Victims, above n. 20, paras. 15, 54 and 78.

of type of harm, urgency of need, availability of proof, etc.[68] Furthermore, the ICC's definition of 'victims and their families' leaves it capable of being adjusted to fit each national situation – even where the atrocities have changed the very definition of 'family' within a culture, such as by increasing the number of female- or child-headed households. A policy paper issued by the ICC Prosecutor in April 2010 expressly supports, for the purpose of reparations, 'participation and representation by a broader range of individuals and entities than those who are linked to the charges for which the accused is ultimately convicted.'[69] Thus, the requirement that court-ordered reparations be only for harm caused by the individual on trial is already being interpreted in a flexible manner and potentially expanding their scope.

If the ICC does trigger the mechanisms available to it through the Trust Fund Regulations, that could add a unique feature to international claims practice, namely a reparations procedure accessible to individuals and anchored in an international court. Claims processes created through out-of-court settlements and funds set up by political branches are often criticised for being launched primarily to prevent or end litigation, thereby 'thwarting the expression of public values found in a court system',[70] and for forcing victims to choose between either the material reparations they seek or a legal determination of their rights. The 9/11 process in the United States is a case in point. Some family members of victims of the terrorist attacks on New York and Washington, DC opted to remain outside the 9/11 settlement fund and continue to press for their wrongful death actions against the airlines in the courts, which allowed them to compel discovery and learn more facts of the case, even if it cost more time and entailed a risk of losing. The overwhelming majority of the victims (97 percent) accepted payment from the fund in exchange for a waiver of legal claims, or had little choice but to do so due to immediate financial needs.[71] But although the announced demand of victims of international crimes is usually to obtain retrospective redress,

[68] *Ibid.*, para. 65.

[69] Policy Paper on Victims' Participation, ICC-OTP April 2010, 16, available at www.icc-cpi.int

[70] See Terry Carter, 'The master of disaster', profile of Kenneth Feinberg, *ABA Journal* (January 2011), 23.

[71] See e.g. Benjamin Weiser, 'Can there be true cost for the pain of Sept. 11?' *International Herald Tribune*, 9 March 2009, www.iht.com, quoting one plaintiff as saying: 'I wanted to know why and how this happened in this country . . . if suing for money is how I have to do it, then that's what I'm going to do.'

the underlying focus of those who do choose the court route is also prospective: to use the harm that befell them to guarantee non-repetition and 'provoke a judicial declaration that the conduct . . . violates a norm of international law.'[72]

The ICC's participation in international claims practice could add some much-needed clarity on the substantive legal issues in this area: it could begin to bridge the disconnect between legal remedies for international law violations and the well-evolved mass claims procedures available for implementing them. Those procedures can accomplish much more than merely handing out amounts of cash; they may offer satisfaction through their ability to be broadly inclusive and review massive numbers of claims individually, unlike in an adversarial setting where defendants can stonewall or block evidence. Meta facts may emerge through patterns of thousands of stories, collected in different locations and languages, as personal accounts are reviewed and verified against historical records and archival data. This can have the accumulative effect of dispelling myths and preconceptions about the underlying causes of conflicts and give a voice to victims who would otherwise not be heard.[73] Whereas international criminal courts focus only on the top-level perpetrators, the victims' experiences may revolve more around their direct tormentors who may remain at large and be anything but 'low-level' in their minds. The ICC is not competent to direct states to hold truth-finding or other symbolic transitional justice processes at the domestic level, but it could in some cases deliver some satisfaction for victims by prompting (through the Trust Fund or partnership with other organizations) processes that allow victims to place their stories and experiences on the record – not merely facts deemed relevant for the trial record of the perpetrator.

5 The need for guidance

The ICC is obligated under the Rome Statute to issue guidelines on reparations. Supporters of the ICC have hoped that it could play a role in standard-setting and provide impetus for states to make reparations available.[74] At the time of writing, guidelines have not been issued.

[72] Koh, 'Transnational Public Law Litigation', at 2369.

[73] Consider e.g. the victims discussed by Christine Byron in this volume (see Chapter 3).

[74] See Redress, *Justice for Victims, the ICC's Reparations Mandate*, 20 May 2011, at www.redress.org/downloads/publications/REDRESS_ICC_Reparations_May2011.pdf, Annex 1: '"REDRESS" Reflections on Draft ICC Reparations Principles'.

As things stand, the ICC need never trigger the Trust Fund ('first mandate') mechanism for conducting a claims process, and states need only do the minimum required (i.e. enforcement and cooperation) if and when the court orders reparations. However, if a state does proceed (as Canada could) to grant reparation to victims for harm that is the subject of an ICC reparations order, there needs at minimum to be guidance on the implications of this for admissibility of the criminal case under article 17 of the Rome Statute (see section 1 above).

After trial and conviction, when weighing whether to order reparation, it would also be useful to know if the ICC will look to whether there is a domestic avenue available to the victims, and whether it will encourage such avenue to be used first (given the primacy of domestic jurisdiction), or instead of, implementation through the Trust Fund. How would the court decide, and on what basis, what constitutes an adequate national procedure for reparations? Specifically, the court could issue guidance on whether and under what circumstances civil cases in domestic courts or other actions on behalf of victims, might adversely affect ICC trials and what criteria would apply.

As the ICC reparations phase is not an exclusive forum, the court might clarify policies concerning double recovery, and define the types of (prior or concurrent) domestic remedies that could count as set-offs against the ICC reparations order. This might encourage states to begin reparation efforts rather than wait and see whether the ICC issues an order. A related question concerns whether it matters if the domestic alternative to ICC reparations is a judicial, legislative, or administrative one. (At the UNCC, for instance, set-offs against awards by the Commission did not have to be judicial in nature. And claimants before the German Forced Labour Compensation Programme had their awards reduced by pensions they had already received from the German state as war reparation.) States need to know whether they can pursue such non-judicial reparations prior to conviction without fear of 'pre-determining any issue to be determined by the court', and whether their expenditures can be recouped to some extent if the ICC subsequently convicts and orders reparations against the defendant.

Last but not least, the court might indicate what victims may reasonably expect as far as reparations if it ever convicts a person of the crime of aggression. Victims of aggression could be the entire population of a state, and they might present to the ICC personal claims for matters that have traditionally fallen within the purview of states to settle through interstate agreements or resolve with the help of the UN. The UNCC, the largest international claims process in history (over 2.7 million claims), established after Iraq's 1990–1 invasion and occupation of Kuwait,[75] serves as an example of the types of efforts that victims of aggression could reasonably expect an international court to make on their behalf.

The ICC is now a decade old and it is far from clear what specifically it will do in terms of victim reparations and what national jurisdictions are expected to do in cases under its jurisdiction. The court's jurisdiction is complementary only to domestic criminal jurisdictions, and there can be no ICC case – hence no reparations ordered by it or processed by the Trust Fund for Victims – if the state in question is genuinely investigating or prosecuting the case, whether or not the state is able or willing to grant reparation to victims. Yet, the expectation was created with the ICC's arrival on the world scene that its novel, permanent, restorative justice feature would respond to victims' demands despite its strictly defined jurisdiction.

The ICC is an attempt to make international justice less ad hoc and arbitrary. Its architects made provision for the growing entitlement of individuals to enforce their human rights rather than have to depend on representation by their state of nationality. But it is important that states, international organizations, victim advocates, and legal scholars continue to innovate and drive forward the development in this field and that the task not be handed over wholesale to the ICC before that court acquires any experience with reparations or has addressed the issue. What should be avoided at all cost is a 'race to the bottom' – where each side detracts from the overall goal by waiting for the other to do what it does not feel able or inclined to do. As Peer Zumbansen put it:

> [O]ur focus on *law* as a contained system of rules guides our perception and our evaluation of what in fact must be recognized as a highly differentiated, fragmented and decentralized interlocking of regulatory and self-regulatory processes . . . Is law's dominion merely the demarcation of *fora* for litigation or is it the establishment of procedural and substantive rules that allow for a universal treatment of human rights issues?[76]

The idea of complementarity as merely a substitution of one court for another – where either the ICC or a state judiciary should act in any given situation – leads to some paradoxes when it comes to reparations.

[75] See generally www.uncc.ch

[76] Peer Zumbansen, 'Globalization and the Law: Deciphering the Message of Transnational Human Rights Litigation', *German Law Journal*, 5(12) (2004), 1499, 1500, 1504 (emphases in original).

First, proactive restorative state action could potentially have an impact on the admissibility of the ICC criminal case, but probably not directly on the ICC's power (in an admissible case) to order reparations after conviction, as it is not an exclusive recourse. Second, even though the ICC is supposed to strike a balance between retributive and restorative justice, the 'stick' of complementarity is missing for the latter: an ICC criminal case need not necessarily result in reparations, nor can the ICC force a state to include reparations in a trial conducted domestically. Finally, the ICC Office of the Prosecutor has indicated that the court's goal is not to have to prosecute but rather be a catalyst for action and strengthen the primacy of domestic jurisdictions, but states seem mostly to be committing to carry out reparations orders handed down by the court rather than asserting their own ability to handle the matter. And, as mentioned, the orders might be carried out in legal systems that do not recognize women's right to inherit or own property, or fall short of human rights protections in other ways.

To conclude on an optimistic note, however, the 'positive complementarity' idea – whereby the ICC, states, international organizations, human rights bodies, alternative justice mechanisms, and donors all live up to their respective spheres of competence and cover the areas that the others cannot reach – is more in line with transnational public law litigation and international claims practice. To add to that mix the ICC's unique 'missing link', of reparation orders based on law and judicial development of the underlying norms, to a permanent trust fund with mass claims competence, and active participation by member states – would do justice to the word 'complementarity'.

PART II

Measuring the impact of non-state actors within international human rights

6

What is to become of the human rights international order in an age of neo-medievalism?

CECILIA M. BAILLIET

> The story of Modernity in the twenty-first century may still be in its opening scenes, yet it seems clear that this is not just another repackaged 1990s tale set at the end of history or in a harmonious stage of non-history. Following closely on the heels of a century noted for its devastating brands of warfare, rationalized violence, and systematized destruction, modernity's triumph over its colonial underside does not look likely. If anything, the global imperial project is intensifying and gaining steam in the midst of a perpetual War on Terror, staggering global inequalities, global corporate hegemony, the steady rollback of established civil liberties, and looming threats of ecological catastrophe. After fuelling some 500 years of colonial violence, the project of modernity remains unfinished and now scuttles frantically towards its self-proclaimed *telos.*
>
> Michael Simpson[1]

The modern human rights institutional and normative system rose from the ashes of World War II.[2] Its conception as a preventive mechanism by which to hinder repetition of similar devastation was confirmed in the UN Charter's preamble calling for reaffirmation of "faith in fundamental human rights, in the dignity and worth of the human person, in the equal rights of men and women and of nations large and small." The explosion of hard and soft law instruments addressing a continually

I wish to express warm thanks to Anne Hellum, Karima Bennoune, Andreas Føllesdal, Ole Kristian Fauchald, Christoffer Eriksen, Malcolm Langford, and Beate Sjåfjell for their insightful commentary on previous drafts.

1 'Other Worlds Are Actual: Tully on the Imperial Roles of Modern Constitutional Democracy', *Osgoode Hall Law Journal*, 46 (fall 2008), 509.

2 Its normative positive roots are the Magna Carta, the French Declaration of the Rights of Man and Citizen of 1789, the American Bill of Rights, treaties, national constitutions, and legislation addressing rights and duties.

evolving catalogue of issues was matched by the development of a plethora of conventional and non-conventional mechanisms by which to monitor state practice. Scholars hailed what they considered to be a progression of the human rights regime from the periphery of international law to the center.[3] ICJ Judge Antonio Cancado Trindade articulated the emergence of a new *jus gentium* (international law for humankind), which would replace statism with a foundation based on human rights.[4] However, a contradiction arises from the fact that human rights have long been interpreted as inextricably being tied to the Westphalian state system. As explained by James Der Derian: "Without the sovereign state there can be no human rights, or any protections granted to groups of people with common identity."[5] Current conceptions of sovereignty highlight a trend towards diffusion of authority in an era of increasing globalization. This may be described as a state of neo-medievalism: "A system of overlapping authority and multiple loyalty, held together by the competing universalistic claims of the nation-state system and the transnational market economy."[6] There are currently 100,000 multinational companies, 50,000 NGOs, hundreds of

[3] Thomas Buergenthal, 'The Normative and Institutional Evolution of Human Rights', *Human Rights Quarterly*, 19(4) (1997), 703–23: "The idea that the protection of human rights knows no international boundaries and that the international community has an obligation to ensure that governments guarantee and protect human rights has gradually captured the imagination of mankind." Consider Anne Peters's assertion that: "The international legal system has since 1999 moved much further in the direction of an individual, centered humanized system . . . It has become clear that the normative status of sovereignty is derived from humanity, understood as the legal principle that human rights, interests, needs and security must be respected and promoted, and this humanistic principle is also the *telos* of the international legal system. Humanity is the Alpha and Omega of sovereignty" ('Humanity as the Alpha and Omega of Sovereignty', *European Journal of International Law*, 20 (2009), 513).

[4] Antonio Augusto Cancado Trindade, *International Law for Humankind: Towards a New Jus Gentium* (The Hague: Academy of International Law, 2010) 27, 158–61. He cites the establishment of the UN and regional organizations and seventy protection treaties as marking the expansion of international law and "the awakening of a universal juridical conscience."

[5] James Der Derian, 'How should sovereignty be defended?' comments in roundtable discussion with Michael W. Doyle and Jack Snyder at Columbia University, New York on 2 December 2005, transcribed in Alex Gourevitch (ed.), *Politics without Sovereignty: A Critique of Contemporary International Relations* (New York: Columbia University Press, 2007), 187–204.

[6] Jörg Friedrichs, 'The Meaning of New Medievalism', *European Journal of International Relations*, 7(4) (December 2001), 475–501. See also: Hedley Bull, *The Anarchical Society* (New York: Columbia University Press, 2002), 254–5; see Stephen Kobrin, 'Back to the Future: Neo-Medievalism and the Post-Modern Digital World Economy', *Journal of*

international, regional, and transnational organizations, and thousands of religious groups which directly or indirectly interact or compete with the state and impact the evolution of human rights.[7] The UN and regional human rights institutions, along with the NGOs that support them, are part of the existing neo-medieval system. They function as subjects of international law and often complement states in provision of protection, as well as interacting with other public and private actors to buttress human security and development within nations. The concept of sovereignty is increasingly malleable and it is suggested that human rights should be released from its tie to sovereignty and reinterpreted via recognition of the individual's fundamental obligations towards oneself, family, community, state, and humanity.

This chapter seeks to correct a trend towards misinterpretation of human rights that has ignored duties within protection policy making. Section 1 addresses the precariousness of human rights within the current global system by reviewing reports, followed by an overview of the main legitimacy challenges facing the international institutional human rights system. Section 2 calls for amelioration of cultural insensitivity within the current human rights system by suggesting adaption, specifically calling for restoration of the balance between rights and duties in order to improve dialogue between international and national societal and state actors. Section 3 identifies normative soft law innovations that recognize the obligations of corporate non-state actors in relation to protection of human rights as exemplifying a new protection approach. Section 4 offers a conclusion, calling for a flexible approach towards articulation and implementation of duties reflecting relational ethics.

1 The enjoyment and protection of human rights

1.1 Reports on freedom and governance

In spite of celebrating over sixty years since the Universal Declaration of Human Rights proclaimed that "recognition of the inherent dignity and of the equal and inalienable rights of all members of the human family is

International Affairs, 51 (1998), 361; Rafael Domingo, *The New Global Law* (New York: Cambridge University Press, 2010).

[7] Parag Khanna, *How to Run the World: Charting a Course to the Next Renaissance* (New York: Random House, 2011).

the foundation of freedom, justice and peace in the world," in 2011 Freedom House declared a state of global freedom recession.[8] The report highlights increased incidences of targeting of journalists, corruption, declines in electoral process, weakness of civil society, infringement of independent media, interference with judicial independence, diminishment of national and local governance, and ethnic divisions. It further confirms consolidation of authoritarian regimes from central Europe to Eurasia, as well as democratic declines due to corruption. Similarly, the Mo Ibrahim Index of African Governance confirmed a decline in political rights, security, and rule of law across Africa in 2010.[9]

Transparency International released a Global Corruption Barometer in 2010 that concluded that corruption levels around the world had increased in the past three years and that government action to fight corruption was often seen as ineffective.[10] A disconcerting overview was provided by the Fund for Peace's Failed State Index of 2011. It identified seventeen states at risk of failing and forty-four states under warning of failing due to indicators including (*inter alia*): mounting demographic pressures, massive movements of refugees and internally displaced persons, uneven economic development along group lines, sharp and/or severe economic decline, criminalization and delegitimization of the state, deterioration of public services, suspension of the rule of law, widespread violations of human rights, dominance of security apparatus, factionalized elites, and intervention of other states or external political actors.[11] This collective data indicates a trend towards diminished enjoyment of freedom and rights, as well as governance challenges within several regions within the world.[12] The next section will highlight challenges facing the international institutional human rights system.

[8] Freedom House, *Nations in Transit* 2011, available online at: www.freedomhouse.org/uploads/nit/2011/NIT2011-Full.pdf. Similarly, the Economist Intelligence Unit announcing a democracy retreat in 2010, characterized by authoritarian trends in the Middle East and former Soviet Union, stagnation of democracy in Sub-Saharan Africa, media restrictions in Latin America, and security-related (war-on-terror) restrictions on civil liberties and low civic participation in the West. See: www.eiu.com/public/topical_report.aspx?campaignid=demo2010

[9] The index is available online at: www.moibrahimfoundation.org/en/section/the-ibrahim-index

[10] See: www.transparency.org/policy_research/surveys_indices/gcb/2010/press#3

[11] See: www.fundforpeace.org/global/library/cr-11-14-fs-failedstatesindex2011-1106p.pdf

[12] Furthermore, this underscores Simon Caney's articulation of variability within the criteria of sovereignty (legality, supremacy, territoriality, and comprehensiveness) which opens for coexistence of both non-statist and statist alternatives for governance

1.2 *Overview of the international institutional human rights system*

The international institutional human rights system is facing legitimacy challenges and limitations, specifically in relation to transparency, effectiveness, and accountability. For the purpose of this chapter, human rights may be conceived as a type of discursive, emancipative vocabulary that varies in accordance with the context in which they are set and the forum in which they are negotiated.[13] Human rights are in part articulated within the top-down processes of norm creation and interpretation by expert bodies within international and regional organizations, NGOs, and academic institutions. They are also elaborated within bottom-up processes involving local actors who engage in local protests and civic actions while also participating in transnational networks often facilitated by the internet and international media channels.[14] The normative frameworks include treaty and customary law, international and regional hard and soft law instruments, as well as national legislation, including constitutions. The international community asserts that human rights are universal, interrelated, indivisible, and interdependent.[15] Human rights are commonly articulated as individual rights, but the collective aspects are protected through recognition of the rights of indigenous peoples, minorities, and peoples.[16] In addition, several rights have communal aspects, such as freedom of association and religion.[17] Duties are primarily directed towards states, but also increasingly towards non-state

(*Justice Beyond Borders: A Global Political Theory* (Oxford: Oxford University Press, 2005), 150). There is presently a dichotomy even within states which externally assert strong sovereignty, such as China and Brazil, but which at times are also de facto limited in their ability to exert internal authority in parts of their vast territory.

13 Conor Gearty characterizes human rights as a language that promotes the visibility or "voice" of persons normally rendered invisible via their marginalization, prompting expressions of compassion by others, and empowering persons to speak for themselves (*Can Human Rights Survive?* (Cambridge: Cambridge University Press, 2006), 42–3).

14 See Boaventura de Sousa Santos, *Toward a New Legal Common Sense* (London: Butterworths, 2002); Margaret E. Keck and Kathryn Sikkik, *Activists Beyond Borders: Advocacy Networks in International Politics* (Ithaca, NY and London: Cornell University Press, 1998).

15 See UN Office of the High Commissioner for Human Rights, available online at: www.ohchr.org/en/issues/Pages/WhatareHumanRights.aspx

16 Robert McCorquodale, 'Rights of Peoples and Minorities', in Daniel Moeckli, Sangeeta Shah and Sandesh Sivakumaran (eds.), *International Human Rights Law* (Oxford: Oxford University Press, 2010), 365.

17 Caney, *Justice Beyond Borders*, at 92.

actors.[18] Obligations include positive and negative variants, including duties to respect, protect, and fulfill human rights.[19]

At the universal level, there are eight principal human rights treaties which have a committee of experts to monitor implementation: the International Convention on the Elimination of All Forms of Racial Discrimination (1965), International Covenant on Civil and Political Rights (ICCPR, 1966), International Covenant on Economic, Social and Cultural Rights (ICESCR, 1966), Convention on the Elimination of All Forms of Discrimination against Women (1979), Convention against Torture and Other Cruel, Inhuman, or Degrading Treatment or Punishment (1984), Convention on the Rights of the Child (1989), International Convention on the Protection of Rights of All Migrant Workers and Their Families (1990), and the Convention on the Rights of Persons with Disabilities (2006).[20] At the regional level, the main conventions are monitored by regional courts: the European Convention on Human Rights (1950), the American Convention on Human Rights (1969), and the African Charter on Human and Peoples' Rights (1981).[21]

The international community seeks enforcement of human rights via issuance of reports, general comments or recommendations, as well as decisions relating to individual complaints. Remedies include: promotion of amendment or adoption of national legislation; education of judges, police, lawyers; provision of benefits and services, and investigation, prosecution, and compensation to victims as part of international, regional, national case processing.[22] Furthermore, long term human rights-based

[18] Walter Kälin and Jörg Künzli, *The Law of International Human Rights Protection* (Oxford: Oxford University Press, 2009), 77–8.

[19] *Ibid.*, at 96–113. Civil and political rights are considered first-generation rights and economic, cultural, and social rights are considered second-generation rights. Third-generation rights include the right to a healthy environment, the right to development, the right to peace, and the right to intergenerational equity. The obligation to respect requires the state to refrain from interfering with the enjoyment of human rights. The obligation to protect requires the state to protect persons from human rights violations from third parties (including private actors). The obligation to fulfill requires adoption of legislation or administrative measures to ensure the realization of the rights (including provision of benefits and services).

[20] Several of the treaties are complemented by optional protocols. For a general overview, see: www.ohchr.org/EN/HRBodies/Pages/HumanRightsBodies.aspx

[21] For an overview of the impact of treaties on a state's human rights practices, see Beth A. Simmons, *Mobilizing for Human Rights: International Law in Domestic Politics* (New York: Cambridge University Press, 2009).

[22] See Moeckli *et al.*, *International Human Rights Law.*

development approaches, including education and empowerment of social actors (such as women) via micro-finance and educational programs seek to complement the protection mechanisms.[23]

Nevertheless, the international human rights system has experienced limitations due to excessive delays in receiving state reports and processing individual cases, as well as weakness in attaining implementation of decisions of its monitoring bodies at the national level.[24] There are legitimacy concerns due to accusations of a lack of transparency, accountability, and imbalances in UN and regional institutional proceedings.[25] At times, UN agencies have been accused of being tempered in their public criticism of states due to concern about loss of funding or denial of access to territory for operations.[26] The interstate complaint system is largely ignored, revealing an important protection gap with respect to enforcement of human rights. There is also disquiet regarding perceptions of bias or selectiveness within forums (such as the Human Rights Council and the Universal Periodic Review) in their treatment of particular countries, politicization and regional blocs in discussion, and their response to humanitarian situations.[27] International and regional human rights courts and committees have been confounded by an inability to counter impunity by ensuring implementation of decisions, views, and recommendations calling for prosecution of those responsible for human rights violations.[28] The UN Security Council's selective

[23] See: Dan Banik, *Poverty and Elusive Development* (Oslo: Scandinavian University Press, 2010); Bård A. Andreassen and Stephen P. Marks (eds.), *Development as a Human Right: Legal, Political and Economic Dimensions* (Antwerp: Intersentia, 2010).

[24] Olivier De Schutter, *International Human Rights Law* (Cambridge: Cambridge University Press, 2010), chs. 9–11.

[25] See e.g. Ved P. Nanda, 'Accountability of International Organizations: Some Observations', *Denver Journal of International Law and Policy*, 33 (2004–5), 379; Philip Alston, 'Hobbling the Monitors: Should UN Human Rights Monitors be Accountable?', *Harvard International Law Journal*, 52(2) (2011), 563.

[26] See e.g. Binaifer Nowrogee and Peter Takirambudde, *Failing the Internally Displaced: The UNDP Displaced Persons Program in Kenya* (New York: Human Rights Watch, 1997).

[27] See Edward R. McMahon and Marta Ascherio, 'Analysis of recommendations of the Universal Periodic Review, sessions I–VI', paper presented at the Human Rights Council's Performance To-Date Conference, Friedrich Ebert Stiftung, Berlin, Germany, October 14–15, 2010, available online at: www.fes.de/gpol/pdf/McMahon_UPR_Analysis.pdf; see also Report from the World Movement for Democracy, 'How to Strengthen the UN Human Rights Council through Cross-Regional Collaboration', available online at: www.wmd.org/assemblies/fifth-assembly/reports/defending-civil-society

[28] See Jo M. Pasqualucci, *The Practice and Procedure of the Inter-American Court of Human Rights* (New York: Cambridge University Press, 2003) 290; Mark W. Janis, Richard S. Kay,

application of economic sanctions and pursuit of humanitarian intervention in response to systematic human rights violations have added fodder to the fire of accusations of politicization of the human rights project.[29] Furthermore, the international economic institutional and normative system (IMF, World Bank, and WTO) has been severely criticized for separating human rights matters from economic policy, regulation, and dispute resolution.[30] This is of particular concern given the obvious impact and relevance of trade and finance upon human rights.

An additional issue relates to the emergence of NGOs which transformed the human rights system through their transnational networking and ability to promote issues (such as the prohibition of torture, the justiciability of socio-economic rights, and the rights of women and children). They mobilize to pursue concrete cases and themes and generate response by the international community.[31] The role of NGOs vis-à-vis international organizations is complex, given the downsizing of the UN and budget constraints of regional human rights bodies. International organizations are increasingly dependent on NGOs for identification of issues for examination, as well as provision of information via shadow reports *and amicus curiae*, as well as analysis delivered via consulting.[32] As a consequence, some human rights issues may benefit from the existence of a well-placed NGO to ensure a more thorough discussion of the topic at the highest

and Anthony W. Bradley, *European Human Rights Law* (Oxford: Oxford University Press, 2008), 103–18.

[29] Mariano J. Aznar-Gómez, 'A Decade of Human Rights Protection by the UN Security Council: A Decade of Deregulation?', *European Journal of International Law*, 13(1) (2002), 223.

[30] Dinah Shelton, 'Protecting Human Rights in a Globalized World', *Boston College International and Comparative Law Review*, 28 (spring 2002), 273; M. Rodwan Abouharb and David Cingranelli, *Human Rights and Structural Adjustment* (New York: Cambridge University Press, 2007); Thomas Pogge, *World Poverty and Human Rights* (Cambridge: Polity, 2008).

[31] See Steve Charnovitz, 'Nongovernmental Organizations and International Law', *American Journal of International Law*, 100(2) (2006), 348–72; Peter Van Tuijl, 'NGOs and Human Rights: Sources of Justice and Democracy', *Journal of International Affairs*, 52(2) (1999), 493–512; Claude E. Welch Jr. (ed.), *NGOs and Human Rights: Promise and Performance* (Philadelphia, PA: University of Pennsylvania, 2001); Peter Willetts (ed.), *NGOs: The Conscience of the World: The Influence of Non-Governmental Organisations in the UN System* (Washington, DC: Brookings Institution, 1996).

[32] See Shamima Ahmed, 'The Impact of NGOs on International Organizations: Complexities and Considerations', *Brooklyn Journal of International Law*, 36 (2011), 817.

levels, while others may remain peripheral due to lack of sufficient advocacy by NGOs.[33] At present, the accountability of NGOs remains an underexplored area, which behoves attention given its obvious implications upon the legitimacy of the international human rights order.[34]

At the national level, human rights are protected by national courts addressing cases involving constitutional rights, national legislation incorporating human rights, as well as universal jurisdiction.[35] There is significant disquietude with respect to limited access to justice among minorities, women, and other vulnerable groups in many countries. They are often stymied by account of excessive delays within court systems, discriminatory practices or regulations, as well as lack of information and financial and/or geographic impediments.[36] There is additional criticism offered that the exercise of universal jurisdiction is an example of legal imperialism, as courts in powerful countries address crimes committed in less powerful countries.[37]

There has been much research on the manifold efforts to reform the international human rights system in order to improve its effectiveness.[38] It is suggested that discussions regarding the legitimacy of the international human rights system requires looking beyond institutions in order to conduct a normative assessment in order to examine to what extent there is a "culture gap" between the international and national levels, specifically with respect to perceptions regarding the roles and relations between "rights" and "duties".

[33] For additional critiques, see Austen L. Parrish, 'Rehabilitating Territoriality in Human Rights', *Cardozo Law Review*, 32 (March 2011), 1099.

[34] George E. Edwards, 'Assessing the Effectiveness of Human Rights Non-Governmental Organizations (NGOs) from the Birth of the United Nations to the 21st Century: Ten Attributes of Highly Successful Human Rights NGOs', *Michigan State Journal of International Law*, 18 (2010), 165. See also Karima Bennoune's chapter in this volume (Chapter 7).

[35] See Oxford Law Reports on International Human Rights in Domestic Courts: www.oxfordlawreports.com

[36] See: UNDP study on Access to Justice: www.undp.org/governance/docs/Justice_PN_English.pdf; also UN Women's report, *In Pursuit of Justice: Progress of the World's Women 2011–2012* (2011) (available online at: http://progress.unwomen.org/pdfs/EN-Report-Progress.pdf).

[37] Parrish, 'Rehabilitating Territoriality'.

[38] See e.g. Mark Toufayan, 'Identity, Effectiveness, and Newness in Transjudicialism's Coming of Age', *Michigan Journal of International Law*, 31 (winter 2010), 307.

2 The need for reevaluation of the normative underpinnings of human rights

2.1 Cultural differentiation in human rights

Some of the most problematic aspects of the conception of human rights in the modern age have been biases pertaining to approaches that favor "equality" over "difference,"[39] "individual" over "communitarian" or collective rights,[40] civil and political rights over socio-economic rights,[41] as well as the trumping of "rights" over "duties".[42] These dilemmas prompted TWAIL (Third World approaches to international law) scholars to characterize human rights as cultural imperialistic examples of Western dominance.[43] According to Mutua, there is a need to resituate the position of the individual vis-à-vis society in order to preserve the legitimacy of human rights.[44] The need for improved harmony between

[39] See Dianne Otto, 'Disconcerting "Masculinities": Reinventing the Gendered Subject(s) of International Human Rights Law', in Doris Buss and Ambreena Manji, *International Law: Modern Feminist Approaches* (Oxford: Hart, 2005), 105. Rachel Kleinfeld states: "In many Islamic societies, giving women equality before the law is opposed by most interpretations of Sharia, the Islamic code. In other cases, equality before the law is de jure, but different justice prevails de facto. For example, even though India has formal equality before the law, caste concepts in villages remain strong; the idea that a low-caste person should be treated as the equal of a high-caste person is 'unjust' in such contexts, as well as irreligious. The idea of equality would be seen as nearly inhuman in less individualistic societies. For example, the notion that a policeman should treat his mother caught in a crime as he would a stranger would be seen in the West as personally difficult but nonetheless a just ideal, whereas elsewhere it would be seen as manifestly unjust" ('Competing Definitions of the Rule of Law', in Thomas Carothers (ed.), *Promoting the Rule of Law Abroad: In Search of Knowledge* (Washington, DC: Carnegie Endowment for International Peace, 2006) 31, 38).

[40] Michael Ignatieff offers a conception of human rights as suggesting a conflict between a rights holder and rights "withholder": "Rights language cannot be parsed or translated into a non-individualistic, communitarian framework. It presumes moral individualism and is nonsensical outside that assumption" (*Human Rights as Politics and Idolatry* (Princeton, NJ: Princeton University Press, 2001), 67). But see M. A. Glendon, *Rights Talk: The Impoverishment of Political Discourse* (New York: Free Press, 1991).

[41] Asbjørn Eide, Catarina Krause and Allan Rosas, *Economic, Social and Cultural Rights: A Textbook* (The Hague: Kluwer Law International, 2001). See also Henry J. Steiner, Philip Alston and Ryan Goodman, *International Human Rights in Context* (Oxford: Oxford University Press, 2007), 370–4.

[42] Steiner *et al.*, *International Human Rights*, at 475–512.

[43] Balakrishnan Rajagopal, *International Law from Below: Development, Social Movements and Third World Resistance* (Cambridge: Cambridge University Press, 2003).

[44] Makua Mutua, 'Human Rights and Powerlessness: Pathologies of Choice and Substance', *Buffalo Law Review*, 56 (2008), 1029, 1033.

the international normative framework and the legal orders espoused by the world's communities is underscored. It may be worthwhile to consider balancing communal-based perspectives when pursuing human rights discussion. Indeed, H. Patrick Glenn reviewed the major legal traditions of the world (Chthonic, Talmudic, civil law, Islamic law, common law, Hindu law, Confucian law) and concluded that: "Most of the tradition which has been captured and retained is aimed at the good or well-being of entire communities, and the largest and greatest of traditions have been directed at very large communities, if not humanity in its entirety."[45] Successful human rights dissemination is contingent on contextual approaches.[46] In accordance with this view, An-Na'im suggests that human rights will not be respected if they are not considered to be culturally relevant.[47] For many societies, discussion of human rights aspirations of social justice are not possible without linkage to religious values, which take as a point of departure recognition of duties, rather than individual rights. Diane Orentlicher states that she supports An-Na'im's conviction that it is preferable to include religious discourse within "the intercultural process of constructing and construing human rights," in part as a check against absolutism and also to enable the idea of human rights "to take root within the deepest commitments of individuals across diverse systems of belief, tradition, and culture."[48] The problem is that some discourses may blend religious teachings with objectives that pursue violence, repression, or exclusion of others. The challenge is to respect religious expressions that uphold peace and human dignity, while supporting reform of extreme discourses that harm individuals or groups. Indeed, during the 2011 uprising against

[45] H. Patrick Glenn, *Legal Traditions of the World* (4th edn., Oxford: Oxford University Press, 2010), 28.

[46] Patrick James Flood, *The Effectiveness of UN Human Rights Institutions* (Westport, CT: Praeger, 1998), 18, cited by Melissa Robbins, in 'Powerful States, Customary Law and the Erosion of Human Rights through Regional Enforcement', *California Western International Law Journal*, 35 (spring 2005), 275, 278.

[47] Abdullahi Ahmad An-Na'im, 'Human Rights in the Muslim World: Socio-Political Conditions and Scriptural Imperatives', *Harvard Human Rights Journal*, 3 (1990), 13, cited by Jason Morgan-Foster in, 'Third Generation Rights: What Islamic Law Can Teach the International Human Rights Movement', *Yale Human Rights and Development Law Journal*, 8 (2005), 67. Morgan-Foster states: "In human rights law, rights are explicit, while corresponding duties are implicit, controversial, and poorly theorized. In several other legal, ethical, and religious systems – such as Islamic law, Jewish law, Christianity, Hinduism, and Confucianism – the reverse is true."

[48] Diane F. Orentlicher, 'Relativism and Religion', in Ignatieff, *Human Rights*, 156.

Mubarak in Egypt, the Muslim Brotherhood published an op-ed in the *New York Times* calling for recognition of the possibility of joining religion with democracy:

> As our nation heads toward liberty, however, we disagree with the claims that the only options in Egypt are a purely secular, liberal democracy or an authoritarian theocracy. Secular liberal democracy of the American and European variety, with its firm rejection of religion in public life, is not the exclusive model for a legitimate democracy. In Egypt, religion continues to be an important part of our culture and heritage. Moving forward, we envision the establishment of a democratic, civil state that draws on universal measures of freedom and justice, which are central Islamic values. We embrace democracy not as a foreign concept that must be reconciled with tradition, but as a set of principles and objectives that are inherently compatible with and reinforce Islamic tenets.[49]

Nonetheless, women's rights commentators are concerned that at present women in Egypt are actually facing threats in the form of potential loss of a quota of seats in the parliament, non-transparent reform of family law, and exclusion from participation in the political transition.[50] Karima Bennoune offers a critical warning: "Religious and cultural claims of particularity do raise a range of significant methodological questions as we try to apply international law norms. However, we must avoid the bizarre privileging and freezing of what is meant by culture and religion that occurs so often in these debates, wherein reified notions are accepted as a singular 'Muslim view' or Muslim reality."[51]

In relation to Africa, Adrien Katherine Wing sets forth that problems relating to both weak and strong states hampered by corruption point to renewed appreciation for tribalism and community-based societies (as well as religion).[52] It is necessary to explore whether the way forward may be to reorient the discussion of the human rights in relation to duties, taking into account the need for analysis of the "contentious

[49] Essam El-Errian, 'What the Muslim Brothers want', *New York Times*, February 9, 2011, available at: www.nytimes.com/2011/02/10/opinion/10erian.html?scp=2andsq=Muslim%20Brotherhoodandst=cse

[50] Carolyn Barnett, 'Egypt: Fighting for Women's Rights in the Aftermath of the Revolution', *Women Living Under Muslim Laws*, June 9, 2011, available online at: www.wluml.org/node/7255

[51] Karima Bennoune, 'Remembering the Other's Others: Theorizing the Approach of International Law to Muslim Fundamentalism', *Columbia Human Rights Law Review*, 41 (2010), 635, 665.

[52] Adrien Katherine Wing, 'Communitarianism v. Individualism: Constitutionalism in Namibia and South Africa', *Wisconsin International Law Journal*, 11 (1992–3), 295, 376.

relationship between human rights and legal pluralism."[53] The discussion seeks to pursue the perspective of responsive communitarianism which seeks to balance pursuit of the common good with respect for autonomy and rights.[54] The point of departure is Alasdair MacIntyre's concept of the "narrative self," in which individuals are defined by their obligations of loyalty or membership of groups that in turn serve to attain a shared good that develops the person's capacity to act rationally and ethically.[55]

2.2 *Duties*

This section seeks to argue that recognition of duties is a central aspect of human rights protection. Duties are the consequence of an individual's identity and membership in a family, community, society, state, and humanity. Duties address actions fulfilling the needs of others and have long formed the basis of societies:

> The interpretation of various forms of social behavior as involving rights and/or duties has depended on cultural factors, such as the existence of a feudal system, or a puritanical religious atmosphere, as well as agricultures which depend on the work of whole families. The balance between a duty-based and a rights-based social order has changed a great deal over

[53] Anne Hellum, Julie Stewart, Shaheen Sardar Ali, and Amy Tsanga, *Human Rights, Plural Legalities and Gendered Realities: Paths are Made by Walking* (Harare: Southern and Eastern African Regional Centre for Women's Law, University of Zimbabwe with Weaver Press, 2007), xix.

[54] Amitai Etzioni, Andrew Volmert, and Elanit Rothschild provide the following definition: "Responsive communitarianism assumes that a good society is based on a carefully crafted balance between liberty and social order, between individual rights and social responsibilities, between particularistic (ethnic, racial, communal) and society-wide values and bonds" (*The Communitarian Reader: Beyond the Essentials* (Lanham, MD: Rowman & Littlefield, 2004), 2).

[55] Alasdair MacIntyre, *After Virtue: A Study in Moral Theory* (London: Duckworth, 1985), 220: "I am someone's son or daughter, someone else's cousin or uncle; I am a citizen of this or that city, a member of this or that guild or profession; I belong to this clan, that tribe, this nation. Hence what is good for me has to be good for the one who inhabits these roles." See also Alasdair MacIntyre, *Dependent Rational Animals: Why Human Beings Need the Virtues* (Chicago, IL: Open Court, 1999). He highlights that we are part of a community of giving and receiving which is a network of duties and obligations. Nevertheless, it is important to recognize that obligations also form an important part of liberal philosophy, but appear to have been neglected in human rights policy circles. For example, Christine M. Korsgaard presents a Kantian perspective on the relation of obligations to oneself and the value of humanity: 'The sources of normativity', Tanner Lecture on Human Value (Cambridge November 16, 1992).

> history. There have been societies based predominantly on duties, and more recently, some which seem to [be] based predominantly on rights. We note again that while the exercise of rights makes no sense unless the correlative duties exist, societies have flourished in which order devolves from reciprocal duties alone.[56]

Moghaddam *et al.* note that the transition from medieval to modern industrial societies resulted in a gradual move away from duties to rights, hence it may be suggested with the advance of neo-medievalism it is logical to reexamine the role of duties in societies.[57] In spite of the Western human rights emphasis on the principles of equality and non-discrimination as fundamental norms, it may argued that in most of the non-Western world (and indeed also within the Western world itself) hierarchical social, political, and economic structures define human relations from the nuclear family level to extended communities.[58] Differentiation according to ability, class, ethnicity, nationality, gender, age, religion, political opinion, and other characteristics result in allocation of status and role within the overall structure (which may be flexible or rigid according to the specific context). The positive aspects of these constructs include:

1. provision of defined roles and connections which solidify identity (perhaps countering modern tendencies towards anomie);

[56] Fathali M. Moghaddam, Nikki R. Slocum, Norman Finkel, Tzili Mor, and Rom Harré, 'Toward a Cultural Theory of Duties', *Culture and Psychology*, 6(3) (2000), 275–302, at 276 and 282. They characterize feudal systems from the medieval period as being based on vertical social divisions in which persons owed duties to those who owed duties to them.

[57] *Ibid.*, at 283. See also: Jordan J. Paust, 'The Other Side of Right: Private Duties Under Human Rights Law', *Harvard Human Rights Journal*, 5 (1992), 51, 63; Ziyad Motala, 'Human Rights in Africa: A Cultural, Ideological, and Legal Examination', *Hastings International and Comparative Law Review*, 12 (1988–89), 373, at 409.

[58] Jack Donnelly characterizes "traditional" societies (Western and non-Western) as having "elaborate systems of duties" that "correspond to values and obligations that we associate with human rights today. But such societies had conceptions of justice, political legitimacy, and human flourishing that sought to realize human dignity, flourishing, or well-being entirely independent of human rights. These institutions and practices are alternatives to, rather than different formulations of human rights" (*Universal Human Rights in Theory and Practice* (Ithaca, NY: Cornell University Press, 2003), 71). The principles of equality and non-discrimination have been characterized as *jus cogens* by the Inter-American Court of Human Rights, Advisory Opinion on the Juridical Condition and Rights of Undocumented Migrants, OC 18/03 (Sept. 17, 2003).

2. transfer of values, knowledge, experience, connections, security, support, and sharing of assets among kith and kin;
3. solidarity, cohesion, and commitment in time of crisis or tension (especially important in the absence or dysfunction of a welfare state);
4. reciprocal, intergenerational obligations addressing responsibility, such as provision of care to the elderly, children, poor, sick; and
5. grant of respect, recognition, and prestige due to performance of obligations to the family/community.

The negative aspects include the subjugation of minority groups and vulnerable persons (including women and children) to exclusion and oppression.[59] They are victimized within contexts that are marked by rigid social stratification, repressive, authoritarian cultures, and domination of political power by a small, ruling class.[60] Although development approaches have focused on rights, the framework of formal equality renders implementation of programs in the field problematic given the difficulty of adjusting entrenched social patterns that are precisely constructed on differentiation among people. It has been noted that "duties are part of an ongoing social life that is sustained, often with little real change, across generations."[61] It is possible to envision the international human rights community developing a framework for adaptation of the notion of equality in order to incorporate the principle of duties within the local context. This would reflect the "beneficent reciprocal relationships" that are considered natural to social systems. Such conception would recognize duties as tying an individual's needs with the needs of others, as leaving another in need results in debasement of oneself.[62]

Devereux suggests adoption of the perspective that "humans could be regarded as bearing a certain level of responsibility for each other, simply

[59] For a review of challenges faced by women seeking access to justice, see the UN Women's report, *In Pursuit of Justice*. See also Anne Hellum in this volume (Chapter 8). In relation to children, for a positive perspective, see J. Sloth-Nielsen and B. D. Mezmur, 'A Dutiful Child: The Implications of Article 31 of the African Children's Charter', *Journal of African Law*, 52 (2008), 159–89.

[60] Sloth-Nielsen and Mezmur, 'Dutiful Child'. See also Frances Raday, 'Culture, Religion, and Gender', *International Journal of Constitutional Law*, 1(4) (2003), 663, discussing asymmetric gender relations and harmful traditional practices within families based on patriarchal culture/religion.

[61] Moghaddam *et al.*, 'Toward a Cultural Theory of Duties', at 282.

[62] Anne Marie Devereux, 'Should "Duties" Play a Larger Role in Human Rights? A Critique of Western Liberal and African Human Rights Jurisprudence', *University of New South Wales Law Journal*, 18(2) (1995), 464, at 474.

because of their shared humanity."[63] Hence, this supports a definition of human identity which is communitarian, recognizing "both individual human dignity and the social dimension of human existence".[64] The standard of respect for human dignity serves as a limitation to the primacy of obligation in social relations. It has been suggested that an African perspective would consider human dignity to be the "product of fulfilling one's role in society," thereby implying that persons would be more likely to provide benefits to others as their interests would coincide (as opposed to a pure rights framework which is antagonistic).[65] In short, the articulation of duties pursues perspectives which are oriented towards reconciliation of interests and acceptance of interdependence as a natural aspect of human experience.[66] This would be compatible with the perspective offered by Sarah Whatmore of "recognizing ethical communities as practically constructed and corporeally embedded points towards a world of fragile heterogeneous networks in which equality (in the sense of an equivalence of being rather than a universal rational ideal) remains the common premise of emancipator subjects or movements."[67]

At the international level, Judge Cancado Trindade considers the identification of duties of individuals as the consolidation of their

[63] *Ibid.*

[64] The Communitarian Network, 'Rights and Responsibilities', available online at: http://communitariannetwork.org. See also: Maku Wa Mutua, 'The Banjul Charter and the African Cultural Fingerprint: An Evaluation of the Language of Duties', *Virginia Journal of International Law*, 35 (1994–5), 363. Devereux states that "promoting a greater emphasis on individual duties and a community outlook is one means by which the existing system could seek to further ensure respect for human dignity" ('Should "Duties" Play a Larger Role in Human Rights?').

[65] Devereux, 'Should "Duties" Play a Larger Role in Human Rights?', at 482. Furthermore, Jack Goody muses: " a too heavy dose of 'individualizing' could reduce a community to a moral desert populated by people in distress" ('Futures of the Family in Rural Africa', *Population and Development Review, Supplement: Rural Development and Population: Institutions and Policy*, 15 (1989), 119–44, at 123).

[66] See Andrew Clapham, 'The Role of the Individual in International Law', *European Journal of International Law*, 21(1) (2010), 25–30, calling for recognition of individual duties: "If we do not want the development of international law to stagnate we should perhaps admit the progressive idea that individuals have, in addition to these rights and criminal law obligations, certain international civil law obligations; this step could help to build an international community which properly recognizes the role of the individual in international law."

[67] Sarah Whatmore, 'Dissecting the Autonomous Self: Hybrid Cartographies for a Relational Ethics', in George Henderson and Marvin Waterstone, *Geographic Thought: A Praxis Perspective* (New York: Routledge, 2009), 109, 119.

international legal personality.[68] Moreover, communitarian values have always been present within the modern human rights normative instruments. The normative foundation for recognition of duties between individuals already exists at the universal level. Consider Article 1 of the Universal Declaration of Human Rights: "All human beings are born free and equal in dignity and rights. They are endowed with reason and conscience and should act towards one another in a spirit of brotherhood." Mary Ann Glendon characterized it as a "declaration of interdependence – interdependence of people, nations, and rights."[69] Indeed, René Cassin, Charles Malik, and other drafters of the UN Declaration of Human Rights conceived human rights as functioning within the context of the family, tribe, city, profession, religion, and human community, thereby underscoring the importance of duties.[70] Thus, the Universal Declaration of Human Rights provides language for recognition of duties between the individual and the community, Article 29 (1) states: "Everyone has duties to the community in which alone the free and full development of his personality is possible." Similarly, the preambles of the ICCPR and the ICESCR recognize that individuals have duties "to other individuals and to the community to which he belongs." Further, the UN Declaration on the Right and Responsibility of Individual Groups and Organs of Society to Promote and Protect Universally Recognized Human Rights and Fundamental Freedoms (1999), Article 18 (1) sets forth:

1. Everyone has duties towards and within the community, in which alone the free and full development of his or her personality is possible.
2. Individuals, groups, institutions and non-governmental organizations have an important role to play and a responsibility in safeguarding democracy, promoting human rights and fundamental freedoms and contributing to the promotion and advancement of democratic societies, institutions and processes.
3. Individuals, groups, institutions and non-governmental organizations also have an important role and a responsibility in contributing, as appropriate, to the promotion of the right of everyone to a social and

[68] Antonio Cancado Trindade, *The Access of Individuals to International Justice (Collected Courses of the Academy of European Law)* (New York: Oxford University Press, 2011), 13.

[69] Mary Ann Glendon, *A World Made New: Eleanor Roosevelt and the Universal Declaration of Human Rights* (New York: Random House, 2001), 174.

[70] *Ibid.*, at 68, 113, 174. Indeed the delegate from China, P. C. Chang, indicated that it was through consciousness of his duties that man reaches a higher level of moral development (at 141).

> international order in which the rights and freedoms set forth in the Universal Declaration of Human Rights and other human rights instruments can be fully realized.[71]

Hence, it may be argued that duty-based protection initiatives have an international framework. Nevertheless, Knox suggests that the lack of specification of duties rendered them subject to the domain of national law. Many initiatives to elaborate the scope of duties are currently found in constitutions, as are human rights. The fact that duties have been left to national interpretation supports recognition that the social context is a necessary element in definition of obligations. It would be beneficial to support a transnational initiative within the global civil society to promote new discourses on duties-based perspectives addressing human rights tied to social justice, development, and a healthy environment.

At the Inter-American level, the American Declaration of the Rights and Duties of Man (1948) established that human rights and duties are on a par with each other.[72] Nevertheless this was not the case with the Universal Declaration of Human Rights or the International Covenants on Civil and Political Rights and Social, Economic, and Cultural Rights, due to concern that states would use duties to limit the exercise of rights. There is a need to reexamine this concern, whether it is no longer considered as valid at present time. If we take a comparative perspective, regional instruments have expressed a higher degree of faith in the possibility of limiting rights in relation to the needs of others. Chapter 2 (Articles XXIX–XXXVIII) of the American Declaration identifies duties to society, towards children and parents, to attain education, to vote, to obey the law, to serve the community and nation, to cooperate with respect to social security and welfare, to pay taxes, to work, and to refrain from political activities in a foreign country. Similarly, the American Convention on Human Rights, Article 32, sets forth personal responsibilities at the nuclear, local, and global levels: "Every person has responsibilities to his family, his community, and mankind. The rights of each person are limited by the rights of others, by the security of all, and

[71] See also Article 10 establishing an obligation not to violate human rights: "No one shall participate, by act or by failure to act where required, in violating human rights and fundamental freedoms and no one shall be subjected to punishment or adverse action of any kind for refusing to do so."

[72] John H. Knox, 'Horizontal Human Rights Law', 102 *American Journal of International Law*, 102 (January 2008), 1. The preamble of the American Declaration states that "the fulfillment of duty by each individual is a prerequisite to the rights of all . . . While rights exalt individual liberty, duties express the dignity of that liberty."

by the just demands of the general welfare, in a democratic society." The key is engaging individuals to effectuate their responsibilities at each level through their own actions as well as placement of demands on state and non-state institutions for fulfillment of duties.

Eric Engle sets forth that the issue of whether rights arise from duties is derived from the North–South debate:

> Representing the global south, Asian schools of thought, whether Islamic, Hindu, Confucian, or Buddhist tend to see not rights, but rather duties as primary, and to recognize rights only as a consequence of duty fulfilled. In contrast, western schools of thought, notably ius natural, tend to see the foundation of human rights on certain inalienable, inherent capacities of humans, generally speaking rationality, though Christian theologians would combine that theory with the idea that rationality is a reflection of divine perfection.[73]

Indeed, the Asian perspective focuses on duties, and the perception of human rights violations often appears to apply to acts conducted by non-state actors against individuals (this is considered a criminal act in the West). This stands in stark contrast to the resistance within several UN human rights bodies to affirm the applicability of human rights to non-state actors.[74] Furthermore, within Chinese society, collective rights generally prevail over the individual.[75] A psychological study discusses the definition of personhood in Asian cultures:

> [W]here the self is defined by one's duties or obligations towards others in one's social network ... There is evidence that in cultures where individuals are expected to accommodate themselves to society's structures and rules, people are highly aware of their collective duties. Similarly, in cultures where society is expected to change to accommodate individuals' needs and aspirations, people are highly aware of their individual rights.

[73] 'Universal Human Rights: A Generational History', *Annual Survey of International and Comparative Law*, 12 (spring 2006), 219, 238.

[74] See e.g. Cecilia Bailliet, 'Towards Holistic Transnational Protection: An Overview of International Public Law Approaches to Kidnapping', *Denver Journal of International Law and Policy*, 38(4)(fall 2010), 581, discussing the resistance by the UN Working Group on Enforced or Involuntary Disappearances to recognize kidnapping by non-state actors as enforced disappearance, stating that such expansion would dilute state responsibility for disappearances.

[75] Randall Peerenboom notes that: "Greater weight should be placed on the interests of specific groups within society, of the society as a whole and of the state itself. In addition, the emphasis on rights should not obscure the importance of duties and the responsibilities of individuals toward others" ('Human Rights and Rule of Law: What's the Relationship?', *Georgetown Journal of International Law*, 36 (spring 2005), 809).

> These cultural variations in lay theories of social organization may account for the East West differences in the conceptions of duty-based versus rights based personhood.[76]

Another psychological study set forth that "Whereas American culture tends to emphasize individual autonomy and freedom of choice, Hindu Indian culture tends to place greater stress on interpersonal interdependence and social obligations."[77] Indeed, Mahatma Gandhi declared that all rights are born of obligations.[78]

Communitarian models vary from "hard" versions in which the state is the primary actor, such as China, and "soft" versions in which civil society are primary drivers. East Asian governments enable fulfillment of duties in various ways, such as China, Japan, and Singapore's legislation that requires children to financially support their elderly parents, or Korea and Hong Kong's provision of tax breaks and housing benefits to support home care.[79] In contrast, within Africa, the Charter on Human and Peoples' Rights, Articles 27–29 set forth duties of the individual towards the family, society, state, and communities, including the international community.[80] Mutua points out that in the African Charter duties are primarily owed to the family (nuclear and extended) and to the community, not to the state (as the family the essential unit of survival):

[76] Ying-yi Hong, Grace Ip, Chi-yue Chiu, Michael W. Morris, and Tanya Menon 'Cultural Identity and Dynamic Construction of the Self: Collective Duties and Individual Rights in Chinese and American Cultures', *Social Cognition*, 19(3) (2001), 251–68, at 253–4. They found that "Apparently, in Chinese culture, duties are central to the conception of the collective self, but rights are not important to the definition of the individual self. In American culture, rights are important components of the individual self, but duties are not strongly linked to the collective self . . . Interestingly, the Chinese participants did not mention any rights in all experimental conditions. It thus appears that among this group of participants, the idea that the self possesses rights was far below the activation threshold, if not cognitively unavailable."

[77] Joan G. Miller, David M. Bersoff, and Robin L. Harwood, 'Perceptions of Social Responsibilities in India and in the United States: Moral Imperatives or Personal Decisions?', *Journal of Personality and Social Psychology*, 58(1) (1990), 33–47, at 34.

[78] Glendon, *World Made New*, at 166.

[79] *Stanford Encyclopedia of Philosophy*, 'Communitarianism' (January 22, 2009).

[80] Furthermore, the African Children's Charter, Article 31, sets forth responsibilities of every child towards his family, society, state, other legally recognized communities, and the international community. It highlights duties to work for the cohesion of the family, to respect his parents, superiors, and elders at all times, and to assist them in case of need. It also calls for service of his physical and intellectual abilities for the national community, support of African cultural values, independence and integrity of the country, and the African Union.

> Crippling economic problems do not allow African states to contemplate some of the programs of the welfare state. The care of the aged and needy falls squarely on family and community members. This requirement – a necessity today – has its roots in the past: it was unthinkable to abandon a parent or relative in need. The family guilty of such an omission would be held in disgrace and contempt pending the intervention of lineage or clan members. Such problems explain why the family is considered sacred and why it would be simply impracticable and suicidal for Africans to adopt wholesale the individualist conception of rights.[81]

In terms of enforceability, only the duties to pay taxes and to support one's parents are considered enforceable.[82] Devereux explains that in Africa: "Duties are regarded as part of the 'law' of the community and are enforced in a similar manner as other laws – primarily through custom and religion."[83] She further explains that: "The duty-based system is not seen as oppressing the individual but as merely providing for the individual's welfare within the proper community setting. The individual's welfare is furthered in harmony, rather than in competition with the welfare of the community."[84] This perspective stands in contrast to separation and alienation which are the negative aspects attributed to individualism.[85]

Within Islam, duties are considered to be central to the conception of human rights: "Individual and group rights are capable of mutually reinforcing each other; a person can fulfill his or her duty to protect the rights of others without undermining his or her individual rights."[86] Indeed, Mohammed's teachings included outright condemnation of the neglect and exploitation of the poor, including orphans and widows.

[81] Makau Mutua, *Human Rights: A Political and Cultural Critique* (Philadelphia, PA: University of Pennsylvania Press, 2002), 88.

[82] Adrien Katherine Wing, 'Communitarianism vs. Individualism: Constitutionalism in Namibia and South Africa', *Wisconsin International Law Journal*, 11 (1992–3), 295, 325. Duties are contained in several African national constitutions, as well as within national civil and penal legislation.

[83] Devereux, 'Should "Duties" Play a Larger Role in Human Rights?', at 476.

[84] *Ibid.*, at 478.

[85] As stated by Josiah Cobbah, "The right of one kinship member was the duty of the other and the duty of the other kinship member was the right of another" ('African Values and the Human Rights Debate: An African Perspective', *Human Rights Quarterly*, 9 (1987), 321), cited by Bonny Ibhawah, *Imperialism and Human Rights: Colonial Discourses of Rights and Liberties in African History* (New York: State University of New York Press, 2007), 23.

[86] Melanie D. Reed, 'Western Democracy and Islamic Tradition: The Application of Shari'a in a Modern World', *American University International Law Review*, 19 (2004), 485.

The Universal Islamic Declaration of Human Rights (1981) states that duties have priority over rights. Preamble (f) states that: "by the terms of our primeval covenant with God our duties and obligations have priority over our rights."[87] The Organization of the Islamic Council promulgated a purported Islamic counter-model of human rights, the Cairo Declaration on Human Rights in Islam (1993). This instrument identifies duties in relation to life, differentiated gender roles, and education.

Anne Elizabeth Mayer criticized the Cairo Declaration's emphasis on equal dignity as opposed to equal rights and its differentiation of obligations assumed by men and women as "a coded way of reaffirming the subordinate role that has been assigned to women in the patriarchal social order that prevails in most Muslim countries."[88] I disagree with the notion that human dignity implies passive adherence to cultural control of behavior. In fact, its merit as a fundamental aspect of the universal human condition is recognized in Article 1 of the European Charter of Fundamental Rights,[89] the preamble of the UN Charter,[90] and the Universal Declaration of Human Rights.[91] Both the ICCPR and the IESCR's preambles recognize that human rights are "derived from the inherent dignity of the human person."[92] Finally, the UN Declaration on the Elimination of Violence Against Women's preamble sets forth "the urgent need for the universal application to women of the rights and principles with regard to . . . dignity of all human beings." Oscar Schachter opines that the notion of human dignity includes: respect for the intrinsic worth of every person pursuant to the Kantian objective that every person is an end in herself (not an object), prohibition of coercion

[87] Similarly, within the Pacific, individuals are obligated to traditional authorities such as chiefs, elders, and village councils, providing labor as a type of "civic" obligation. Guy Powles, 'Duties of Individuals: Some Implications for the Pacific of Including "Duties" in "Human Rights" Documents', *Victoria University Wellington Law Review*, 22 (1992), 49, citing Western Samoa and Tuvalu.

[88] Ann Elizabeth Mayer, 'Universal versus Islamic Human Rights: A Clash of Cultures or a Clash with a Construct?', *Michigan Journal of International Law*, 15 (1993–4), 307, 331. She notes that the duties pertaining to women are only referred to generally, not specified, as opposed to those pertaining to men. Non-specification need not be a risk, it may potentially be a benefit.

[89] Article 1: Human dignity is inviolable. It must be respected and protected.

[90] "To reaffirm faith in fundamental human rights, in the dignity and worth of the human person."

[91] The Declaration characterizes recognition of human dignity as one of the components of freedom, justice and peace in the world. Article 1 states that "All human beings are born free and equal in dignity and rights."

[92] See also the Helsinki Accords, Principle VII.

and humiliation, recognition of autonomy and responsibility, and access to distributive justice.[93] He agrees that at times it would be possible to uphold human dignity by identifying concrete violations of human rights, but there would also be situations in which dignity may be "more appropriately and effectively attained through social processes such as education, material benefits, political leadership and the like . . . Informal channels for dealing with alleged affronts to dignity might be more suitable and effective than litigation in many cases."[94]

This perspective illuminates an alternative road for protection, one that focuses more on the role of civil society and its cultivation of empathy and social justice, as well as reliance on conciliatory dispute resolution mechanisms. These are mechanisms oriented towards recognition of a common good and the interconnections of individuals and communities with each other.

The emphasis of the international human rights community on rights, often to the exclusion of duties, may well be one of the factors behind widespread rejection/marginalization of human rights within Africa, the Middle East, and Asia. Several regimes and social actors view NGOs with accompanying individual-focused human rights policies as sources of instability and antagonism, actually challenging the larger communitarian or collective interest.[95] At essence is the concern that overemphasis of individualism over communal identity delegitimizes the normative regime as overriding the local context in which it is to be applied. Protection strategies should be evaluated from the perspective of to what extent do the objectives match the interest of the community in ensuring its collective aspirations – and whether the program ignores, violates, or supports the underlying network of reciprocal duties and benefits within

[93] Oscar Schachter, 'Human Dignity as a Normative Concept', *American Journal of International Law*, 77(4) (Oct. 1983), 848–54.

[94] *Ibid.*, at 854.

[95] Moghaddam *et al.*, 'Toward a Cultural Theory of Duties', at 277: "A sense of duty involves the recognition of responsibilities for others, opening up the possibility of freedom for those others. However, since a duty is an obligation to fulfill the needs, commands, and expectations of someone else, it can be seen as a form of oppression, in that those who are dutiful surrender some measure of their freedom to those to whom the duty is owed. It may even be that an excessive sense of duty can indeed lead to officious interference in the lives of others. Rights are structured on the opposite valency. Thus, a pervasive assumption, sometimes made explicit, is that liberation can only come about through a dismantling of traditional duties, which are often tied into hierarchical social structures. However, too strong an anti-duties stance undercuts one of the necessary conditions for the possibility of rights."

the social structure. Discussion of rights-based protection of vulnerable individuals and groups within a community should not occur in a vacuum, but rather elaborated with full recognition and respect for the bonds sustaining the community.

As noted by Sylvia Tamale, "For many African women the sustainable solutions to their oppression, exploitation and subordination hardly lie in vague, alien legal rights, but in a careful and creative deployment of the more familiar cultural norms and values."[96] Should human rights institutions and NGOs take into account duties in conjunction with rights, they may well find increased spaces for dialogue with societal and state actors, thereby setting a foundation for increased legitimacy. Enjoyment of human rights is not to be conditioned on fulfillment of duties, but duties may alternatively support or limit the exercise of rights in pursuit of the common good and adhering to standards of proportionality.[97] The key will be to pursue pluralistic, contextual approaches that maintain allegiance to the core value of human dignity. Fulfillment of duties should not result in violation of personhood or coercion. Hence, the participation of vulnerable individuals or groups in the articulation, interpretation, and implementation of duties is essential. There is also a need for accountability of both state and non-state actors for violations of human rights, whether it be in public or private settings, or within the "hard" and "soft" variants of communitarianism which will continue to evolve concurrently. The next section will examine the impact of the emergence of new norms establishing indirect human rights obligations for transnational corporations.

[96] Sylvia Tamale, 'The Right to Culture and the Culture of Rights: A Critical Perspective on Women's Sexual Rights in Africa', *Feminist Legal Studies*, 16 (2008), 47–69, at 64. But see Fareda Banda, *Women, Law and Human Rights: An African Perspective* (Oxford: Hart, 2005), 262, who underscores the importance of ensuring participation of women in the formulation of cultural and national policies and law, but also in the enjoyment of socio-economic rights and the benefits of development. Indeed, the Protocol to the African Charter on Human and Peoples' Rights on the Rights of Women in Africa, Article 17 (1) sets forth: "Women shall have the right to live in a positive cultural context and to participate at all levels in the determination of cultural policies." In contrast, Bennoune cites the case of Sudanese women human rights activists referring to international human rights (as opposed to religious or cultural argumentation) to protest flogging of women on account of wearing trousers ('Remembering the Other's Others', at 663–4). A caveat is offered by Hellum *et al.*, *Human Rights, Plural Legalities*, who counter that the needs of women and girls are overridden or compromised in processes in which rights, culture, and religious values are negotiated (at xix).

[97] Sloth-Nielsen and Mezmur, 'Dutiful Child'.

3 Corporate responsibility for human rights

Corporations have long been criticized for enjoying the protection of rights, akin to those of human beings, such as due process and freedom of speech.[98] The failure of the human rights system to address corporate responsibility for human rights violations is a primary weakness within the system. At present, there are increased efforts to hold states responsible for failing to control violations of human rights by non-state actors. Further, non-state actors are being regulated directly and prosecuted (e.g. pursuant to the Alien Torts Claims Act in the United States), and codes of conduct have arisen to influence corporate responsibility.[99] It is suggested that the current epoch will be marked by increased collective demands against states, as well as corporations, to effectuate rights, enjoy autonomy and freedom, or request reparation for harm. Furthermore, these initiatives may be linked to third-generation rights, such as self-determination and autonomy, development, and healthy environment; as well as articulation of related intergenerational duties.[100] Whether or not state institutions will be amenable to collective actions in pursuit of social justice, it is interesting that societal actors appear to be mobilizing in response to state inaction or stagnation in the face of global inequality and challenges (such as the stalled initiatives to address climate change in Copenhagen and Mexico). The emergence of institutionalized societal pluralism is revealing some progressive discourses accompanied by the implementation of new programs. For example, we may consider joint initiatives from NGOs, the UN, and individual actors, such as

[98] The personification of corporations within US jurisprudence dates back to 1886, when the US Supreme Court declared that a corporation was a "person" for purposes of the Fourteenth Amendment (*Santa Clara County* v. *Southern Pacific Railroad Co.* 118 US 394 (1886)). The Court also guaranteed the right of corporations to make donations to political parties under the guise of freedom of speech (*Citizens United* v. *Federal Election Commission*, 558 US 08–205 (2010)).

[99] See Andrew Clapham, *Human Rights Obligations of Non-State Actors* (Oxford: Oxford University Press, 2006). A notable example of innovative institutions is the Norwegian Petroleum Fund's Council of Ethics which advocates disinvestment in the event of human rights violations by corporations (at: www.regjeringen.no/en/sub/Styrer-rad-utvalg/ethics_council.html?id=434879). See also Beate Sjåfjell in this volume (Chapter 12).

[100] See the 2011 judgment by an Ecuadoran court against Chevron for environmental damage which ordered reparation to the community, including provision of health care and cultural reconstruction, available online at: http://opiniojuris.org/2011/02/14/ecuador-court-fines-chevron-86-billion. Chevron sought injunctions from a NY court and a BIT arbitral tribunal against enforcement of the judgment, revealing the complexity of collective actions in pursuit of reparation in a fragmented judicial order.

philanthropists such as Ted Turner in the area of environmental protection and biodiversity, or Bill Gates and the UN Millennium Development Goals, as well as the World Economic Forum 2011 in relation to poverty and climate change.[101] Human rights discourses will be deemed legitimate when they reflect the values and beliefs of peoples and the social complexity and nuances of human experience.[102] Instead of only discussing the relation of individuals and groups to the state, it is imperative to discuss the relations between individuals and groups with each other, their communities, and humanity at large, moving beyond sovereignty. These discourses are more likely to pursue reconciliation of interests under a rubric of common obligations, rather than only articulation of rights. This will entail departing from the traditional international human rights institutional framework, instead exploring the elaboration of pluralistic networks which recognize the primacy of community based initiatives to define, implement, and enforce obligations. As an example of possible reforms, one may consider the creation of principles on human rights and transnational corporations.

3.1 New soft law on human rights and transnational corporations

There is recent normative evolution in the form of new soft law which indicates the international community's recognition of a need to address non-state actor responsibility in the arena of human rights. In 2011, the UN Special Representative of the Secretary-General on the issue of Human Rights and Transnational Corporations and other Business Enterprises, John Ruggie, created guiding principles based on a "protect, respect, and remedy" framework.[103] The principles set forth the state's

[101] The World Economic Forum reports from 2011 are available online at: www.weforum.org/events/world-economic-forum-annual-meeting-2011. Consider Elizabeth Ashford, 'The Duties Imposed by the Human Right to Basic Necessities', in Thomas Pogge (ed.), *Freedom from Poverty as a Human Right* (Oxford: Oxford University Press, 2007), 183, 218: "In particular, until just institutions have been brought about that specify and enforce both (positive and negative) kinds of duty, the onus is often on individual agents in affluent countries to take the initiative in accepting responsibility for fulfilling these duties and in deciding how to do so."

[102] Bonny Ibhawoh, *Imperialism and Human Rights: Colonial Discourses of Rights and Liberties in African History* (New York: State University of New York Press, 2007), 18.

[103] UN Human Rights Council, Report of the Special Representative of the Secretary-General on the issue of human rights and transnational corporations and other business enterprises, John Ruggie, Guiding Principles on Business and Human Rights:

primary duty in protecting "against human rights abuse within their territory and/or jurisdiction by third parties, including business enterprises. This requires taking appropriate steps to prevent, investigate, punish, and redress such abuse through effective policies, legislation, regulations and adjudication."[104] States are expected to have oversight over companies they contract with. The commentary sets forth that states that contract with companies for services should clarify human rights expectations and ensure independent monitoring and accountability mechanisms.[105] A significant problem is that many companies are present in territories classified as failed states or failing states. Reliance on the state as the primary source of protection is impossible, as it may be tribes, communities, warlords, and/or the corporations themselves that in practice influence respect for human rights. The principles are unclear with respect to home state accountability for corporate violations of human rights abroad, identifying a "role" for home states to assist corporations and host states to prevent human rights abuses in conflict-affected areas.[106] The vagueness of accountability in the situation of a failed/failing state highlights the existence of a protection gap.[107]

As pertaining corporate responsibility, the principles set forth a due diligence obligation to avoid violating human rights: "Business enterprises should respect human rights. This means that they should avoid infringing on the human rights of others and should address adverse human rights impacts with which they are involved."[108] Knox states this type of corporate responsibility may be characterized as indirect and grounded on societal expectations instead of human rights law, thereby rendering it soft in effect.[109] The principles call upon businesses to issue a public policy commitment to respect human rights, conduct human

Implementing the UN "Protect, Respect, Remedy" Framework, UN Doc. A/HRC/17/31 (March 21, 2011), available online at: www.business-humanrights.org/media/documents/ruggie/ruggie-guiding-principles-21-mar-2011.pdf

104 Principle 1. 105 Commentary to Principle 5. 106 Commentary to Principle 7.

107 This issue has prompted some scholars to argue in favor of amending the International Criminal Court's jurisdiction to address corporations. See Kathyrn Haigh, 'Extending the International Criminal Court's Jurisdiction to Corporations: Overcoming Complementarity Concerns', *Australian Journal of Human Rights*, 14(1) (2008), 199.

108 Principle 11. The principles define human rights as at minimum those contained within the International Bill of Human Rights and the ILO Declaration on Fundamental Principles and Rights at Work. The principles also call upon corporations to adhere to international humanitarian law in situations of armed conflict.

109 John H. Knox, 'The Ruggie rules: applying human rights law to corporations', paper (August 16, 2011), on file with the author.

rights impact assessments, and track the effectiveness of their response.[110] Companies are encouraged to consult stakeholders, taking into account language barriers, and other issues. Tracking is to be based on qualitative and quantitative indicators, and utilizing internal and external reporting sources. The commentary to the principles calls for companies to communicate how they impact human rights, and indicate the importance of state encouragement of accurate and accessible communication via policy or legislation.[111]

Companies are called upon to demonstrate transparency and accountability in reporting and communication.[112] The principles also recognize a duty on the part of transnational corporations to provide or cooperate for remedy in the event of human rights violations that they have caused or contributed to.[113] Causation responsibility is narrower than communitarian responsibility;[114] hence the true test will be whether corporations will move beyond the normative language to address remediation in spite of absence of proof of causation in the interest of improving community relations.

In addition to ordinary access to justice, the principles additionally recognize the value of non-judicial grievance mechanisms.[115] Transnational corporations have experience with alternative dispute resolution mechanisms that may be more adaptable to a complex, contradictory, decentralized global governance system.[116] In practice, what this will mean is that allegations of human rights violations may be assessed and reparation offered in forums that are neither national courts, nor international committees or tribunals. They may well be settled at the local level at a mediation meeting organized by the company itself, the village chief, or other relevant actor. In some respects, this may prove more effective than traditional channels which were previously described

110 Principles 16–20.

111 Commentary to Principle 3. Nevertheless, the commentary also notes that: "Any stipulation of what would constitute adequate communications should take into account risks that it may pose to safety and security of individuals and facilities; legitimate requirements of commercial confidentiality: and variations in companies' size and structures. Financial reporting requirements should clarify that human rights impacts in some instances may be 'material' or 'significant' to the economic performance of the business enterprise."

112 Principle 21.

113 Principle 22.

114 See David Miller, 'Distributing Responsibilities', in Thomas Pogge and Keith Horton (eds.), *Global Ethics: Seminal Essays* (St. Paul, MN: Paragon, 2008), 481.

115 Principles 25–31.

116 See Dan Danielsen, 'Corporate Power and Global Order,' in Anne Orford (ed.), *International Law and its Others* (New York: Cambridge University Press, 2006), 85.

as suffering from corruption, delays, or faulty implementation of decisions. The principles call for non-judicial grievance mechanisms to meet the criteria of legitimacy, accessibility, predictability, equity, transparency, compatibility with human rights, value as a source of learning, and foundation on engagement and dialogue.[117]

This soft law is a welcome initiative that signals that the international community is slowly moving towards recognition of diverse sources of responsibility and accountability. Protection of human rights is contingent on direct action by both state and non-state actors.[118] Whether this soft law will prove effective will depend on the extent to which it is able to generate a culture change within the transnational business and legal communities, as well as conform to local expectations relating to social justice. Nevertheless, an essential point is the fact that the current principles do not have a provision regarding international monitoring, as was present in a previous draft instrument that sought to impose human rights obligations directly on companies.[119]

The current principles rely on state monitoring in accordance with its own policy and legislation, as well as self-monitoring by the companies. It remains to be seen to what extent this will suffice to meet basic standards of transparency, participation, and accountability that the UN system itself has struggled to comply with.

4 Conclusion

Human rights are undergoing new interpretations and applications, and the starting point for future dialogue between international and local actors (both state and non-state) may well be linked to concepts relating

[117] Principle 31.

[118] See Major Christopher E. Martin, 'Sovereignty, Meet Globalization: Using Public–Private Partnerships to Promote the Rule of Law in a Complex World', *Military Law Review*, 202 (winter 2009), 91. See also Eric Engle, 'Corporate Social Responsibility (CSR): Market-Based Remedies for International Human Rights Violations?', *Willammette Law Review*, 40 (winter 2004), 103; see also Steven R. Ratner, 'Corporations and Human Rights: A Theory of Legal Responsibility', *Yale Law Journal*, 111 (2001–2), 443.

[119] UN Sub-Commission on the Promotion and Protection of Human Rights, Human Rights Principles and Responsibility for Transnational Corporations and other Business Enterprises, UN Doc. E/CN.4/Sub.2/2002/WG.2/WP.1 (February 2002), available online at: www1.umn.edu/humanrts/principlesW-OutCommentary5final.html. "Transnational corporations and other businesses enterprises shall be subject to periodic monitoring by national, international, governmental, and/or nongovernmental mechanisms regarding their application of the Principles. This monitoring shall be transparent, independent, and take into account input from relevant stakeholders."

to duties owed each other, forming a new *telos* that may prove more viable for this epoch. Although MacIntyre suggests that a practical approach to advancing greater social justice within the world is to commence with network initiatives at the local community level, I advocate parallel recognition of the evolution of transnational solidarity actions and policies that reflect and respond to the neo-medieval order.[120] Human rights protection strategies in the current epoch should confirm the principle of human dignity as the central value in the elaboration of frameworks that take as a point of departure the recognition of duties towards oneself, family, community, society, state, and humanity. The creation and implementation of policy should include the effective participation of vulnerable individuals and groups, as well as accountability mechanisms for human rights violations. Responses to particular issues will place variable emphasis on different duties contingent on the context – hence rather than articulate universal binding standards, this perspective opens for flexible articulation and implementation of relational ethical agency.[121] Notwithstanding the fact that conflicts will always arise between the obligations persons owe to different groups and communities (as well as to oneself), we may be comforted by the view that overall there appears to be a greater potential for harmonization of interests than discord, and that is the aspiration of humanity.

120 Alasdair MacIntyre, *Whose Justice? Which Rationality?* (Notre Dame, IN: University of Notre Dame, 1988), 99.

121 See Whatmore, 'Dissecting the Autonomous Self'.

7

Productive tensions: women's rights NGOs, the "mainstream" human rights movement, and international lawmaking

KARIMA BENNOUNE

Introduction

Non-governmental organizations (NGOs) are among the most discussed non-state actors involved in the creation, interpretation, and application of international law. Yet, scholars of international law have often overlooked the critical issue of diversity among NGOs, and the differing stances they may take on key international law issues and controversies. This oversight exemplifies the ways in which international law scholarship sometimes takes overly unitary approaches to its categories of analysis. Feminist international law questions the accuracy of such approaches.[1] When one unpacks the "NGO" category, one often discovers multiple NGO constituencies reflecting conflicting concerns and perspectives. Hence, feminist international law theories should reflect a view of NGOs as international lawmakers that is equally complexified.

This chapter will focus on one example of such NGO diversity, namely the inter-NGO dynamic sometimes found between women's human rights NGOs and what is often termed the "mainstream" human rights movement. These relationships have long been complicated. At times these constituencies are allies with the same international law priorities. At other times they are opponents or at least involved in what might be described as a tense dialogue. Sometimes the "mainstream" human rights groups become themselves the targets of the lobbying of women's human rights groups. Indeed, women's human rights NGOs and other

The author would like to thank Jennifer Berman for research assistance.

[1] The need for complexity in analyzing international law is a subtext of Hilary Charlesworth, Christine Chinkin and Shelley Wright, 'Feminist Approaches to International Law', *American Journal of International Law*, 85 (1991), 613.

human rights NGOs may have very different views of particular international law questions. Over time, however, the women's rights groups have often – though not always – prevailed on human rights groups to evolve their view of international law in a more gender-sensitive direction.

This dialectical relationship between women's groups and other human rights groups has played out in numerous arenas, including in the 1990s debate over the definition of torture, and, most recently in regard to the need to (also) respond to atrocities by fundamentalist non-state actors in the context of critiquing the "war on terror." In each instance, women's groups and other human rights NGOs have sometimes had uneasy, multifaceted and shifting relationships that have shaped critical international lawmaking processes and debates. Groups within both of those broad categories of NGOs have also taken diametrically opposed positions at times. All of these sets of complexities, these putatively productive tensions, have both enriched and rendered more difficult the role of NGOs as lawmakers, and must be reflected in any meaningful theorizing of the issue.

What then should these layered inter-NGO dynamics tell us about our conception of "NGO" as a category of analysis, and about the role of NGOs in the creation and practice of international law? What can analyzing these dynamics tell us about how progress can most successfully be made toward a feminist reshaping of international law? This chapter will consider each of these questions in light of several case studies.

I come at this subject from a range of vantage points, having been an Amnesty International legal adviser, having also worked closely with a range of women's NGOs, and currently as an academic. Hence, I will try to look at these questions at the intersection of both academic and these various practitioner perspectives. To that end, this chapter begins with a brief overview of NGOs and their roles on the international law stage, as described in the literature. An examination of the categories used here follows, interrogating the meaning of the terms, "women's human rights NGO" and "mainstream human rights NGO." Subsequently, the chapter reviews the case studies drawn from practice, first with regard to NGO interaction concerning the definition of torture, and then bearing on responses to the "war on terror." It then concludes with a brief application of the lessons learned from these case studies about the meaning of NGO participation in international lawmaking.

1 NGO-ology: the many faces of NGOs

International lawyers often like to define entities by what they are not – non-state actors, non-governmental entities, non-governmental organizations. In light of the centrality of the state to international law, it is perhaps unsurprising that this practice is most common when the thing that they are not is the state. While the fact of *not* being the formal state or government undoubtedly does have certain kinds of legal meaning and consequences (sometimes this has been to women's detriment in international law),[2] defining crucial categories in this fashion can produce vague results. We may think we are saying more than we are actually saying by employing such terms.

The term NGO is, in fact, variously defined in the literature.[3] Even the UN Charter, which gives the Economic and Social Council explicit power to "make suitable arrangements for consultation with non-governmental organizations which are concerned with matters within its competence,"[4] does not define these same organizations. The precise meaning of the term "human rights NGO" is even more rarely clarified. Henry Steiner writes that at a 1991 gathering of human rights NGO activists, the majority of participants concluded that "self-perception and self-definition by NGOs constitute the only sensible method of identifying human rights organizations."[5] This was due to a fear that any definition would be too limiting over time. "NGO" is then a very general category, with many different groups that are "not the government" jockeying for position within it. Even just the alphabet soup of acronyms used to

[2] See Frances Olsen, 'Feminist Critiques of the Public/Private Distinction', in Dorinda Dallmeyer (ed.), *Reconceiving Reality: Women and International Law* (Washington, DC: American Society of International Law, 1993), 157.

[3] See Kerstin Martens, 'Mission Impossible? Defining Nongovernmental Organizations', *International Journal of Voluntary and Nonprofit Organizations*, 13 (2002), 271, 272. Martens quotes Archer who writes that the term NGO remains, "an awkwardly negative title coined by the United Nations to describe a vast range of international and national citizens organizations" (*ibid.*, at 274).

[4] UN Charter, Art. 71.

[5] Henry Steiner, *Diverse Partners: Non-Governmental Organizations in the Human Rights Movement* (Cambridge, MA: Harvard Law School Human Rights Program, 1991), 5. Aryeh Neier took a contrary approach to this, suggesting that there should be objective criteria that distinguish "partisan efforts from genuine efforts to promote human rights" ('Not All Human Rights Groups are Equal', letter to editor, *New York Times*, May 27, 1989, 22). He focuses on impartiality, criticism of a full range of states and all sides in a conflict, and acknowledgement of counter-evidence.

denote different types of NGOs makes this clear, GONGOs,[6] DONGOs,[7] INGOs,[8] and BINGOs,[9] being but a few of them.

Yet, international lawyers often write about NGOs' international law-making roles as if NGOs constituted a more-or-less monolithic category that does one thing (or a few things) with the archetype seemingly my former employer Amnesty International (AI). The international human rights law literature does not often enough reflect that not only do NGOs work on different things in very different ways, they may even have very different views about the same things, and they are as likely to compete and clash as to collaborate. Many practitioners know this all too well from sometimes bitter experience. However, academic writing – and international law textbooks – often seems to find this a much too complicated reality to reflect upon. Of course, this is par for the course in an international law that "speak[s] of sovereignty as a uniform quality with respect to Andorra and the United States," what Martti Koskenniemi has termed "not an impressive piece of sociological analysis."[10] In other words, we have made some of the same formal generalizations when employing "state" as our category of analysis, as we have made with regard to some of those entities defined simply as not being the state.

In the last twenty years or so, NGOs have been variously heralded as *the* solution for all manner of international law difficulties,[11] and lambasted as undemocratic manifestations of global inequality, political puppets, and dangerously unaccountable at that.[12] Of course, like most academic assertions, each of these things has been true in particular instances, and each completely false at many other times.

As Catharine MacKinnon recently said at a conference about her work at the University of Tulsa College of Law, perhaps what is needed is the

[6] Governmentally organized non-governmental organizations.

[7] Donor-organized NGOs. [8] International NGOs.

[9] Business and industry NGOs.

[10] Martti Koskenniemi, 'The Wonderful Artificiality of States', *Proceedings of the American Society of International Law*, 88 (1994), 28.

[11] See e.g. Mary Kaldor, *Global Civil Society: An Answer to War* (Cambridge: Polity, 2003); Richard Falk, 'The Global Promise of Social Movements: Explorations at the Edge of Time', *Alternatives*, 12 (1987), 173.

[12] See, e.g., 'The Non-Governmental Order', *The Economist*, December 18, 1999, 23; Kenneth Anderson, 'The Ottawa Convention Banning Landmines, The Role of International Non-Governmental Organizations and the Idea of International Civil Society', *European Journal of International Law*, 11 (2000), 92.

ability to think more than one thing at the same time.[13] I am increasingly convinced that that seemingly simple remark is actually a critical feminist insight into the ways we need to retheorize international law. A unitary paradigm rarely provides a thorough or coherent explanation by itself – and that is certainly true of the way that international women's human rights law is made and how NGOs have helped (and hindered) its making. However, challenging the grand paradigmatic approach to international law theory poses conceptual difficulties in the legal academy, perhaps in the United States in particular, where having *a* paradigm, *a* solution, a straightforward and comprehensive analysis dominates in the literature, and is often the *sine qua non* for publication in elite journals. This often means that we academics are left trying to fit the world to our unitary paradigm, rather than shaping our paradigm in messy ways that might better reflect the multifaceted world.

2 NGOs as international legal actors

Taken as a group, NGOs have a variety of roles as makers of international law. Of course, given that I am talking about NGO diversity, I should note that many entities one might label an NGO, including some in the human rights and women's human rights spheres respectively, do not engage with international law or international legal process at all. In any case, when considering NGOs collectively as international legal persons, Steve Charnovitz's catalogue of their international law functions in the *American Journal of International Law* (*AJIL*) is helpful.[14] NGOs contribute to the making of hard and soft law, through participation in the drafting of treaties and non-treaty standards. For example, their participation in the major UN Conferences of the 1990s was vital in producing the documents that resulted, even if those documents did not meet these same groups' full expectations.[15]

[13] See Catharine MacKinnnon, 'Foreword', in 'Scholarship Symposium Honoring Catharine MacKinnon', *Tulsa Law Review*, 46 (2010), 1, 6.

[14] Steve Charnovitz, 'Nongovernmental Organizations and International Law', *American Journal of International Law*, 100 (2006), 348, 352–5. See also the discussion of these functions in Karsten Nowrot, 'Legal Consequences of Globalization: The Status of Non-Governmental Organizations Under International Law', *Indiana Journal of Global Legal Studies*, 6 (1998–9), 579, 590–601.

[15] See generally, Ann Marie Clark, Elisabeth J. Friedman, and Kathryn Hochstetler, 'The Sovereign Limits of Global Civil Society: A Comparison of NGO Participation in UN World Conferences on the Environment, Human Rights, and Women', *World Politics*, 51 (1998), 1.

NGOs help to launch entirely new sub-fields of international law, such as women's human rights law itself. They contribute to the interpretation of international law in a range of ways. They shape international adjudication either by bringing cases where that is possible, or by serving as *amici* where such status is available (a topic authoritatively described by Dinah Shelton),[16] or through other forms of less formal participation, such as by submitting written information or making statements. In addition, NGOs assess the compliance of states with international law, and where it proves insufficient, promote such compliance. What I would add to this litany of international lawmaking tasks of NGOs would be the crucial symbolic functions of agenda-setting and the setting of priorities in international law debates.

In the human rights arena, the international law role of NGOs is arguably enhanced given the limited enforcement capacity of the legal system, and the under-resourcing of the UN human rights machinery, as well as the very nature of the human rights project.[17] NGOs contribute to intergovernmental reports, to the adoption of general comments and to the elaboration of the jurisprudence of treaty bodies through shadow reporting and other submissions. Some human rights mechanisms allow NGOs themselves to submit complaints.[18] Thus, while human rights NGOs may not have always the kind of power they would like to have, i.e. to actually change government policy and effectively hold perpetrators accountable, they may represent very powerful actors in the domain of international law nonetheless. This is a good thing in many respects, but it also carries with it heavy responsibilities, and means that NGO mistakes or inter-NGO conflicts may have very serious international law and policy consequences. It is this power of NGOs, which should be neither overstated nor understated, that has led to calls for NGO accountability from both the enemies of the NGO enterprise, as well as from friendlier voices.[19]

In his interesting work on NGO activity in the context of the World Trade Organization (WTO), Daniel Esty has looked beyond the formal

[16] Dinah Shelton, 'The Participation of Nongovernmental Organizations in Judicial Proceedings', *American Journal of International Law*, 88 (1994), 611.

[17] See, e.g., Theo van Boven, 'The Role of Non-Governmental Organizations in International Human Rights Standard-Setting: A Prerequisite of Democracy', *California Western International Law Journal*, 20 (1989–90), 207.

[18] Nowrot, 'Legal Consequences of Globalization', 628.

[19] See, e.g., Peter Spiro, 'Accounting for NGOs', *Chicago Journal of International Law*, 3 (2002), 161.

functions of NGOs as international law-makers, to the symbolic meaning of their actions in this sphere.[20] He sees NGOs as "analytic 'competition'"[21] for governments in intergovernmental organization settings as they "play a co-operative role in assisting international decision processes."[22] Thus, they broaden the pool of information and analysis on which decisions in such bodies are made.

While Esty is clearly focused on NGO participation as a means of improving the functioning and representativity of the WTO, he also recognizes the enhanced role of NGOs in such a context as one which can legitimize the intergovernmental organization (IGO) in question itself.[23] (And he uses that to sell NGO participation to its critics.) For example, he argues that:

> [r]egular contact with groups around the world also might help governments to mobilize public opinion in favour of freer trade when it comes time to hold congressional or parliamentary votes on free trade agreements or other trade and investment liberalization efforts.[24]

For NGOs that engage with the WTO precisely because they are highly critical of the institution or of the impact of "free trade" on human rights, such a reading of their increased involvement in the international legal process might be highly worrying. Yet, his insight is easily transposable to the UN human rights system where NGOs fill in many of the gaps in the relatively insufficient resourcing of the Office of the UN High Commissioner for Human Rights, and add a dynamic and participatory component to otherwise stultifying fora such as the Human Rights Council. These roles can enhance the work of NGOs and the IGOs in question and lead to greater human rights law enforcement and development; they can also offer an alibi to dysfunctional aspects of a still largely intergovernmental international human rights legal system.

The scholarly assessments of the meaning of NGO involvement in international legal process are themselves varied. A group of scholars sees this participation as representing a radical change in the way international law is created. For example, Karsten Nowrot went so far as to say that NGO activities constitute part of "a variety of new lawmaking processes by non-State actors, undermining the former monopoly of

[20] Daniel Esty, 'Non-Governmental Organizations at the World Trade Organization: Cooperation, Competition or Exclusion', *Journal of International Economic Law*, 1 (1998), 123.

[21] *Ibid.* [22] *Ibid.*, at 129. [23] *Ibid.*, at 128. [24] *Ibid.*, at 134.

States."[25] On the other hand, writing in the Simma commentary on the UN Charter, Lagoni and Chaitidou conclude that NGOs play a "limited" role within the UN system and that there is no "general international law of NGOs."[26]

While most human rights scholars see NGO engagement in international lawmaking as an inherently and only positive phenomenon which is critical to the success and validity of international legal process itself,[27] the critics of NGOs worry that this same participation will lead to non-democratic special interests having undue influence in the making of international law.[28] There should also be room for some other readings of NGO roles between these poles, perhaps beginning where Esty does by reading the symbolic meaning of these roles, but adding a critical spin. As I will argue below, in light of NGO diversity, the role of NGOs in making international law merits a more nuanced reading.

3 Defining the women's human rights movement and the "mainstream" human rights movement

This chapter looks at only one manifestation of NGO diversity, and there are admittedly many others. My frame of analysis is the relationship between women's human rights NGOs and what I refer to (for lack of a better term) as the "mainstream" human rights movement, in particular the high-profile INGOs that sometimes dominate that movement. Though these terms are used regularly in the field, it is perhaps worth pausing to ponder the meaning and implications of this language.

The precursors to the contemporary international women's human rights movement have a long and proud history stretching back at least to the Hague Peace Conferences, though the movement was only formally conceptualized as such around a human rights framework at the global level in the 1980s and especially the 1990s. By women's human rights NGOs, I am referring to NGOs working to advance women's

25 Nowrot, 'Legal Consequences of Globalization', 642.

26 Bruno Simma (ed.), *The Charter of the United Nations: A Commentary* (2nd edn., Oxford: Oxford University Press, 2002), 1081–2.

27 See, e.g., van Boven, 'Role of Non-Governmental Organizations'; Dianne Otto, 'Non-governmental Organizations in the United Nations System: The Emerging Role of International Civil Society', *Human Rights Quarterly*, 18 (1996), 107.

28 See, e.g., Kenneth Anderson and David Rieff, '"Global Civil Society": A Skeptical View', in Helmut Anheier, Marlies Blasies, Mary Kaldor (eds.), *Global Civil Society* (London: Sage, 2005).

rights within a human rights framework. Of course, this terminology is challenging since some feminists are highly critical either of notions of rights in general, or of human rights in particular.[29] Hence, I use the term "within" because some of these groups do not consciously purvey "human rights," though many others do.

Archetypal examples of women's human rights groups include the Center for Women's Global Leadership (CWGL), the Network of Women Living Under Muslim Laws (WLUML), Equality Now, the Women's Human Rights Defenders International Coalition, the Association for Women's Rights in Development (AWID) and Women in Black, at the international level. Regional analogues are found in the Asia Pacific Forum on Women, Law and Development, Women in Law and Development in Africa (WiLDAF) and Latin America's CLADEM (Comité de América Latina y El Caribe para la Defensa de los Derechos de la mujer). National counterparts such as Bangladesh's Ain o Salish Kendra, Senegal's Grefels, and the Fiji Women's Rights Movement round out the picture. These groups, and many others, work transnationally or at least with a clear global perspective, sometimes work closely together in coalition and work on a wide range of issues that affect women's lives.

But, if this may indeed be termed a movement in the sociological rather than purely symbolic sense, it is loosely structured and extremely diverse. Some groups one might put in the women's human rights defender[30] category work only within a single national, regional or local context, work without significant international connection or involvement and may work on only one or a handful of issues. Some reject considering themselves as NGOs at all, but prefer to be seen as forums, collectives or social movements through which activists collaborate.

What then is the "mainstream"[31] human rights movement? Here I am referring to human rights groups that focus more generally across the

[29] See, e.g., Lisa Schwartzman, 'Liberal Theory and Social Inequality: A Feminist Critique', *Hypatia*, 14 (1999), 26. These critiques are beyond the scope of this chapter.

[30] The website of the Women's Human Rights Defenders International Coalition explains that "those advocating for women's human rights – no matter what gender or sexual orientation they claim – are in fact human rights defenders." See www.defendingwomen-defending-rights.org/about.php. The Coalition's twenty-one institutional members include women's human rights organizations such as the Urgent Action Fund for Women's Human Rights and Women's Initiatives for Gender Justice, but also "mainstream" human rights groups such as AI. Clearly, the organizational categories here are porous.

[31] As the UN's Economic and Social Council defined it, "Mainstreaming a gender perspective is the process of assessing the implications for women and men of any planned

diverse areas covered by the Universal Declaration of Human Rights and its progeny, on the broader spectrum of human rights of both men and women. Historically, they were often more concerned with the former than the latter, and this de facto orientation sometimes prevails. Like the women's human rights groups, these NGOs too are diverse. They include prominent INGOs such as Amnesty International, Human Rights Watch, the International Federation for Human Rights (FIDH), the International Commission of Jurists, as well as less resourced organizations that have also had to battle for attention to their issues within the so-called "mainstream" like the Center for Economic and Social Rights, as well as regional and national groups. In this paper, I will mostly be focusing on INGOs in the mainstream human rights field.

I am cognizant of the fact that using this dichotomous schema, with women's human rights groups on one side and "other" human rights groups on another, lends itself to a number of fallacies. These include the unfortunate notion that women's rights and human rights are non-overlapping ideas, that the women's rights movement is not part of the human rights movement and vice versa, and that women are not "mainstream" and other human rights groups are. Given the diversity among the organizations in both of these categories, another possibility would be to see all these NGOs as situated along an axis of centre–periphery, with an intersecting axis that reflects the degree to which they focus on women's rights or not within their work. Nevertheless, for purposes of clarity, given the focus of this chapter, I will employ the notion of clusters of NGOs – women's human rights groups and "mainstream" groups – while recognizing the considerable heterogeneity of each one.

Despite my use of distinct categories here, it is also clear that the women's human rights movement has made profound contributions to human rights in general – both because women are (or should be)[32] half

action ... It is a strategy for making women's as well as men's concerns and experiences an integral dimension of the design, implementation, monitoring and evaluation of policies and programmes ... so that women and men benefit equally and inequality is not perpetuated." Report of the Economic and Social Council for the Year 1997, UN GAOR, 52nd Sess., Supp. No. 3, at 24, UN Doc. A/52/3/Rev. 1 (1997). For a thoughtful critique of mainstreaming, see Hilary Charlesworth, 'Not Waving but Drowning, Gender Mainstreaming and Human Rights in the United Nations', *Harvard Human Rights Journal*, 18 (2005), 1.

[32] See, e.g., A. Sen, 'More Than 100 Million Women Are Missing', *New York Review of Books*, December 20, 1990, 61.

the human race, but also because their experiences both of rights and of violations have a profound impact on men as well. Moreover, I would be remiss if I did not point out the significant contributions which the so-called mainstream human rights movement has sometimes made to the creation of women's human rights law and the advancement of the women's human rights legal agenda.[33] However, these positive affirmations are certainly not the end of the story. The awkward reality is that at times groups within these two clusters of NGOs have found themselves at loggerheads, fighting against one another for the soul of human rights, rather than simply standing side by side against perpetrators of abuse. Some social scientists have alluded to this as the problem of "'unaligned' NGO frames."[34] Yet, far too little attention has been paid in international human rights scholarship to this framing disconnect[35] which at times has had significant consequences for human rights protection, or lack thereof. The case studies that follow demonstrate these fractious debates.

4 Case studies of "productive tensions"

It is perhaps most useful to think about these dynamic NGO relationships, and their international law meanings and impacts, through the prism of concrete case examples. I propose to survey two such examples, namely (a) the interpretation of the definition of torture and (b) recent debates regarding the stance of human rights NGOs toward fundamentalist non-state actors in the context of their work on the "war on

[33] Note, for example, the success of AI-Australia during the Stop Violence Against Women campaign in pushing for a national plan of action on violence against women as a way of implementing the Beijing Declaration and Platform for Action and the UN Declaration on Violence against Women. See www.amnesty.org.au/svaw/comments/14454/ and National Plan to Reduce Violence against Women and Their Children, available at: www.fahcsia.gov.au/sa/women/progserv/violence/nationalplan/Pages/default_new.aspx

[34] Clark *et al.*, 'Sovereign Limits', 23.

[35] Even Clark and her co-authors, in their sophisticated discussion of NGO participation in world conferences, glide over important layers of dissonance when they explain straightforwardly that "[o]ngoing relationships between key players within large human rights groups and women's rights activists in different countries had solidified in the late 1980s. This fostered the 'mainstreaming' of women's human rights within human rights discourse and action, leading to the emergence of the movement for women's human rights" (*ibid.*, at 24). This is part of the story, but the road was significantly bumpier at times.

terror."[36] Each of these topics represents a complex subject well beyond the scope of this short paper. Hence, for these purposes, I will offer only a brief overview, highlighting issues of relevance to a rethinking of the role of NGOs in shaping international law. I will spend more time on the second example as it was most recently the subject of sharp controversy among diverse NGO constituencies.

4.1 *"Going after husbands": the reconceptualization of torture*

In 1995, the then-UN Special Rapporteur on violence against women, Radhika Coomaraswamy, argued in her report to the then-Commission on Human Rights that under certain circumstances, domestic violence should be considered to be a form of torture or ill-treatment under international law.[37] She was led in this direction by the work of prominent feminist international lawyers, including Catharine MacKinnon[38] and Rhonda Copelon.[39] Further inspiration clearly came from the campaigning of some women's human rights groups such as the Center for Women's Global Leadership that worked with the Global Campaign for Women's Human Rights to organize the ground-breaking tribunal on violence against women at the Vienna World Conference on Human Rights.[40]

In concluding her discussion of conceptualizing violence in the family as torture, the Special Rapporteur explicitly invoked the role of NGOs (without distinguishing among them), politely suggesting that:

> [t]he argument that domestic violence should be understood and treated as a form of torture and, when less severe, ill-treatment, is one that deserves consideration by the rapporteurs and treaty bodies that investigate these violations together perhaps with appropriate NGO experts and jurists.[41]

36 One could study a range of other areas of dissonance, such as around the drafting of the Rome Statute of the International Criminal Court, or the pace at which some mainstream human rights groups have embraced economic, social and cultural rights.

37 *Report of the Special Rapporteur on Violence against Women, Its Causes and Consequences*, UN Doc. E/CN.4/1996/53, Feb. 6, 1996, paras. 42–50.

38 Catharine MacKinnon, 'On Torture: A Feminist Perspective on Human Rights', in Kathleen Mahoney and Paul Mahoney (eds.), *Human Rights in the Twenty-First Century: A Global Challenge* (Leiden and Boston, MA: Martinus Nijhoff, 1992), 21.

39 Rhonda Copelon, 'Recognizing the Egregious in the Everyday: Domestic Violence as Torture', *Columbia Human Rights Law Review*, 25 (1993–4), 291.

40 See the discussion of the history and impact of this Tribunal in Elisabeth Friedman, 'Women's Human Rights: The Emergence of a Movement', in Julie Peters and Andrea Wolper (eds.), *Women's Rights, Human Rights: International Feminist Perspectives* (New York: Routledge, 1995), 30.

41 *Report of the Special Rapporteur* (1996), para. 50.

Initially, this call from the Special Rapporteur provoked consternation on the part of some mainstream human rights NGOs as it was so outside their contemporaneous paradigm of how human rights are harmed. I remember a senior colleague of mine at Amnesty International during the planning of Amnesty's third major international campaign against torture in 1996 asking in horror, "Are we going to have to go after husbands now?" "Going after husbands" (at least *qua* husbands) has not traditionally been something that mainstream human rights NGOs did. To quote MacKinnon's contribution in this volume, the discomfort seemed to be in part related to "how utterly familiar the acts are," how "normal in everyday life."[42] In fact, the discomfort was so great with considering such normalized violence as torture that I was initially prohibited from even circulating a memo containing the excerpt from the Special Rapporteur's report quoted above to the staff working group organizing the campaign against torture.

The women's human rights movement worked hard to change these approaches to international law within mainstream human rights groups. Women's NGOs worked to show human rights NGOs that "husbands" could also be perpetrators worthy of their scrutiny.[43] Some of these education and lobbying efforts were highly successful so that we now see major initiatives such as AI's recent, important Stop Violence Against Women (SVAW) campaign which *inter alia* recognized domestic violence and other forms of violence against women by non-state actors as torture or other forms of human rights *violation* (the dreaded "v" word that some still claim applies only to action by the state).[44]

[42] Chapter 2, in this volume, p. 17.

[43] One example would be the critical participation of feminist experts and women's human rights NGOs in Amnesty International's internal expert meeting on the torture of women in 1997.

[44] See, e.g., Amnesty International, Amnesty International Response to Andrés Ballesteros, Jorge A. Restrepo, Michael Spagat, Juan F. Vargas, *The Work of Amnesty International and Human Rights Watch: Evidence from Colombia*, CERAC, Colombia, February 2007, AI Index: AMR 23/2007, February 21, 2007. This document states that "AI's position . . . is that non-state actors 'abuse' human rights . . . while state actors 'violate' human rights (because only states are party to human rights treaties) . . . Although such language may appear legalistic . . . it does correspond to legal definitions in international human rights law." What is interesting is that at the same time, AI's SVAW campaign was challenging these very boundaries, as was its program on corporations and human rights.

Historically, Human Rights Watch was out in front on these issues thanks to its innovative Women's Rights Division which was founded in 1990. The division could perhaps be seen as a hybrid women's human rights organization within a mainstream human rights group. It was and is institutionally embedded in a mainstream human rights organization but with substantive commitments to women's human rights and additional loyalties and ties to the women's human rights movement, further challenging the framing of these constituencies as being necessarily separate. The Women's Rights Division was willing and able to tackle issues such as rape, trafficking and domestic violence as human rights abuses back in the early 1990s, meaning that Human Rights Watch institutionally championed these issues before other mainstream human rights groups were doing so. However, according to Women's Rights Division founding director Dorothy Thomas, this too was often the product of feminist pressure from within and without the organization, producing a kind of triangular dynamic that created space for this work. She notes that the use of human rights methodology by women's rights groups was critical to this development, as was pressure on Human Rights Watch from feminists in the United States.[45] Nevertheless, even the advanced approach of the Women's Rights Division, often did not alter the way in which the organization's other work was done outside the focal point of the division, at least not in the 1990s.[46]

In any case, what is most interesting to me for this study in looking back at the dynamics of this controversy in the 1990s, is that international law was arguably out in front of how most mainstream human rights NGOs were interpreting it on this question. Mainstream human rights NGOs were not leading the progressive development of international law in this regard, a role which is often ascribed to them in the human rights law literature on NGOs.[47] The UN Convention against

[45] Cited in Friedman, 'Women's Human Rights', 26.

[46] For example, Middle East Watch issued an ironically titled report, 'Human Rights Abuses in Algeria: No One Is Spared', in January 1994 which did not even mention the treatment of women in the conflict there, notwithstanding the fundamentalist assault on women, including unveiled women and women human rights defenders, and the use of sexual slavery by armed groups, all of which was at the heart of the conflict. Human Rights Watch, *Human Rights Abuses in Algeria: No One Is Spared* (New York: January 1994). Meanwhile, these practices were being vigorously documented and opposed on the ground by the local women's human rights movement. See M. Shahin, 'Algerian women fight terror', *Jordan Times*, November 13, 1994, 1.

[47] See above text at nn. 15–27.

Torture and Other Cruel, Inhuman or Degrading Treatment or Punishment already defined torture not only as action by the agents of the state, but also with its consent or acquiescence.[48] The first report of the first UN Special Rapporteur on torture Peter Kooijmans already listed things such as female genital mutilation (FGM) as among the kinds of violations he might be able to consider under the rubric of torture.[49] As he noted back in the now seemingly prehistoric year of 1986:

> [t]he authorities' passive attitude regarding customs broadly accepted in a number of countries (i.e. sexual mutilations and a number of other tribal traditional practices) might be considered as "consent or acquiescence," particularly when these acts are not prosecuted as criminal offences under domestic law, probably because the state itself is abandoning its function of protecting its citizens from *any kind of torture.*[50]

Notwithstanding the somewhat archaic language about "tribal practices" and the accompanying assumption that this paradigm only applies in such "faraway" tribal contexts, Rapporteur Kooijmans was already making clear, in 1986, that torture could include "private" acts of violence against women. Of course, neither successive Special Rapporteurs on torture nor the UN Committee against Torture took this important insight to heart or applied it in their practice much at all until nearly another decade had passed.

[48] UN Convention against Torture and Other Cruel, Inhuman or Degrading Treatment or Punishment, New York, art. 1(1), 10 December 1984, in force June 26, 1987, S. Treaty Doc. No. 100-20 (1988), 1465 UNTS. 85. Moreover, in 1988 the Inter-American Court of Human Rights had held that states are responsible under international law when they fail to act with due diligence to prevent and punish abuses by non-state actors. *Velásquez Rodriguez* v. *Honduras* [1988] Inter-American Court of Human Rights, Ser. C, 4(9) (1988)*Human Rights Law Journal*, 212.

[49] In his 1986 report, the Special Rapporteur on torture further noted that "attention must be paid to so-called 'traditional practices', such as sexual mutilation in certain tribal societies that might constitute 'severe pain or suffering' according to international law. States shall provide appropriate protection under law against such treatments even when the perpetrators are 'private' persons rather than public officials. In this connection, the Human Rights Committee indicated ... that 'it is also the duty of public authorities to ensure protection by the law against such treatment even when committed by persons acting outside or without any official authority.' It should be recalled that the Convention ... [against Torture's] definition of torture includes pain or suffering when it is 'inflicted by ... or with the consent or acquiescence of a public official ...' (art. 1 para. 1)" (Report by the Special Rapporteur, Mr. P. Kooijmans, appointed pursuant to Commission on Human Rights resolution 1985/33, UN Doc. E/CN.4/1986/15, February 19, 1986, para. 49).

[50] *Ibid.*, at para. 38 (emphasis added).

Nevertheless, on this issue, key players in the mainstream human rights movement itself such as Amnesty International were not ahead of international law or making international law develop progressively, but instead looking backward at a stale and formalistic notion of the boundaries of torture shaped by their own practice and by the vision of those who led these groups, and who held key legal and policy positions within them, well into the 1990s. What changed is that the women's human rights movement pushed these NGOs forward, and women activists – often with links to those women's NGOs – but formally situated within the mainstream human rights movement, did so as well. The international discourse developed by women's NGOs grew from Cairo to Vienna to Beijing, until it became embarrassing to be openly retrograde.[51] The pressure from within and without began to make significant changes in the late 1990s.

Since then, much progress has been made on rendering the human rights notion of torture increasingly gender inclusive, thanks to international tribunals, feminist international lawyers, women's NGOs and indeed human rights NGOs themselves beginning to catch up.[52] The challenge remains the "mainstreaming" of that perspective. Feminists can write their reports about rape and domestic violence as human rights violations, and even as forms of torture and ill-treatment, within mainstream human rights NGOs now. The question which remains is whether or not these issues will be included in other initiatives on torture and ill-treatment carried out within human rights NGOs at moments when women's human rights advocates are not in the driver's seat, outside what Hilary Charlesworth has termed the "women's ghettoes"[53] within those groups. This continuing limitation comes into stark relief in the subsequent case study.

4.2 *Human rights, Muslim fundamentalism and the "war on terror"*

Another area where tension between some women's NGOs and some other human rights groups has been palpable of late has been in relation to the contours of human rights work on the "war on terror" (WOT).

[51] See discussion in Friedman, 'Women's Human Rights'.

[52] Note for example the detailed treatment of the torture of women, including by non-state actors in Committee Against Torture, General Comment No. 2, Implementation of article 2 by states parties, UN Doc. CAT/C/GC/2, 24 January 2008, at paras. 18 and 22–24. This is a vast improvement on the past practice of the Committee against Torture.

[53] Charlesworth, 'Not Waving But Drowning', 1.

In this context, the major international human rights groups have focused their attention on gross abuses committed by governments fighting against Muslim fundamentalist[54] non-state actors such as the various permutations of Al Qaeda or the Taliban.[55] Meanwhile, some women's human rights groups and women human rights defenders, and sometimes other local human rights groups in Muslim, Asian, Arab, and African contexts, while sharing the concern about the detrimental nature of some practices associated with the WOT have pleaded with their NGO compatriots to remember that so-called "war" often has two sides, both of which gravely threaten human rights, and both of which are deserving of human rights scrutiny, criticism and opposition.[56]

This dispute first flared in relation to events in Algeria in the 1990s when the Algerian state backed by the military fought the forces of armed fundamentalism. The mainstream international human rights movement focused on the very real harms committed by the state, but had much less (sometimes nothing whatsoever) to say about much more widespread violence by Muslim fundamentalist non-state armed groups whose misogynist ideology and practices were gendercidal.[57] The Algerian

[54] On the definition of fundamentalism, see Karima Bennoune, 'Remembering the Other's Others: Theorizing the Approach of International Law to Muslim Fundamentalism', *Columbia Human Rights Law Review*, 41 (2010), 335–98. Marieme Hélie-Lucas, an Algerian sociologist who founded the Network of Women Living Under Muslim Laws, has defined fundamentalisms as "political movements of the extreme right, which, in a context of globalization … manipulate religion … in order to achieve their political aims" ('What Is Your Tribe?: Women's Struggles and the Construction of Muslimness', *Women Living Under Muslim Laws Dossier*, 49 (2001), 23–4, available at: www.wluml.org/english/pubs/pdf/dossier23-24/D23-24.pdf).

[55] See, e.g., International Commission of Jurists, *Assessing Damage, Urging Action: Report of the Eminent Jurists Panel on Terrorism, Counter-Terrorism and Human Rights* (The Hague: ICJ, 2009), which despite its title focuses largely on state violence, an important concern surely, but not the only one in this field.

[56] See, e.g., Association for Women's Rights in Development, *Religious Fundamentalisms on the Rise: A Case for Action* (Toronto: AWID, 2008); Cherifa Kheddar, Dir., Djazairouna Assoc. of Families of Victims of Islamist Terrorism, 'Oui, c'est cette terreur que nous avons vécue seuls et isolés', address before the International Conference Against Terrorism (September 11, 2007), at 5 (on file with author). This plea has also come from feminist scholars. See, e.g., Seyla Benhabib, 'Unholy Wars', in Betsy Reed (ed.), *Nothing Sacred: Women Respond to Religious Fundamentalism and Terror* (New York: Nation Books, 2002), 397.

[57] See, e.g., Human Rights Watch, 'No One Is Spared'. Contrast this with Leila Hessini, *From Uncivil War to Civil Peace: Algerian Women's Voices* (New York: Population Council, 1998), 28. Hessini, and many other Algerian feminists, have been very critical of what they see as the failures of mainstream human rights organizations to document armed group abuses against women during the conflict (*ibid.*, at 26–7).

women's movement, literally under siege from the fundamentalist armed groups, was sharply critical of the major international human rights organizations – not because those groups were critiquing the state (many of these feminists were also critics of successive Algerian governments) – but because they seemed to be oblivious to the meaning of the fundamentalist agenda itself for women's human rights in the local context, and to take non-state fundamentalist crimes less seriously than those by the state.[58]

Another failing of the mainstream human rights groups in the view of some Algerian and other women's groups was that the mainstream groups were very quick to attribute specific atrocities to the state (their usual paradigm) but were very reluctant to attribute them to the fundamentalist non-state actors, even when those actors may have claimed responsibility at the local level.[59] While there is no question that attributing abuses to non-state actors in conflict situations raises difficult research challenges, this practice also reflects the same theoretical problem found in the torture dispute – the mainstream human rights sense that harms by the state are always worse, or always in a separate and legally privileged category.

In the most recent public manifestation of this split on the significance of abuses by non-state fundamentalists, Amnesty International recently forced out the head of its gender unit, the Indian feminist Gita Sahgal, after her public criticism of the organization's overly close relationship with a British former Guantánamo detainee Moazzam Begg[60] and his organization Cage Prisoners.[61] While Begg had clearly

[58] Louisa Ait Hamou, 'Women's Struggle Against Muslim Fundamentalism in Algeria: Strategies or a Lesson for Survival?', in Ayesha Imam *et al.* (eds.), *Warning Signs of Fundamentalisms* (London: WLUML, 2001), 117.

[59] See, e.g., Amnesty International, Algeria: *When the State Fails*, AI Index MDE 28/47/97, 23 December 1997, and Human Rights Watch, 'No One Is Spared'. For a discussion of the legal consequences of such stances, see Karima Bennoune, 'The Paradoxical Feminist Quest for Remedy: A Case Study *of Jane Doe* v. *Islamic Salvation Front and Anwar Haddam*', *International Criminal Law Review*, 11 (2011), 579–87.

[60] See R. Kerbaj, 'Amnesty International is "damaged" by Taliban link', *Sunday Times*, February 7, 2010, available at: www.timesonline.co.uk/tol/news/world/afghanistan/article7017810.ece; M. Driscoll, 'The conscience stifled by Amnesty', *The Times*, February 14, 2010, available at: www.timesonline.co.uk/tol/news/uk/article7026143.ece. Amnesty International's official responses to these concerns are available at: http://livewire.amnesty.org/2010/02/15/letter-to-the-sunday-times/#more-1771; http://livewire.amnesty.org/2010/02/14/amnesty-international-response-to-the-sunday-times/ and www.amnestyusa.org/document.php?id=ENGNAU2010021115380

[61] Cage Prisoners, the organization with which he works, defends the rights of only detainees in the context of the "war on terror," including many salafi jihadists convicted

suffered abuse, including protracted arbitrary detention, at the hands of US authorities from which he unquestionably deserved defense while detained, he himself had a nasty track record of expressing support for the Taliban, of running an extremist bookshop in the UK[62] and of numerous visits to jihadi training camps.[63] Begg described himself as "leftwing on equality and conservative on family values" in the program for AIUSA's annual general meeting (AGM) in 2008 where he gave a keynote address via video link. (One wonders whether someone who described himself as left-wing on equality but conservative on race relations would have been invited to keynote the AGM.)

When Begg says he is "conservative on family values," in Muslim majority contexts that can mean anything from justification of women's subordination in general terms to support for gender apartheid or honor crimes, though he is careful not to be specific.[64] Hence, ratifying his human rights credentials also impacts women human rights defenders in Muslim populations in Britain and beyond. This does not imply that Begg deserved to have his human rights violated. The question is: what

in fair trials. The organization has also offered a platform for the most extreme views such as those of the late Anwar al Awlaki. See Fahad Ansari, 'Beyond Guantanamo – Review of Cage Prisoners Fundraiser Dinner', February 10, 2009, www.cageprisoners.com/articles.php?id=30493. Awlaki was suspected of links to the Christmas day 2009 attempted airliner bombing, and has openly justified this attack, and indeed the killing of all civilian unbelievers (which includes "bad" Muslims). See 'Interview: Anwar al-Awlaki,' AlJazeera.net, February 7, 2010, available at: http://english.aljazeera.net/focus/2010/02/2010271074776870.html. The Quilliam Foundation has made the charge that Cage Prisoners has "[a]cted as a conduit between convicted extremists such as Abu Hamza [a well-known Al Qaeda and Armed Islamic Group supporter currently imprisoned in the UK] and their supporters and sympathizers outside prison" (James Brandon, 'Unlocking Al-Qaeda: Islamist Extremism in British Prisons', available at: www.quilliamfoundation.org/images/stories/pdfs/unlocking_al_qaeda.pdf, at 30.

62 On the significance of this network of bookshops, see Chetan Bhatt, 'The "British Jihad" and the Curves of Religious Violence', *Ethnic and Racial Studies*, 33 (2010), 39, 49–50.

63 The *Guardian* reported in November 2001 that a "photocopy of a money transfer in sterling asking a London branch of the Pakistani firm Union Bank to credit an account in Karachi held by a man named Moazzam Begg," was among the documents discovered when "a secret toxins and explosives laboratory operated by Arab fighters at an al-Qa'ida military training camp near the eastern Afghan city of Jalalabad" was raided during the US invasion of Afghanistan. See Rory McCarthy, 'Inside Bin Ladin's chemical bunker', *The Guardian* (UK), November 17, 2001, www.guardian.co.uk/world/2001/nov/17/afghanistan.terrorism9. Such reports should at least be investigated and considered by human rights actors that continue to support and partner with Begg now that he is no longer a detainee.

64 See George Valentine Corr, 'Interview: Moazzam Begg on Guantanamo', Cage Prisoners, January 8, 2009, www.cageprisoners.com/articles.php?id=27368

does it mean for the human rights movement to give someone such as Begg the kind of prominent platform he has received because he has been a victim of a state, without looking at what he stands for and how that might affect the rights of others?

When Gita Sahgal went public with her concerns, large sectors of the organized international women's human rights movement, especially Asian, Muslim and black feminist groups such as Southall Black Sisters and Women Against Fundamentalism, championed her. Several of South Asia's leading women's human rights defenders, including Sunila Abeysekera, of the INFORM documentation center in Sri Lanka, and Sara Hossain, an advocate at the Supreme Court of Bangladesh, wrote an open letter to Amnesty International which became a global petition signed by several thousand people around the world.[65] The 2,213 signatories include prominent women's rights defenders such as Yakin Erturk, former UN Special Rapporteur on violence against women from Turkey, the leading Pakistani human rights lawyer Hina Jilani, pioneering Egyptian feminist writer Nawal El Saadawi, as well as prominent women's NGOs such as the Network of Women Living Under Muslim Laws, and the Center for Women's Global Leadership.

Meanwhile, Sahgal was pilloried by some in the mainstream human rights movement and their allies, and accused of justifying human rights abuses against people such as Begg – something she has never done.[66] Again, the suggestion is that it is impossible to think more than one thing at a time – i.e. that international law holds both that governments should not commit abuses in the WOT *and* that non-state terrorist groups such as Al Qaeda and their fundamentalist sympathizers gravely harm human rights and should be actively opposed in accordance with international law.

[65] *Global Petition to Amnesty International: Restoring the Integrity of Human Rights*, February 13, 2010, available at: www.human-rights-for-all.org/spip.php?article15 (last visited Sept. 2, 2011).

[66] See, e.g., Victoria Brittan: 'Dangerous Game: A Reply to Gita Sahgal and Her Supporters', Open Democracy, June 30, 2010, available at: www.opendemocracy.net/victoria-brittain/dangerous-game-reply-to-gita-sahgal-and-her-supporters. The most surprising part of this piece is when Brittain lectures the signatories of the global petition (some of whom live in places such as Algeria, Bangladesh, and Pakistan or are originally from Iran) that they should be working on real abuses such as those committed by the UK government in the "war on terror," rather than worrying about relatively trivial matters such as fundamentalism or women's rights. This is similar to a recurring human rights refrain that abuses by states are worse than those committed by non-state actors (though fundamentalism is sometimes the ruling ideology, as in Iran).

International law actually grounds both principles, and provides many tools for doing both things.[67] For example, the International Covenant on Civil and Political Rights (ICCPR) in its second article calls on states to both "respect and ensure" the rights in the Covenant.[68] This means states have to take affirmative action to protect the rights of those within their jurisdiction from impingement by others (ensure rights).[69] But, in so doing, the state cannot violate rights itself (respect rights). In the face of terrorism, the double burden of respecting and ensuring rights requires states to take active steps to safeguard their populations from violent attack by non-state armed groups as, *inter alia*, a matter of human rights law. However, in so doing, the state cannot itself trounce the rights guaranteed in the ICCPR. International lawyers often seem to think they must choose one task or the other, or at least prioritize one significantly over the other. Gita Sahgal was actually saying we should take the respecting part and the ensuring part equally seriously, a recurring theme of the women's human rights movement.

While this particular human rights dispute concerned personnel and policy, it also reflected an approach to the WOT that has serious international legal ramifications. These same mainstream human rights groups have shaped the international human rights law agenda in international organizations using all of their roles as lawmakers described above in ways that have reflected the same exclusionary tendencies. For example, human rights NGOs have proudly celebrated their success in ensuring that only state violence and not the violence of non-state actors could be examined by the UN Special Rapporteur on promoting and protecting human rights while countering terrorism.[70]

[67] In addition to the international law protecting human rights, there is also a far-reaching body of international law on terrorism which seeks to facilitate its prevention, and the punishment of those involved. See, e.g., Andrea Bianchi (ed.), *Enforcing International Law Norms Against Terrorism* (Oxford: Hart, 2004).

[68] International Covenant on Civil and Political Rights, art. 2(1), New York, December 16, 1966, in force March 23, 1976, 999 UNTS. 171, 6 ILM 368 (hereafter ICCPR).

[69] Manfred Nowak, *UN Covenant on Civil and Political Rights: CCPR Commentary* (Arlington, VA: N.P. Engel, 1993), 38.

[70] The mandate of the UN Special Rapporteur on the promotion and protection of human rights while countering terrorism focuses only on the human rights violations committed by states, rather than also looking at the impact of terrorism itself on human rights. UN Commission on Human Rights Resolution 2005/80, Protection of Human Rights and Fundamental Freedoms while Countering Terrorism, para. 14, July 2, 2005. Mainstream human rights NGOs were heavily involved in the lobbying process that led to this result. While there is no question that some governments that wanted non-state activities included in the mandate were pushing this for their own reasons, the outcome is a loss

They have submitted shadow reports and information to human rights treaty bodies and special procedures that have been heavily relied upon in the counter-terrorism area, shaping that jurisprudence in ways that have diminished its reflection of the fundamentalist assault on women's rights.[71] They have brought cases in a one-sided way that undermines the work of many women's human rights NGOs, and efforts by other NGOs to challenge the violence of non-state actors.[72]

Work against counter-terror abuses is utterly vital. However, this work has paradoxically been divorced from work against terrorism itself, state atrocity disconnected from non-state atrocity. Feminist international law again serves as a vital reminder that all of these things

for a holistic vision of human rights that considers the complex web of state and non-state atrocities. The discipline of women's human rights tries to make these linkages clear. Hence, the brief of the Special Rapporteur on violence against women, who can look at violence by the state, in the community and in the family, stands in sharp contrast to this mandate.

Recently, the limit on the counterterrorism rapporteur's mandate inhibited an important report to the General Assembly on gender and counter-terrorism. See Report of the Special Rapporteur on the promotion and protection of human rights and fundamental freedoms while countering terrorism, UN Doc. A/64/211, Aug. 3, 2009, 7–23. The Special Rapporteur rightly "observes with grave concern the extent to which terrorist groups commit significant gender-based abuses, which may in their effects be similar to human rights violations committed by the State . . ." but concedes that "consistent with the mandate . . . the focus of this report is on the gendered impact of States' counter-terrorism measures" (*ibid.*, at para. 22).

71 On this problem generally, see Gianluca Rubagotti, 'Non-Governmental Organisations and the Reporting Obligation under the International Covenant on Civil and Political Rights', *Non-State Actors and International Law*, 5 (2005) 59, 73–74.

72 For example, the US-based Center for Constitutional Rights (CCR) chose to represent pro bono the interests of the late Anwar al-Awlaki, the reported number two in Al Qaeda in the Arabian Peninsula, who was targeted for assassination by the US government in a civil suit against US officials. However, Awlaki was himself openly advocating assassination of writers, artists and others, and was not in detention at the time. Meanwhile, the CCR described him simply as a "Muslim cleric". This author, at the time a member of the CCR Board of Trustees, publicly dissented from this move. See Mark Tran, 'Legal challenge to assassination policy divides rights groups', *The Guardian*, November 15, 2010, available at: www.guardian.co.uk/world/2010/nov/15/us-assassination-policy-rights-awlaki. A group of Algerian NGOs representing victims of fundamentalist terrorism, and a number of prominent individual victims and survivors of terrorism, sent a sharply critical letter to CCR criticizing this decision. 'Letter to the Center for Constitutional Rights' (English translation), 14 November 2010, *available at* www.siawi.org/article2308.html. WLUML also condemned the organization's move. WLUML, 'Letter to CCR regarding decision to represent Anwar al-Awlaki's interests', November 25, 2010, available at: www.wluml.org/node/6813

are on the same spectrum of horror that constrains women's lives. They must be tackled holistically by international lawyers. This is not to say that these things are exactly alike or entail precisely the same kind of international legal responsibility or obligation. But feminists have understood for a long time that the state is not the only kind of legal or other person that can harm human rights, and that the law should not be just about what the state does. These abuses of these "husbands" matter also. And it must be a supreme paradox that some entities defined as not being the state (human rights NGOs) but that are claiming a significant role on the international law stage nonetheless must still sometimes struggle so hard against the notion that the actions of an entity not-the-state (an armed group or non-governmental entity that engages in or advocates violence against civilians or systematic discrimination against women) can actually matter in international law terms.

While in the area of torture, as described above, women's human rights groups have prevailed upon "mainstream" human rights groups to evolve their view of international law in a more feminist direction, that has not happened yet in relation to the WOT. I have recently written in detail about the reasons for the failures of international human rights lawyers in this particular area[73] and will not rehearse them here. Undoubtedly, the tools of a feminist international law that take entities that are not the state seriously, whether they are NGOs, NGEs (non-governmental entities), or mere "husbands," that analyzes these entities and their conduct with complexity, will be critical to improving international law interpretation and practice in this area in future.[74] Such a possibility of "mutual agenda formation"[75] will require continued intensive inter-NGO dialogue, a dialogue in which NGO diversity can be a strength if basic human rights principles are respected and universality is applied rigorously. This process is, however, likely to be frustratingly slow.

[73] See Bennoune, 'Remembering the Other's Others'.

[74] There has been significant progress in international law in this regard in the last twenty years, and mainstream human rights NGOs have undertaken some work on non-state actor abuses. However, this case study suggests that we have not yet cured the problem diagnosed in 1991, namely that "greater significance is attached to the public, male world than to the private, female one" (Charlesworth *et al.*, 'Feminist Approaches to International Law', 621). For an overview of the evolution in international law in this area, see Clapham, *Human Rights Obligations.*

[75] Clark *et al.*, 'Sovereign Limits', 23.

5 Conclusion: rethinking the role of NGOs in international legal process, re-conceptualizing the process of women's human rights lawmaking

I now return to consider the theoretical questions with which I began in light of these case studies. There have been some nods to the general problem of NGO diversity in the literature, but little significant consideration of its theoretical meaning. In his *AJIL* article, Steve Charnovitz acknowledges that:

> Measuring NGO success has become more complicated because for many important issues, competing NGOs have been positioned on all sides of any debate. Years ago, the most involved NGOs were reliable advocates of a stronger world public order. Today, overwhelming NGO support for the international rule of law can no longer be assumed. NGOs follow their own stars.[76]

The challenge to conceptualizing the role of NGOs may be even more difficult, for even many NGOs that share a commitment to a notion of "world public order" and the international rule of law may still have vastly different understandings of what that order should look like and what the rule of law can mean, as the examples above make clear. This is perhaps a further example of the fragmentation described by Fionnuala Ní Aoláin in this volume with which international lawyers must come to terms (see Chapter 4).

There is no question that mainstream human rights groups have made great contributions toward the development of women's human rights law, and this is also true of Amnesty International in particular. To give but a few examples, Amnesty actively lobbied for the drafting of the Optional Protocol to CEDAW in the Commission on the Status of Women (though arriving a bit late to the process) and today AIUSA continues to push for US ratification of CEDAW itself. The organization went on to carry out an important global campaign to Stop Violence Against Women from 2004–10 which worked to raise the profile of violence against women as a "mainstream" human rights issue.[77]

[76] Charnovitz, 'Nongovernmental Organizations', 348.

[77] For the assessment of the campaign by reviewers commissioned by AI, see *A Synthesis of the learning from the Stop Violence Against Women Campaign*, available at: www.amnesty.org/en/library/asset/ACT77/008/2010/en/6e25f263-fa84-4cd9-8a76-a9ea15bb1e8c/act770082010en.html

However, we need to contemplate how to confront situations when differences in the stances of NGOs instead cause problems for women's human rights advocacy, and arguably shape international law process and discourse in ways that are harmful to women's human rights or are at odds with the views of women's human rights defenders (who may of course themselves have diverse positions). Too little attention has been paid to this concern in international law theorizing about the role of NGOs in the "creation of international law." Social scientists writing in the area have been perhaps more attuned to this phenomenon, what some have labeled "a 'parallel repertoire' of NGO-to-NGO interactions."[78] As Diana Hortsch has written in light of the Gita Sahgal affair, "[w]hether human rights organizations attend to their multiple accountabilities, and whether they champion a nuanced understanding of human rights that acknowledges the potential for conflict within the human rights agenda is a question that goes to the heart of the organization's mission and legitimacy."[79] The question remains as to how these sets of relations, and potential axes of conflict, should shape our thinking about the ways NGOs contribute to making women's human rights law. I will make a few concluding observations about this below.

What becomes clear to me from this review is that interaction among NGOs sometimes has as much impact on the trajectory of international human rights law as the interaction between NGOs and other international legal persons such as states and international organizations. The NGO category is no monolith, even within specific issue areas, and the term "NGO" then should be understood as a generic category, not as a trope for particular substantive positions within international law.[80]

[78] Clark *et al.*, 'Sovereign Limits', 4. See also the discussion of the tense relations between women's human rights NGOs and "pro-family" groups during the drafting of the Rome Statute in Marlies Glasius, 'Who Is the Real Civil Society?: Women's Groups versus Pro-Family Groups at the International Criminal Court Negotiations', in Jude Howell and Diane Mulligan (eds.), *Gender and Civil Society: Transcending Boundaries* (London: Routledge, 2005), 222.

[79] Diana Hortsch, 'The Paradox of Partnership: Amnesty International, Responsible Advocacy and NGO Accountability', *Columbia Human Rights Law Review*, 42 (2010), 119, 155.

[80] As Glasius rightly notes, "global civil society is not the exclusive domain of 'progressive' human rights, environmental, social justice and women's rights activists, it is a space co-inhabited by conservatives, anti-abortionists, and religious fundamentalists" ('Who Is the Real Civil Society?', 3). For example, both pro-choice and anti-abortion NGOs have made submissions to the European Court of Human Rights in cases such as *Open Door and Dublin Well Women* v. *Ireland*. See discussion in Shelton, 'Participation of Nongovernmental Organizations', 637. This view contrasts sharply with assumptions about a coherent progressive NGO agenda made in the human rights literature at times.

As I always remind my students, while the American Civil Liberties Union (ACLU) is an NGO, so too are the National Rifle Association (the US pro-gun lobby) and Operation Rescue (a leading US anti-abortion group). And in any case, parts of the women's movement sometimes disagree with both sets of groups (i.e. the ACLU defends pornographers).

Nevertheless, one often hears the terms "*the* NGOs" or "the NGO community" in particular contexts as if they constitute a lobby or a bloc.[81] This is sometimes true, sometimes not at all, and should not be presumed. Moreover, just like any other international legal person, NGOs may sometimes improve international law, but they may also hinder those improvements or make overtly negative contributions. They may be a part of the solution, or they may be a part of the problem at different moments. What seems to be critical is that we apply complexity to these issues, and not be afraid of recognizing the reality of politics, which is after all what we are talking about here at its root. Women's human rights law has been pushed forward by both mainstream human rights groups and by women's groups. However, at times the women's groups have had to target the other human rights groups first as an obstacle to progress before they could move forward more broadly in reshaping international law and process.

The destabilizing potential of non-governmental organizations to traditional international law by the mere fact of being non-national actors has been an important reality, and has at times opened a new kind of space, movement and potential for the creation of international law. However, the mere invocation of the category of NGO itself should no longer be presumed as an automatic win for human rights, or women's rights. It is what is done through the NGO space in particular instances that matters. This practical distinction that invokes politics and substantive judgment – whether we are comfortable as a discipline with these things or not – is critical to any theorizing of NGOs as makers of international law on women's human rights. Ultimately, one hopes that greater attention to this complex problem of inter-NGO dynamics in our theorizing can create more space for these tensions to be in fact "productive" and to make a positive contribution to the ongoing creation of international law.

See, e.g., Chadwick Alger, 'The Emerging Roles of NGOs in the UN System: From Article 71 to a People's Millennium Assembly', *Global Governance*, 8 (2002), 93.

[81] See, e.g., Otto, 'Nongovernmental Organizations', 139; Alger, 'Emerging Roles of NGOs'.

8

Transnational challenges to international and national law: Norwegian-Pakistani women at the interface

ANNE HELLUM

1 Transnational challenges to international and national law

> Wanting to promote women's rights we are walking a tight rope. Some families do not allow women to contact us. We try to send out a message to the wider community that we accord due respect to our religion and culture. This makes it easier for the women to contact us and for us to promote women's rights in a less hostile environment.

This statement made by the leader of a Norwegian-Pakistani women's organization in Oslo illustrates the complex legal situations that women embedded in transnational relationships have to handle. As citizens, migrant women are entitled to equal protection under national law. However, as members of transnational families and religious communities, women are often expected to follow the moral and religious codes of the group. This chapter explores how migrant women from the Norwegian-Pakistani community in Oslo negotiate the legal pluralities that in practice have a bearing on their access to law. It analyzes the complex relationship between the right to legal information, choice, and autonomy in the context of migrant women's mixed identities as individual citizens and members of transnational families.

I would like to thank Cecilia Bailliet for insightful comments. The research for this article was carried out in cooperation with Professor Shaheen Saradar Ali and Research Fellow Farhat Taj as part of the research project 'From Formal to Real Rights: Immigrant Women's Protection against Discrimination'. It is led by Anne Hellum, funded by the Norwegian Research Council's Immigration Program (IMER) and based at the Institute of Women's Law, Child Law and Discrimination Law at the Department of Public and International Law at the University of Oslo.

Equal access to justice and the right to legal information is a human right that, in principle, applies to all individuals regardless of time and place. In practice, the availability of legal information and subsequently access to justice, is dependent on people's class, gender, race and religion. Addressing mechanisms of legal exclusion, the United Nations Commission on Legal Empowerment of the Poor estimates that at least four billion people are excluded from the rule of law. The Commission understands legal empowerment as 'a process of systemic change through which the poor and excluded become able to use the law, the legal system and legal services to protect and advance their rights and interests as citizens and economic actors'.[1]

The failure of state legal orders to translate basic human rights principles into attainable entitlements for women and men on the ground is today addressed by a large body of socio-legal research examining the interaction between international law, state law and coexisting social and religious norms in different parts of the world.[2] This article takes a bottom-up approach and explores how migrant women embedded in transnational relationships involved in local struggles for justice and dignity are manoeuvering in a legal landscape made up by international law, Norwegian state law, Pakistani state law, religious and customary norms.[3] The overall aim is to demonstrate how a grounded, pluralist and relational women's law approach can contribute to an understanding of what it takes to initiate and sustain a process through which migrant women as individual citizens and members of an ethnic or religious

[1] Commission on Legal Empowerment of the Poor, *Making the Law Work for Everyone*, vol. 1 (New York: United Nations Development Programme, 2008).

[2] A. An-Na'im, 'State Responsibility under International Human Rights Law to Change Religious and Customary Laws', in R. Cook (ed.), *Human Rights of Women: National and International Perspectives* (Philadelphia, PA: University of Pennsylvania Press, 1995); S. S. Ali, *Gender and Human Rights in Islam and International Law* (The Hague, London and Boston, MA: Kluwer Law International, 2000); A. Hellum, *Women's Human Rights and Legal Pluralism in Africa: Mixed Norms and Identities in Infertility Management in Zimbabwe* (Oslo and Harare: TANO/MHOND, 1999); S. E. Merry, *Human Rights and Gender Violence* (University of Chicago Press, 2006); A. Hellum *et al.* (eds.), *Human Rights, Plural Legalities and Gendered Realities: Paths Are Made by Walking* (Harare: Weaver Press, 2007); B. Derman *et al.*, 'Intersections of Law, Human Rights and Water Management in Zimbabwe: Implications for Rural Livelihoods', in B. Van Koppen *et al.* (eds.), *Community-based Water Law and Water Resource Management Reform in Developing Countries* (Oxford: CABI, 2008), 248–70.

[3] For a review of the literature critiquing human rights approaches that favour 'equality' over 'difference,' 'individual' over 'communitarian' or collective rights as well as the trumping of 'rights' over 'duties', see Cecilia Bailliet in this volume (Chapter 6).

group become able to use the law.[4] Towards this end, this chapter explores how international, national and civil society actors involved in legal education engage with the multiplicity of national, religious and customary norms that are at work in the lives of migrant women. Through engagement with the complex identities of women within the Norwegian-Pakistani community in Oslo, it addresses challenges related to making law accessible in the context of plural legalities.

The chapter unfolds in seven sections. The second section sets out a legal pluralist framework to analyze the complex legal situations that legal educators addressing migrant women embedded in transnational relationships have to confront. The third section describes the evolving jurisprudence of international human rights treaty bodies with the overall focus on the right to legal literacy of vulnerable groups, including migrants and minorities. Current trends in international law calling for linguistically and culturally appropriate, gender-sensitive methods are given attention. The fourth section situates the case study in the context of the changing social, cultural and legal Norwegian landscape that is characterized by accumulating international legal obligations, unprecedented cultural diversity and increasing transnationalism. The fifth section addresses Norway's response to the CEDAW Committee's concluding comments on Norway's fifth, sixth and seventh periodical reports, urging the Norwegian state to take steps to increase awareness of the availability of social services and legal remedies for migrant women. Turning to the experiences of a Pakistani women's organization in Oslo and its interaction with Norwegian non-governmental organizations, Norwegian legal institutions and Islamic institutions in Oslo, section 6 demonstrates how smaller non-state entities may provide space for women who have been marginalized both by state law and the religious and customary legal orders. Section 7 discusses the strengths and weaknesses of the woman-focused and pluralist legal literacy and counselling approach that has been developed in response to the concerns and values of migrant women embedded in transnational relationships in the light of the right to substantive equality.

[4] T. S. Dahl, *Feminist Jurisprudence* (Oslo: Norwegian University Press 1986); A. Bentzon *et al.*, *Pursuing Grounded Theory in Law: South–North Experiences in Developing Women's Law* (Oslo: TANO Aschehoug and Harare: Mond Books, 1998); A. Hellum *et al.*, 'Paths Are Made by Walking: Introductory Thoughts', in. Hellum *et al.* (eds.), *Human Rights, Plural Legalities and Gendered Realities: Paths Are Made by Walking* (Harare: Weaver Press, 2007).

2 Challenges for international feminist jurisprudence: gender and legal pluralities

The embodiment of both universality and diversity within international human rights law is considered at present to be the key to the challenges that increased mobility, cultural diversity and complexity have sparked in most parts of the world.[5] The rapidly growing body of international and regional human rights instruments and institutions has become the receptor of claims for welfare, freedom, justice and dignity from women, refugees, migrants and ethnic, religious and sexual minorities in all parts of the world. Yet the human rights arena is only one of the multiple avenues that people who fall outside the scope of international and national law pursue. Globalization, in terms of mobility and flows of people, capital, technology, ideas and norms, has had the effect of creating transnational social, economic and religious communities that to a large extent regulate their own affairs.[6] For people living transnational lives, neither international nor national laws are the sole mechanisms for regulating their affairs. The concept of legal pluralism draws attention to the coexistence of more than one body of law within the same social space, pertaining to the same set of activities.[7]

In North Atlantic countries, such as Norway, national law is challenged both from above and below. From above it is faced with a growing body of international and regional human rights obligations protecting the rights of minorities, immigrants and refugees. From below an unprecedented cultural and normative diversity, embedded in transnational personal, social and religious relations, challenge the assumption of homogeneity that often underpin both national legislation and the coexisting customary and religious norms of different minority groups. North Atlantic states are today facing an accelerating stream of claims invoking cultural and religious rights and, in some

[5] International Council on Human Rights Policy (ICHRP), *When Legal Orders Overlap: Human Rights, State and Non-state Law* (Geneva: Switzerland, 2009).

[6] A. Hellum *et al.*, 'Introduction: Transnational Law in the Making', in Hellum *et al.* (eds.), *From Transnational Relations to Transnational Laws: Northern European Law at the Crossroads* (Surrey: Ashgate, 2010).

[7] J. Griffiths, 'What Is Legal Pluralism?', *Journal of Legal Pluralism*, 24 (1986), 1–55; F. von. Benda-Beckmann, 'Who Is Afraid of Legal Pluralism?', *Journal of Legal Pluralism*, 47 (2002), 37–82; A. Griffiths, 'Legal Pluralism', in R. Banakar and M. Travers (eds.), *An Introduction to Law and Social Theory* (Oxford: Hart, 2002).

instances, a quest to make informal religious and customary norms and institutions a part of the formal legal system.

In order to bridge the gap between state law and the legal pluralities on the ground, international and national law and policy makers have in recent years turned their attention to the informal justice sector. The UN Commission on Legal Empowerment, for example, calls for liberalization of the justice sector and recommends recognition of non-state legal services and informal justice systems.[8] Current trends to recognize religious and customary norms may, on the one hand, enlarge different social, ethnic and religious groups' space for local autonomy. On the other hand, recognition may also reinforce existing inequalities within these groups in terms of gender, status and age.[9] Human rights standards responding to the quest for recognition have developed furthest in respect of indigenous people's and minority rights. Standard setting in this area has, however, occurred largely without reference to standard setting concerning the individual rights of women and children.[10]

These current trends suggest that globalization may affect women's right to equality and choice under international and national law in complex and contradictory ways. As pointed out by Christine Chinkin, Shelly Wright and Hillary Charlesworth, the way in which centralization of power within the sovereign state has been fragmented by globalization is not necessarily supportive of equality between women and men.[11] The relationship between gender, human rights, and legal pluralities thus raises fundamental questions about the construction of female subjectivity, agency and empowerment, all key issues in international feminist jurisprudence.[12]

In order to set out an approach that bridges these gaps this article takes Norwegian-Pakistani migrant women involved in local struggles for equality, dignity and justice as starting point. It explores how migrant women themselves, civil society organizations and state authorities

[8] Commission on Legal Empowerment of the Poor, *Making the Law Work*, vol. 1.

[9] R. Sieder, 'Legal Globalization and Human Rights: Constructing the Rule of Law in Post-conflict Guatemala', in P. Pitarch and S. Speed (eds.), *Human Rights in the Maya Region: Global Politics, Moral Engagements, and Cultural Contentions* (Durham, NC: Duke University Press, 2008).

[10] ICHRP, *When Legal Orders Overlap.*

[11] C. Chinkin *et al.*, 'Feminist Approaches to International Law: Reflections from another Century', in D. Buss and A. Manji (eds.), *International Law: Modern Feminist Approaches* (Oxford: Hart, 2005).

[12] Buss and Manji, 'Introduction', in *International Law.*

involved in legal literacy and legal aid navigate a socio-legal terrain in which international and national law interact with a multiplicity of norms and expectations deriving from relatives and religious networks. In order to describe and understand the complex legal situations migrant women and legal educators have to confront, legal pluralism is used as an analytical framework. The theory of legal pluralism focuses the interaction of more than one body of law within the same social space, pertaining to the same set of activities.[13] It is a descriptive approach that facilitates analysis of how women and men as actors in transnational social space are subject to a multitude of restricting, conflicting and incoherent bodies of international law, state law, religious norms and customary practices that govern their lives. Taking international law down from the plane of abstract principles and situating it in the plural legalities that women embedded in transnational relationships have to negotiate helps us to come to grips with the mixed and porous character of law in the era of globalization that Boaventura de Sousa Santos has termed 'interlegality'.[14]

From a pluralist perspective, legal literacy is not a simple question of making information about the law available and understandable. It is a complex process of translation aimed at making human rights both understood and accepted in the light of the norms and values that already exist within the group. To connect human rights ideals to local social and moral values while simultaneously ensuring that they retain their core content is a delicate balancing act. There is always a risk that human rights principles are transformed to fit local norms and values, promote cultural relativism, and justify practices that are not accepted for women from the majority.[15] In order to distinguish between processes in which human rights are appropriated and adopted to local circumstances from situations in which human rights are made resonant with dominant cultural or religious norms, the legal anthropologist, Sally Engle Merry, uses the terms 'vernacularization' and 'indigenization'.[16] The process of appropriation and local adaptation of globally

[13] Griffiths, 'What Is Legal Pluralism?'; Benda-Beckmann, 'Who Is afraid of Legal Pluralism?'; Griffiths, 'Legal Pluralism'.

[14] B. de Sousa Santos, 'Law: A Map of Misreading. Towards a Postmodern Conception of Law', *Journal of Law and Society*, 14(3) (1987), 279–99.

[15] M. Helie-Lucas, 'What Is Your Tribe? Women's Struggles and the Construction of Muslimness', in *Dossier 26 Identity Politics* (London: Women Living Under Muslim Laws, 2004).

[16] Merry, *Human Rights*, at 216.

generated norms, ideas and strategies is called 'vernacularization'.[17] 'Vernacularization', according to Levitt and Merry, depends on factors such as the content of rights at stake, the social position of the vernacularizor, the channel of transmission, and the local geographies of history and culture.[18] 'Vernacularization', in my view, provides a valuable analytical tool. It adds a normative dimension to John Griffith's descriptive approach to legal pluralism as 'that state of affairs, for any social field, in which behavior pursuant to more than one legal order occurs'.[19]

There is, however, more to these processes than a mere translation among coexisting norms and values. In a situation in which the relationship between women's right to equal status under international and national law and local norms based on gender difference is contested, a key question is who within a local community has the power to define, interpret, implement, and enforce law at the multiple levels it operates? Of particular interest is how the NGOs that mediate between women's rights under national and international law and local religious and customary norms are situated in the local hierarchy of status and power. A related question is how the power structures that inform unequal gender relations at the family level, the local community level, and at the level of state law are handled? Addressing all these levels, I turn to Luke's definition of power, which includes the visible power embedded in state law, the hidden power embedded in institutions that not formally are part of government, and the invisible power embedded in social and religious norms and institutions.[20] The aim is to come to a better understanding of how engagement with the legal pluralities that are at work in migrant women's lives may change or reinforce existing relations of inequality, domination and control, and as such strengthen or undermine women's access to justice. What awareness do the different actors that are involved in legal literacy have of power structures at the household and local community level, and in what way are they they challenging power-holders in these spheres? How is this awareness translated into measures aimed at assisting women as individuals and as members of transnational migrant communities? To what extent are unequal power structures challenged and changed?

[17] P. Levitt and S. Merry, 'Vernacularization on the Ground: Local Uses of Global Women's Rights in Peru, China, India and the United States', *Global Networks*, 9(4) (2009), 441–61.

[18] *Ibid.*, at 441 [19] Griffiths, 'What Is Legal Pluralism?'.

[20] S. S. Lukes, *Power: A Radical View* (Basingstoke: Macmillan, 1974).

3 The right to legal information without discrimination: emerging international trends

The jurisprudence of international human rights treaty bodies constitutes a dynamic attempt to facilitate access to justice for the poor and marginalized through increased attention to the right to legal information. The Human Rights Committee considers the duty to provide legal information as an inherent part of the state obligation embedded in Article 2 in the International Covenant on Civil and Political Rights. To fulfil this obligation, states parties, according to the Human Rights Committee, are required to adopt legislative, judicial, administrative, educative and other appropriate measures.[21] Following suit, the Committee on Economic, Social and Cultural Rights has outlined a set of criteria that also apply to legal education: 'Fundamental education included the elements of availability, accessibility, acceptability and adaptability which are common to education in all its forms and at all levels.'[22] Contributing to the contextualization of the right to legal information, the CEDAW Committee has, considering the situation of women migrant workers, emphasized the need for context-specific education programmes ensuring 'that linguistically and culturally appropriate gender-sensitive services for women migrant workers are available'.[23]

Leaning towards a contextual approach to legal literacy that engages with the gendered, socio-cultural diversity on the ground, these treaty bodies' evolving jurisprudence speaks to migrant women's mixed identities and belongings. The need for a woman-focused human rights approach that moves beyond the legal text has also been emphasized by the Special Rapporteur on Violence against Women. Discussing how to take legal action against honour killing, she emphasizes women's wariness of the 'arrogant gaze of critical outsiders' who suggest simplistic legalistic solutions. Rights must, in her view, be asserted in a manner which takes cognizance of the social embeddedness of women's identity. According to the Special Rapporteur: 'Where international attention and

[21] HRC, General Comment No. 31 *The Nature of the General Legal Obligation Imposed on State Parties to the Covenant*, 26 May 2004, UN Doc. CCPR/C/21/Rev.1/Add.13.

[22] ICESCR Committee, General Comment No. 13, 8 December 1999, UN Doc. E/C.12/1999/10.

[23] CEDAW Committee, General Recommendation No. 26, 5 December 2008, UN Doc CEDAW/C/2009/WP.1/R, para. 24 b.

leverage are rooted in culturally-sensitive strategies and locally supported, they can give strong underpinning to situation-specific approaches and interventions on the ground'.[24]

The international equality and non-discrimination standard embedded in the Convention on the Elimination of All Forms of Discrimination against Women (CEDAW) and other international conventions offers scope for effective engagement with legal pluralism in general and pluralist approaches to legal literacy in particular. It sets the international standard to assess the outcome of justice delivery initiatives that engage with legal pluralism. The four dimensions of discrimination – direct, indirect, structural and multiple – embedded in Article 1 of the Convention, bespeak and reflect the diverse and complex relationships in which women are involved. How the Committee is responding to this diversity so as to promote substantive, as opposed to formal, equality, is illustrated by its interpretation of the object and purpose of the Convention:

> In the Committee's view, a purely formal legal or programmatic approach is not sufficient to achieve women's *de facto* equality with men, which the Committee interprets as substantive equality. In addition, the Convention requires that women are given an equal start and that they be empowered by an enabling environment to achieve equality of result. It is not enough to guarantee women treatment identical to that of men. Rather, biological as well as socially and culturally constructed differences between women and men must be taken into account.[25]

In line with this overarching concern, the Committee has moved beyond both the formalized and individualized notion of discrimination. It defines 'direct discrimination' as occurring when a difference in treatment relies directly and explicitly on distinctions based exclusively on the basis of sex and characteristics of men or of women, which cannot be justified objectively. 'Indirect discrimination', according to the Committee, occurs where laws, policies and programs – based on apparently gender-neutral criteria – fail to take into account social, economic and cultural gender differences.[26]

[24] R. Coomaraswamy, 'Preface: Violence against Women and Crimes of Honour', in L. Welchman and S. Hossain (eds.), *'Honour' Crimes, Paradigms, and Violence against Women* (London: Zed Books, 2005).

[25] CEDAW Committee, General Recommendation No. 25 on Article 4, paragraph 1 of the Convention, 2004.

[26] *Ibid.*

Recognizing the social and cultural structures that often underlie acts of discrimination, Article 5(a) of the Convention addresses 'structural discrimination'. Understanding direct and indirect discrimination as informed by gender stereotypes that have no objective justification, it obliges state parties to take all appropriate measures to:

> modify the social and cultural patterns of conduct of men and women, with a view to achieving the elimination of prejudices and customary and all other practices which are based on the idea of the inferiority or superiority of either of the sexes or on stereotyped roles for men and women.

Gender stereotypes, according to Rebecca Cook and Simone Cusack, degrade women when they assign them subservient roles in society.[27] Prejudices about women's inferiority generate disrespect and devaluation of women. When societies fail to recognize and eliminate stereotypes they are, according to Cook and Cusack, 'exacerbating a climate of impunity with respect to women's rights.'

The concept of direct, indirect and structural discrimination protects the right to individual identity and, as such, the right to be different. At the core of the equality and non-discrimination norm is the protection of the individual against gender stereotypes that lack an objective justification. Yet the CEDAW Committee's call for socially and culturally appropriate measures to make migrant women's rights real demonstrates a constructive engagement with difference as a means of achieving substantive equality.

4 Situating the case study: the Norwegian context

In Norway, international human rights obligations, particularly the equality and non-discrimination principle applying to inequalities based on gender, ethnicity, religion, disability and sexuality, have in recent years called the assumed cultural homogeneity underlying national law into question. Challenging privileged positions of identity, status and power, international human rights law is met with increasing state resistance in Norway as in the other Nordic countries. There is, among state lawyers, an increasing concern about the dynamic interpretation of regional human rights treaty bodies challenging national laws, policies

[27] R. Cook and S. Cusack, *Gender Stereotyping* (Philadelphia, PA: University of Pennsylvania Press, 2010), at 1.

and practices. In Norway, a recent study on power and democracy raised concerns about incorporating international conventions into national law which served to undermine national sovereignty.[28] When presenting the government's proposal to incorporate CEDAW into the Human Rights Act in 2009, after ten years of battle, the Minister of Justice Knut Storberget, assured parliament that preserving national sovereignty was an overall political concern and that the CEDAW was the very last international convention that would be incorporated into the Human Rights Act.[29] One hypothesis purporting to explain this growing state resistance towards incorporating international human rights in the Nordic countries' legislation is the prevalence of communitarian narratives that depict these countries as ethnically and culturally homogeneous and egalitarian nations with a strong emphasis on grass-roots movement and participatory local democracy.[30]

Norway, like other nation-states in Northern Europe, is in the throes of rapid and uneven socio-cultural change. Faced with accumulating international legal obligations, unprecedented cultural diversity, and increasing transnationalism a revitalization of traditional nationalism is taking place in Norway, as elsewhere in Europe.[31] Immigrants account for 8 per cent of the Norwegian population and 25 per cent of the population in Oslo has a minority background. Pakistanis are the second largest immigrant group in Norway with 29,000 people. The highly gendered migration patterns reflect strong transboundary family and marriage networks.[32] Most Pakistani male and female immigrants marry a spouse from the country of origin.[33] The majority of the male migrants are workers who migrate independently while most of the women join their spouses or other members of their families who have formal employment. These patterns are reflected in occupational gender

[28] NOU 2003: 19 Makt og demokrati.

[29] Article by Minister of Justice Knut Storberget and Minister of Equality and Children's Affairs Anniken Huitfeldt i Dagbladet, 7 May 2009.

[30] A. Føllesdal and M. Wind, 'Introduction: Nordic Reluctance towards Judicial Review under Siege', *Nordic Journal of Human Rights* 2:2009 (Oslo: Norwegian University Press, 2009), at 132.

[31] S. Algashi *et al.*, 'Introduction', in S. Algashi *et al.* (eds.), *Paradoxes of Cultural Recognition: Perspectives from Northern Europe* (Farnham: Ashgate, 2009), at 283.

[32] Available statistics show that immigrants from Sri Lanka, Somalia and Pakistan keep close economic ties through regular remittances to family members in the home country (*Samfunnsspeilet* nr. 6, 2004).

[33] Of the 11,000 Pakistani immigrants who were married and living in Norway, only 200 married a Norwegian spouse (*Samfunnsspeilet* nr. 3, 2004).

segregation and unequal language skills, particularly for first-generation immigrants.[34] Most Norwegian-Pakistanis are followers of Hanafi Islam which contains personal and family law within its teaching that categorizes women as people in need of protective rights rather than equal rights with men.[35] This school of Islamic thought does not sit well with the gender equality principle embedded in CEDAW and in Norwegian family law.

While in principle applying to all women living in Norway, Norwegian state law is in practice often overruled by informal religious and customary norms of the immigrant's country of origin when disputes related to family and personal matters are resolved through family negotiations or on the basis of informal counselling of an imam. There are a growing number of Pakistani mosques in Oslo that are involved on an informal basis in counselling and dispute resolution. The process whereby the right to legal information, embedded in international law, is translated into laws, policies and practices that have a bearing on women from the Norwegian-Pakistani community in Oslo is thus a well-suited case to engender the encounter between international, national and imported religious and customary norms. The gendered character of migration and the religious and customary norms that operate within this group of immigrants represents a challenge for state actors and NGOs that are involved in making the right to equality and non-discrimination in the family, in the public sphere, and in the labour market real for migrant women.

5 Norwegian state law: between the international and the local

An area of increasing concern for the CEDAW Committee, which monitors state compliance with the Convention, is migrant women's vulnerability to intersecting forms of gender, race and class discrimination. In order to provide access to justice and prevent these intersecting forms of discrimination, the Committee emphasizes that 'state parties should ensure that linguistically and culturally appropriate gender-sensitive services for women migrant workers are available'.[36] In its

[34] Gender differences regarding occupation and language are greatest among immigrants from Pakistan, Irak, Serbia and Montenegro (*Statistisk sentralbyrå, Levekår blant innvandrere*, 2005/2006).

[35] Ali, *Gender and Human Rights.*

[36] CEDAW Committee, General Recommendation No. 26, 5 December 2008, UN Doc. CEDAW/C/2009/WP.1/R, para. 24b.

concluding comments on Norway's fifth and sixth reports, the CEDAW Committee urged the Norwegian state to take steps to increase awareness of the availability of social services and legal remedies for migrant women.[37]

Norway has incorporated the International Covenant on Civil and Political Rights, the International Covenant on Social, Economic and Cultural Rights, and the Convention on the Elimination of All Forms of Discrimination against Women into its Human Rights Act. This implies that the obligation to provide legal literacy in a manner that makes law available, accessible and acceptable through linguistically and culturally appropriate, gender-sensitive methods is part and parcel of national law.

Access to justice is in Norway, as elsewhere in the world, in practice highly dependent on people's class, gender, ethnicity, race or immigrant status.[38] The few measures that the Norwegian government so far has taken to ensure equal access to legal information have been piecemeal and fragmented. The Norwegian government has lacked any systematic analysis of the complex relationship between gender, law, society and culture in the new Norway.[39] National information campaigns directed at migrant and minority women and their families have by and large focused on female genital mutilation, forced marriages and honour killings.[40]So far, not a single public information campaign has been carried out to inform migrant women about the laws that protect them against discrimination on the basis of gender and ethnicity. This suggests that the inequalities between majorities and minorities in Norway to a large extent appear to be ascribed to the migrant's own culture and not to any discrimination related to the majority's stereotypical perception of migrant women. It illustrates how the Norwegian notion of equality, as pointed out by the anthropologist Marianne Gullestad, appears to be premised on the notion that 'people have to be more or less the same to

[37] CEDAW Committee, Draft General Recommendation No. 26 on Women Migrant Workers, 31 January 2003, UN Doc. CEDAW/C/2003/I/CRP.3/Add.2/Rev.1 para. 25.

[38] T. Mathiesen, *Retten I samfunnet* [*Law in Society*] (Oslo: Pax, 2010).

[39] T. S. Nordstrøm, 'Innvandrerkvinners Rett til Rettighetsinformasjon: Hva Gjøres og Hva Krever FNs Kvinnekonvensjon?' ['Immigrant Women's Right to Legal Information: What Is Done and What Is Required by CEDAW?'] *Kritisk Juss* [*Critical Legal Studies*] 2 (2010).

[40] Norwegian Ministry of Children and Equality 2008. *Action Plan against Forced Marriages* (2008–11) (Oslo: Government of Norway); Norwegian Ministry of Foreign Affairs 200. *Action Plan for Women's Rights and Gender Equality in Development* (2007–9) (Oslo: Government of Norway).

get along'.[41] Egalitarian ideas, in her view, are often 'used to marginalize specific groups by simultaneously creating dichotomies asking for sameness'.[42]

Dissemination of legal information to immigrants has by and large been carried out by non-governmental institutions on a voluntary basis. Committed legal scholars at the faculties of law at the universities of Oslo, Bergen and Tromsø have set up programmes for vulnerable groups, including women, prisoners, immigrants and minorities such as the Sami and the Roma, with funding from national and local government. These university clinics provide information and advice in areas such as refugee law, immigration law, housing law, women's rights, children rights and minority rights.[43] Since its formation in 1974, JURK (Free Legal Advice for Women) at the University of Oslo has made dissemination of legal information to women one of its priority areas. Realizing that its service fell short of non-Western women's needs, JURK started an outreach programme for immigrant women in 1997. It offers this programme at language classes for newly arrived women with different national, ethnic and religious backgrounds.

Emphasizing the importance of dialogue and cooperation, the Norwegian government is funding an increasing number of non-governmental organizations where immigrant women of the same national background assist each other.[44] A characteristic feature of these organizations' engagement with law is that information about rights is not dealt with in isolation but in response to concrete problems related to family, health and education issues.[45] Many of these initiatives are premised on the assumption that information about Norwegian society and law must be transmitted through a socio-cultural lens if it is to be seen as relevant and acceptable according to the women concerned.

41 M. Gullestad, 'Imagined Sameness: Shifting Notions of Us and Them', in L. A. Ytrehus, *Forestillinger om den andre* [*Images of Us and Them*] (Oslo: Norwegian Academic Press, 2001), at 37.

42 *Ibid.*, at 54.

43 In Oslo these programmes are two student schemes at the faculty of law at the University of Oslo, Juss Buss and JURK (Free Legal Advice for Women).

44 See 'Turning Point', the *Action Plan against Domestic Violence* (2008–11), Ministry of Justice and Police, Government of Norway; and *Action Plan against Forced Marriages* (2008–11), Ministry of Children and Equality, Government of Norway.

45 An example is Primærmedisinsk Verksted [Primary Medical Workshop] PMV (Thune 2007).

6 Taking the law to women in the Pakistani community in Oslo

Addressing challenges involved in making legal education available, accessible and acceptable, we now turn to the experiences of a Pakistani women's organization, PAKWOM, and its interaction with Norwegian non-governmental organizations, Norwegian legal institutions and Islamic institutions in Oslo.[46]

6.1 The Norwegian-Pakistani NGO PAKWOM

PAKWOM is a non-governmental organization that receives state support with the aim of promoting women's rights embedded in CEDAW and Norwegian state law. It arranges social events, classes and discussion groups to support women from the Pakistani community in Oslo and promote gender equality. External resource persons are invited to give talks on topics ranging from religion and literature to politics and law. PAKWOM is a membership organization with about 150 members who come from different parts of Punjab. Most of them belong to Jatt and Butt biradries (sub-clans or extended families). Their period of residence in Norway varies greatly – some members have been living in Norway for twenty-five years, others for ten or twenty years, while some only arrived in 2007.

Through the action research project, 'From formal to real rights', I have been involved in the dissemination of legal information to women from the Norwegian-Pakistani community in Oslo. Through cooperation with JURK which disseminates legal information to members of PAKWOM, I and other researchers within this project have been able to observe how law is made accessible, acceptable and available to women on the ground.[47] Through our interaction with these NGOs we have been both observing and participating in the process of taking law to women in the Norwegian-Pakistani community.[48]

[46] The sessions which took place in Oslo in April 2008 and April 2009 were attended by Anne Hellum and Farhat Taj. Both sessions were videotaped with the permission of the leader of the non-governmental organization and transcribed by Farhat Taj.

[47] Farhat Taj's research, based on participating in the day-to-day work of the organization, their meetings and social events and individual counseling, provides a window into the way in which PAKWOM seeks to make law accessible for members facing problems and conflicts.

[48] On legal advice as research method, see A. Hellum, 'Legal Advice as Research Method', in Hellum *et al.* (eds.), *Methodology of Women's Law: Norwegian Perspectives in an African Context* (Oslo: Norwegian University Press, 1991).

6.2 *Between legal centralism and legal pluralism: making law available and accessible*

To make law available to its members, PAKWOM has included legal literacy and awareness in its social program. The Norwegian organization JURK is regularly invited to disseminate information about women's rights under Norwegian law.

In the sessions we observed, Norwegian state law relating to marriage, divorce, domestic violence, inheritance law and discrimination law was presented by female Norwegian students from JURK. Their presentations were translated into Urdu by one of the leaders of the organization. By means of practical cases JURK actively engaged the women in discussions about their legal rights in different situations. The strength of this approach is that it situates legal information in an environment where women feel confident and in a language they understand. It gives concrete content to abstract principles and encourages engagement and discussion about real-life issues. In the course of the discussion the women in the audience talked about problems that they or women they knew were facing. Several of them reported that the Norwegian legal system had not rendered them justice in their encounters with it. Most queries related to the division of matrimonial property and matters relating to the children in connection with divorce.

Rights awareness does not automatically translate into legal action. While women in this way are becoming aware of their rights under Norwegian law they are often held back by moral and religious constraints. PAKWOM, according to its leader, strives for women's rights at two levels.[49] On one level it seeks to protect women's rights and on the other it strives not to be seen as violating religious and cultural limits. Well aware of the power relations in the local community, they are not networking with Pakistani women's NGOs who are part of the transnational network Women Living under Muslim Law. The reason according to PAKWOM's leader is that these women are regarded as "bad women" both in Pakistan and Norway. To ensure that information about Norwegian law is conveyed in a way that makes it acceptable to the broader community, PAKWOM keeps close contact with the *imam* in one of the nearby Oslo mosques. According to the leader, this contact carries the symbolic message to the wider community that the

[49] Interview conducted by Farhat Taj with the caseworker at her office in Oslo on 15 March 2007.

organization's work is not violating Islam. Explaining the rationale behind this approach, she recounted:

> We have a perception problem within the local community. It is often assumed that we are out there to instigate divorces and break up marriages. Wanting to promote women's rights we are walking a tight rope. Some families do not allow women to contact us. We try to send out a message to the wider community that we accord due respect to our religion and culture. This makes it easier for the women to contact us and for us to promote women's rights in a less hostile environment. At least this is our aim.

Observing the challenges that the coexisting and sometimes conflicting norms at work in Norwegian-Pakistani women's lives pose, our research team, in cooperation with JURK and PAKWOM started to arrange legal literacy classes that engaged with both Norwegian and Islamic law. To reconcile the women's identities as Norwegian citizens with their identity as Muslims, Professor Ali started to give literacy classes where she compared information on women's rights under Norwegian law with Islam and Pakistani law.[50]

In the literacy classes that were arranged in cooperation with Free Legal Advice for Women, Professor Ali addressed the ambiguities many of the women experienced in relation to their identity as Norwegian citizens and as Muslims. In the two presentations of women's rights under Muslim family law that the research team observed, she focused on issues related to the acceptability of women's rights under Norwegian law. Her presentations started out with the relationship between Norwegian civil law and religious norms from the perspective of Islamic international law:

> Islam believes in universality of humanity and is not tied down to a specific country or place. Yet Islam sees us as duty-bound to obey the laws of the country that has offered us citizenship, this is what Islam demands of us. So long as the laws of our acquired countries do not contradict the main pillars of our faith, such as saying prayers, fasting during Ramadan, *haj*, *zakat* and so on.

Addressing forced marriages, she emphasized the similarities between Islam and Norwegian law:[51]

[50] All of these classes have been observed by Anne Hellum as part of the research project From Formal to Real Rights. Some of them have also been observed and recorded by Farhat Taj who recorded and translated from Urdu to English.

[51] Hellum, research notes, Oslo (April 2010).

> Forced marriages as we all know are completely unIslamic and illegal in Pakistan as well as Norway. In Islam marriage is a civil contract and both parties must freely consent to it. So we have a rather sophisticated Islamic position on this issue. Forcing girls and boys into marriage against their will is to my mind a greedy, economic ploy because we feel that if we get someone over from Pakistan, we are fulfilling an economic promise made to some relative some years ago. There are other ways of helping relatives and loved ones than to make your own child a sacrificial lamb! So please let us take this message to the men in our families.

Emphasizing basic principles underlying Norwegian law, Pakistani law, and different versions of Islam in terms of justice and integrity, she attempted to build a conceptual bridge between Norwegian state law and Islam. The following statement from one of the women who participated in the comparative legal literacy sessions speaks to the potential of this approach:

> As Muslims we believe we have to be accountable and answerable to God on the Day of Judgement about what we do in this world. We follow the Norwegian law to get social benefits or some relief, such as divorce or having our human rights protected. But it would be psychologically very difficult to follow the law if we know that the law violates Islam. We think we get benefits from the Norwegian law, but at the same time make our life hereafter very difficult. We then think it is better not to follow the Norwegian law because Norwegian law is only for this worldly life which is short and rather make sure to protect ourselves from perpetual punishments on the Day of Judgement. Dr Shaheen's lectures and our discussions with her beautifully convince us that going by the Norwegian law is not a violation of Islam. This is such a relief in terms of concerns about the life hereafter.[52]

Considering both similarities and differences among the plurality of norms at work in women's lives, these insights suggest an open space for active and inclusive engagement with core issues related to the acceptability of law. Through these discussions about equal rights in marriage, human rights law was adapted to Islam and local circumstances and as such 'vernacularized', in the legal anthropologist Sally Engle Merry's terms.[53] To understand the process whereby women's human rights and Islam is reconciled, it is important to pay attention to relations of power and control. The women's NGO is a space which is controlled by women who seek greater choice and equality. The NGO is a member of a broader network of NGOs that receive economic support

[52] Taj, research notes, Oslo (24 March 2009). [53] Merry, *Human Rights.*

from the Norwegian states to promote equality and integration. The leader of the NGO was educated in the UK. She is respected in the local community and deeply committed to assist the individual members of the organization. A related factor is the social status of the mediator. As a former professor at the faculty of law at the University of Peshawar, the first chair of the Pakistani Commission of the Status of Women and former Minister of Health in the provincial government in North West Frontier Province Shaheen Sardar Ali is an elite actor that is well placed to negotiate socially and culturally legitimate innovations. When challenged by the wife of one of the local imams on issues concerning marriage and divorce she would use her legal authority and refer to court cases concerning the relationship between the Muslim Family Law ordinance and Islam that had been decided by the High Court of Pakistan. In spaces controlled by male religious authorities, such as the informal Shariah councils in Britain, the outcome of the negotiations is, as described in Samia Bano's research, often less favourable for women.[54]

6.3 *Making law accessible: options and limits of a pluralist approach*

Through individual counselling, PAKWOM seeks to enable women to act on the knowledge they have gained through legal literacy.[55] To make women's equal rights under Norwegian law real, PAKWOM seeks ways to overcome the constraining stereotypes posed by different versions of Islamic law at work in the family network and in the local community. Depending on the circumstances of a case and subject to the consent of the woman concerned, the case may be referred to an *imam* for religious counselling, or to a lawyer to be pleaded in a court of law, or to both. The following two case studies draw attention to the options and limits of the pluralist approach that is adopted by PAKWOM.

[54] S. Bano, 'Cultural Translations and Legal Conflict: Muslim Women and the Shari'a Councils in Britain', in Hellum *et al.*, *From Transnational Relations to Transnational Laws.*

[55] These two cases referred to here are based on Taj's fieldwork notes and her paper presented at two conferences: Transnational Law and Transnational relations in Oslo in June 2007 and American Anthropologists Association in Washington in December 2007. The two cases are referred to in Hellum and Taj, 'Taking What Law Where and to Whom?', in Hellum *et al.*, *From Transnational Relations to Transnational Laws.*

6.3.1 Claiming rights and being a good Muslim

Asma's case demonstrates how the selective use of Norwegian and Islamic norms in the context of a counselling process, where the women themselves are in control, may enable women to claim their rights under Norwegian law and feel confident that they also are good Muslims.

Asma married her first cousin under Pakistani law before she came to Norway. Her husband became interested in another woman and divorced her after a few years. After the divorce her parental family and the husband's family married her off to her husband's younger brother in Oslo. Some years later he married another woman in Pakistan. He had applied for a divorce under Norwegian law but it had not yet been granted. After a quarrel Asma was thrown out of their home in Oslo by her husband and her in-laws. One of Asma's acquaintances took her to PAKWOM and they accompanied her to the social welfare office which arranged for accommodation and financial help. Asma had been subjected to violence, sexual abuse and humiliation and wanted assistance from a lawyer to sue her husband for bigamy in a Norwegian court of law. She and her husband had contracted a marriage under Norwegian law which makes bigamy a criminal offence. On the advice of the lawyer, the organization collected video clips of her husband's marriage and marriage documents from Pakistan to substantiate her case in court. The Norwegian court heard the evidence, found the husband guilty of bigamy and handed down a penalty of twenty-one days in jail and a fine of 7,000 kroner. A mitigating circumstance was that the husband had not intended to be polygamous since he had already applied for divorce.

Interviews with Asma and the caseworker revealed Asma's strong desire to restore the self-respect she felt she had lost in the humiliation inflicted on her by her in-laws and former husband:

> They [the in-laws and the husband] battered me. They tortured me, physically and mentally. They used to say I was a good for nothing, useless, mindless creature. I descended into having an inferiority complex. I have lost my self-esteem. I feel everyone in the world is better than me. I am good for nothing. I have no children, not much formal schooling and I can't speak the Norwegian language. I live alone. The only thing that will restore my self-respect is to get him behind bars. This will re-establish confidence in myself. It will prove them wrong – with their repeated assertion that I am good for nothing.

> It will prove to them and to the extended family that I can set goals and achieve them single-handedly.[56]

One reason she sought the assistance of PAKWOM and the Norwegian court to reassert her dignity was that there was no family who could assist her:

> My brother in Denmark has almost no time to care for me. The only person who cares is my ailing mother who lives alone thousands of miles away in Pakistan. I have no children to turn to. My husband married my cousin and this alienated me from the family of that cousin. So I had no relatives in Norway to turn to for help. I felt I stood humiliated in the eyes of my relatives both in Pakistan and in Norway. There was no one to avenge my humiliation. It befell on me to stand up and reassert myself.[57]

An important reason for turning to Norwegian state law was that both Asma and the caseworker who assisted her believed there was no point in asking the *imam* to reconcile the case. According to the caseworker, the *imam* that the organization regularly turned to in matters of dispute resolution did not consider polygamy illegal:

> We knew what the *imam* would say. He would say what the problem is. Polygamy is legal in Islam. There is no violation of God's law. There can be no punishment for polygamy. Keeping in view Asma's strong wish, I and she agreed to keep the *imams* out of the issue.[58]

Yet Asma's decision to pursue Norwegian law was also grounded in Islam:

> Islam may permit it. But the Norwegian law does not. He is a citizen of Norway and lives in Norway. He must not violate the law of Norway. But he did. Any citizen of this country who violates the law of this country must face the law and so must he. The religion of Islam that I understand does not obligate its followers to violate the law of a country that they have freely chosen to live in.[59]

By linking Islam with Norwegian state law and responsibilities of citizenship, Asma felt she could answer any criticism of her decision. When Asma and the caseworker decided to keep the *imam* out of the case, they knew that polygamy was a disputed issue and that there are different interpretations of the Qur'anic verses regarding polygamy. Notwithstanding the

[56] Taj, interview with Asma, Oslo (September 2006). [57] *Ibid.*
[58] Taj, interview with NGO caseworker, Oslo (November 2006).
[59] Taj, interview with Asma, Oslo (September 2006).

local Oslo *imam*'s view on polygamy, women members of the organization continue to question polygamy in their group discussions and seminars. Some women members also surf the internet to look for Islamic arguments against polygamy.

As demonstrated by this case the *imams* are not the only 'experts' that the women's organization consults on family disputes. They also hold seminars with liberal Muslim legal scholars, such as Professor Ali, who argues against polygamy from an Islamic perspective. Thus the organization provides a milieu where Muslim personal law, as upheld by the *imams*, is debated and questioned. This, the leader argues, is in line with the inbuilt pluralism of the Muslim legal tradition. It is, according to the leader, the pluralist nature of Islam that provides the conceptual potential to extend the limits of Muslim personal law, as shown by Asma's case. According to the leader of the organization, this case was 'PAKWOM's contribution towards the elimination of gender discrimination in the Norwegian-Pakistani community'. Asma's case demonstrates how engagement with gender stereotypes embedded in dominant discourses under the circumstances can be bypassed through alternative interpretations offered by feminist interpretations. Whether and to what extent Islam's pluralist nature facilitates 'vernacularization' of women's human rights is, as shown by Asma's case, highly dependent on who does the translation and who controls the process where women decide what path to pursue.

6.3.2 Reinforcing hierarchic gender stereotypes

Ayesha's case shows how archaic patriarchal interpretations of Islam may be mobilized to reinstate women's honour while simultaneously upholding the very understanding of Islam that is at the root of her oppression. It demonstrates how human rights through engagement with Islam easily can become 'indigenized' rather than 'vernacularized'.

Ayesha lived in a violent marriage. Angry and under the influence of alcohol her husband had divorced her through 'triple talaq' at least five times since 1998. Their youngest son was conceived and born after his pronouncement of the third 'triple talaq'. According to Ayesha the in-laws argued that the child was a 'bastard' child. The consultations with the caseworker made it clear that Ayesha wanted to maintain her marriage but at the same time, she wanted her husband and her in-laws to respect her. Towards this end they agreed to seek religious advice from an *imam*. The *imam*, with reference to Hanafi Islam, upheld the husband's unilateral right to terminate the marriage through 'triple talaq'. In

Pakistan, this type of divorce is curtailed by the Muslim Family Law Ordinance which lays down a procedure for divorce involving the local marriage authorities. Yet in diasporic communities in Norway or the United Kingdom, marriages are often terminated unilaterally through 'triple talaq'. The Oslo imam who was contacted reaffirmed the validity of the triple talaq with reference to Verse 230 of Chapter 2 of the Qur'an:

> If a man divorces her again (a third time). She becomes unlawful for him (and cannot remarry her) until she has married another man.[60]

The *imam* maintained that Ayesha could not legitimize her relationship through remarriage without hilala – a second marriage. The second marriage (hilala) is an intervening marriage which is contracted with the intention of dissolving it by divorce. However, according to the *imam*:

> It is unIslamic to perform hilala marriage as a formality to remarry the first husband. It is forbidden for a woman to marry a second man with the intention to be divorced by him and remarried by the first husband.

The outcome of the consultations with the non-governmental organization and the *imam* was that Ayesha wanted her husband to concede to hilala but he opposed this solution. Her 'public' reason for the hilala was that it would legitimize her son in the eyes of her in-laws who called him a 'bastard'. Her personal reason was that she wanted to punish her husband through the humiliation of hilala. During an interview she stated:

> I want to torture my husband through hilala. I want him to feel how much I suffered because of him, first due to his violence and now because I have to pass through the humiliation of hilala. He does not want hilala and I wish to make him accept what he is not ready to accept. It is only through the humiliation of hilala that he will feel the equivalent torture he put me through.[61]

The caseworker explained how her client felt that this would make a difference in her life:

> She wants hilala to make her husband realize what he has done to her. That she had been with another man without his consent. She wants to make him realize that he always brought torture on her, including the torture of hilala. She wants to hurt his male honour for the miseries he had been inflicting on her in the past.[62]

[60] *Ibid.* [61] Taj, interview with Ayesah, Oslo (August 2006).
[62] Taj, interview with PAKOM caseworker, Oslo (August 2006).

In the course of the process the standards of equality and freedom that PAKWOM sets out to promote were 'indigenized' to resonate a version of Islam that has been used to invoke female submission and inequality.[63] It shows how the pluralist approach, under the circumstance may be to the effect that the very gender stereotypes that are at the root of the women's problems are reinforced. Individual women, it must be borne in mind, are often more concerned with an outcome that suits their personal aims and goals than with changing the structures that constrain their course of action. In such situations the organization, which receives funding from the Norwegian state to promote women's rights and gender equality, is faced with difficult choices. How should the loyalty between the demands of the donor (in this case the Norwegian state) and the diverse expectations of the members seeking advice and support be divided? In Asma's case the mediator respected the woman's choice although it came into conflict with the principle of equality and the wider aims and goals of the organization. In a long-term perspective the decision to respect the woman's choice, however, achieved positive results. Through continued support from PAKWOM, Asma, after some time, gained the strength to divorce her husband and abandoned the hilala approach.

7 Woman-centred innovations from below

Both religious groups and women's groups are, as demonstrated in this case study, in search of justice beyond the confines of state, customary or religious laws. The appropriation of space provided by state law to religious groups and women's groups, such as legal literacy and conflict mediation provides a vehicle for solutions that mediate beyond the confines of the prescribed rules associated within the particular domains of state, religious or customary law. Yet the interests of the religious group and the interests of women within the group are, as demonstrated, often coming into conflict.

The study of PAKWOM's work illustrates how smaller non-state entities, under the circumstances, may provide space for women who have been marginalized both by state law and the religious and customary legal orders applying within their group. It demonstrates constructive ways of promoting pluralism, choice and recognition within a human

[63] Merry, *Human Rights*, at 216.

rights framework. To reconfigure socio-legal relationships that constrain their course of action, individual women and women's organizations in the Norwegian-Pakistani community in Oslo are, as we have seen, mobilizing a multiplicity of norms and institutions ranging from *imams* to Norwegian courts. The outcome of this process is an innovative and responsive legal literacy and counselling approach that invokes both Norwegian and Islamic law to make basic human rights available, acceptable and accessible. Yet, engagement with legal pluralism can, as shown by the case studies, be a double-edged sword. When women, in response to Professor Shaheen Sardar Ali, say they feel at ease because she enables them to claim their rights under Norwegian law and still be good Muslims, dominant religious stereotypes are challenged. Yet engagement with Islamic norms and institutions may also, as demonstrated by the hilala case, have the consequence that the very stereotypes that limit women's right to equality are reinforced.

Drawing on multiple sources and networks both within the local Pakistani community and the Norwegian legal community, PAKWOM provides an enabling environment that facilitates choice and empowerment. A space where women are assisted by women in the spirit of free and informed choice so as to define a place for themselves in the context of the conflicting expectations and pressures deriving from husbands, in-laws, religious institutions and Norwegian authorities has been created. Established customary and religious paradigms that restrict women's opportunities and choices are challenged by demonstrating the multiple normative avenues that are available. Facilitated through cooperation between Pakistani and Norwegian women's organizations, *where women themselves are in control*, the process stands in contrast to the confined normative repertoire that often is at work within male-dominated religious institutions, such as the Sharia Councils in the UK as described in Samio Bano's empirical research.[64]

To be seen as a morally acceptable organization, PAKWOM is set up as a social centre where women come together to cook, sew, socialize and celebrate religious events. Acceptance of norms that ascribe separate spaces for men and women are, as demonstrated by the case studies a double-edged sword. Separate social and educational spaces may reinforce existing gender stereotypes. As shown by these case studies, separation may also, provide an entry point for the attainment of basic

[64] Bano, 'Cultural Translations and Legal Conflict'.

human rights such as protection against domestic violence and equal divorce rights. By creating a space where women are setting the agenda and are in control, PAKWOM is in practice providing support for women who seek to overcome religious or customary stereotypes that bar their access to law and justice. While, on the one hand, conforming to the stereotypical gender views in the local community PAKWOM is, on the other hand, providing a platform for empowerment and substantive equality which is CEDAW's overall goal. The case studies demonstrate that equal access to justice calls for careful analysis of how engagement with difference and sameness under the circumstances may enhance or undermine substantive gender equality.

PART III

Confronting the challenge of environmental protection, climate change and sustainable development: new actors and shifting norms

9

The creation of the international law of climate change: complexities of sub-state actors

HARI M. OSOFSKY

1 Introduction

As a formal matter, international legal efforts to address climate change fit within a traditional model for the creation of international law. The dominant multilateral climate change regime consists of the United Nations Framework Convention on Climate Change (UNFCCC)[1] and agreements negotiated under that convention. The UNFCCC provides general commitments and a structure for achieving more specific targets and timetables.[2] Parties to the UNFCCC meet regularly in conferences under its auspices, most recently in Durban 2011, to attempt to negotiate additional agreements. The 2011 Conference of the Parties (COP) in Durban resulted in an agreement to reach a universal agreement by 2015 and established an "Ad Hoc Working Group on the Durban Platform for Enhanced Action," to begin negotiating toward this 2015 goal.[3] In addition, thirty-five of the parties to the Kyoto Protocol, the

This chapter has benefited greatly from the dialogue at the conference Creation of International Law an Exploration of Normative Innovation, Contextual Application, and Interpretation in a Time of Flux hosted by Department of Public and International Law, University of Oslo. I would like to thank all of the participants for their helpful feedback. The draft also has been improved by feedback and suggestions of additional scholarly literature from Cecilia Bailliet, Hilary Charlesworth, Brad Karkkainen, Alexandra Klass, Fiona de Londras, and Christina Voigt. In addition, I am grateful for a summer research grant from the University of Minnesota Law School that helped to support this work. As always, I deeply appreciate the love, support, and patience of Josh, Oz, and Scarlet Gitelson.

1 See United Nations Framework Convention on Climate Change, New York, May 9, 1992, in force March 21, 1994 S. Treaty Doc. No. 102–38, 1771 UNTS 107 (hereafter UNFCCC).

2 See *ibid.*

3 See Draft Decision-/CP 17. Establishment of an Ad Hoc Working Group on the Durban Platform for Enhanced Action/Advance unedited version, Nov./Dec. 2011, available online at: http://unfccc.int/meetings/meetings/durban_nov_2011/decisions/application (hereafter Durban Platform).

only agreement agreement negotiated under the UNFCCC which provides binding targets and timetables, committed to a second commitment period, which begins in January 2013, when the first one ends.[4]

However, an analysis of the international law of climate change which focused only on the UNFCCC and its progeny would be significantly impoverished. Not only do these negotiations seem unlikely to achieve results quickly enough to prevent the risks of severe climate change,[5] but they also fail to include many key players in the effort to mitigate emissions and adapt to impacts. A large number of other entities – from nongovernmental organizations, to corporations, to cities and states – meet at the same time in separate fora, create transnational agreements, and try to influence the primary dialogue among nation-states. However, those other entities are excluded from the main negotiating table, except when they serve on nation-state delegations (in which case they are representing the national rather than subnational governments) and the agreements among nation-states only include their input indirectly.[6]

The meetings at Copenhagen in December 2009 and developments since reflect this pattern. Non-state and sub-state actors had extremely limited formal involvement in the meetings and struggled even to gain access to the negotiating venue. The Copenhagen Accord emerged from last-minute negotiations among nation-states, and its language focuses on those countries as the key actors.[7] The mostly contingent commitments

[4] Kyoto Protocol to the United Nations Framework Convention on Climate Change, Kyoto, Dec. 11, 1997, in force February 16, 2005, 2303 UNTS 148, 37 ILM 22; Draft Decision-/CMP.7, Outcome of the work of the Ad Hoc Working Group on Further Commitments for Annex I Parties under the Kyoto Protocol at its sixteenth session/Advance unedited version, Nov./Dec. 2011, available online at: http://unfccc.int/file/meetings/meetings/durban_nov_2011/decisions/application/pdf/awgkp_outcome.pdf

[5] See Kelly Levin and Rob Bradley, 'Comparability of Annex I Emission Reduction Pledges', World Res. Inst., Working Paper (2010), 21; available online at: http://pdf.wri.org/working_papers/comparability_of_annex1_emission_reduction_pledges_2010-02-01.pdf

[6] Gavin Newsom analyzed these issues in his response to a question that I posed to him following his keynote address at a 2008 conference. Gavin Newsom, Mayor of San Francisco, Remarks following his Keynote Address at the University of California Hastings College of the Law Conference: Surviving Climate Change: Adaptation and Innovation (April 4, 2008) (notes on file with author). For a discussion of nation-states as the primary international legal actors, see Ian Brownlie, *Principles of Public International Law* (6th edn., New York: Oxford University Press, 2003), 287–8.

[7] See Draft Decision-/CP 15: Proposal by the President, Copenhagen Accord, Copenhagen, December 18, 2009, UN Doc. FCCC/CP/2009/L.7. (hereafter Copenhagen Accord); Arthur Max, 'Obama brokers a climate deal, doesn't satisfy all', *Daily Record* (Morristown, NJ), December 19, 2009, 1; Andrew C. Revkin and John M. Broder, 'A grudging accord in climate talks', *New York Times*, December 20, 2009, A1; Michael Gerrard, 'Copenhagen

of nation-states under the Copenhagen Accord treat countries as singular decision-making entities in dialogue with other nation-states.[8] The Cancún and Durban Agreements similarly view nation-states as at the center of the conversation.[9]

As with a broader climate change legal narrative focused on the UNFCCC, a narrative of the COP negotiations that focuses description of nation-states and their struggle to make progress through the UNFCCC is significantly incomplete. Even though non-nation-state entities have a limited role in the formal treaty process, they have long collaborated transnationally on climate change and have chosen to form their own agreements in parallel to the main sessions. This chapter will focus on a particular set of those non-nation-state entities – cities, states, and provinces – and the agreements that they made during the Copenhagen COP. These sub-state actors have governmental authority and control significant amounts of emissions through their transnational coalitions.[10]

report: Monday, December 14', December 14, 2009; available online at: http://blogs.law.columbia.edu/climatechange/2009/12/14/michael-gerrards-copenhagen-report-monday-december-12; Michael Gerrard, 'Copenhagen report: Tuesday, December 15', December 15, 2009; available online at: http://blogs.law.columbia.edu/climatechange/2009/12/15/copenhagen-report-tuesday-december-15; Michael Gerrard, 'Copenhagen report: Wednesday, December 16', December 16, 2009; available online at: http://blogs.law.columbia.edu/climatechange/2009/12/16/copenhagen-report-december-16; Michael Gerrard, 'Copenhagen report: Thursday, December 17', December 17, 2009; available online at: http://blogs.law.columbia.edu/climatechange/2009/12/17/copenhagen-report-thursday-december-17; Michael Gerrard, 'Copenhagen report: Sunday, December 20', December 20, 2009; available online at: http://blogs.law.columbia.edu/climatechange/2009/12/20/copenhagen-report-saturday-december-20-2009

8 See United Nations Framework Convention on Climate Change, Information Provided by Parties to the Convention Relating to the Accord, at: http://unfccc.int/home/items/5262.php

9 See Cancún; Durban Platform; Further Kyoto commitments; United Nations Framework Convention on Climate Change, United Nations Climate Change Conference in Cancún, COP 16/CMP 6, November, 26–December 10, 2010, Decisions adopted by COP 16 and CMP 6 (hereafter Cancún Agreements); available online at: http://unfccc.int/meetings/cop_16/items/5571.php; Cesare Romano and Elizabeth Burleson, 'The Cancún Climate Conference', *American Society of International Law Insight*, 15 (January 21, 2011), 1.

10 Global Climate Solutions Declaration (November 19, 2008), at: www.wisgov.state.wi.us/docview.asp?docid=15325; United States Conference of Mayors, Mayors Climate Protections Center – Mayors Leading the Way on Climate Protection, at: www.usmayors.org/climateprotection/revised; European Commission Energy, Covenant of Mayors, at: www.eumayors.eu/mm/staging/library/CoM_text_layouted/Texte_Convention_EN.pdf; Local Government Climate Roadmap, Climate Roadmap – About the Roadmap, at: www.iclei.org/index.php?id=9639; ICLEI Global, at ICLEI Climate Program, www.iclei.org/index.php?id=800

Their Copenhagen agreements involved commitments among themselves which will impact nation-states' ability to meet the goals articulated in the Copenhagen Accord, and also involved pushing nation-states to make progress on these issues.[11]

In a previous essay, I considered how different approaches to international legal theory might characterize these developments and use them as a basis for future action.[12] This chapter builds upon that work by focusing on the international-law-creating moment at Copenhagen – the Copenhagen Accord – and comparing its significance to that of these agreements. As section 2 explores, although the agreements among substate entities are nonbinding as a formal international legal matter, they contain more substantive commitments than the nation-state submissions pursuant to the Copenhagen Accord.

Section 3 explores the conceptual implications of this juxtaposition of limited formal progress at a national level with significant subnational efforts, a phenomenon which is mirrored in the United States at a domestic level as a number of its cities and states attempt to address climate change more aggressively than the federal government, and which raises serious normative questions about international lawmaking. On the one hand, the negotiations among nation-states are so complex that is it hard to envision a more inclusive approach to UNFCCC negotiations themselves. On the other hand, denying any international lawmaking role for these transnational gatherings of sub-state entities seems like an incomplete portrayal. Section 3 draws from my previous law and geography work on international legal theory generally and the Copenhagen negotiations in particular to argue that one's perspective on the geography of the nation-state importantly influences how one resolves this conundrum.[13]

[11] Press release, Office of the Governor of California, 'Gov. Schwarzenegger announces new coalition of subnational leaders to combat climate change' (December 14, 2009), available online at: http://gov38.ca.gov/press-release/14032/ (hereafter R20 press release); Copenhagen Climate Summit for Mayors, 'Cities Act: Copenhagen Climate Communiqué' (December 16, 2009), available online at: www.kk.dk/Nyheder/2009/December/~/media/B5A397DC695C409983462723E31C995E.ashx; City Climate Catalogue, List of Commitments, at: www.climate-catalogue.org/index.php?id=6870

[12] Hari M. Osofsky, 'Multiscalar Governance and Climate Change: Reflections on the Role of States and Cities at Copenhagen', *Maryland Journal of International Law*, 25 (2010), 64.

[13] See *ibid.*; Hari M. Osofsky, 'Climate Change and Environmental Justice: Reflections on Litigation over Oil Extraction and Rights Violations in Nigeria', *Journal of Human Rights and the Environment*, 1 (2010), 189; Hari M. Osofsky, 'The Geography of Climate Change Litigation Part II: Narratives of *Massachusetts* v. *EPA*', *Chicago Journal of International Law*,

Section 4 narrows from this broader comparison to draw from perspectives in the new governance[14] and global legal pluralism[15] literatures and to consider a model for international law creation that might be more inclusive. It examines how these sub-state negotiations might be accorded more significance both in the formal process of the UNFCCC and in other complementary fora. It explores the benefits and limitations of more inclusive approaches and their implications for how we might conceptualize international law creation more broadly.

2 Formal and informal international legal commitments on climate change

At first blush, climate change presents a relatively straightforward model for international law creation, which fits a traditional international law narrative. A large number of nation-states, including major emitters and countries at greatest risk from impacts, created a framework convention to address this problem in 1992.[16] They have met regularly since in conferences of the parties (COP), and many of the major developed country emitters – with the significant omissions of the United States

8 (2008), 573; Hari M. Osofsky, 'The Geography of Justice Wormholes: Dilemmas from Property and Criminal Law', *Villanova Law Review*, 53 (2008), 117.

14 For examples of the new governance literature, see Gráinne de Búrca and Joanne Scott (eds.), *Law and New Governance in the EU and US* (Portland, OR: Hart, 2006); Bradley C. Karkkainen, '"New Governance" in Legal Thought and in the World: Some Splitting as Antidote to Overzealous Lumping', *Minnesota Law Review*, 89 (2004), 471; Orly Lobel, 'Setting the Agenda for New Governance Research', *Minnesota Law Review*, 89 (2004), 498 and 'The Renew Deal: The Fall of Regulation and the Rise of Governance in Contemporary Legal Thought', *Minnesota Law Review*, 89 (2004), 342; J. B. Ruhl and James E. Salzman, 'Climate Change, Dead Zones, and Massive Problems in the Administrative State: A Guide for Whittling Away', *California Law Review*, 98 (2010), 59.

15 For examples of the global legal pluralism literature, see Robert B. Ahdieh, 'Dialectical Regulation', *Connecticut Law Review*, 38 (2006), 863; Diane Marie Amann, 'Abu Graib', *University of Pennsylvania Law Review*, 153 (2005), 2085; Diane Marie Amann, 'Calling Children to Account: The Proposal for a Juvenile Chamber in the Special Court for Sierra Leone', *Pepperdine Law Review*, 29 (2001), 167; Elena A. Baylis, 'Parallel Courts in Post-Conflict Kosovo', *Yale Journal of International Law*, 32 (2007), 1; Paul Schiff Berman, 'Global Legal Pluralism', *Southern California Law Review*, 80 (2007), 1155; William W. Burke-White, 'International Legal Pluralism', *Michigan Journal of International Law*, 25 (2004), 963; Janet Koven Levit, 'A Bottom-up Approach to International Law Making: The Tale of Three Trade Finance Instruments', *Yale Journal of International Law*, 30 (2005), 125; Ralf Michaels, 'The Re-State-Ment of Non-State Law: The State, Choice of Law, and the Challenge from Global Legal Pluralism', *Wayne Law Review*, 51 (2005), 1209.

16 See UNFCCC.

and initially Australia – agreed to more specific targets and timetables under the Kyoto Protocol five years later.[17] Moreover, since President Obama has replaced President Bush at the helm in the United States, that major emitter has been playing a significant role in negotiating the regime that will follow the expiration of the first Kyoto Protocol commitment period in 2012, including a lead role by the president in the compromise that undergirded the Copenhagen Accord and constructive participation by the US delegation in the subsequent Cancún and Durban negotiations.[18]

As noted in the introduction, the issues that such a narrative of international law creation pose are two-fold, which this section explores. First, and least problematically for a traditional account, the existing regime and negotiations are struggling to achieve their goals.[19] Many nation-states are having difficulties meeting their Kyoto Protocol commitments, and those commitments do not go as far as scientific consensus suggests is needed to prevent the most severe risks of climate change.[20] Moreover, the United States, Canada, Japan, and Russia were not among the thirty-five countries committing to this period, the United States never committed to the first one, and the potential 2015 universal agreement will not result in the reductions needed now.[21]

The Copenhagen Accord and commitments under it exemplify this difficulty. The Accord has limited and somewhat ambiguous binding obligations contained within it, and the parties noted it rather than

[17] See Kyoto Protocol.

[18] See above nn. 3, 7, and 9 and accompanying text.

[19] I have explored these failures in my prior scholarship. See, e.g., Hari M. Osofsky, 'Is Climate Change "International"?: Litigation's Diagonal Regulatory Role', *Virginia Journal of International Law*, 49 (2009), 585.

[20] For analyses of Kyoto Protocol compliance, including issues facing particular countries, see David Freestone and Charlotte Streck (eds.), *Legal Aspects of Implementing the Kyoto Protocol Mechanisms: Making Kyoto Work* (Oxford and New York: Oxford University Press, 2005); Anna Korppoo *et al.* (eds.), *Russia and the Kyoto Protocol: Opportunities and Challenges* (London: Chatham House, 2006); Alastair R. Lucas, 'Mythology, Fantasy and Federalism: Canadian Climate Change Policy and Law', *Pacific McGeorge Global Business and Development Law Journal*, 20 (2007), 41, at 52–6; Mindy G. Nigoff, 'The Clean Development Mechanism: Does the Current Structure Facilitate Kyoto Protocol Compliance?', *Georgetown International Environmental Law Review*, 18 (2006), 249. For an analysis of the ways in which the Copenhagen Accord commitments are insufficient to bring the reductions that scientists say are needed, see Levin and Bradley, 'Comparability of Pledges'.

[21] See Further Kyoto Commitments. For an analysis of the gap in addressing emissions as of the Durban COP, see United Nations Environment Programme, Bridging the Emissions Gap: A UNEP Synthesis Report (Nov. 2011), at: wwwunep.org/pdf/UNEP_briding_gap_pdf

adopting it at the meeting.[22] Although many nations did make submissions pursuant to it at the end of January 2010, those commitments largely were contingent on other nations acting.[23] The United States added the further contingency of the US Congress passing climate change legislation, which is looking extremely unlikely in the short term.[24] The end result – as Sumudu Atapattu also analyzes in the context of her chapter's discussion of hard law and soft law[25] – is many key countries failing to commit themselves in significant ways at the national level, a state of affairs that the limited Cancún Agreements and the subsequent agreement to make a universal agreement at Durban did not fundamentally change.[26]

These difficulties do not necessarily suggest the need for innovative theorizing about international law creation. A Westphalian[27] narrative of international law creation, in which international law arises from the consent of sovereign and equal nation-states, would likely acknowledge the regime as creating limited international legal obligations and assess it as not entirely successful in achieving its goals.[28] But the substantive problem of addressing climate change effectively through international law would remain. A core question that this chapter asks is whether current international legal efforts should focus primarily on achieving better agreements in negotiations among nation-state parties, or whether more inclusive conceptions of international law creation which shift that focus somewhat might actually serve as a tool in solving this problem.

[22] See *ibid.*

[23] See United Nations Framework Convention on Climate Change, Information Provided by Parties to the Convention Relating to the Accord, at: http://unfccc.int/home/items/5262.php

[24] See *ibid.* Even before the mid-term elections changed the political balance in the US Congress, the Democrats conceded defeat on comprehensive climate change legislation. See Carl Hulse and David M. Herzenhorn, 'Democrats call off Climate Bill effort', *New York Times*, July 23, 2010, A15.

[25] See Chapter 10, in this volume.

[26] See Romano and Burleson, 'Cancún Climate Conference'.

[27] By Westphalian, I mean guided by the core notions of nation-states as primary subjects and objects of international law and of international law being created through the consent of sovereign and equal nation-states. For expositions of Westphalian understandings of international law, see Brownlie, *Principles*, 287–8; Michael J. Kelly, 'Pulling at the Threads of Westphalia: "Involuntary Sovereignty Waiver" – Revolutionary International Legal Theory or Return to Rule by the Great Powers', *University of California, Los Angeles Journal of International Law and Foreign Affairs*, 10 (2005), 361, 383.

[28] See section 3 below.

Second, and more fundamentally, there is a great deal of activity with legal significance on climate change outside of the UNFCCC structure. Some of this activity includes a wide range of additional formal international legal agreements among nation-states which should be included for completeness in even a traditional account of international law creation.[29] For example, the Montreal Protocol's[30] efforts to address ozone impact greenhouse gas emissions significantly.[31] In addition, and less acknowledged in most of the commentary on the UNFCCC, nations have crafted many bilateral and multilateral agreements (with fewer parties) on relevant issues such as alternative/renewable energy.[32] These agreements arguably should also be included in almost any account of the creation of international law relevant to climate change.

The conceptual conundrum comes not from these additional formal agreements among nation-states, but from the many other agreements among nation-states which are less formally binding and among a wider range of governmental and nongovernmental entities. Specifically, this chapter focuses on the example of transnational agreements among subnational governments, something that would not even qualify as the soft law between nation-states that is the focus of Atapattu's analysis.[33] It considers, in particular, the agreements reached among cities, states, and provinces at Copenhagen in December 2009 because they include subnational governments from nation-states which were having difficulty reaching agreement and the pledges within them represented massive quantities of emissions reductions.[34]

[29] I have discussed some of this activity in Hari M. Osofsky, 'Diagonal Federalism and Climate Change: Implications for the Obama Administration', *Alabama Law Review*, 62 (2011), 237.

[30] Montreal Protocol on Substances that Deplete the Ozone Layer, Article 5, Montreal, September 16, 1987, in force January 1, 1989, 1522 UNTS 3, 26 ILM 1550 (1987).

[31] For an analysis of the relationship between the Montreal Protocol and climate change and a proposal for the future, see Mark W. Roberts and Peter M. Grabiel, 'A Window of Opportunity: Combating Climate Change by Amending the Montreal Protocol to Regulate the Production and Consumption of HFCs and ODS Banks', *Georgetown International Environmental Law Review*, 22 (2009), 99.

[32] See, e.g., press release, 'US–Mexico announce bilateral framework on clean energy and climate change', at: www.whitehouse.gov/the_press_office/US-Mexico-Announce-Bilateral-Framework-on-Clean-Energy-and-Climate-Change; International Council on Clean Transportation, 'Athens Resolution' (2010), at: www.theicct.org/documents/0000/1220/Athen_ICCT_2009-2.pdf; White House, Office of the Press Secretary, 'US–China energy announcements' (November 17, 2009), at: www.whitehouse.gov/the-press-office/us-china-clean-energy-announcements

[33] See Chapter 10, in this volume.

[34] I have previously analyzed these agreements and dilemmas that they pose for international lawmaking in Osofsky, 'Multiscalar Governance'.

Subnational governmental leaders made a variety of commitments while the nation-states were meeting separately during the Copenhagen COP. More than fifty mayors from a wide range of nation-states, as well as some governors, signed the Copenhagen Climate Communiqué. This document illustrates the significant steps taken at a local level on climate change and calls for nation-state action.[35] In addition, at the time of the conference, local government leaders from 59 countries registered 3,232 targets in the Copenhagen City Climate Catalogue, a transnational effort to compile local targets and achievements.[36] At a somewhat larger scale, leaders from states and provinces within Algeria, Canada, France, Nigeria, and the United States held a joint press conference to announce the planned launch of a Club of 20 Regions (R20) in September 2010, an arrangement which builds upon the October 2009 Governors' Climate Summit and the Global Climate Solutions Declaration signed there.[37] At more recent COPs, this trend continued, with local leaders signing the 2010 Mexico Pact and Durban Adaptation Charter for Local Government.[38] Localities have also taken action through the World Mayors Council on Climate Change and the carbon*n* Cities Climate Registry.[39]

These actions have no formal international legal significance under traditional notions of international law. They are formed among subnational actors who, as a matter of international law, are not subjects and objects of international law and could rescind their commitments at any time. The commitments themselves involve subnational, not international, legal action. Moreover, under the Statute of the International Court of Justice, they would not serve as sources of international law. They are not treaties, and are unlikely to be treated as evidence of nation-states' customary international law obligations or of the general legal principles that they recognize.[40]

However, these agreements have great potential significance for UNFCCC nation-state parties achieving the goals laid out in that

[35] Copenhagen Climate Summit for Mayors, 'Copenhagen Climate Communiqué'.

[36] City Climate Catalogue, 'List of Commitments'.

[37] See R20 press release.

[38] Mexico City Pact, Signatories, at: www.mexicocitypact.org/en/the-mexico-city-pact-2/list-of-cities; Durban Adaptation Charter for Local Governments, at: www.iclei.org/fileadmin/user_upload/documents/Global/initiatives/LG_roadmap

[39] World Mayors Council on Climate Change, Members' List, at: www.worldmayorscouncil.org/members/members-list.html; carbon*n* Cities Climate Registry, Reporting Cities, at http://citiesclimateregistry.org/cities/reporting-cities

[40] Statute of the International Court of Justice, Art. 38, June 26, 1945, 59 Stat. 1055.

convention and agreements under it. For example, the Communiqué notes that signatory cities together include more than half of the world's population and that up to 75 percent of global greenhouse gas emissions originate from urban areas.[41] Governor Schwarzenegger's press release announcing the formation of the R20 includes estimates by the United Nations Development Programme that the subnational level will provide up to 80 percent of the pollution reduction policies needed to meet a new international commitment.[42] These statements take place in the context of broader transnational efforts among mayors; as of August 2011, 2,854 European cities have signed the Covenant of Mayors, with targets that surpass the European Union's 2020 goals,[43] and 1,054 US mayors have committed to meeting or exceeding Kyoto Protocol targets and timetables.[44]

As with the first problem of insufficient formal international law, this second issue could be understood through a traditional, Westphalian approach to the creation of international law. These subnational agreements do not need formal international legal significance to help supplement the international legal efforts by nation-states under the UNFCCC. The subnational efforts can be treated as part of the nation-state meeting its commitments. However, such an understanding captures the transnational aspects of the subnational activities in a rather limited fashion. The transnational agreements are legally insignificant, and the coalitions only matter to international lawmaking to the extent that they influence nation-states' behavior in the UNFCCC meetings or help them to meet their commitments.[45] Section 3 asks whether such a limited understanding is appropriate by exploring the ways in which different conceptual approaches to the geography of the nation-state might alter this account.

3 The geography of the nation-state and international climate change law creation

In my prior work, I explored how different theoretical approaches – Westphalian, modified Westphalian, pluralist, and critical – might view the international legal significance of subnational agreements at

[41] See Copenhagen Climate Summit for Mayors, 'Copenhagen Climate Communiqué'.
[42] See R20 press release.
[43] European Commission Energy, Covenant of Mayors, at: www.eumayors.eu/index_en.html
[44] United States Conference of Mayors, Mayors Climate Protections Center – Mayors Leading the Way on Climate Protection, at: www.usmayors.org/climateprotection/revised
[45] See n. 6 and accompanying text above.

Copenhagen and might approach more inclusive strategies to international lawmaking on climate change. These four approaches differ significantly from one another in the extent to which they would be open to a broader conception of international lawmaking and how they would frame more inclusive strategies. I argued that whether one chooses one of these conceptual approaches or tries somehow to combine them, exploring all of them helps to create a richer dialogue about subnational participation in climate governance.[46]

This section builds upon that work by engaging the way in which one's conceptual approach to the geography of the nation-state influences that narrative. Specifically, in my law and geography work on other topics, I have developed three potential models of the nation-state – enclosed, permeable, and enmeshed – and considered how choosing among them influences possibilities for greater justice.[47] This part interweaves these three models of the nation-state with the four conceptual approaches to international legal theory in order to analyze the issues raised in section 2; it explores how a more open and interconnected conception of nation-state geography might change the traditional account of the current failures in the negotiations and of the efforts of subnational entities. This section analyzes how one's perspective on the openness of the nation-state influences one's understanding of the problems articulated in section 2, and demonstrates how that perspective enters into four of the primary categories of international legal theory and their views of international law creation in the context of climate change.

One's geographic understanding of the nation-state foundationally shapes one's narrative of international law creation. Treating the nation-state as an enclosed space, as stricter Westphalian accounts tend to, means viewing it as a singular entity with clearly delineated boundaries and viewing its internal workings as generally irrelevant to its international law commitments. Such a view of the nation-state is generally intertwined with a strong belief in the notion of sovereign equality. International law recognizes that, with very limited exceptions, states are sovereign over the space within them, which is treated as domestic and only relevant to international law as part of the national entity. States can protect themselves against intrusions upon that

46 Osofsky, 'Multiscalar Governance'.

47 Osofsky, 'Geography of Justice Wormholes' and 'Climate Change and Environmental Justice'.

enclosed space and generally can choose when to enter into consensual agreements with other states to abide by treaties and establish customary international law norms.[48] As described in section 2, under such an account, the limitations of the UNFCCC process and other climate change agreements among nation-states are an unfortunate example of international law not yet fully addressing the problem. The non-nation-state agreements only have potential international legal relevance if they influence the behavior of states.[49]

But what if that portrayal of nation-state geography is inaccurate and incomplete? A number of scholars in different fields have grappled with this question. For the purposes of this section, I focus on two such accounts, each of which challenges this narrative in different ways.[50] Judith Resnik, a legal scholar, has argued that international legal norms move across sovereign borders continuously and become part of internal, domestic understandings whether or not they are formally accepted. She claims that battles over the use of international law in domestic courts, for example, miss the fact that international norms enter domestic decisions regardless of whether the international law is formally accepted as part of them.[51] Julie Cidell, a geographer, has focused on the role of the individual in the creation of scale. Her work demonstrates that our delineation into scalar levels – international, national, state, local, community, individual – should take into account that the individual is not simply the smallest level, but a part of every level.[52]

Bringing together these two insights provides the basis for what I have termed a permeable model of the nation-state. The basic account of what formally constitutes international law creation does not change, but the view of the nation-state within it does. The nation-state becomes a less monolithic entity, as international legal norms flow in and out of its borders and individuals (and other entities) within it shape its course.[53] This change in viewpoint has significant implications for the narrative of international law creation generally and in the context of climate change in particular. The formal moment of international law creation becomes

[48] See sources in n. 27 above. [49] See section 2 above.

[50] I have explored these accounts in my previous work on nation-state spaces. See Osofsky, 'Geography of Justice Wormholes' and 'Climate Change and Environmental Justice'.

[51] Judith Resnik, 'Law's Migration: American Exceptionalism, Silent Dialogues, and Federalism's Multiple Ports of Entry', *Yale Law Journal*, 115 (2006), 1564, 1627–33.

[52] Julie Cidell, 'The Place of Individuals in the Politics of Scale' (2006) 38 *Area* 196, 202.

[53] See Osofsky, 'Geography of Justice Wormholes''.

less central as one describes the myriad of interactions and of norm evolution that precedes it and influences its implementation.

Once one recognizes the nation-state as permeable, however, further questions arise about the traditional model of international law creation. Namely, if the nation-state is constituted by individuals and entities and has borders that can be informally permeated, does the formal story also need to be changed? Should a view of the nation-state as fully enmeshed with and constituted by a wide range of actors and entities in multiple arenas change the way in which international law is created? In response to questions such as these, scholarship on global legal pluralism, which has an intellectual debt to the New Haven School, and on new governance (among other potentially relevant literatures) begins to rethink the formal story.[54] Section 4 focuses on these approaches in more depth, but for current purposes, the key point is that this scholarship decenters the nation-state and allows for a broader conception of what might constitute law. It provides the basis for a narrative of international law creation in which the UNFCCC negotiations might be approached more inclusively and in which agreements by subnational governments might be integrated more with treaties among nation-states.

This trio of perspectives of nation-state geography maps well onto categories of legal theory. I have argued in my prior work that the spectrum from strict Westphalian, to modified Westphalian, to pluralist, to critical (which does not fit quite as neatly as the other three, as described below) represents a movement towards a gradually less enclosed view of the nation-state and towards more questioning of its legitimacy. Strict Westphalians have an enclosed view of the nation-state,

[54] For examples of global legal pluralism, New Haven School, and new governance scholarship, see above nn. 14–15 and accompanying text. I first developed this enmeshed model of the nation-state in Osofsky, 'Geography of Justice Wormholes'. Other strands of international legal theory, such as regulatory institutions theory, also grapple with the mix of formal and informal law and actors. For examples of scholarship from the Regulatory Institutions Network at Australia National University, see: Valerie Braithwaite, 'Ten Things You Need to Know about Regulation and Never Wanted to Ask', RegNet Occasional Paper No. 10 (2006), available at: http://ctsi.anu.edu.au/publications/occasionalpapers.htm; Charlotte Wood, Mary Ivec, Jenny Job, and Valerie Braithwaite, 'Applications of Response Regulatory Theory in Australia and Overseas', RegNet Occasional Paper No. 15 (2010), available at: http://ctsi.anu.edu.au/publications/occasionalpapers.htm. Integrating the wide range of potentially relevant theories is beyond the scope of this chapter, but I explore the possibilities for creating a more comprehensive theory by integrating additional strands in Hari M. Osofsky, 'The BP *Deepwater Horizon* Oil Spill and Multidimensional Governance', *Florida Law Review*, 63 (2011), 1077.

which supports a focus on formal international law creation by nation-states. Modified Westphalians have a more permeable view of the nation-state, in which the formal international law story does not change but more interactions among a broader range of entities are incorporated into that story. Pluralists, as discussed above, take an enmeshed view of the nation-state and, as a result, decenter it, focusing on a more inclusive conception of international lawmaking in which formal agreements among nation-states form only part of that lawmaking. Finally, critical legal scholars question the legitimacy of the entire international legal system – which could be viewed as the final move away from the enclosed nation-state – but may view the current system as having enclosed, permeable, or enmeshed nation-states.[55]

As I have noted in this work, such categorization of scholarship becomes messy at the boundaries. The distinction between modified Westphalians and pluralists, in particular, is often particularly difficult to make because once one begins opening up the nation-state and decentering it somewhat, the fullness of the decentering is sometimes unclear and may depend on circumstance. In addition, some theories may have elements of more than one category.[56] This complexity of categorization applies to the three basic categories of nation-state enclosure articulated above as well. If one recognizes the nation-state as at least somewhat permeable, the distinction between that permeability and full enmeshment may be hard to pinpoint. But this messiness does not diminish the central point, which is that the geography of the nation-state – especially its level of enclosure – impacts how one should conceptually approach dilemmas of international law creation. These conceptual differences translate into normative and practical possibilities for progress on climate change, which section 4 explores.

4 Possibilities for pluralist and new governance approaches

This section brings together pluralist and new governance approaches to sketch the beginning of an alternative model for international law creation in the context of climate change which I plan to explore in more depth in future work.[57] Legal pluralism's enmeshed view of nation-state

[55] See Osofsky, 'Geography of Climate Change Litigation Part II'. [56] See *ibid.*

[57] That work will also integrate additional intellectual streams beyond new governance and global legal pluralism, as I have begun to do in the context of the BP *Deepwater Horizon* oil spill. See Osofsky, 'BP *Deepwater Horizon* Oil Spill'.

geography allows for the possibility of considering subnational agreements as international law-creating acts in a more direct way than a strict Westphalian model would. New governance approaches provide an ideal complement for pluralism's decentering because they engage how one might structure more inclusive governance structures. Together, they can assist in crafting a dual approach to rethinking climate change governance which is the focus of this section: (a) making the UNFCCC and other treaty-making process more inclusive of non-nation-state actors, such as subnational governments; and (b) including subnational climate change agreements as part of the international lawmaking on climate change.

This section begins by providing a fuller conceptualization of pluralist and new governance approaches to international law creation. It then analyzes how they potentially provide alternative solutions to the problem raised in section 2 of addressing climate change effectively and holistically. In the process of this analysis, the section raises core questions that need to be addressed in crafting such alternative approaches.

Global legal pluralism emerges from several conceptual approaches which have a shared notion that international lawmaking involves more actors and more arenas than the traditional strict Westphalian account. Although I do not have the space in the chapter to trace all of these conceptual approaches in depth, I would like to highlight two that are particularly relevant in this context. First, to the extent that global legal pluralism is a subset of legal pluralism more broadly, legal pluralism views lawmaking as being constituted by multiple normative communities which have shared social and legal space.[58] When this notion is applied at a larger, global scale, as a number of leading scholars have recently done in different variations, a picture emerges of law creation through a range of simultaneous formal and informal processes among stakeholders.[59]

Second, although many scholars analyzing global legal pluralism would not necessarily identify themselves as part of the New Haven

[58] See Robert M. Cover, 'The Supreme Court 1982 Term Foreword: Nomos and Narrative', *Harvard Law Review*, 97(4) (1983), 4; Ambreena Manji, '"Like a Mask Dancing"': Law and Colonialism in Chinua Achebe's Arrow of God', *Journal of Law and Society*, 27 (2000), 626; Emmanuel Melissaris, 'The More the Merrier? A New Take on Legal Pluralism', *Social and Legal Studies*, 13 (2004), 57; Sally Engle Merry, 'Legal Pluralism', *Law and Society Review*, 22 (1988), 869; Dalia Tsuk, 'The New Deal Origins of American Legal Pluralism', *Florida State University Law Review*, 29 (2001), 189.

[59] See sources in n. 15 above.

School, the ideas of these two partially overlapping groups have significant synergies and global legal pluralism scholars at times acknowledge an intellectual debt to the New Haven School.[60] The New Haven School treats law as authoritative decisionmaking through which community members clarify and secure their interests in multiple arenas. In so doing, New Haven School accounts of international law creation focus not only on the formal processes among nation-states, but also on a wide range of other interactions that have those elements of authoritative decisionmaking.[61]

As I have analyzed previously in the context of climate change litigation, pluralist accounts of international law do not necessarily have to change the formal story. One could acknowledge agreements among states as the formal core of international law creation, but then engage the many other interactions taking place as also an important part of the international lawmaking story. However, pluralism's decentering of the nation-state shifts the focal point of discussion about how to achieve more effective transnational and international action on climate change. Instead of having a primary focus on the nuances of the UNFCCC process, as a large portion of the international law dialogue on climate change still does, it views the agreements – or lack thereof – among nation-states as only one important piece of a broader international lawmaking process.[62] Such a shift opens the possibility for the agreements among cities, states, and provinces to be treated as part of international lawmaking on climate change and for a more holistic narrative that includes both these and other steps by a wide range of actors as needed to make international-level progress on climate change.

60 See, e.g., Paul Schiff Berman, 'A Pluralist Approach to International Law', *Yale Journal of International Law*, 32 (2007), 301, at 301–2.

61 For examples of the New Haven School approach, see: Harold D. Lasswell and Myres S. McDougal, *Jurisprudence for a Free Society: Studies in Law, Science and Policy* (New Haven, CT: New Haven Press, 1992), xxi; Richard A. Falk, 'Casting the Spell: The New Haven School of International Law', *Yale Law Journal*, 104 (1995), 1991; Myres S. McDougal and Harold D. Lasswell, 'The Identification and Appraisal of Diverse Systems of Public Order', *American Journal of International Law*, 53 (1959), 1; Myres S. McDougal *et al.*, 'The World Constitutive Process of Authoritative Decisions', *Journal of Legal Education*, 19 (1967), 253; W. Michael Reisman, 'International Lawmaking: A Process of Communication', *American Society of International Law Proceedings*, 75 (1981), 101.

62 See Hari M. Osofsky, 'Climate Change Litigation as Pluralist Legal Dialogue?', *Stanford Environmental Law Journal*, 26 (2007) and 43 *Stanford Journal of International Law*, 181.

New governance approaches provide an important complement to global legal pluralism in this context. These law and policymaking approaches focus on creating innovative partnerships among a range of state and non-state actors, which are often voluntary, to accomplish regulatory goals. They represent a movement away from "old governance," which, according to Professors Kenneth Abbott and Duncan Snidal, is governance that is state-centric, centralized, reliant on bureaucratic expertise, and focused on mandatory rules. In contrast, they characterize new governance as state orchestrated, decentralized, reliant on dispersed expertise, and more inclusive of soft law.[63]

In the transnational environmental context, in particular, scholars have used new governance to propose creative, inclusive institutional arrangements. For example, in the US Great Lakes management context, Professor Brad Karkkainen has argued:

> We need better interagency and intergovernmental coordination along both horizontal (federal–federal, state–state–provincial, local–local) and vertical (federal–state/provincial–local) dimensions. We need to identify and fill the gaps, and at the same time eliminate the redundancies among mission-specific agencies and sometimes among narrow-gauged programs even with a single agency. And finally, we need institutions that are more nimble, flexible, and adaptive, capable of generating and rapidly assimilating new learning and adjusting course in response to that learning and changing conditions. In short, we need an institutional architecture better suited to integrated and adaptive ecosystem management.[64]

New governance approaches cross-cut traditional orderings and power structures and, in so doing, design and maintain an institutional flexibility which might allow for greater incorporation of subnational activity on climate change.

Like with global legal pluralism, employing new governance approaches does not have to result in a different understanding of formal international law creation. One could accept the strictures of formal international law, and also propose complementary structures which would not be recognized as international law. However, rethinking institutional design in these ways also allows for the possibility of reconstituting formal institutions to allow for more holistic, inclusive approaches to problem-solving.

[63] Kenneth W. Abbott and Duncan Snidal, 'Strengthening International Regulation Through Transnational New Governance', *Vanderbilt Journal of Transnational Law*, 42 (2009), 501.

[64] Bradley C. Karkkainen, '"New Governance" in the Great Lakes Basin: Has Its Time Arrived?', *Michigan State Law Review* (2006) 1249, at 1254–5.

Together, these theories open the door for nontraditional answers, which might be more effective, to the dilemmas proposed in section 2. Regarding the inadequacy of the UNFCCC processes in achieving reductions at the rate scientists say are needed, gaining further nation-state support for more serious mitigation and adaptation plans may not simply be a matter of better proposed agreements and COP-negotiating strategies. Rather, a more inclusive UNFCCC process might put additional pressure on the nation-states and on other actors, such as subnational governments, which control a lot of emissions. If subnational governments were included more directly in negotiations, (a) they might convince nation-states of the possibility of achieving greater reductions and (b) commitments by nation-states based explicitly on subnational commitments would make those cities, states, and provinces more legally accountable.[65]

Crafting such structures would face many obstacles. Since the UNFCCC negotiations take place under a treaty signed by nation-states, those nation-states would have to agree to establish such a process for subnational coalitions to become a formal part of the negotiations beyond their current observer status.[66] If the nation-states do not do so, such a process could at most be a complementary side process, which might not have enough weight to accomplish the kind of integrated dialogue and agreements described above. In the scenario in which such a structure is informal, careful structuring would be needed to give it more direct impact on the UNFCCC negotiations than the current side forums do.[67]

Practical considerations would also be daunting. Who should decide who is included and excluded, and how should those decisions be made?[68]

[65] Subnational governments are not all leaders. As I have discussed in my previous work, some of them push against larger-scale efforts to address climate change. See Osofsky, 'Is Climate Change "International"?' and 'Diagonal Federalism and Climate Change'. However, at this stage in the climate change negotiations, the leader cities, states, and provinces are the primary ones meeting and forming agreements to try to supplement international negotiations and there are no signs of subnational governments that oppose more stringent regulation organizing in a similar fashion at an international level. A more comprehensive exploration of including subnational entities in international negotiations more directly would need to engage this divide in more depth and how that divide would be expressed in a representative inclusion of subnational voices.

[66] See UNFCCC. [67] See *ibid.*

[68] Erin Ryan has explored these interesting meta-questions of "who should decide who should decide" in her recent federalism work; see 'Negotiating Federalism', *Boston College Law Review*, 51 (2011), 1.

In those decisions around inclusion, how can representation be simultaneously manageable and comprehensive and avoid both democratic deficit problems and accompanying difficulties of over- and under-representation?[69] To what extent does this valuation of these smaller scale voices hinge on the presumption that they are pro-regulatory and how should our model address the possibility that fair representation likely would include anti-regulatory voices as well?[70] Who would be bound, formally or informally, and through what mechanisms? In a process centered around the governmental entities at different levels that are the focus of this piece, would nation-states and subnational governments have the same status? Should we consider such a multi-government agreement to be international law because of the agreements among nation-states or not to be international law because of its inclusion of non-nation-state actors or partially to be international law and partially not because of its hybrid status?[71] However, these difficulties may be worth wading through, to explore the potential that pluralist and new governance approaches have to produce more effective commitments on climate change from key actors, especially given the urgency of the problem and limited successes emerging from nation-state negotiations.

Similarly, these pluralist and new governance approaches would be more open to according some sort of international legal status to the subnational agreements that took place at Copenhagen, Cancún, and Durban. Like with the example of the negotiations, that acknowledgment of legal status might not take the form of adding to what would count as formal international law. Rather, these approaches could also have value in their treatment of both the formal and informal as part of the overall process of international lawmaking. Such treatment would address the problem raised in section 2 of the formal negotiations among nation-states having minimal space for meaningful acknowledgement or incorporation of subnational agreements.

[69] Assuming there is a fair approach to representation, the democratic deficit problem should not be more severe than in a nation-state context since the subnational governments, like national ones, are sovereign representatives of the people (though like at a national level, democratic deficit may be a problem due to not very democratic forms of government).

[70] See above n. 63.

[71] For an exploration of some of these issues, see Abbott and Snidal, 'Strengthening International Regulation'.

This acknowledgement is a different and complementary solution to changing the negotiations themselves, and may be easier to achieve than an inclusive process under the treaty system itself. Treating transnational agreements among subnational governmental entities as a more meaningful part of the creation of the international law of climate change – even if that part is not a formal one – opens up space for the mutual pressure on both nation-states and subnational entities described above. The subnational agreements, if considered in the national negotiations more directly, might both put more pressure on the nation-states and reinforce to them the plausibility of further commitments. In turn, the national agreements, if explicitly relying upon those subnational agreements, might make them more binding upon those subnational entities as a matter of national law.

As in the context of changing the treaty-negotiating process, such an approach to the subnational agreements raises questions that lack straightforward solutions. What does it mean to take those agreements more seriously as a practical matter? How would this approach differ from allowing side programs to take place at the time of the main meeting and including language about national governments in the agreements among nation-states? To what extent do the extensive informal ties between subnational and national governments already accomplish this dynamic and, if this dynamic already exists, why is it not creating more forward motion in the negotiations? Is there any way to make transnational agreements among subnational entities binding at an international level or would doing so simply require too much reconceptualization of international law? What exactly, as a legal matter, is being created through these processes if they are not treated as formal international law? Like with the context of reconfiguring treaty negotiations, addressing these and other practical questions is critical for developing meaningful alternative approaches.

Although pluralist and new governance approaches require creative reconceptualization and careful crafting, such an effort is worthwhile. The current reliance on traditional Westphalian notions of international law is not solving the problem of climate change quickly enough. Perhaps alternative approaches would not either. But given the urgency of the problem, some conceptual blockbusting is needed. In the context of international law creation in particular, an openness to more inclusive approaches puts more possibilities on the table. These possibilities may not solve the problem of climate change, but they increase the hope of doing so.

5 Concluding reflections

This chapter aims to contribute to the scholarly dialogue regarding both international legal theory and climate change policy by modeling how a law and geography analysis of international law creation can allow for a reconceptualization of current strategies. Certainly, a law and geography approach is not a prerequisite for innovative international legal theory; for example, the emerging body of global legal pluralism and new governance scholarship makes a significant contribution, and generally does so without explicit reference to the discipline of geography.[72] But thinking geographically helps to delineate more clearly the differences among the various perspectives on international law creation, and in particular, the ways in which their view of the nation-state shapes the legal and institutional possibilities for progress.

Climate change will pose a daunting governance challenge regardless of one's perspective on international law creation. However, exploring approaches, such as global legal pluralism and new governance, which rely upon an enmeshed view of nation-state geography allows for creative policy-making that the current process, grounded in Westphalian strictures, does not permit. Such creativity is critical in the face of the potential risks we face if our solutions to climate change continue to fall short.

[72] For examples of this work, see above nn. 14–15, 61, and 63–4. I have previously explored how drawing explicitly from the discipline of geography could contribute to New Haven School scholarship. Hari M. Osofsky, 'A Law and Geography Perspective on the New Haven School', *Yale Journal of International Law*, 32 (2007), 421.

10

International environmental law and soft law: a new direction or a contradiction?

SUMUDU ATAPATTU

1 Introduction

One of the features of modern international law is the remarkable development of the law governing the environment in recent years. From a very modest start with virtually no law at law, international environmental law has grown into a very sophisticated field encompassing many treaties, some general principles, and a few customary international law rules. It is no secret that this remarkable development is due, to a considerable extent, to the contribution made by soft law[1] instruments. The journey that started with the Stockholm Declaration on the Human Environment in 1972[2] culminated in the adoption of the Johannesburg

The original version of this chapter was prepared for the conference Creation of International Law: An Exploration of Normative Innovation, Contextual Application and Interpretation in a time of Flux, organized by University of Oslo, Faculty of Law, August 6–7, 2010. Revised for publication.

[1] There is a considerable amount of literature on soft law. See generally: John J. Kirton and Michael J. Trebilcock (eds.), *Hard Choices, Soft Law: Voluntary Standards in Global Trade, Environment and Social Governance* (Farnham: Ashgate, 2004); Prosper Weil, 'Towards Relative Normativity in International Law?', *American International Law Journal*, 77 (1983), 413; Hartmut Hillgenberg, 'A Fresh Look at Soft Law', *European Journal of International Law*, 10 (1999), 499; Mark Drumbl, 'Actors and Law-making in International Environmental Law', Washington and Lee Public Legal Studies Research Paper Series, available online at: http://ssrn.com/abstract=1022363; Kal Raustiala, 'Form and Substance in International Agreements', *American Journal of International Law*, 99 (2005), 581; Jon Birger Skjærseth, Olav Schram Stokke, and Jorgen Wettestad, 'Soft Law, Hard Law, and Effective Implementation of International Environmental Norms', *Global Environmental Politics*, 6(3) (August 2006), 104–20; Andrew T. Guzman and Timothy L. Meyer, 'International Soft Law', *Journal of Legal Analysis*, 2 (2010), 171; Pierre-Marie Dupuy, 'Soft Law and the International Law of the Environment', *Michigan Journal of International Law*, 12 (1991), 420.

[2] (1972)11 ILM 1416.

Declaration on Sustainable Development[3] in 2002. During a rather short span of thirty years, the development of international environmental law can be described as "phenomenal." The instrument that laid the foundation for this development is the non-binding Stockholm Declaration on the Human Environment adopted by the international community in 1972.

Article 38(1) of the ICJ statute, considered as embodying the sources of international law, recognizes treaties, customary international law, and general principles of law as main sources while writings of jurists and court decisions are considered as subsidiary sources. This list does not contain any reference to resolutions of international organizations, declarations of international conferences, voluntary codes of conduct, and similar instruments that have played an important role in developing law in many areas, particularly, international environmental law and international human rights law. What does this development mean? Are they a separate source of international law or do they facilitate the development of international law through the traditional means?

This chapter seeks to discuss the seminal role played by soft law instruments in the field of international environmental law through the lens of three soft law instruments that have played a significant role in this field: the Stockholm Declaration on the Human Environment (1972); the Rio Declaration on Environment and Development (1992); and the Johannesburg Declaration on Sustainable Development (2002). While it is impossible to do justice to all the soft law instruments in this field within the confines of this chapter, mention must be made of other important soft law instruments in this field: the World Charter for Nature,[4] the New Delhi Principles on Sustainable Development,[5] and the draft articles on sustainable development proposed by the Experts Group of the World Commission on Environment and Development.[6] It then discusses the pros and cons of using soft law instruments vis-à-vis hard law. Finally, it uses the Copenhagen Accord adopted at the UN Summit on Climate Change in 2009 as a case study to evaluate its implications for the future climate change legal regime.

[3] A/CONF.199/20, available online at: www.un-documents.net/jburgdec.htm

[4] (1983) 22 ILM 455.

[5] Available at: www.springerlink.com/content/v52m758047k73q41/fulltext.pdf

[6] Robert Munro and Johan Lammers (eds.), *Environmental Protection and Sustainable Development*, Experts Group on Environmental Law of the World Commission on Environment and Development (London: Graham and Trotman, 1987).

2 What is "soft law"?

What is soft law? Some contend that this is an oxymoron as law is necessarily "hard."[7] They contend that if law is soft, it is not law at all.[8] Hard law is defined as "a regime relying primarily on the authority and power of the state . . . in the construction, operation, and implementation, including enforcement, of arrangements at international, national, or subnational level."[9] Thus, according to this definition, at the heart of hard law is the state, whether in adopting the law, its implementation or its enforcement. However, the present international legal regime has moved away from this traditional state-centric approach to encompass non-state actors, with international organizations and civil society actors being the most prominent. The increasing adoption of, and the reliance on, soft law may be the result of the expanding nature of international law both in terms of its actors as well as its reach.

Soft law, by contrast, has been identified as "regimes that rely primarily on the participation and resources of nongovernmental actors in the construction, operation, and implementation of a governance arrangement."[10] This definition, while being useful for its distinction with hard law, is not helpful to define declarations adopted by states at international conferences by an overwhelming majority (sometimes without a single dissenting vote) which clearly lay down principles – declarations such as Stockholm, Rio and Universal Declaration of Human Rights (UDHR) are prime examples of this phenomenon. Thus, a broader definition of soft law becomes necessary. Sometimes it is useful to think of the hard law–soft law phenomenon as a continuum rather than a dichotomy[11] and as complementing rather than competing with each other.

In this chapter we refer to soft law in a broad sense, encompassing all instruments that do not fall within the realm of binding law.[12] Thus,

[7] See Raustiala, 'Form and Substance', who argues that "there is no such thing as 'soft Law.' The concept of soft law purports to identify something between binding law and no law."

[8] See Guzman and Meyer, 'International Soft Law', at 172 who point out that while soft law is not law, most legal scholars agree that they are not simply politics either. Some have quasi-legal character but this too is problematic because it is not clear what separates quasi-legal soft law rules from non-legal ones.

[9] See Kirton and Trebilcock, *Hard Choices*, at 9. [10] *Ibid.* [11] *Ibid.*

[12] See Skjærseth *et al.*, 'Soft Law, Hard Law', who define soft law as "international norms that are deliberately non-binding in character but still have legal relevance, located 'in the twilight between law and politics'" (quoting Daniel Thurer, 'Soft Law', in R. Bernhardt ed., *Encyclopaedia of Public International Law* (2000), vol. 4, 452–60).

declarations of conferences, resolutions of international organizations (except decisions of the Security Council which are binding on its members under Article 25 of the UN Charter), general comments of various treaty bodies, guidelines, interpretative documents, plans of action, decisions of conferences of parties adopted by consensus, good practices, documents aimed at non-state actors and codes of conduct all fall into the category of soft law.[13] By contrast, any soft or vague obligations in treaties are, by this definition, hard law, although in terms of their legal effect, there is hardly any distinction between hard commitments in non-binding instruments and soft obligations in binding instruments. If this is so, what is the real distinction between soft law and hard law? While at the beginning, soft law instruments were not taken very seriously by states, states now pay meticulous attention to the drafting language[14] and have even begun to enter reservations to these soft law instruments. A good example is the US "reservation" to the Declaration on the Right to Development adopted by the General Assembly in 1986 stating that the US government considers economic development to be a goal and not a right. Another example is the US "reservation" to Principle 7 of the Rio Declaration on the common but differentiated responsibility principle (CBDR) wherein the US specifically said that acceptance of Principle 7 does not mean the acceptance of historic responsibility for environmental problems by the US.[15] Thus, the entering of reservations, hitherto reserved for treaties, is no longer a yardstick to measure whether a document is binding or not. Moreover, weak obligations in binding instruments and strong obligations in non-binding instruments can have the same legal effect under international law.

Similarly, some contend that another way to ascertain whether a commitment is binding or not is to see whether the failure to fulfill it

[13] See Dinah Shelton, 'Soft Law', in *Handbook of International Law* (2008), available online at: http://ssrn.com/abstract=1003387. See also, Guzman and Meyer, 'International Soft Law', at 173 who point out that "soft law is best understood as a continuum, or spectrum, running between fully binding treaties and fully political positions. Viewed in this way, soft law is something that dims in importance as the commitments of states get weaker, eventually disappearing altogether."

[14] See Geoffrey Palmer, 'New Ways to Make International Environmental Law', *American Journal of International Law*, 86 (1992), 259, 274.

[15] This is called an interpretative statement, not a reservation. See David Hunter, James Salzman, and Durwood Zaelke, *International Environmental Law and Policy* (4th edn., New York: Foundation Press, 2011), 348.

would give rise to any legal ramifications under the law of state responsibility.[16] According to the law of state responsibility, the failure to fulfill an international obligation will give rise to an internationally wrongful act.[17] Thus, given this definition, everything hinges on what an "international obligation" is. Under traditional international law, an international obligation is generally considered as a binding obligation and, therefore, could arise under a treaty, customary law or a general principle of law. Soft law instruments are not mentioned as a source of legal obligations under Article 38(1) of the ICJ statute.

It has been suggested that the term soft law implies that it is a type or variant of law[18] or legal norms that fall short of the classical definition of law.[19] On the other hand, it has been critiqued for including the word "law" in the term on the ground that if a rule is not binding, it should not have the word law in its name[20] and that it gives more fuel to those who criticize international law as a system of law: "Given, in particular, the disdain with which international law is held by some international relations scholars, the concept of soft law seems to serve no purpose except to confuse matters and dilute the distinctive nature of legal rules."[21]

The main criticism aimed against soft law seems to be terminological.[22] The phenomenon itself – that there are norms that fall short of legal obligations or principles – is not really contested. Dividing norms into legal and non-legal norms, Blutman argues that one needs a sharp and formal distinction between law and non-law which she calls the "binary approach."[23] Although Blutman argues that soft law theories share a misconception about the traditional approach relating to its

16 See Shelton, 'Soft Law'.

17 See ILC Draft Articles on State Responsibility, 2001, available online at: http://untreaty.un.org/ilc/texts/instruments/english/draft%20articles/9_6_2001.pdf

18 See Laszlo Blutman, 'In the Trap of a Legal Metaphor: International Soft Law', *International and Comparative Law Quarterly*, 59 (2010), 605, 609.

19 *Ibid.*, quoting A.T. Guzman, 'The Design of International Agreement', *European Journal of International Law*, 16 (2005), 579, 583–4.

20 *Ibid.*, quoting A. C. Arend, *Legal Rules and International Society* (New York: Oxford University Press, 1999), 25.

21 *Ibid.*

22 See Blutman, 'Trap of a Legal Metaphor', at 610 who contends that "The real problem, however, is that the expression is not only incorrect but it is also meaningless" and that every non-legal norm may be described as soft law.

23 *Ibid.* Others prefer to treat this as a continuum; cf. Guzman and Meyer, 'International Soft Law', at 173.

assessment of legal norms, she accepts that lack of legal form does not necessarily mean a 'diminished function' but questions why they are called soft law if social norms play an important regulatory role.[24]

Shelton distinguishes between primary and secondary soft law instruments.[25] According to her, primary soft law consists of those normative texts that are addressed to the entire international community that declare new norms. These often precede the adoption of a later treaty on the subject. Secondary soft law includes recommendations and general comments of international supervisory organs, jurisprudence of courts and decisions of rapporteurs and ad hoc bodies.[26] Arguing that "soft law agreement is not a coherent concept, nor does it accord with state practice," Raustiala nonetheless distinguishes between two types of soft law agreements: (a) those that are nominally non-binding but have some soft legal qualities; and (b) those that are nominally binding but lack precision or enforcement provisions.[27] Some of the criticisms against soft law instruments can be aimed at treaties too – some treaties, particularly framework treaties lack precision and enforcement mechanisms. From this point of view, the mere fact that certain commitments are included in a treaty does not mean that they are binding. Much would depend on what the parties intended. However, while a commitment lacking in precision whether embodied in a soft law instrument or a binding one will remain a "soft" commitment, it has been cautioned that calling imprecise provisions in soft law muddles several issues.[28]

Another feature of soft law instruments is that they encompass the activities of non-state actors, while binding documents generally encompass only states. Shelton also points out that more recently even supervisory bodies have been created to oversee compliance with non-binding instruments – the creation of the UN Commission on Sustainable Development (CSD) to supervise the implementation of Agenda 21, a non-binding instrument, is cited as an example.[29] States are required to submit periodic reports to the CSD – this is an example of a hard obligation

[24] See Blutman, 'Trap of a Legal Metaphor', at 612. [25] See Shelton, 'Soft Law'.

[26] *Ibid.* [27] See Raustiala, 'Form and Substance', at 587.

[28] *Ibid.*, at 589. See also Blutman, 'Trap of a Legal Metaphor', at 606, who makes the same distinction but notes that there could be soft commitments in soft instruments, in which event they are considered as "double soft law." We can safely exclude this type of instrument from our discussion because it is very unlikely that vague commitments in soft law instruments will give rise to any subsequent legal developments.

[29] See Raustiala, 'Form and Substance'.

arising out of a soft law instrument. This is a very important development and merits further analysis beyond what is feasible in this chapter. If non-binding instruments have no legal effect, why are international institutions being created to supervise the implementation of these non-binding instruments?

According to another categorization, soft law instruments fall into three groups: (a) non-binding decisions of international organizations; (b) non-obligatory agreements and declarations adopted by states; and (c) recommendations of non-governmental organizations (NGOs).[30] Sometimes there could be an overlap between these categories and some soft law instruments may not fall neatly within any category. Thus, for example, the draft articles on Human Rights and the Environment were drafted by Sierra Club in 1986 for a workshop convened by the UN Special Rapporteur on Human Rights and the Environment.[31] It is not clear where the Equator Principles[32] adopted by financial institutions would fall as they cannot be termed as NGOs. Nonetheless, some resolutions sponsored by NGOs in the field have had much influence. A good example is the New Delhi Resolution on Sustainable Development adopted by the International Law Association.[33]

Not everybody considers soft law as being devoid of all legal effect. Soft law has been identified as international norms that are "deliberately non-binding in character but still have legal relevance, located in the twilight between law and politics."[34] Other dimensions that are sometimes considered include precision and delegation of authority to third parties.[35] On the other hand, it is contended that states often weaken the substance and structure of multilateral agreements when they are uncertain about compliance costs by weakening monitoring or watering down commitments.[36] Another reason for this tendency is the need for widespread adherence.

The creation of the United Nations Environment Programme (UNEP) is another interesting example. UNEP, a subsidiary body of the UN, was created by a General Assembly resolution in 1972 as a direct result of the Stockholm Conference. As such, UNEP has no charter of incorporation

[30] See Blutman, 'Trap of a Legal Metaphor'.

[31] See Final Report of the Special Rapporteur, Fatma Zohra Ksentini, E/CN.4/Sub.2/1994/9, 6 July 1994, available online at: www.unhchr.ch/Huridocda/Huridoca.nsf/0/eeab2b6937bc-caa18025675c005779c3?Opendocument

[32] Available at: www.equator-principles.com

[33] See n. 5 above.

[34] See Skjærseth *et al.*, 'Soft Law, Hard Law', at 452–4.

[35] *Ibid.*

[36] See Raustiala, 'Form and Substance', at 582.

as other international bodies have. Despite its origin, UNEP has been successful in adopting binding instruments under its auspices – good examples are the conventions relating to hazardous wastes and ozone depletion. UNEP has also been instrumental in adopting many soft law instruments – good examples are the UNEP guiding principles on shared natural resources[37] and the regional seas program[38] which have facilitated further action in these areas.

Soft law instruments play several roles at the international level: similar to treaties, they can codify customary international law; they can crystallize a trend towards a particular norm; they can facilitate the emergence of new customary international law principles; consolidate political opinion in relation to a new problem; fill gaps in existing treaties; provide interpretative guides to treaties; give rise to new state practice on a particular issue; and help shape domestic law. As the subsequent discussion shows, soft law instruments have had a great influence at the national level as well.

Another interesting feature of the environment field is the adoption of a combination of instruments to address various environmental issues facing the international community. The ozone regime is a good example where the combination of a framework convention and a protocol as well as numerous soft law instruments was adopted. The legal regime required flexibility as it was totally dependent on scientific developments relating to ozone depletion. Thus, for example, no sooner than the Montreal Protocol was adopted did it became clear that the phase-out obligations were inadequate and needed to be amended in light of the developments relating to scientific evidence.[39] A combination approach can be seen in relation to many other environmental issues ranging from climate change[40] to biodiversity.[41]

[37] Environmental Law Guidelines and Principles on Shared Natural Resources, available online at: www.unep.org/law/PDF/UNEPEnvironmental-Law-Guidelines-and-Principles.pdf

[38] For details, see: www.unep.org/regionalseas; see also Hunter *et al.*, *International Environmental Law*, at 224.

[39] See Palmer, 'New Ways', at 274.

[40] The UNFCCC and Kyoto Protocol provide the binding legal regime, while a multitude of soft law instruments supplement this regime – the Bali Action Plan and the Copenhagen Accord are some examples.

[41] The Convention on Biological Diversity, 1992, the Biosafety Protocol and the recently adopted Nagoya Protocol on Access to Genetic Resources are the binding documents while Bonn Guidelines on Access to Genetic Resources, Interim Guiding Principles for the Prevention, Introduction, and Mitigation of Impacts of Alien Species are some of the soft law instruments in this area.

3 Seminal soft law instruments in the field of international environmental law

The watershed of modern international environmental law is considered as the Stockholm Conference on the Human Environment held in 1972. Prior to this, international law hardly had any rules governing the environment, apart from the seminal decision in the *Trail Smelter Arbitration* in 1941[42] and a handful of treaties.[43] The Stockholm Conference saw the adoption of two instruments – the Stockholm Action Plan and the Stockholm Declaration on the Human Environment. It also gave rise to a flurry of activity at both international and national levels, including the creation of UNEP, the adoption of national laws on the environment and the creation of environmental institutions at the national level.

The Stockholm Declaration is considered as the foundation of modern international environmental law as prior to its adoption there were virtually no laws governing the international environment. Despite being adopted without a single negative vote by the international community, the Stockholm Declaration remains a soft law instrument. It contains several important principles, including rational planning, prior assessment of the impact of development activities on the environment, integration of environment into the development process planting the early seeds of sustainable development, the duty not to cause damage beyond national borders and the right to exploit resources according to environmental policies. It was a carefully crafted instrument that, for the first time, sought to lay down principles relating to the environment.

Another milestone in the history of international environmental law is the Rio Conference on Environment and Development convened to mark the twentieth anniversary of the Stockholm Conference. By this time environmental problems had become much more complex and intertwined with the global economy, giving rise to the emergence of the discourse on sustainable development. There is no doubt that the report issued by the World Commission on Environment and Development in

[42] *USA* v. *Canada*, 3 RIAA 1905 (1941).

[43] The early treaties include the International Convention for the Regulation of Whaling, 1946 (available online at: http://iwcoffice.org/commission/convention.htm#convention); Treaty for the Preservation and Protection of Fur Seals, 1911; and Convention on Certain Questions Relating to the Law on Watercourses, 1929. See Hunter *et al.*, *International Environmental Law*, at 140.

1987 had a great influence on the Rio Declaration adopted in 1992. It embodies several important principles relating to the environment with sustainable development providing the overarching framework.[44]

Other important principles in the Rio Declaration include the principle of integration,[45] the polluter pays principle,[46] the precautionary principle,[47] the common but differentiated responsibility principle,[48] and environmental impact assessment and participatory rights.[49] While it does not provide a definition of sustainable development, it clearly endorses that concept and elaborates on its components. In addition, it embodies linkages[50] and tools to achieve sustainable development.[51] At the debate held on the link between climate change and security and the role of the UN Security Council, many states referred to the need to implement Rio principles, specifically, the common but differentiated responsibility principle, the precautionary principle and sustainable development.[52] The fact that the Rio Declaration was a soft law instrument seemed immaterial to the debate.

Ten years later, the international community saw the adoption of yet another declaration at yet another conference – the World Summit on Sustainable Development in 2002. This declaration was markedly different from its predecessors, in that it was clearly labeled a "political document" leaving us in no doubt that no legal effect was intended. Nonetheless, it explicitly endorsed the notion of sustainable Development and articulated the three pillars of sustainable development as economic development, social development, and environmental protection.[53] Marking a clear departure from its predecessors, the Johannesburg Declaration contains no principles. As can be seen, even among similar instruments, the normative effect can be very different.

[44] Hunter *et al.*, *International Environmental Law*, at 171, who argue that sustainable development provided the framework for a hitherto ad hoc body of principles governing the environment: "More than anything perhaps, Rio marked the formal acceptance of sustainable development as the goal of modern economy. Sustainable Development was the organizing conceptual framework for the entire North–South dialogue and is integrated throughout the various Rio texts."

[45] Principle 4, Rio Declaration. [46] Principle 16, Rio Declaration.

[47] Principle 15, Rio Declaration. [48] Principle 7, Rio Declaration.

[49] Principle 10, Rio Declaration.

[50] Linkages include: poverty (Principle 5), warfare (Principle 24), and peace and development (Principle 25).

[51] Tools include: the EIA process (Principle 10), the precautionary principle (Principle 15) and the polluter pays principle (Principle 16).

[52] The debate is available online at: www.un.org/News/Press/docs/2007/sc9000.doc.htm

[53] See n. 3 above; Hunter *et al.*, *International Environmental Law*, at 172.

The field of international environmental law is replete with soft law instruments, too numerous to enumerate here. Be it climate change, biodiversity, desertification or rights of nature, soft law instruments have played a seminal role in developing these areas of law from virtually nothing in many instances.[54]

4 Soft law: pros and cons

Despite their differences, one feature is common to all three instruments discussed above: they are all non-binding, thus falling into the realm of soft law.[55] This, however, is an oversimplification – to say that a particular instrument is non-binding is to ignore the important role that soft law instruments have played and continue to play in international law. They have played a particularly important role in the field of international environmental law from forming its foundation to articulating legal principles governing this area. There is no doubt that the three instruments discussed above have played a significant role in shaping the direction of international environmental law.

Despite these developments, many questions remain in relation to soft law: why do states opt for soft law instruments? Do states feel more comfortable adopting them because they are non-binding? Do they prefer soft law instruments because they do not require protracted negotiations and a lengthy drafting process? Is it because soft law instruments are flexible and can be adopted speedily? Or is it because no ratification or approval is necessary at the national level? The reasons may be a combination of all these factors.

As Professor Dupuy pointed out in 1991:

> "Soft" law certainly constitutes part of the contemporary law-making process but, as a social phenomenon, it evidently overflows the classical and familiar legal categories by which scholars usually describe and explain both the creation and the legal authority of international norms. In other words, "soft" law is a trouble maker because it is either not yet or not only law."[56]

[54] See Hunter *et al.*, *International Environmental Law*, at 344.

[55] See Drumbl, 'Actors and Law-making', who notes that these major international conferences have "a social constructivist value in that they generally are preceded by years of planning and discussion, public dissemination of information, receive extensive media coverage, and lead to the adoption of important instruments."

[56] See Dupuy, 'Soft Law and the International Law', at 420.

While he notes that "soft" law is a paradoxical term for defining an ambiguous term, he nonetheless concedes that "a new process of normative creation which jurists feel uncomfortable analyzing does exist and has been developing for more or less twenty years."[57] Writing over twenty years ago, Dupuy referred to soft law as a troublemaker. However, its impact in the environment field has been much more positive. While some may still contend that soft law is a troublemaker, soft law has played a key role in developing and shaping the law at least in the environment field. It will continue to play a vital role where action cannot await a protracted treaty negotiating process. For example, negotiations leading up to the third Law of the Sea Convention spanned over a period of ten years and it took another twelve years for the convention to enter into force. Granted that the Law of the Sea Convention was a very ambitious undertaking encompassing all aspects of the law of the sea, the international community cannot afford to spend twenty years to adopt a treaty governing the environment. Thus, international environmental law has adopted various tools and techniques to deal with flaws inherent in the international lawmaking process such as protracted treaty negotiations. Another problem specific to the environmental field is lack of scientific evidence relating to various environmental problems and how to adopt legal instruments faced with that uncertainty. The framework–protocol approach, the soft law approach and the development of principles such as the precautionary principle have all contributed to speedy action in the environment field. The ozone legal regime is a good example of adopting novel legal strategies to deal with a novel environmental problem.[58]

Soft law instruments do not need ratification at the national level and for politically controversial issues, adopting a soft law instrument may be the answer. Moreover, soft law instruments often pave the way for hard law developments[59] and as Dupuy pointed out soft law today may be the hard law of tomorrow.[60] While some contend that states do not pay as meticulous attention to drafting soft law instruments as they do to hard

[57] *Ibid.*

[58] This was the first global environmental problem that confronted the international community.

[59] See Skjærseth *et al.*, 'Soft Law, Hard Law', at 105.

[60] See Dupuy, 'Soft Law and the International Law'.

law instruments,[61] this is not strictly true.[62] As Palmer points out, states pay attention to the drafting language of soft law instruments and may even enter reservations if they do not agree with some provisions in the instrument. As discussed above, a case in point is the US reservation to the General Assembly resolution on the Right to Development.[63] It is probably easier to reach agreement on ambitious soft law than mediocre hard law.[64]

Another reason for the proliferation of soft law instruments in the field of environmental protection is the active role played by non-state actors in this field. Several NGOs have played a significant role in drafting new principles and most of these have been included in soft law instruments. The World Charter for Nature adopted by the General Assembly in 1982 is a good example – it was drafted by the IUCN, a prominent international environmental NGO. Although it is a soft law instrument, it is so far the only instrument that specifically embodies rights of nature. Some of the provisions in the Charter have now entered into the realm of hard law – the EIA process and participatory rights are considered part of customary law governing the environment.[65] Thus, far from being a troublemaker, soft law has contributed to the development of legal norms in this field. While it is not the instrument itself that creates law, rather subsequent state practice, what shapes such state practice is the soft law instrument.

The advantages of a soft law approach have been identified as: "timely action when governments are stalemated; bottom-up initiatives that bring additional legitimacy, expertise, and other resources for making and enforcing new norms and standards; and an effective means for direct civil society participation in global governance."[66] Other advantages are flexibility and speedy adoption.

[61] See Skjærseth *et al.*, 'Soft Law, Hard Law', at 105.

[62] Both Dupuy ('Soft Law and the International Law') and Palmer ('New Ways') point out that states pay close attention to the drafting language of soft law instruments.

[63] A/RES/41/128, Annex (December 1986), available online at: www.un-documents.net/a41r128.htm. See Hunter *et al.*, *International Environmental Law*, at 452. Again, this is called an interpretative statement, rather than a reservation: "Development is not a right. On the contrary, development is a goal we all hold, which depends for its realization in large part on the promotion and protection of human rights set out in the Universal Declaration of Human Rights."

[64] See Skjærseth *et al.*, 'Soft Law, Hard Law', at 115.

[65] See Sumudu Atapattu, *Emerging Principles of International Environmental Law* (New York: Transnational, 2006).

[66] See Kirton and Trebilcock, *Hard Choices*, at 5.

4.1 *Application by international tribunals*[67]

International courts and arbitral tribunals have relied on soft law instruments, particularly, General Assembly resolutions in some instances. Thus, in their *Advisory Opinions on Namibia*,[68] and *Western Sahara*,[69] the ICJ referred to the General Assembly declarations on self-determination and independence of peoples in territories that have not yet attained independence as having legal effect. In *Nicaragua* v. *USA*,[70] the ICJ found evidence of *opinion juris* on the part of the US in its voting for the resolution of the 6th International Conference on American States on Aggression, and acceptance of the prohibition of use of force in the declaration on principles governing the mutual relations of States participating in the Conference on Security and Co-operation in Europe. The Court also relied on the General Assembly Declaration on Principles of International Law Concerning Friendly Relations and Co-operation among States as providing evidence of the lesser forms of the prohibition of use of force formulation found in the UN Charter as well as the principle governing non-intervention in internal affairs of states.[71] The Court articulated that this principle has been included in many declarations of international organizations and conferences which have been endorsed by both parties to the dispute[72] and noted its relevance as an acceptance of the validity of the rule declared by the resolution:

> Texts like these, in relation to which the Court has pointed to the customary content of certain provisions such as the principles of the non-use of force and non-intervention envisage the relations among States having different political, economic and social systems on the basis of coexistence among their various ideologies; the United States not only voiced no objection to their adoption, but took an active part in bringing it about.[73]

The Court also noted that these instruments play a role in relation to *opinion juris*:

[67] While there is considerable literature on the adoption of soft law instruments by the EU, this chapter will not attempt to analyze that literature, as that would involve a discussion of the structure of the EU itself. See generally, David Trubek, Patrick Cottrell, and Mark Nance, '"Soft Law," "Hard Law," and European Integration: Toward a Theory of Hybridity', available online at: http://eucenter.wisc.edu/OMC/Papers/EUC/trubeketal.pdf, who point out that soft law in the EU refers to a variety of processes. They rely on Francis Snyder's definition of soft law: "rules of conduct which in principle have no legally binding force but which nevertheless may have practical effects."

[68] 1971 ICJ 31. [69] 1975 ICJ 12. [70] 1986 ICJ 14. [71] *Ibid.*, 91, para. 191.

[72] *Ibid.*, 97, para. 203. [73] *Ibid.*, para. 265.

> This *opinion juris* may, though with all due caution, be deduced from, *inter alia*, the attitude of the Parties and the attitude of States towards certain General Assembly resolutions, and particularly resolution 2625 (XXV) entitled "Declaration on Principles of International Law concerning Friendly Relations and Co-operation among States in accordance with the Charter of the United Nations." The effect of consent to the text of such resolutions cannot be understood as merely that of a "reiteration or elucidation" of the treaty commitment undertaken in the Charter. On the contrary, it may be understood as an acceptance of the validity of the rule or set of rules declared by the resolution by themselves.[74]

Similarly, the arbitral tribunal in *Texaco* v. *Libya*[75] relied on the UN resolutions on permanent sovereignty over natural resources. With regard to Resolution 1803 (XVII) of December 1962 the Tribunal articulated that: "The principles stated in this Resolution were therefore assented to by a great many States representing not only all geographical areas but also all economic systems." The tribunal even looked at the *travaux préparatoires* of the Charter of Economic Rights and Duties of States adopted by the General Assembly in 1974. Noting that UN resolutions have "a certain legal value" the Tribunal stressed that this legal value differs considerably depending on the type of resolution and the conditions attached to its adoption.[76]

Perhaps the concept that has attracted most attention at both national and international levels is the concept of sustainable development, coined by the WCED, a commission appointed by the UN General Assembly: "Sustainable Development is development that meets the needs of the present without compromising the ability of the future generations to meet their own needs."[77] It is ironic that it is this definition of sustainable development that the international community has consistently relied on despite allegations that it is a vague term[78] and

[74] *Ibid.*, 89–90, para. 188.

[75] International Arbitral Awards, Jan. 19, 1977 (1978), 17 ILM 1.

[76] Referred to in Henkin *et al.*, *International Law: Cases and Materials* (4th edn., Minnesota, MN: West Publishing, 2001), 150. However, in similar cases, the arbitral tribunals refused to attach any legal significance to these resolutions. See: *BP* v. *Libya* (1973) 53 ILR 297; *Liamco* v. *Libya* (1981) 29 ILM 10.

[77] See *Our Common Future: The Report of the World Commission on Environment and Development* (Oxford: Oxford University Press, 1987), at 43. For the mandate given to the WCED, see *ibid.*, chairman's foreword.

[78] See: Michael McCloskey, 'The Emperor Has No Clothes: The Conundrum of Sustainable Development', *Duke Environmental Law and Policy Forum*, 9 (1999), 153; Atapattu, *Emerging Principles*, ch. 2, on sustainable development.

which has subsequently crept into hard law.[79] It is even more ironic that even the ICJ has relied on this definition:

> Throughout the ages, mankind has, for economic and other reasons, constantly interfered with nature. In the past, this was often done without consideration of the effects upon the environment ... new norms and standards have been developed, set forth in a great number of instruments during the last two decades. Such new norms have to be taken into consideration, and such new standards given proper weight, not only when States contemplate new activities but also when continuing with activities begun in the past. *This need to reconcile economic development with protection of the environment is aptly expressed in the concept of sustainable development.*[80]

In his separate opinion in this case, Justice Weeramantry relied extensively on soft law instruments. He was of the opinion that sustainable development was not a mere concept but a principle of international law:

> The concept of sustainable is thus a principle accepted not merely by the developing countries, but one which rests on the basis of worldwide acceptance ... The principle of sustainable development is thus a part of modern international law by reason not only of its inescapable logical necessity, but also by reason of its wide and general acceptance by the global community.[81]

In the *Advisory Opinion on the Legality of the Threat or Use of Nuclear Weapons*,[82] the ICJ referred to both Principle 21 of the Stockholm Declaration and Principle 2 of the Rio Declaration and noted that: "The existence of the general obligation of States to ensure that activities within their jurisdiction and control respect the environment of other States or of areas beyond national control is now part of the corpus of international law relating to the environment."[83] Thus, the Court endorsed that Principle 21 of the Stockholm Declaration which laid down this principle and replicated almost verbatim in Principle 2 of the Rio Declaration is now part of customary international law governing the environment. Stressing that respect for the environment is one of the elements that go to assess whether the action in question is in conformity with the principles of necessity and proportionality, the

[79] See UNFCCC, Article 3; Convention on Biological Diversity refers to sustainable use of biological resources.

[80] *Case Concerning the Gabčíkovo–Nagymaros Project* (*Hungary* v. *Slovakia*) 1997 ICJ Rep 7 (emphasis added).

[81] *Ibid.* [82] 1996 ICJ 226. [83] *Ibid.*

Court specifically said that this approach is supported by Principle 24 of the Rio Declaration which calls upon states to respect international law providing protection for the environment during armed conflict.[84]

4.2 *Application by domestic courts*

Moreover, soft law instruments have contributed to the development of domestic law and national judiciaries have sometimes relied on these instruments. Thus, in *Filartiga* v. *Pena-Irala*,[85] the US Court of Appeals relied on the General Assembly Declaration on Torture and noted that the Declaration, similar to the UDHR, was adopted without dissent by the General Assembly:

> These UN declarations are significant because they specify with great precision the obligations of member nations under the Charter. Since their adoption "[m]embers can no longer contend that they do not know what human rights they promised in the Charter to promote." Moreover, a UN Declaration is, according to one authoritative definition, "a formal and solemn instrument, suitable for rare occasions when principles of great and lasting importance are being enunciated" ... Thus, a Declaration creates an expectation of adherence, and "insofar as the expectation is gradually justified by State practice, a declaration may by custom become recognized as laying down rules binding upon States."[86]

Soft law instruments have also influenced the decisions of national courts in other parts of the world. Thus, in the words of the Supreme Court of Sri Lanka in a case involving a proposed agreement to exploit a phosphate mine in Sri Lanka:

> In my view, the proposed agreement must be considered in the light of the foregoing principles [the court referred to various principles of the Stockholm and Rio Declarations]. Admittedly, the principles set out in the Stockholm and Rio De Janeiro Declarations are not legally binding in the way in which an Act of our Parliament would be. It may be regarded merely as 'soft law'. *Nonetheless, as a Member of the United Nations, they could hardly be ignored by Sri Lanka.* Moreover, they would, in my view, be binding if they have been either expressly enacted or become a part of the domestic law by adoption by the superior Courts of record and by the Supreme Court in particular, in their decisions.[87]

[84] *Ibid.* [85] US Court of Appeals, Second Circuit, 1980, 630 F. 2d 876. [86] *Ibid.*
[87] *Bulankukama and others* v. *Secretary, Ministry of Industrial Development and others* (2000) *Sri Lanka Law Reports*, 243, at 274–5 (emphasis added).

The Court relied on several principles of the Stockholm and Rio Declarations[88] as well as the WCED Report with regard to the definition of sustainable development,[89] all of which are non-binding instruments. The Supreme Court of the Philippines in *Minors Oposa* case articulated the intergenerational equity principle as: "every generation has a responsibility to the next to preserve the rhythm and harmony of nature for the full enjoyment of a balanced and healthy ecology."[90]

Similar pronouncements have been made by the Indian Supreme Court in various fundamental rights cases that have come before it. Thus, in *MC Mehta* v. *Kamal Nath and others,*[91] the Indian Supreme Court relied on various principles including the polluter pays principle and discussed its evolution at the international level, particularly its adoption by the OECD as a recommendation and as a binding principle by the EU. The *Vellore Citizens Welfare Forum* v. *Union of India*[92] involved the environmental damage and public health hazard caused by tanneries in the State of Tamil Nadu. The Court noted that while the tanneries brought in a considerable amount of foreign revenue and generated employment, the industry has no right to destroy the ecology and create a health hazard. It noted that: "Sustainable development, and in particular the polluter pays principles and the precautionary principle, have become part of customary international law."[93]

In *Karnataka Industrial Areas Development Board* v. *Sri C. Kenchappa and others,*[94] the court again reiterated the principle of sustainable development and referred to the Stockholm Declaration as the "*Magna Carta of our environment.*"[95] The court further discussed the history of international environmental law, paying extensive attention to the provisions of the Rio Declaration. It noted that in keeping with the principle of sustainable development, a serious effort has been made "to strike a golden balance between industrial development and ecological preservation."[96]

[88] These include Principles 14 and 21 of the Stockholm Declaration and Principles 2, 4, and 10 of the Rio Declaration.

[89] See *Our Common Future,* n. 77 above.

[90] Reprinted in (1994) 33 ILM 173.

[91] Supreme Court of India (1997) 1 Supreme Court Cases 388.

[92] Supreme Court of India, AIR 1996 SC 2715. [93] *Ibid.*

[94] Supreme Court of India (2006), available online at: www.nlsenlaw.org/environmental-protection/case-laws/supreme-court-1/karnataka-industrial-areas-development-board-vs-sri-c-kenchappa-and-ors-2006

[95] Emphasis added. [96] *Ibid.*

In *Shehla Zia and others* v. *WAPDA*[97] the Supreme Court of Pakistan noted that where life of citizens is degraded, the quality of life is adversely affected and health hazards are created affecting a large number of people. With regard to scientific uncertainty, the Court noted that the precautionary principle should be applied[98] and that a balance should be struck between economic progress and prosperity and to minimize possible hazards. Thus, the court confirmed that a policy of sustainable development should be adopted.[99] With regard to the Rio Declaration the Court articulated:

> The Rio Declaration is the product of hectic discussion among the leaders of the nations of the world and it was after negotiations between the developed and the developing countries that an almost consensus declaration had been sorted out. Environment is an international problem having to [sic] frontiers creating trans-boundary effects. In this field every nation has to cooperate and contribute and for this reason the Rio Declaration would serve as a great binding force and to create discipline among the nations while dealing with environmental problems.[100]

4.3 *Challenges and advantages*

It is thus obvious that soft law instruments have had a significant influence on the development of law not only at the international level but also at the national level. They can give rise to new customary international law norms, consolidate emerging principles as well as give rise to new treaties. A good example is Principle 21 of the Stockholm Declaration. Since its adoption in 1972, it has been included in numerous instruments, both binding and non-binding. It has, since then, become one of the few customary international law principles in the environment field.[101]

[97] PLD 1994 SC 693, referred to in Parvez Hassan and Azim Azfar, 'Securing Environmental Rights through Public Interest Litigation in South Asia', *Virginia Environmental Law Journal*, 22 (2004), 215.

[98] The court relied on Principle 15 of the Rio Declaration and noted that it envisages a rule of precaution and prudence.

[99] The court noted the importance of economic development but stressed that "in the quest of economic development, one has to adopt such measures which may not create hazards to life, destroy the environment and pollute the atmosphere."

[100] See Hassan and Azfar, 'Securing Environmental Rights'.

[101] See Philippe Sands, *Principles of International Environmental Law* (Cambridge: Cambridge University Press, 2003); Patricia Birnie, Alan Boyle, and Catherine Redgwell, *International Law and the Environment* (3rd edn., Oxford, Oxford University Press, 2009).

Similarly, the WCED definition of sustainable development has been relied upon by the entire international community including the ICJ despite its origin being a non-binding document, embodying a vague definition. Like Principle 21, it has been included in both binding[102] and non-binding[103] instruments. What is significant is that none of these instruments have deviated from the original definition articulated by the WCED.

Despite these advantages, soft law has its share of flaws. Precisely because they are non-binding, states can simply ignore them even if they have voted for their adoption. Since they are not legally binding, no legal recourse can be taken against states that ignore the commitments in these instruments, except perhaps exerting political pressure. Another disadvantage is the effect on non-state actors. If some non-state actors decide to follow codes of conduct or similar documents, while others do not, then those who follow these non-binding instruments will be at a comparative disadvantage vis-à-vis those who do not follow them, particularly in relation to international trade. This is a major disadvantage of soft law instruments. It may be recalled that with regard to ozone depletion, industries in the US lobbied for international controls on ozone-depleting substances because they were subject to national controls[104] and, therefore, were at a disadvantage when competing internationally.

The challenges posed by soft law are summarized as:

> It may lack the legitimacy and strong surveillance and enforcement mechanism offered by hard law. With a broader array of stakeholders, soft law may promote compromise, or even compromised, standards, less stringent than those delivered by governments acting with their full authority all alone. And soft law can lead to uncertainty, as competing sets of voluntary standards struggle for dominance, and as actors remain unclear about the costs of compliance, or its absence, and about when governments might intervene to impose a potentially different, mandatory regime.[105]

While the comments about legitimacy, lack of enforcement and uncertainty are definite challenges of a soft law regime, hard law often

[102] Examples include the UNFCCC, the Biodiversity Convention.

[103] The whole Rio Declaration is based on sustainable development; Johannesburg Declaration and Doha Declaration of the 4th Ministerial Conference (2001) are some examples.

[104] The US banned all non-essential use of CFCs in 1978 under the Clean Air Act. See Hunter *et al.*, *International Environmental Law*, at 545.

[105] See Kirton and Trebilcock, *Hard Choices*, at 6.

embodies compromises and even compromised standards similar to soft law. A good example is the Geneva Convention on Long Range Transboundary Air Pollution[106] adopted by the ECE in 1979 which embodies terms such as "shall endeavour to limit and as far as possible, gradually reduce"[107] and use "best available technology which is economically feasible."[108] Most environmental treaties are replete with compromises which is a feature of international negotiations.

After a careful analysis, Blutman summarizes the function of soft law as follows:

> Norms under soft law are essentially (in a broad sense) social norms (political, moral, technical and other non-legal requirements) that can carry out an extremely important function in the coordination of actions of States or other international actors: they can raise expectations towards the arrangement of conduct of international participants; they can outline political, moral and technical (but not legal) requirements as well as mediate in the interactions of international participants. Of course, the regulatory function of these international norms is a complex issue of sociology, international relations theory and organization theories. The relationship of these social norms to international law is wide-ranging, multifaceted, nonetheless ever-changing and hard to classify. Several of these social norms have become the indispensable condition of the operation of the international legal system, especially in some branches of international law (e.g. protection of the environment, international trade and financial matters).[109]

In the field of international commercial law, soft law instruments have played a variety of roles from model laws to guidance to tribunals.[110] Similarly, in the human rights field soft law instruments abound[111] and indeed, the foundation document of modern international human rights law – the UDHR – is itself a non-binding instrument. The provisions in the Declaration have since been embodied in two treaties[112] and there is general consensus that many provisions in the UDHR are part of

[106] 18 ILM 1442, 1302 UNTS 217. [107] Article 2. [108] Article 6.

[109] See Blutman, 'Trap of a Legal Metaphor', at 623 (footnotes omitted).

[110] See Henry Deeb Gabriel, 'The Advantages of Soft Law in International Commercial Law: The Role of UNIDROIT, UNCITRAL and the Hague Conference', *Brooklyn Journal of International Law*, 34 (2009), 655.

[111] A recent addition is the UN Declaration on the Rights of Indigenous Peoples, available online at: www.un.org/esa/socdev/unpfii/documents/DRIPS_en.pdf. The Convention on the Rights of the Child was preceded by a Declaration on the subject.

[112] International Covenant on Civil and Political Rights and the International Covenant on Economic, Social and Cultural Rights both adopted in 1966.

customary international law.[113] Thus, the role that was played by the Stockholm Declaration in the environment field has been played by the UDHR in the human rights field.

Moreover, the traditional distinction between binding and non-binding norms is blurring[114] and binding documents can contain "soft" obligations while non-binding instruments can embody features that are traditionally found only in binding documents, such as supervisory mechanisms and compliance procedures.[115] Shelton offers a good explanation for the role of soft law instruments pointing out that there seems to be "a dynamic interplay between soft and hard obligations similar to that which operates between international law and national law:"[116]

> Indeed, soft law rarely stands in isolation; instead, it is used most frequently either as a precursor to hard law or as a supplement to a hard-law instrument. Soft-law instruments often serve as an authoritative way to allow treaty parties to resolve ambiguities in a binding text or fill in gaps. This function is part of an increasingly complex international system with variations in forms of instruments, means, and standards of measurement that interact intensely and frequently, with the common purpose of regulating behavior within a rule-of-law framework.[117]

International environmental issues have become increasingly complex. So have international relations and politics. The international legal system, considered less sophisticated than national legal systems,[118] has responded to this changing structure and increasing complexity by adopting an increasing variety of instruments by a variety of institutions to embody commitments, forms of behavior, and even legal principles. These instruments have given them greater flexibility, common fora, as well as common meeting of minds to address these increasingly complex issues that the international community now faces. While the entire field of international environmental law provides a rich, fertile canvas to

[113] See David Bederman, *International Law Frameworks* (New York: Foundation Press, 2001), 96. It is interesting to note that the US issued a statement after the Declaration was adopted to the effect that it is not a treaty and it "does not purport to be a statement of law or legal obligation," (*ibid.*). See also, Henkin *et al.*, *International* Law, at 594.

[114] Dinah Shelton points out that if and how the term soft law should be used depends on whether one adopts a binary approach or a continuum view of international law (see 'Normative Hierarchy in International Law', *American Journal of International Law*, 100 (2006), 291).

[115] *Ibid.* [116] *Ibid.* [117] *Ibid.*

[118] See Bederman, *International Law Frameworks*, ch. 1, on sources and methods of international law.

study the phenomenon of soft law, we will now turn to the Copenhagen Summit of December 2009 at which the international community adopted yet another soft law instrument.

5 Case study: lessons from Copenhagen

A good example to study the role of soft law is provided by the Copenhagen Accord[119] adopted by a group of states at the UN Summit on Climate Change in December 2009. A total of 136 countries have now signed on to the Copenhagen Accord.[120] Despite much anticipation by the international community that legally binding targets will be agreed upon as a successor to Kyoto commitments, what emerged at the Summit was a non-binding document totally devoid of any binding targets. The conference resulted in a political document negotiated by a group of twenty-nine countries[121] led by the US president. Unfortunately, due to the objections by a small group of states, the Conference was unable to formally "adopt" the Accord[122] and merely took note of it.[123] Thus, in the hierarchy of soft law instruments, the Copenhagen Accord would fall onto the lowest rung.

While noting that climate change is one of the "greatest challenges of our times"[124] the parties to the Accord agreed that "deep cuts" in global emissions are required. The Accord notes that the parties "should cooperate in achieving the peaking of global and national emissions as soon as possible."[125]Annex I parties have committed to implement individually or jointly the quantified economy-wide emissions targets for 2020, to be submitted to the Secretariat[126] by January 31, 2010. Non-Annex I parties will implement nationally appropriate mitigation actions (NAMAs) including those submitted to the Secretariat by January 31, 2010. Essentially, the Accord endorsed the continuation of the basic framework of the Kyoto Protocol maintaining the same distinction

[119] FCCC/CP/2009/L.7, Dec. 18, 2009. [120] http://unfccc.int/home/items/5262.php

[121] See Lavanya Rajamany, 'Neither Fish nor Fowl', available at: www.india-seminar.com/2010/606/606_lavanya_rajamani.htm

[122] See Daniel Bodansky, 'The Copenhagen Climate Change Conference: A Post-Mortem', *American Journal of International Law*, 104(2) (2010), 230.

[123] *Ibid.*

[124] This, of course, is not a new realization, and seems more like window-dressing.

[125] Copenhagen Accord, n. 119 above.

[126] This is the Climate Change Secretariat established under Article 8 of the UNFCCC, see: http://unfccc.int/secretariat/history_of_the_secretariat/items/1218.php

between Annex I and non-Annex I countries. However, unlike Kyoto, the Accord leaves emission reduction targets to the discretion of each country. The deadline set by the Accord – January 31, 2010 – passed virtually unnoticed by the international community. Moreover, by keeping the distinction between Annex I and non-Annex I countries, the Accord preserves the status quo. Although it indicates that non-Annex I countries should also implement mitigation actions, no differentiation is made among non-Annex I countries. Thus, it treats high emitters such as China, India, Brazil, and South Africa in the same manner as small island states. This was one of the main contentions of the Kyoto regime. Indeed, China overtook the US as the highest emitter of carbon dioxide in 2007.[127] The question has been raised whether it is equitable to continue to treat emerging high emitters such as China and India as non-Annex I countries or whether the time has come to differentiate among non-Annex I countries?[128] However, the Accord does not recognize new categories of states and no emission reduction targets are set forth for non-Annex I countries.

Bodansky identifies the key elements of the Copenhagen Accord as follows: due to the strong objections from developing countries for setting a date for the peaking of their emissions, no target date or the level of reduction of emission levels are mentioned in the Accord. Instead, the parties agreed that "deep cuts" are necessary to limit the temperature rise to 2 degrees Celsius. Rather than set rigid emission levels for developed countries, the Accord "establishes a bottom-up process that allows each Annex I party to define its own target level, base year and accounting rules."[129] They have committed to implement their targets, individually or jointly, subject to international monitoring, reporting and verification.[130] With regard to developing countries, the main contentious issue was with regard to international review of their NAMAs. China specifically rejected international review. Ultimately, the Accord reflects a compromise. Evaluating the outcome of Copenhagen, Bodansky notes thus:

[127] See E. Rosenthal, 'China increases lead as biggest carbon dioxide emitter', *New York Times*, June 14, 2007.

[128] See Sumudu Atapattu, 'Climate Change, Differentiated Responsibilities and State Responsibility: Devising Novel Legal Strategies for Damage Caused by Climate Change', in Benjamin Richardson, Yves Le Bouthillier, Heather McLeod-Kilmurry, and Stepan Wood (eds.), *Climate Law and Developing Countries: Legal and Policy Challenges for the World Economy* (Cheltenham: Edward Elgar, 2009), 37, 50.

[129] See Bodansky, 'Copenhagen Climate Change Conference'.

[130] *Ibid.*

> Although many negotiators left Copenhagen with a sense that the UNFCCC process is broken, there is no viable alternative at the moment, so the AWGs will continue to meet and the negotiations will continue to revolve around the COPs. But if world leaders were unable to make further process through direct negotiations, under an intense international spotlight, there is little reason to expect mid-level negotiators to be able to achieve a stronger outcome anytime soon. As a result, the Copenhagen Accord may well represent the high-water mark of the climate change regime for some time to come.[131]

In a harsh critique of the Copenhagen Accord Rajamany notes that: "The Copenhagen Accord can plausibly be characterized as 'rotten' not just because it is weak and will not contain climate change in its current form, but also because even in this weak form it faces considerable legal and procedural challenges to its operationalization. As a definitive answer to the climate challenge the accord leaves much to be desired."[132] She identifies several legal and procedural challenges with the Accord[133] and notes that these are merely the tip of the iceberg.[134]

6 Conclusion

Thus, what does the Copenhagen Accord tell us? To be sure, it is a non-binding document devoid of any binding effect. Is it advisable to leave something as serious as emission reduction levels to the discretion of states? On the other hand, the track record of Kyoto has not been very encouraging either: even a mere 5 percent reduction of greenhouse gas emissions below 1990 levels mandated by the Kyoto Protocol was unachievable by most Annex I countries during the first commitment period (2008–12).[135] Therefore, given this bad track record of Kyoto,[136]

131 *Ibid.* 132 See Rajamany, 'Neither Fish nor Fowl'.

133 See Lavanya Rajamany, 'The Making and Unmaking of the Copenhagen Accord', *International and Comparative Law Quarterly*, 59 (2010), 824. These challenges are: it is unclear who the addressees are (Annex I, non-Annex I, developing or developed); the parts of the Accord rely on COP engagement, while others do not, which results in some parts being immediately operable while others are not; since the Accord is not part of the UNFCCC process, some of the normative presumptions it was based on no longer apply; and given the Accord's questionable legal basis and its connection to the UNFCCC, the Secretariat's ability to facilitate further action is debatable.

134 *Ibid.*, at 835.

135 Only the UK and Germany were able to meet this target, but this was because of the policies put in place by these two countries well before Kyoto was adopted.

136 The negotiations leading up to the adoption of the Kyoto Protocol were protracted and contentious. See Hunter *et al.*, *International Environmental Law.*

the question arises whether the international community is looking for an alternative means of creating obligations for states. Granted that treaty negotiations involving almost 200 states with differing priorities, needs, development levels, and emission levels can become overwhelming, protracted and often deadlocked as negotiations relating to other issues have shown. However, there are success stories too. The adoption of legal instruments relating to the ozone layer within a short span of time comes to mind.[137] Moreover, given that climate change is an unprecedented global problem implicating also future generations, the question arises whether it is advisable to adopt commitments through soft law instruments where the Conference of Parties or the international community has no legal say in the matter? Or has the time come to change our mindset about the traditional sources of international law and the distinction between binding and non-binding norms? Are we moving away from the traditional way of creating international law? The field of environmental protection certainly offers us a rich array of examples that shows that the traditional distinction between binding and non-binding instruments is indeed getting blurred as this field seeks to adopt norms to cover changing situations, to respond to uncertain science and to encompass non-traditional actors. Given this reality, time may have come to recognize this emerging source of international law.[138] However, without amending other branches of law such as the law of state responsibility, the mere recognition of the normative quality of non-binding documents may not be sufficient for the further development of international law.

There is no doubt that at least in certain areas of international law, soft law and hard law have accommodated each other without too much disharmony. They fulfill distinct roles feeding on each other. The harsh critiques of soft law seem aimed more toward the terminology rather than its existence. It is hard to deny the important role soft law has played in creating and molding the law in certain areas.

It seems logical to end this discussion with the succinct summing up of the soft law–hard law debate by Kirton and Trebilcock:

> To be sure, hard law and soft law are each the conceptual antithesis of the other, and each brings distinctive advantages and disadvantages from its

[137] *Ibid.*, ch. 10, on ozone depletion.

[138] Even international courts have not been immune to this development, as they have referred to the role of these non-binding instruments in many cases.

separate identity. Yet in the real world, hard law and soft law approaches might be more complementary than competitive. Each can have its own empirical domain where it is destined to flourish, and does. Yet the two might also blend and overlap in a single regime, or combine separately to reinforce each other and fill the gaps in an overall tableau of global governance as a whole.[139]

[139] See Kirton and Trebilcock, *Hard Choices*, at 11–12.

11

Assuming away the problem? The vexing relationship between international trade and environmental protection

REBECCA M. BRATSPIES

With development comes destruction[1]

What does global trade mean for the environment of any particular place? The struggle to forge locally meaningful engagement with global trade can produce place-based transformations that are both positive and negative. The trade literature frequently points to the positive – in particular the financial resources generated by trade liberalization – positing that these trade-generated resources enable states to make previously unaffordable investments in environmental protection and that wealth generates interest in sustainability.[2] Critics, by contrast, focus on the proliferation of environmental problems that follow

This research was supported by a PSC–CUNY grant and the generous support of the CUNY School of Law. It benefitted greatly from the thought-provoking dialogue at the conference Creation of International Law: An Exploration of Normative Innovation, Contextual Application, and Interpretation in a Time of Flux hosted by Department of Public and International Law, University of Oslo. I am indebted to Jonathan Saxon, Kathy Williams and Raquel Gabriel for their assistance in obtaining obscure and hard-to-find documents, and to Sarah Lamdan, Mik Kinkead and Bianca Cappelini for assistance with citations and formatting, to Emily Shalcross, Paula Segel, Casey Bryant and Anna Arstein-Karslake for excellent research help, to Nadia Bood and Mauricio Mejia of the World Wildlife Fund for the access they gave me, to Fiona de Londras, Hari Osofsky, Michelle Anderson, Dr. Beate Sjåfjell and Dr. Christina Voigt for substantive feedback, and to Naomi Florence and B. Allen Schulz for their endless patience and support.

[1] Roderick P. Neumann, *Making Political Ecology* (London: Hodder Arnold, 2005), 80. Neumann describes Marshall Berman's analysis of Faust in *All that Is Solid Melts into Air: The Experience of Modernity* (Toronto: Penguin, 1988), 40.

[2] Anna Strutt and Kym Anderson, 'Will Trade Liberalization Harm the Environment? The Case of Indonesia to 2020', at: www.adelaide.edu.au/cies/papers/sp9804.pdf. The article argues that trade generates a surplus that can be used for environmental protection.

production for the global market, and the attendant degradation of ecosystem services. Instead of embracing the complexity of the relationship between trade and environmental protection, discourse too often devolves into equating trade with either destruction or progress: either approach is so gross an oversimplification that it represents a failure of analysis.

Both sides of this tug of war invoke the legacy of colonialism in support of their position. Of the many complex motivations that drove colonialism, the one of most relevance to this chapter was the desire to secure access to the mineral, timber and biological wealth of the colonized states for the benefit of the colonial masters. Because this kind of exploitation focused on the needs and desires not of the inhabitants of a place, but of producers and consumers elsewhere, attention to the externalities of pollution, social instability, resource depletion or loss of biodiversity was rare (and of course much of this exploitation occurred when attention to those issues in general was lacking). In the rush to extract wealth from colonial holdings, local environments and societies were devastated. Explorations of the contours of a right to development, and its relationship to environmental rights, would become a central issue only with widespread decolonization and the emergence of the Third World.

Both sets of rights are deeply embedded in decolonization's intellectual legacy. Where some perceive free trade as a form of recolonization, others characterize the embrace of "sustainable development," particularly by the Bretton Woods Institutions, as merely a new, more intrusive set of reasons justifying intervention into the governance of developing countries.[3] As a result, the colonial shadow still influences all sides of the international discourses surrounding both trade and environmental protection.

The self-determination impetus behind decolonization clearly encompassed the desire to make choices about resource exploitation and preservation that took the needs of the actual inhabitants into account. Nevertheless, independence did not necessarily mark significant changes in policy with regard to export-oriented trade. For many developing

[3] Balakrishnan Rajagopal, *International Law from Below: Development, Social Movements and Third World Resistance* (Cambridge: Cambridge University Press, 2003), 114–34. To the extent this concern resonates, globalization – and in particular the spectacular rise of transnational corporations – begs the question of who is doing the colonizing. The answer may not be states.

countries, the clearest path to economic growth came from accepting the baton handed off by former colonial masters and continuing the intensive exploitation of natural resources. Prevailing development strategies encouraged these countries to enter the global market by producing commodities intended for export.[4] The lending policies of multilateral and bilateral development institutions fostered and funded this trend.[5] As a strategy for obtaining foreign exchange,[6] export-oriented commodity production can be quite successful, at least for a little while. Over time, however, the price of that success can be widespread environmental degradation.[7] Moreover, the pressure to repay foreign debt, incurred to develop these export industries, too often tempts developing countries to 'mine', rather than sustainably manage their renewable resources.[8] This approach thus reinscribed the fundamental principle from the colonial era that resources were to be exploited not based on the interests of a places' inhabitants, but based on the interests of producers and consumers elsewhere.

As a result, export-led development strategies often placed burdens on ecosystems that exceeded their ability to regenerate. Called the

[4] Jasper Goss, David Burch and Roy E. Rickson, 'Agri-Food Restructuring and Third World Transnationals: Thailand, the CP Group and the Global Shrimp Industry', *World Development*, 28 (2000), 513, 514–15.

[5] Pascal Raux and Denis Bailly, 'Literature Review on World Shrimp Farming', Individual Partner Report for the Project: Policy research for sustainable shrimp farming in Asia (2002), part 4. The Asian Development Bank and the World Bank were the largest sources of loans and grants for development of shrimp farming in developing countries. Other development banks also participated significantly in funding shrimp farming projects in developing countries; at: www.port.ac.uk/research/cemare/publications/pdffiles/sustainableshrimpfarminginasia/filetodownload,28780,en.pdf. Solon Barraclough and Andrea Finger-Stich, 'Some Ecological and Social Implications of Commercial Shrimp Farming in Asia', United Nations Research Institute for Social Development (1996), 18.

[6] Of course, trade policies are closely related to wider resource mobilization and investment strategies. But, the crucial need to generate foreign exchange to meet the needs for imports of capital goods and equipment essential for growth and diversification mean that developing countries are very interested in expanding exports.

[7] Rimjhim M. Aggarwal, 'Globalization, Local Ecosystems and the Rural Poor', *World Development*, 38 (2006), 1405. See generally, James Boyle, *The Public Domain: Enclosing the Commons of the Mind* (New Haven, CT: Yale University Press, 2008). There are also significant social justice concerns associated with this strategy as it entails the privatization and enclosure of areas that were traditionally common-property resources.

[8] Arthur E. Neiland *et al.*, 'Shrimp Aquaculture: Economic Perspectives for Policy Development', *Marine Policy*, 25 (2001), 265, 267.

"resource curse" or the "paradox of plenty," states with an abundance of natural resources often find themselves caught in a cycle of environmental degradation that destroys human health and economic well-being along with the environment.[9] In many states, this degradation has reached such a point that it compromises overall environmental resilience.[10] Indeed, because it depends so heavily on implicit environmental subsidies[11] that come from drawing down environmental goods, some suggest that export-oriented resource extraction is inherently unsustainable.[12] If so, that raises an interesting conundrum for international law, which walks a fine line between facilitating international trade[13] and encouraging environmental protection; between

[9] World Trade Organization, *World Trade Report 2010: Trade in Natural Resources* (2010), 90–96, available at: www.wto.org/english/res_e/publications_e/wtr10_e.htm

[10] Resilience is typically defined as "the buffer capacity or the ability of a system to absorb perturbations, or the magnitude of disturbance that can be absorbed before a system changes its structure" (W. Neil Adger, 'Social and Ecological Resilience: Are They Related?', *Progress in Human Geography*, 24 (2000), 347, 349. Another aspect of resilience focuses on the "capacity for renewal, re-organization and development" (Carle Folke, 'Resilience: The Emergence of a Perspective for Social-Ecological Systems Analyses', *Global Environmental Change*, 16 (2006), 253). Many ecologists consider resilience the key to ecosystem stability and functioning: Harold A. Mooney and Paul R. Ehrlich, 'Ecosystem Services: a Fragmentary History', in Gretchen Daily (ed.), *Nature's Services: Societal Dependence on Natural Ecosystems* (Washington, DC: Island Press, 1997), and to its ability to cope with and adapt to changed circumstances; Folke, 'Resilience', 254. Thus, fostering resilience is a central aspect of much work on sustainability. See generally, Michael S. Common, *Sustainability and Policy: Limits to Economics* (Cambridge: Cambridge University Press, 1995).

[11] See, for example: reports by the Global Alliance for Workers and Communities, an international coalition dedicated to improving the workplace experiences, particularly in Asia, at wwww.theglobalalliance.org; Michael Rauscher, 'On Ecological Dumping', *Oxford Economic Papers*, 46 (1994), 822. There has been a great deal of work exploring social dumping in the EU context, see, e.g., Tito Cordella and Isabel Grilo, 'Social Dumping and Relocations: Is there a Case for Imposing a Social Clause?', *Regional Science and Urban Economics*, 31 (2001), 645.

[12] Marta G. Rivera-Ferre, 'Can Export Oriented Aquaculture in Developing Countries Be Sustainable and Promote Sustainable Development: The Shrimp Case', *Journal of Agricultural and Environmental Ethics*, 22 (2009), 301; see also Daniel Bergquest, 'Colonized coasts', Ph.D. thesis, Uppsala University (2008), at: www.cemus.uu.se/cefo/Manuscript%2020070903.pdf; Partha Dasgupta, 'Is Contemporary Economic Development Sustainable?', *Ambio: A Journal of the Human Environment*, 31 (2002), 269; Jonas Larsson, Carle Folke and Nils Kautsky, 'Ecological Limitations and Appropriation of Ecosystem Support by Shrimp Farming in Columbia', *Environmental Management*, 18 (2004), 663.

[13] The premier international organization devoted to trade is, of course, the World Trade Organization (www.wto.org).

recognizing a state's right to development,[14] and promoting the human right to a healthy environment.[15]

International law clearly embraces both development and environmental rights. The profusion of multinational environmental treaties reflects a growing consensus that human activities are threatening the integrity of the earth's ecosystems, and that environmental degradation is among the most serious threats to global stability.[16] At the same time, the World Trade Organization (WTO) embodies international law's investment in free trade. Both environmental and trade values are repeatedly asserted to be at the core of international law and international civil society. Indeed, the United Nation's Millennium Declaration identifies "respect for nature" as one of the fundamental values for the twenty-first century (along with freedom, equality, solidarity, tolerance and shared responsibility),[17] and environmental sustainability was identified as one of the eight Millennium Development Goals alongside the goal of halving poverty by 2015. Thus the international community explicitly recognized environmental protection as a concern on par with ending poverty.[18]

The WTO conceives of itself as contributing to the achievement of these Millennium Development Goals.[19] This self-conception is

[14] See, e.g., Declaration on the Right to Development, UN GOR, 41st Sess., UN Doc. A/RES/41/128 (Dec. 4, 1986), Annex, at 186; Subrata Roy Choudhury *et al.* (eds.), *The Right to Development in International Law* (Dordrecht: Kluwer Academic, 2002) (exploring the ideological and theoretical grounding for a right to development); Arjun Sengupta *et al.* (eds.), *Reflections on the Right to Development* (New Delhi: Sage Publications, 2001) (containing essays discussing the theoretical and historical aspects of the right to development and empirical case studies examining national development policies from right to development perspective, and explaining links between social choice and right to development).

[15] See Xiaobing Xu and George Wilson 'On Conflict of Human Rights', *Pierce Law Review*, 5 (2006), 38–9 (discussing a broad construction of human rights "based on the totality of international human rights efforts in the United Nations" and including "not only traditional civil and political rights, but also ... so-called 'third generation rights,' such as the right to development and the right to the environment"). See generally Luis E. Rodriguez-Rivera, 'Is the Human Right to Environment Recognized under International Law? It Depends on the Source', *Colorado Journal of International Environmental Law and Policy*, 12 (2001), 1 (tracing the various arguments for a human right to environment).

[16] The Secretary-General, *High-level Panel on Threats, Challenges and Change, A More Secure World: Our Shared Responsibility*, 12, 53–4, UN Doc. A/59/565 (Dec. 2, 2004).

[17] United Nations Millennium Declaration, GA Res. 55/2, UN GAOR, 55th Sess., UN Doc. A/Res/55/2 (Sept. 18, 2000).

[18] Millennium Development Goals (www.un.org/millenniumgoals).

[19] www.wto.org/english/news_e/news10_e/tnc_chair_report_29jul10_e.htm

particularly important because the WTO has been repeatedly asked to weigh in on the balancing act between environmental protection and free trade, beginning with the pre-WTO Dolphin–Tuna case,[20] and most recently in the GMO case.[21] Given the comparative enforcement strength between the various multinational environmental agreements and the agreements administered by the WTO, it is not surprising that these disputes often wind up in that trade-oriented forum.[22] However, it should raise concerns that fundamental choices about a hierarchy of values in international law are being resolved in a forum dedicated to one of the contested sets of values. This concern is heightened by a persistent strain of analysis that would subsume environmental concerns into trade and development entirely. Known as the environmental Kuznets curve hypothesis, this line of thinking assumes away the conflict between international law's trade promotion and environmental protection priorities. It does so by purporting to demonstrate that increasing overall social wealth through trade inevitably produces increased environmental protection. If true, this relationship between trade and environmental protection would encourage developing states interested in protecting their environments to abandon environmental protection regulation and sustainable development initiatives in favor of rapidly promoting maximum economic development.

This chapter disputes the putative relationship between global trade and environmental protection embodied by the environmental Kuznets curve hypothesis. Section 1 describes the growth of the Kuznets curve meme, and the influence this approach has had on legal and policy choices surrounding development and environmental protection. Section 2 details the flaws inherent in a Kuznets curve-influenced development strategy, leveling both practical and theoretical critiques of its central thesis that economic development inherently creates a more sustainable society. Having rejected the environmental Kuznets curve hypothesis,

[20] This case predates the WTO and was decided under the GATT. United States – GATT Dispute Panel Report on Restrictions on Imports of Tuna, Sept. 3, 1991, GATT BISD (39th Supp.), at 155 (1993).

[21] Panel Report, European Communities – Measures Affecting the Approval and Marketing of Biotech Products, WT/DS291/R, WT/DS292/R, WT/DS293/R (Sept. 9, 2006), available at: http://tiny.cc/p5g8p

[22] For an in-depth exploration of these tensions, see Christina Voigt, *Sustainable Development as a Principle of International Law: Resolving Conflicts between Climate Measures and WTO Law* (Leiden and Boston, MA: Martinus Nijhoff, 2008).

section 3 briefly highlights some possible alternatives for addressing the tensions between global trade and sustainability.

1 The Kuznets curve and its influence

The term Kuznets curve comes from an influential Cold-War era paper in which economist Simon Kuznets theorized that income inequality in a developing market economy would follow an inverted U-shaped curve.[23] According to Kuznets, income inequality would initially rise precipitously in such a community as the market's winners amassed wealth. But, as the society grew wealthier, Kuznets theorized that citizens would begin to demand education and social welfare programs from their government. These programs would then rectify the intense inequality of the earlier period, and would produce rough economic equality at a new, higher level.

Four decades later, economists Gene Grossman and Alan Krueger theorized that environmental protection might follow a Kuznets curve.[24] They asserted that while pollution levels increase as a society grows wealthier, societies eventually reach the Kuznets "turning point" as the now-wealthier society begins to invest in environmental protection. Economists began proposing inverted U-shaped relationships between income and a wide variety of environmental ills ranging from air pollution, water pollution, annual deforestation, carbon intensity and so on.[25] There has been much speculation over the income level at which the turning point is reached.

[23] Simon Kuznets, 'Economic Growth and Income Inequality', *American Economic Review*, 45 (1955), 1. In 1971, Kuznets's work was recognized with the award of the Nobel Prize for Economics.

[24] Gene M. Grossman and Alan B. Krueger, 'Economic Growth and the Environment', *Quarterly Journal of Economics*, 110 (1995), 353, 354.

[25] See: Christoph Martin Lieb, 'The Environmental Kuznets Curve and Flow versus Stock Pollution: The Neglect of Future Damages', *Environmental and Resource Economics*, 29 (2004), 483; Matthew A. Cole *et al.*, 'The Environmental Kuznets Curve: An Empirical Analysis', *Environmental and Development Economics*, 2 (1997), 401; Thomas M. Seldon and Daqing Song, 'Environmental Quality and Development: Is There a Kuznets Curve for Air Pollution Emissions?', *Journal of Environmental Economics and Management*, 27 (1994), 147; Douglas Holtz-Eakin and Thomas M. Selden, 'Stoking the Fires? CO_2 Emissions and Economic Growth', *Journal of Public Economics*, 57 (1995), 85; Gene M. Grossman and Alan B. Krueger, 'Environmental Impacts of a North American Free Trade Agreement', Working Paper No. 3914, National Bureau of Economic Research (1991).

This environmental Kuznets curve thesis fits nicely with the UN's 1987 Brundtland Commission Report, *Our Common Future*,[26] which identified poverty as a major cause of environmental degradation, and proposed that greater economic growth through increased international trade would improve environmental conditions. If pollution in fact followed a Kuznets curve,[27] then there was an easy answer to these seemingly contradictory internationally identified imperatives. Growth alone would reconcile the perceived conflict between the international priorities of environmental protection and economic development, thereby harmonizing the WTO's trade liberalization agenda with the goals of multilateral environmental agreements.

The business community eagerly embraced the environmental Kuznets curve, which offered them a theoretical rationale for continuing business as usual, and a tactical weapon for blunting civil society calls for a transformative approach to international trade. Suspicious that the Northern environmental agenda would reinscribe the hierarchy of colonization, many developing countries also signed on. The environmental Kuznets curve hypothesis rapidly gained traction in policy circles, and by the early 1990s, had become standard fare on op-ed pages[28] and

[26] UN Environment Program Governing Council, Report of the World Commission on Environment and Development, *Our Common Future*, UN Doc. UNEP/GC.14/13, ES-7 (Mar. 20, 1987). Even before that, the Stockholm Declaration urged states to "adopt an integrated and co-ordinated approach to their development planning so as to ensure that development is compatible with the need to protect and improve [the] environment for the benefit of their population" (Report of the United Nations Conference on the Human Environment 1972, Stockholm Declaration of the United Nations Conference on the Human Environment, Prin. 13, 1, 4, UN Doc. A/ CONF. 48/14/Rev. (1973), reprinted in 11 ILM 1416 (1972)). Principle 9 of the Stockholm Declaration urged nations to adopt environmental policies that "enhance" the "development potential of developing countries," (*ibid.*), while Principal 2 emphasized the compelling need for intergenerational equity ("[t] he natural resources of the earth . . . must be safeguarded for the benefit of present and future generations through careful planning or management").

[27] The foundational paper for this claim purported to demonstrate that the relationship between sulfur oxide (SO_2) pollution and GDP followed a Kuznet curve. Gene M. Grossman and Allen B. Krueger, 'Economic Growth and the Environment', *Quarterly Journal of Economics*, 110 (1991), 353–77. It was rapidly followed by numerous other articles purporting to find a Kuznet curve, or a related variant curve for a host of pollution issues. See Arik Levinson, 'The Ups and Downs of Environmental Kuznet Curves', Working Paper, Georgetown University (2000), at: www9.georgetown.edu/faculty/aml6/pdfsandzips/ups%20and%20downs.pdf (arguing for the more modest claim that the data proves only that environmental degradation need not accompany economic growth).

[28] See: John Tierney, 'Use energy, get rich and save the planet', *New York Times*, April 21, 2009, D1, available at: www.nytimes.com/2009/04/21/science/earth/21tier.html?_r=3; Bruce Barlett, 'The High Cost of Turning Green', *Wall Street Journal*, September 14, 1994, A18.

policy briefings worldwide.[29] Many international institutions embraced the notion that the best way to ensure environmental protection was through the increased prosperity that global trade would bring.[30] The WTO recently went one step further, asserting that free trade of natural resources ensures their long-term sustainability.[31]

This vision of trade-induced sustainability offers a counter-narrative to civil society pressure on extractive industries to reduce their ecological footprint. After all, if environmental degradation is a necessary stage that states must go through as a precursor of later vigorously protecting their environment,[32] there is little reason for the World Bank, the IMF, or, for that matter private capital, to heed civil society's call that they bring an environmental sensibility to their activities, or that they recognize when their trade-liberalization activities are incompatible with preserving the integrity of ecosystems, natural resources, animal and plant life or human health. In fact, according to the prevailing reading of environmental Kuznets curves, incorporating environmental concerns at early

[29] Bruce Yandle, Maya Vijayaraghavan and Madhusudan Bhattarai, 'The Environmental Kuznets Curve: A Primer', *Property and Environment Center Research Study 02–1*, at: www.perc.org/files/Yandle_Kuznets02.pdf (2000). See generally: International Bank for Reconstruction and Development (World Bank), *World Development Report 1992: Development and the Environment* (New York: Oxford University Press), 11, 38–40, available at: www-wds.worldbank.org/external/default/WDSContentServer/IW3P/IB/2000/12/13/000178830_9810191106175/Rendered/PDF/multi_page.pdf

[30] Indeed, there is an entire school of so-called "free-market environmentalism," which espouses this belief that economic development alone will ensure increased protection for the environment. See e.g., John Baden and Robert Ethier, 'Free Trade Pact Links Prosperity and Environment', *Seattle Times*, September 28, 1992, A9, available at: www.free-eco.org/articleDisplay.php?id=334

[31] The WTO makes a nod toward environmental impacts of trade in natural resources, but by carefully massaging the assumptions and preconditions it employs, the WTO manages to conclude that trade actually increases rather than decreases sustainability (*World Trade Report 2010: Trade in Natural Resources*, at: www.wto.org/english/res_e/booksp_e/anrep_e/wtr10–2f_e.pdf).

[32] See e.g., Wilfred Beckerman, 'Economic Growth and the Environment: Whose Growth? Whose Environment?', *World Development*, 20 (1992), 481 (claiming that "there is clear evidence that, although economic growth usually leads to environmental degradation in the early stages of the process, in the end the best – and probably the only – way to attain a decent environment in most countries is to become rich"). This approach is embodied by the World Bank's 1992 *World Development Report*, which characterized the perceived conflict between economic activity and environmental protection as "based on static assumptions about technology, tastes and environmental investments" and asserted that "[a]s incomes rise, the demand for improvements in environmental quality will increase, as will the resources available for investment" ((New York: Oxford University Press, 1992), 38–9).

development stages might actually work against the ultimate goals of sustainability and environmental protection.

2 Critiquing the Kuznets curve as an accurate description of the relationship between increased trade and increased sustainability

The theory of comparative advantage flows from the premise that all trading partners gain from trade when each specializes in the goods that it can produce most efficiently. From this basic Ricardian premise, an entire theoretical edifice supporting free trade has been built. Unfortunately, this basic theory does not consider environmental externalities associated with the production or consumption of goods. Thus, the environmental Kuznets curve hypothesis comes in handy. Rather than offering any reason to internalize these environmental externalities, thereby getting a truer sense of the cost of production, which might shift or negate the comparative advantage assessment, environmental Kuznets curves encourage decision-makers to bracket sustainability concerns. From the premise that economic growth will inevitably spur environmental improvements, it is not much of a theoretical leap to assuming that a stage of environmental degradation is a necessary precursor to the prosperity that will achieve environmental goals.[33] This convenient and important assumption allows decisionmakers to discount the environmental harms associated with production for global trade on the ground that these problems will inevitably take care of themselves as a state becomes wealthier. As such, environmental Kuznets curves invite policymakers to avoid hard thinking about potentially incommensurable values.[34] But there are both practical and theoretical objections to depending on environmental Kuznets curves to bring about sustainability and environmental protection outcomes.

2.1 Practical objections

Poverty alleviation is often an explicit goal and justification for developing countries to support the creation of export-led resource extraction

[33] Susmita Dasgupta *et al.*, 'Confronting the Kuznets Curve', *Journal of Economic Perspectives*, 16 (2002), 147, 158, 163–4 (critiquing this assumption and proposing that with proper regulation, environmental quality and economic prosperity can increase together).

[34] For a discussion of the incommensurability point, see Carmen E. Pavel, 'Normative Conflict in International Law', *San Diego Law Review*, 46 (2009), 884, 892–3.

industries. States, investors and donors claim that the increased revenues will lift entire communities out of poverty, thereby making other goals, like sustainability, more possible. That environmental protection follows a Kuznets curve is presumed to be undisputed fact.

Yet, there are some significant practical objections to the environmental Kuznets curve hypothesis. First, the evidence for such a relationship is the result of a few limited and wholly academic studies that used carefully selected variables. Very little empirical data undergirds the environmental Kuznets curve hypothesis. Even for those pollutants most often touted as clear examples of the environmental Kuznets curve in action, empirical researchers disagree as to whether the environmental Kuznets curve hypothesis provides a good fit for the available data.[35] Indeed, some economists reject the theory entirely, asserting that there is little evidence that a Kuznets curve relationship between trade and environmental protection actually exists.[36] Other thinkers point out that the environmental Kuznets curve hypothesis blurs the line between correlation and causation, noting that drawing and reading environmental Kuznets curves in reverse would be just as easy, and fit the data just as well. Reorienting the curve along these lines would reverse the hypothesis, leading to the conclusion that "since higher levels of pollution control are correlated with higher wealth among developed countries, the key to future economic growth is cutting pollution."[37]

In addition to noting the thinness of the data supporting the environmental Kuznets curves hypothesis, critics also point to mounting evidence that for many environmental issues, like biodiversity conservation, fisheries management, greenhouse gas emissions, and overall ecological footprint, results do not fit within the environmental Kuznets curve theory.[38] There is a growing recognition that the aggregate

[35] David I. Stern, 'Progress on the Environmental Kuznets Curve?', *Environmental and Development Economics*, 3 (1998), 175 (describing the data behind Kuznets curves claims as limited and unsystematic).

[36] David I. Stern: 'The Environmental Kuznets Curve', in Eric Neumayer (ed.), *Ecological Economics Encyclopedia* (London: London School of Economics, 2003), at: www.ecoeco.org/pdf/stern.pdf (raising serious methodological and theoretical flaws in research finding environmental Kuznet curves); and 'The Rise and Fall of the Environmental Kuznets Curve', *World Development*, 32 (2004), 1419.

[37] Daniel Farber, 'Rethinking the Role of Cost–Benefit Analysis', *University of Chicago Law Review*, 76 (2009), 1355, 1368.

[38] Kenneth Arrow *et al.*, 'Economic Growth, Carrying Capacity, and the Environment', *Ecological Economics*, 15 (1995), 91–5; Arik Levinson, 'The Ups and Downs of Environmental Kuznet Curves' (2000) UCF/CentER Conference, at: www9.georgetown.edu/

growth statistics touted by global trade's most vocal supporters can and often do mask increasing inequality and further environmental degradation.[39] While it is possible that the increased income associated with export-focused resource extraction, *could* translate into increased sustainability, decreased poverty, or a new focus on environmental protection, it does not seem to do so with any regularity.[40] For example, aquaculture, an industry heavily promoted to developing countries by the multilateral investment agencies, tends to focus on producing high-value luxury commodities (such as salmon and lobster) for sale in wealthy, developed markets rather than on producing food for local consumption.[41] Mining and ore-smelting activities often inflict a terrible pollution toll on local residents and their

faculty/aml6/pdfsandzips/ups%20and%20downs.pdf (demonstrating that a U-shaped pollution–income curve can be fully consistent with sub-optimal environmental policies, and cannot, by itself, justify a laissez-faire approach to pollution control). See Peter Uvin, 'On Moral High Ground: The Incorporation of Human Rights By Development Organizations', *Praxis*, 17 (2002), 1, 2, at: http://fletcher.tufts.edu/praxis/archives/xvii/Uvin.pdf (pointing out, in the human rights context, that development organizations sometimes co-opt language in order to validate existing practices); Jack Donnelly, 'Human Rights, Democracy and Development', *Human Rights Quarterly*, 21 (1999), 611.

39 Dolagobinda Pradhan and Mark Flaherty, 'National Initiatives, Local Effects: Trade Liberalization, Shrimp Aquaculture and Coastal Communities in Orissa, India', *Society and Natural Resources*, 21 (2008), 63, 63–5; Calogero Carletto, Angeli Kirk, Paul Winters and Benjamin Davis, 'Nontraditional Crops, Traditional Constraints: The Adoption and Diffusion of Export Crops Among Guatemalan Smallholders', *World Bank Policy Research Working Paper*, 2–4 (2007), 4347; Fantu Cheru, 'Transforming Our Common Future: The Local Dimensions of Global Reform', *Review of International Political Economy*, 7 (2000), 353.

40 For example, Henry Tucker of the Asian Development Bank's Agriculture, Environment and Natural Resources Division, characterized the Bank's withdrawal from shrimp aquaculture funding by pointing out that "shrimp culture is primarily a commercial enterprise that is not so appropriate as a means of poverty reduction" (quoted in Christophe Bene, 'The Good, The Bad and the Ugly: Discourse, Policy Controversies and the Role of Science in the Politics of Shrimp Farming Development', *Development Policy Review*, 23 (2005), 590). China may be the exception to this rule. In China, aquaculture, though not necessarily of shrimp, has dramatically increased protein availability on a per capita basis. What remains unclear is whether this translates into greater availability of protein to the food insecure, or merely mirrors the global situation of increased production from aquaculture translating into increased consumption of high-status fish by wealthy elites and a growing middle class. FAO (2010), State of World Fisheries and Aquaculture 2010, FAO Fisheries and Aquaculture Department, Food and Agriculture Organization, Rome 63–5, at: www.fao.org/docrep/013/i1820e/i1820e.pdf (SOWFA).

41 SOWFA, n. 40 above, 61(noting that the consumption of high-priced commodities like shrimp is concentrated mainly in affluent economies).

environment.[42] Petroleum extraction is notorious for devastating local environments while also failing to benefit the local communities in which it occurs.[43] The multinational companies engaged in these industries often cite the pressures of competing in a global market as justification for not installing even readily available pollution control equipment.[44]

The relationships between global trade, local development and sustainability are complex, multidirectional, and not always easy to predict. Thus, it should not be surprising that export-driven extraction activities, even when profitable and productive, do not reliably produce real improvement in the conditions of life for local poor people.[45] Instead, there is some evidence that this kind of development reinforces inequality in the areas in which it occurs.[46] It is quite possible to have a highly profitable export industry, like shrimp farming, timber or oil extraction, bringing significant foreign exchange and investment to the state without the local community benefitting much, if at all. Moreover, allowing environmental pollution/destruction today in the hopes of preservation/restoration tomorrow allows unsustainable practices to become the default – the "normal" way to do things.

42 Anna K. Cederstav and Alberto Barandiaran G., *La Oroya Cannot Wait* (Oakland, CA: Inter-American Association for Environmental Defense, 2002), describing pollution and health effects from the Doe Run Smelter in Peru, which is owned by the American Company Doe Run; Pratap Chatterjee, 'Human Rights – Indonesia; US Mining Giant Implicated in Indonesian Atrocities', online article, *Ecological Enterprises* (1995), describing the environmental degradation caused by Freeport mine operations in Indonesia.

43 *Nigeria: Petroleum, Pollution and Poverty in the Niger Delta* (London: Amnesty International, 2009).

44 For example, the Doe Run smelter La Oroya, Peru has repeatedly cited cost pressure from Chinese smelters as the reason it refuses to install legally mandated pollution control equipment, even though virtually all of the children in the town of La Oroya have blood lead concentrations that vastly exceed WHO safety guidelines. Cederstav and Barandiaran G., *La Oroya Cannot Wait*, documenting the environmental and health catastrophe in La Oroya. In 2009, the Inter-American Commission on Human Rights accepted a case brought on behalf of the city's residents alleging that the failure to control pollution at the smelter amounted to a deprivation of the right to life and the right to bodily integrity. Inter-American Commission on Human Rights, 'Admisibilidad Comunidad de la Oroya Peru', available online (2009), at: www.aida-americas.org/sites/default/files/admisibilida-d_La_Oroya_09–08.pdf. This case is one of many highlighting how global competitive pressures discourage capital investment in environmental and safety technology.

45 Rivera-Ferre, 'Can Export Oriented Aquaculture', 301.

46 Nyguyen L. Lebel *et al.*, 'Industrial Transformation and Shrimp Aquaculture in Thailand and Vietnam: Pathways to Ecological, Social and Economic Sustainability?', *Ambio: A Journal of the Human Environment*, 31 (2002), 311.

Any change to that normalized approach is then perceived as a costly add-on, rather than an inherent cost of doing business.

That the underlying data provides at best mixed evidence for environmental Kuznets curves has not prevented interested parties from making sweeping claims for this approach in the policy arena. Even if economic growth, in and of itself, may provide the impetus for solving some environmental problems, as the environmental Kuznets curve hypothesis suggests, there is nothing inevitable about such a result. When there are generalized local costs, and substantial local benefits, there is a reasonable possibility that increased resources from trade will produced the posited increase in environmental protection. (Whether the steps taken as a result of increased resources, be they pollution control devices or clean up activities, are capable of actually increasing environmental welfare, rather than merely slowing its erosion is a separate question, discussed in the next section below.) However, when the costs of environmental degradation are borne not by those who benefit economically from the activity but by others, especially the poor or otherwise marginalized groups, increased wealth from trade brings few incentives to alter damaging behaviors. In most circumstances, active public intervention in the form of regulation, and rigorous civil society oversight will be critical to achieving environmentally desired results.

Moreover, the environmental Kuznets curve hypothesis presumes an extremely optimistic vision of what remedial technologies can actually accomplish vis-à-vis resolving the environmental crises created by the development/trade portion of the Kuznets curve analysis. It relies on the dangerous premise that humans have the capacity to retroactively cure the environmental problems we create. This is of particular concern for environmental challenges stemming from overexploitation of resources and the attendant pollution externalities. To the extent that trade-mediated growth draws down environmental capital and converts it into financial capital, those trade-offs may be irreversible. For example, there is no way to "un-exterminate" a species driven to extinction by habitat destruction, nor is there any clear way to restore the world's atmospheric CO_2 concentrations to pre-industrial levels.[47]

[47] For a critique that highlights the missing parties in the internationally negotiated agreements responding to the problems of climate change, see Chapter 9, in this volume.

Such an approach also overlooks the tensions between the sustainability and free trade approaches to problem-solving,[48] and ignores the role that global trade concerns play in shaping domestic regulatory policy. The ecological problems associated with export-oriented resource extraction are, at their core, social and political problems rather than technical or managerial ones.[49] Too often, environmental harms are defined as technical challenges, amenable to technical solutions,[50] rather than structural problems implicating fundamental social and economic choices. A parallel narrative seeks to cast environmental costs of these activities as a reflection of the differing environmental preferences of citizens in sovereign states.[51] Climate change, and anthropogenic greenhouse gas generation are perhaps the clearest examples of the dangers of relying on technical fixes to solve systemic environmental problems. The scale of the problem is so immense, and the level of complexity is so high, that technical solutions proposed to "solve" the problem (typically in lieu of fundamentally changing behavior) risk creating even more harm.[52]

If, instead of assuming that trade-induced prosperity will solve environmental problems, we consider those problems to be the inevitable outcome of a set of structural and organizational choices at the core of global trade,[53] we see that not only does this dominant, export-led development model shape the available technologies and methods for resource extraction, it also defines the very possibilities for environmental regulatory innovation as

[48] Judith A. Giles and Cara L. Williams, 'Export Led Growth: A Survey of the Economic Literature and Some Noncausality Results', Working Paper, at: http://papers.ssrn.com/sol3/papers.cfm?abstract_id=146208 (1999), 1, 26.

[49] For a full description of the field of political ecology, see Roderick P. Neumann, *Making Political Ecology* (Oxford: Oxford University Press, 2005), defining environmental problems as simultaneously political and ecological, social and biophysical.

[50] See e.g., Global Aquaculture Alliance, *Feeding the World through Responsible Aquaculture* (2001); Claude E. Boyd and Jason W. Clay, 'Shrimp Aquaculture and the Environment: An Adviser to Shrimp Producers and an Environmentalist Present a Prescription for Raising Shrimp Responsibly', *Scientific American*, 42 (1998), 9.

[51] Andrew P. Morriss and Roger E. Meiners, 'Borders and the Environment', 31 *Environmental Law*, 141, (2009), 175–8.

[52] As Professor Dan Tarlock presciently warned a decade ago in the climate change context, "adaptation is based on the ideology of scientific progress, a faith that is open to question . . . Science and technology may not always prevent serious harm or make things better" ('Now Again Think about Climate Change', *Arizona Journal of International and Comparative Law*, 9 (1992), 169, 170).

[53] For a discussion of the political choices incorporated into the collection and processing of nominally scientific information, see Piers Blaikie, 'Changing Environments or Changing Views? A Political Ecology for Developing Countries', *Geography*, 348 (1995), 203, 208.

developing nations seek to enter the global market. It does so in part using the power of definition to exclude entire categories of concerns from the discourse surrounding the desirability of trade and the accuracy of comparative advantage assessments. Not only will these definitional choices limit a state's ability to use its domestic regulatory apparatus to respond to environmental concerns, they also mean that the scientific information and technical capacities generated in this context will be incomplete – because those capacities will exclude critical considerations that were defined out of the problem.[54] This is particularly troubling because the manner in which export-led growth curbs the state's regulatory flexibility has a strong environmental justice component.[55]

The relationship between global trade and environmental protection is much more complex than a simple curve drawn onto a chart.[56] Simply conflating environmental protection with free trade pays no heed to the obstacles that stand in the way of achieving either or both. Effective management of environmental burdens generated by trade needs to respond to, not merely to note, that the costs associated with export-oriented growth are borne disproportionately by the rural poor, while the benefits tend to flow elsewhere.[57]

2.2 *Theoretical objections*

The conventional story, embodied in the environmental Kuznets curve hypothesis has developed countries leading the way, with less-developed countries following in their wake. To the extent this relationship is portrayed as desirable or natural, it shores up the global power status quo by ignoring the developing world's experience with Northern colonialism, environmental exploitation, protectionism and overconsumption.

[54] For an in-depth exploration of this point, see Rebecca Bratspies, 'Regulatory Trust', *Arizona Law Review*, 53 (2009), 575.

[55] These environmental justice concerns are entwined with, but distinct from the more ecosystem-based environmental concerns explored in this chapter. For a discussion of the social justice implications of shrimp farming, see Susan C. Stonich, 'The Environmental Quality and Social Justice Implications of Shrimp Mariculture', *Human Ecology: An Interdisciplinary Journal*, 23 (1995), 143, 149–56 (making the case that shrimp farming in Honduras fosters economic growth at the expense of environmental destruction and worsening rural poverty).

[56] See Julianne H. Mills and Thomas A. Waite, 'Economic Prosperity, Biodiversity Conservation and the Environmental Kuznet Curve', *Ecological Economics*, 68 (2009) 2087, 2092–3.

[57] *Ibid.*

These experiences must be part of any genuine conversation about sustainability, trade and environmental protection if only because drawing the boundaries between trade policy and environmental decisionmaking implicates state sovereignty.[58]

Ignoring or denying this context gives rise to the suspicion that sustainability discourse is just another way for the developed countries to exert power over developing countries. A predictable drama plays out when developed states advocate for particular production techniques deemed "sustainable" as a condition of trade, or when workers in developed countries object to what they see as unfair competition from exploited, underpaid labor in the developing world. Developing countries push back, labeling Northern attempts to impose environmental protection measures as environmental protectionism[59] or even neo-colonialism in a new guise.[60] This phenomenon is clearly at play in the climate change discourse.[61]

At the core of this concern is the critical question of *who* shapes a state's sustainability policies: the state through its regulatory powers, or the collection of individual and systemic choices we call "the market."

58 See Benedict Kingsbury, 'The Tuna–Dolphin Controversy, the World Trade Organization, and the Liberal Project to Reconceptualize International Law', *Yearbook of International Environmental Law*, 5 (1994), 29.

59 See: Achim Korber, *The Political Economy of Environmental Protectionism* (Northampton, MA: Edward Elgar Publishers, 2000); Piritta Soursa, *Environmental Protectionism, North–South Trade and the Uruguay Round*, IMF Working Paper No. 95/6 (1995), at: http://papers.ssrn.com/sol3/papers.cfm?abstract_id=883156, 1–2, 9–12; Katie A. Lane, 'Protectionism or Environmental Activism? The WTO as a Means of Reconciling the Conflict Between Global Free Trade and the Environment', *University of Miami Inter-American Law Review*, 32(2001), 103, 105.

60 See: Elli Louka, *International Environmental Law: Fairness, Effectiveness and World Order* (Cambridge: Cambridge University Press, 2006), 28–30 (describing the roots of this thinking); some have argued that the efforts by developed nations to codify international environmental law is merely a "ploy to keep the developing world economically and politically subservient to Western capitalist and neocolonial interests" (e.g., Olusegun Areola, 'Comparative Environmental Issues and Policies in Nigeria', in Uday Desai (ed.), *Ecological Policy and Politics in Developing Countries* (New York: State University of New York Press, 1998), 241); Howard Taubenfeld, 'Environment and Development', *Proceedings of the Annual Meeting (American Society of International Law)*, 77 (1983) 411; Joao Augusto de Araujo Castro, 'Environment and Development: The Case of the Developing Countries', *International Organization*, 26 (1972), 401 (claiming that environmental protection would tend "to perpetuate the existing gap in socioeconomic development between developed and developing countries and so promote the freezing of the present international order"). Others have made use of this argument for their own ends, e.g., Robert H. Nelson, 'Environmental Colonialism: Saving Africa from Africans', *Independent Review*, 8 (2003), 65, 65–70 (making this claim as part of a free-market argument critical of conservation measures).

61 For an excellent exploration of this issue, see Voigt, *Sustainable Development*.

Unfortunately, this core concern is often suppressed. For example, the WTO jurisprudence addressing environmental trade disputes does not acknowledge that it is choosing between contested and alternative value frames, but instead systematically normalizes one of those frames as the natural and inevitable way of viewing these problems. Thus, free trade becomes the overarching lens through which other values gain or lose legitimacy, regardless of the arguments that these other values are co-equal, rather than subordinate to free trade.

2.2.1 Who decides: states or the market?

The authority to formulate and enforce environmental policies exists primarily at the national level. Dating back at least as far as the *Trail Smelter* arbitration, there has been significant attention devoted to the problem of transboundary harms associated with industrial production.[62] Of equal or even greater concern has been the question of how the dynamics of global trade affect sustainability and environmental protection policies within national jurisdictions. In particular, the concern about a race to the bottom has haunted theorists and policy-makers alike. Because trade agreements contain no provisions concerning environmental protection, there is little to prevent a state from deciding that its competitive advantage lies in increasing the pollution load accepted by its citizens and its territory. In short, states can, by allowing greater levels of pollution, provide implicit environmental subsidies to industry. For this reason, the specter that market actors will play states off against each other by demanding implicit environmental subsidies is a very real one. Thus we see extensive discussions about whether free trade pressures states with developed environmental protection regimes to lower their standards.

The specific contours of meaning for trade barrier, subsidy and tariff embedded in the WTO's Global Agreement on Tariffs and Trade (GATT)[63] create a particular vision of trade subsidies that not only categorically excludes implicit environmental subsidies from trade discourses but actually renders those subsidies invisible. With environmental subsidies safely hidden from view, the relationship between trade and environmental protection can be framed as whether "non-trade matters" should be linked

[62] Rebecca Bratspies and Russell Miller, *Transboundary Harm in International Law: Lessons from the 'Trail Smelter' Arbitration* (Cambridge: Cambridge University Press, 2006).

[63] The full text of the GATT agreement is available at: www.wto.org/english/docs_e/legal_e/legal_e.htm

to trade and included in the WTO.[64] As such, this question assumes its own answer – it begins by labeling the environmental (and labor) consequences of trade as "non-trade" matters. Yet that is precisely the definitional issue in question. Because the boundary between "trade" and "non-trade" issues is itself an articulation of values, rather than merely a landscape onto which value can be mapped, it is possible to draw a very different set of boundaries for trade and non-trade issues. Rather than acknowledge this, the WTO doubles back on itself, creating its own jurisdictional competency through a self-fulfilling and subjective set of value judgments. In the process, it buries a host of unacknowledged disagreements about the proper lens through which to view the legal, political and economic interests implicated by both environmental protection and economic development. The most significant problem with this circular reasoning is that it obscures even the recognition of implicit environmental subsidies as a major practical as well as theoretical problem.

A more appropriate question would be to ask why the inherent environmental aspects of trade are currently excluded from WTO consideration. Answering this latter question involves surfacing the key points at which the global trade system is structured to allow, or even require states to provide implicit environmental subsidies. For example, in the Tuna–Dolphin case, the GATT dispute panel ruled that the United States could not use its domestic legislation to protect dolphins outside its territorial limits because, in the panel's view, differences in the way that the tuna were caught could not possibly affect tuna *as a product*.[65] Thus, environmental externalities surrounding the extraction of tuna from the ocean were deemed to be wholly irrelevant to the trade conversation. In a similar 1999 case, the WTO ruled that the United States could not prohibit shrimp imports from countries using fishing methods that killed endangered sea turtles.[66]

These decisions raised concern that international trade law would undercut the ability of states to increase their domestic environmental protection standards. This worry about international trade law curtailing state freedom to develop rigorous environmental protection programs

[64] See e.g., Magda Shahin, 'To What Extent Should Labor and Environmental Standards Be Linked to Trade?', *Law and Development Review*, 2 (2009), 1, 4.

[65] United States – GATT Dispute Panel Report on Restrictions on Imports of Tuna, Sept. 3, 1991, GATT BISD (39th Supp.), at 155 (1993).

[66] Panel Report, United States – Import Prohibition of Certain Shrimp and Shrimp Products, WT/DS58/R (May 15, 1998).

heightened the pre-existing concerns that globalization and free trade would create a relentless race to the bottom for environmental protection. Worse, this approach shut down discussion entirely by rejecting the very idea that accounting for environmental externalities could be part of the trade discourse – rendering important choices about environmental burdens associated with trade invisible. Only if these choices are made visible, does it become possible to consider whether they are ill-advised, or whether alternative choices might be preferable.

Ever since the Dolphin–Tuna decision, there have been major concerns that global trade would compel developed states to lower their environmental standards in order to compete in the global market. Two decades later, responses to the Obama administration's offshore drilling moratorium after the BP oil spill catastrophe demonstrated just how salient that concern remains. Industry spokespeople were quick to suggest that increased oversight might prompt them to move rigs out of the Gulf of Mexico to areas that impose fewer environmental regulations.[67] This kind of thinly veiled threat frequently produces the desired results – weakening or abandonment of proposed environmental protections. Indeed, opposition politicians explicitly cited the specter of job losses in the Gulf Region as grounds for opposing stricter offshore drilling regulation.[68] Thus, global trade can be a weapon for achieving results exactly opposite of the environmental Kuznets curve prediction.

2.2.2 Implicit environmental subsidies: a case study of Belize

In addition to concerns about downward pressure on developed countries' regulatory regimes, there is often significant discussion about the appropriateness (or not) of demanding that developing states implement domestic legal measures to meet higher environmental standards as a precondition for participating in global trading regimes. Developing states point to environmental Kuznets curves as proof that it is inappropriate to expect them to impose high environmental standards until they reach the curve's tipping point (wherever that may be.) These countries

[67] See, e.g., Monica Hatcher, 'Disaster in the Gulf: Drillers may go where the rules matter less', *Houston Chronicle*, June 27, 2010; Tim Webb, 'Gulf drilling ban ruins "job ecosystem"', *The Guardian*, June 22, 2010.

[68] Richard Simon, 'House approves oil spill legislation', *Los Angeles Times*, July 31, 2010; Matthew Daly, 'House approves bill to crack down on offshore drilling, remove liability cap in oil spills', *Newser*, July 30, 2010.

often couple this economic-based argument to a fairness-based argument, pointing out that many of the world's environmental problems (ranging from deforestation to pollution loads to atmospheric greenhouse gas concentrations) are largely the result of earlier uncontrolled growth by the now-developed countries. Yet because the burden of responding to these problems often seems to fall primarily on developing countries, who are now being asked to curb or retool their development, environmental protection policies reinscribe the unequal distribution of wealth between developed and developing world. This is where the neo-colonialist critique comes into play.

The unspoken assumption of this discourse is that Northern trading partners unidirectionally pressure developing countries toward increased environmental protection. Very little attention is paid to the possibility that international trade does the exact opposite: that it limits the ability of developing states to use their own domestic legal systems to achieve better environmental protection within their own borders. But, very often, global markets demand major implicit environmental subsidies as a price of entry. Thus, to participate in global markets for commodities and natural resources, developing states have no choice but to accept market behaviors that lead to pollution loads, and degraded natural resources. Thus, participation in global trade limits the freedom of developing countries to adopt higher standards for environmental protection. The nascent shrimp-farming industry in Belize provides a clear example of how global markets can, and do, demand implicit environmental subsidies from developing countries.

The shrimp farming community in Belize is somewhat atypical. There is an unusually high level of environmental awareness, and a willingness to consider employing more sustainable shrimp-farming methods. The World Wildlife Federation has been working closely with the Belize aquaculture industry to develop coral reef friendly industry practices. The industry is still developing, and beginning with reef friendly practices is much easier and less expensive than retrofitting existing facilities. Nevertheless, constructing reef-friendlier shrimp farming facilities and adopting more sustainable practices requires an upfront investment in technology that increases the capital costs associated with production. That puts Belizean producers at a price disadvantage that prevents them from profitably selling their sustainably produced shrimp into the globalized commoditized shrimp market.

The preference of Belizean shrimp farmers is to farm shrimp in a fashion that protects the reef. This is the Belizean government's preference as well, and reflects a national commitment to protecting the environment while also creating space for economic development. The costs invested in sustainable production simply internalize costs that are otherwise subsidized by the broader society in the form of degraded water supplies, devastated mangrove forests, and harmed coral reefs. As such, these are classic externalities, costs of economic activity that are not accounted for in the private decisions of producers and consumers. Because these effects involve costs to third parties in the form of loss of access to traditional resources, and costs to society as a whole in the form of degraded ecosystems, conventional shrimp farmers' production decisions are not optimal from the perspective of society as a whole.

The problem is that there has historically been no way to sell sustainably produced shrimp into the global commodity market. Because using sustainable technologies prices them out of the global market, it is the global market, rather than the Belize shrimp farmers themselves, or the community in which they operate, that sets the possible conditions under which shrimp farming will be conducted.

Not only does the global trading system not recognize that lower environmental standards for shrimp farms are actually a trade subsidy from the state to the producer – allowing externalization of a cost that should properly be internalized – but the WTO system prohibits countervailing duties under these circumstances.[69] The relentless logic of the global market which seeks out only the least cost provider (cost to consumer that is) without considering total cost of production, forces Belize away from its preference into an unending competition with other shrimp producers who might also have the same preference but have no way to express that collective preference.

This paradox is at the heart of using a "willingness to pay" model to analyze success or failure of shrimp farming – it puts into the hands of the end consumer the ultimate power to decide what the producer will have to accept in terms of environmental degradation. When this problem is viewed through the economic lens of offer and demand, there is no room for producers to assert their preferences for preserving mangrove swamps, even though a number of studies have documented that the overall economic costs of conventional

[69] Amy Sinden, 'The Preference for Pollution and Other Fallacies, or Why Free Trade is Not Progress', in Russell A. Miller and Rebecca M. Bratspies (eds.), *Progress in International Law* (Boston, MA: BRILL, 2008) (making this point).

shrimp farming (if environmental externalities are internalized) significantly exceeds the economic return.[70]

Because the consumer's preference that others subsidize the price of their shrimp dictates the result, the producer is left merely with the illusion of choice. It seems that the narrow, price-driven commodity market for shrimp either cannot make, or refuses to allow space for Belize's actual preference for a sustainable shrimp industry *and* a healthy reef.[71] Instead, the relentless search for lowest-cost production signifies that for Belize to participate in the global shrimp market, it must agree to subsidize production in the form of externalized costs borne by the Belizean environment, particularly the coral reef. Were this Hobson's choice limited to shrimp farming, Belize, and like-minded states might simply eschew the industry for other development opportunities. Yet, each available opportunity comes with the same price of entry – states seeking to enter just about every possible global commodity market have no choice but to provide producers with implicit environmental subsidies by allowing their production to pollute and degrade the environment. The rules of engagement are structured to offer Belize only a false choice: either healthy reefs and mangrove swamps, *or* a successful shrimp-farming industry. If there were room for Belize and other producers to set their own terms of production, they could have both.

3 What to do going forward

Careful examination of development endeavors around the world makes it clear that the conventional wisdom that focusing on export-led development inevitably (or even probably) produces a more sustainable society is wrong. In fact, because they demand implicit environmental subsidies in the form of degrading the environment, many export-oriented activities touted as economic engines of growth are actually economically inefficient – they represent a sale of goods at a price well below the cost of production, if environmental costs are

[70] David Whitmarsh and Maria G. Palmeri, 'Aquaculture in the Coastal Zone: Pressures, Interactions and Externalities', in M. Holmer (ed.), *Aquaculture in the Ecosystem* (New York: Springer, 2008): M. Gunawardena and John S. Rowan, 'Economic Valuation of a Mangrove Ecosystem Threatened by Shrimp Farming', *Environmental Management*, 36 (2005), 535.

[71] Sinden, 'Preference for Pollution'.

included.[72] Every such trade actually transfers wealth away from the state that is providing the implicit subsidy. To begin to remedy this situation, we need to first understand it. That means exploring the role that the world economy plays vis-à-vis the state, as well as the relationship between the state and local resource managers and groups within society that affect resource management.

Entering a global trading regime should not add to the environmental burdens of individuals and communities of any country, be it developed or developing. A sounder, more appropriate understanding of the relationship between trade and the environment begins with the better integration of the obligation to protect against environmental degradation with the desire to promote economic development into a sustainable vision of progress. The question, of course, is how to operationalize such a vision. There are three basic alternatives: (1) create a new market for sustainably produced products; (2) change the existing market; or (3) change the underlying trade rules that structure markets more generally.[73]

3.1 *Creating a new market*

One possibility is to create a new market for sustainably produced products. This initiative is already fairly well developed for timber, coffee and other industries that have developed private certification schemes. Although reliable data is hard to come by, it is clear that these schemes have successfully attached a price premium to sustainability for quite a few produced consumer goods.

A major disadvantage of this approach is that it proceeds commodity by commodity, making progress slow. This approach works best for products sold directly to the end consumer – for example, paying a price premium for sustainably grown coffee is a much easier pitch than paying a price premium for a gold necklace extracted from a sustainably run mine. The longer the chain of custody between producer and consumer, the more difficult it becomes to develop and apply a certification scheme. In part, this is because the host of coordination problems that arise in attempting to create private certification schemes

72 Larsson *et al.*, 'Biological Limitations', 673 (making this claim with regard to shrimp farming); Raux and Bailly, 'Literature Review on World Shrimp Farming', 4.

73 Space constraints mean that this chapter can do no more than to hint at the outlines of what those alternatives might entail.

across a global market can be daunting. It is not clear how this approach can be adapted to production far removed from the final consumer.

Moreover, the relationship between these private commitments and public law remains murky. Are there legal consequences for violating voluntarily-adopted sustainability commitments? Will the very existence of these commitments stave off regulatory efforts, thereby ensuring that voluntary commitments do not harden into legal obligations? Even if these voluntary commitments are viewed as legally binding obligations, it does not necessarily follow that any consequences will follow a breach of these commitments. Coupled with the absence of a clear governance chain along the supply chain[74] from local producers to overseas buyers and consumers, this lack of consequences can create a temptation to cheat, particularly since the burdens of compliance typically fall most heavily on resource-poor workers engaged in the initial commodity production or extraction.[75]

It remains to be seen whether self-regulation and environmental safeguards through voluntary codes of practice can be an effective form of governance in the absence of binding legal obligations, or a state entity tasked with enforcing the rules. The possibility exists that "sustainable production" could dwindle into an advertising gimmick, producing little or no actual environmental or social change. That is always a risk with this kind of a solution – rather than challenging the production system itself, it merely tinkers at the margins to make the existing production process more palatable.

Moreover, the emergence of a wide range of private certification schemes and accreditation bodies can be a source of confusion among producers and consumers alike.[76] Instead of providing useful information, a proliferation of private certification schemes, each emphasizing different aspects of sustainability, can further muddy the water.[77] But,

[74] Louis Lebel, Phimphakan Lebel, Po Garden, Dao Huy Giap, Supaporn Khrutmuang and Sachiko Nakayama, 'Places, Chains, and Plates: Governing Transitions in the Shrimp Aquaculture Production–Consumption System', *Globalization*, 5 (2008), 211–26.

[75] See Food and Agriculture Organization of the United Nations (FAO), *Implications of International Standards and Certification Scheme for Aquaculture on Small-scale Producers* (Rome: FAO, 2008).

[76] FAO, *State of the Worlds Fisheries and Aquaculture* (Rome: FAO, 2010), 103.

[77] Brian O'Riordan, 'Certifying the Uncertifiable?', *Samudra Report*, 48 (2007), 30–4; Julie A. Caswell, 'Quality Assurance, Information Tracking and Consumer Labelling', *Marine Pollution Bulletin*, 53 (2006), 650–6; Shabbar Jaffry, Helen Pickering, Yaseen Ghulam, David Whitmarsh and Premachandra Wattage, 'Consumer Choices for Quality and Sustainability Labelled Seafood Products in the UK', *Food Policy*, 29 (2004), 215–28.

perhaps the most fundamental critique is that responding to the problem created by demands for implicit environmental subsidies ignores the systemic nature of the problem.

3.2 *Changing the market: upward harmonization of environmental management practices*

Many international organizations and industry groups claim that best management practices (BMPs) are the appropriate framework for promoting and supporting export-oriented extractive resource industries while resolving the environmental and social problems associated with them.[78] This approach emphasizes technical improvements, and good management. There is much to be said for this approach. Solving the pollution and habitat destruction problems associated with many such industries would certainly make a positive difference. One major advantage of creating and promoting industry-wide BMPs is that changes can be coordinated across the industry, and need not depend on any particular government's regulatory initiative. This is particularly important because there is often confusion over the legal and institutional position of extractive industries within domestic legal regimes, with overlapping or conflicting jurisdictions common.[79] This confusion is sometimes a major obstacle to effective legal oversight. These problems are then compounded by lax enforcement regimes. All in all, it is not a recipe for effective governmental oversight.

The main drawback of this approach is that by framing the challenges as technical ones, best management practices render the contributions made by the underlying trade regime invisible. Industry-generated standards typically focus on improving the technical aspects of production, without addressing these deeper structural concerns.[80] And, these initiatives rarely push for the *best* available technology. Instead, these initiatives typically embrace a lower common denominator of improvements viewed as "achievable."

[78] For example, the World Wildlife Fund has developed global sustainable aquaculture standards for a range of aquacultured species; see: www.worldwildlife.org/what/globalmarkets/aquaculture/dialogues-shrimp.html

[79] Many countries in which shrimp aquaculture takes place are still struggling with the rule of law more generally. Confusion over aquaculture's institutional status only makes that struggle more difficult.

[80] For an exploration of the relationship between the two sets of concerns, see generally, Bene, 'The Good, The Bad and the Ugly'.

Yet, even if these initiatives help make extractive industries less ecologically damaging, they do nothing to confront or resolve the ultimate issue – the splitting off of trade concerns into a body of law divorced from their inevitable environmental consequences. Without directly confronting the incentive system at the heart of global trade, moves toward sustainability will always be an afterthought – nice if you can do it, but an unaffordable luxury most of the time.

3.3 *Integrating international law: embracing sustainability*

Recognizing the definitional nature of the conflict created by dividing the world into "trade" and "environment" is ultimately the best way to respond to the tensions identified in this paper. Thus integrating the disparate strands of international law will be necessary to create a comprehensive solution to the root problem that environmental costs are excluded from economic calculations and are externalized on the wider society. By surfacing and accounting for these formerly excluded considerations, international law would force choices about conflicting values into the public arena for discussion and debate. Although the logistics would be daunting, fully integrating environmental and economic considerations is the only way to achieve true sustainability.

12

Quo vadis, Europe?

The significance of sustainable development as objective, principle and rule of EU law

BEATE SJÅFJELL

1 EU law and the international goal of sustainable development

What is the role of supranational law in making national law disciplines such as company law comply with and work towards objectives and principles of international treaties?

Sustainable development is an overarching societal goal which integrates the objectives of environmental protection, social justice and economic development. The essence is balance, and the goal is a preservation of our ecosystems as the very basis of our existence and the achievement of the best possible world for all of humanity. In *Our Common Future* sustainable development is famously defined as a development that 'meets the needs of the present without compromising the ability of the future generations to meet their own needs'.[1]

In international law and politics, there is a growing recognition of sustainable development as an all-important objective and a general principle of international law. Sustainable development has a strong legal position among the ultimate objectives of the European Union (EU), underpinned by the growing recognition in the EU of the inextricable entity of humanity, our natural environment and our economic system. In the search for the balancing that this goal requires within the non-negotiable limits of our planet, the principle of sustainable development is the key. This principle requires the integration of environmental

I am grateful to Cecilia Bailliet for encouraging me to write this piece, to Christina Voigt and Mads Andenæs for inspiring discussions, and to Rebecca Bratspies for insightful comments.

[1] World Commission on Environment and Development, *Our Common Future* (Oxford: Oxford University, Press, 1987), 43.

protection requirements in all areas, with the aim of achieving a sustainable development.[2] The threat of climate change and to global biodiversity accentuates the necessity of recognizing and respecting the ecological limits within which all social and economic development must take place. The principle of sustainable development is codified, following the changes made by the Lisbon Treaty, in an enhanced version of the rule now enacted in Article 11 of the Treaty on the Functioning of the European Union (TFEU).[3]

In practice, however, on national, supranational and international levels, actions speak louder than words. In practice the focus is on economic growth and efficiency in a narrow and short-term sense, leading to environmental degradation, loss of biodiversity and dangerous climate change. Although progress is made in some areas, the regulation of companies, these all-important components of our economies, is to a great extent shielded. Talk about voluntary corporate social responsibility seems to be the closest law-makers dare to get to regulating these entities, without which we cannot hope to achieve the overarching global goal of a sustainable development. Modern company law is often seen as matter of private law only, seeking efficient regulation of an instrument perceived to have as its only goal the profit-maximization of shareholders. The fundamental freedoms of EU law are seen by some as an argument in favour of such a narrowing of the scope of company law and for restricting the room for encompassing other interests.

EU law is, however, not just about free movement and market integration. On a Treaty level, the general objectives of the EU have a strong legal significance, and the codification of the principle of sustainable development entails an all-encompassing legal duty to integrate environmental protection requirements in the policies and activities of the Union. What does this entail for the EU institutions and for the Member States, and specifically for the regulation of companies – and what is the broader, global significance?

In a tentative answer to these questions, this paper first introduces sustainable development as an EU law objective, principle and rule (section 2).

2 As Rebecca Bratspies rightly concludes in Chapter 11, in this volume, fully integrating environmental and economic considerations is the only way to achieve true sustainability.

3 The Treaty on the functioning of the European Union, last amended by the Treaty of Lisbon, OJ 2008 C115 (consolidated version), formerly the EC Treaty, which it will be referred to as in historical contexts and otherwise abbreviated TFEU in accordance with the new reference style of the Lisbon Treaty.

The argument is presented that particularly the codification of the sustainable development principle in Article 11 TFEU has significant legal implications for the institutions of the European Union (section 3), entailing direct obligations on all levels: lawmaking, administration, supervision and judicial control (section 4). For EU company law, this requires a whole new approach. The implications for the Member States are rather more indirect, but nevertheless highly relevant, influencing the interpretation, implementation and application of EU law; the justification of Member State initiatives that restrict free movement; entailing a possible duty to act to promote overarching objectives under certain circumstances, and perhaps also indicating a coming general principle of sustainable development on Member State level (section 5). The chapter thereby shows how EU treaty law, taken seriously, may be used as a tool to ensure that EU law itself and the national laws of its Member States truly work towards a global, sustainable development. The paper concludes with some reflections on how EU law already may be influencing national law also beyond the scope of the direct requirements for EU law implementation in national legislation, and how this could impact on both national law and international law (section 6).

2 Sustainable development as an EU law objective, principle and rule

Sustainable development is an overarching, global societal goal, encompassing the search for a balance between economic development, social justice and environmental protection. Sustainable development has a strong legal position among the ultimate objectives of the EU,[4] underpinned by the growing recognition in the EU of the inextricable entity of humanity, our natural environment and our economic system.

The ultimate objectives of the EU are stated in the relevant provisions of the Treaties.[5] These are the objectives of EU law, based on the premise

[4] As of the Treaty of Lisbon amending the Treaty on European Union and the Treaty establishing the European Community, OJ 2007 C 306/01, in force 1 Dec. 2009, the European Union replaces and succeeds the European Community. This article will therefore only use 'Community' and related terms in a couple of historical contexts.

[5] Until 1 Dec. 2009 particularly Article 2 of the former EC Treaty, i.e. the Treaty establishing the European Community (1957), last amended (and name-changed to TFEU) by the Treaty of Lisbon, OJ 2008 C115 (consolidated version); as well as the former Art. 2 and Art. 6 of the Treaty on European Union (1992), last amended by the Treaty of Lisbon,

that the general point of EU law is to facilitate the achievement of the objectives of the EU.[6] Discussing the legislative objectives is important for several reasons. In EU law, with its teleological approach, objectives have a special status.[7] Analysing the objectives may tell us the direction that EU law is taking or, should the perception of the objectives have become unclear or out of focus, the analysis may highlight the objectives, indicating the direction that EU law should be taking.[8] The position of environmental protection and sustainable development as general objectives of EU law therefore is highly significant. The general objectives of EU law may be summed up as the ultimate goal of the good society, the achievement of which may be said to consist of five main elements: economic development; social development; environmental protection; the respect for human rights; and contributing to global development.[9] Much of these elements are encompassed by the overarching objective of sustainable development.[10]

In the search for the balancing that the goal of a sustainable development requires, within the non-negotiable ecological limits of our planet, the principle of sustainable development is the key. The codification of the principle of sustainable development in the environmental integration rule, now in Article 11 TFEU, has enhanced the position of sustainable development as an overarching objective and especially that of its environmental dimension.

The Lisbon Treaty has strengthened sustainable development as an overarching goal and expanded the scope of the environmental integration rule in Article 11 TFEU. The Lisbon Treaty emphasizes the position of sustainable development, in Europe and globally, as an overarching objective:

> The Union shall . . . work for the *sustainable development of Europe* based on balanced economic growth and price stability, a highly competitive

OJ 2008 C115 (consolidated version), hereafter referred to as the EU Treaty (abbreviated TEU in accordance with the new reference style of the Lisbon Treaty). See notably the new Art. 3 TEU (ex Art. 2 EU).

6 Ultimate, overarching and general objectives will be used as interchangeable terms throughout this chapter.

7 See B. Sjåfjell, *Towards a Sustainable European Company Law. A Normative Analysis of the Objectives of EU Law, with the Takeover Directive as a Test Case* (Alphen aan den Rijn: Kluwer Law International, 2009), pt. III.

8 Discussing the objectives also serves to shed light on the underlying values of the particular area of law.

9 See Sjåfjell, *Towards a Sustainable European Company Law*, sects. 10.2 and 10.3–10.8.

10 See particularly *ibid.*, sect. 10.7.

> social market economy, aiming at full employment and social progress, and a high level of protection and improvement of the quality of the environment.[11]

The global aspect is enhanced in an unprecedented manner on Treaty level, in the same article:

> In its relations with the wider world, the Union shall uphold and promote its values and interests and contribute to the protection of its citizens. *It shall contribute to peace, security, the sustainable development of the Earth, solidarity and mutual respect among peoples, free and fair trade, eradication of poverty and the protection of human rights*, in particular the rights of the child, as well as to the strict observance and the development of international law, including respect for the principles of the United Nations Charter.[12]

This is underlined further in the article dealing with the relationship between the Union and the international community, where the Union expresses its will to work to:

> foster the *sustainable economic, social and environmental development of developing countries*, with the primary aim of eradicating poverty;
>
> [. . .]
>
> help develop international measures to preserve and *improve the quality of the environment and the sustainable management of global natural resources*, in order to ensure *sustainable development*.[13]

The codification of the principle of sustainable development in the environmental integration rule has been strengthened through the removal of the reference to (then) Article 3 EC, making it applicable for absolutely all of the Union's activities, and giving us the following clear legal basis:

> Environmental protection requirements *must* be integrated into the definition and implementation of the Union policies and activities, in particular with a view to promoting sustainable development.[14]

The changes made through the Lisbon Treaty thereby bring to the forefront the important question of what Article 11 TFEU – taken seriously – actually entails. In dealing with the legal significance of

[11] Art. 3(3) TEU (emphasis added). [12] Art. 3(5) TEU (emphasis added).

[13] Art. 21(2)(d) and (f) TEU (emphasis added).

[14] (Emphasis added.) Art. 11 TFEU, ex Art. 6 EC, where the wording was the same except for the reference to (then) Art. 3 EC. See also Art. 37 of the EU Charter of Fundamental Rights.

sustainable development as an EU law objective, principle and rule, the main emphasis will accordingly be on Article 11 TFEU, as it encompasses all three levels: it is the rule that refers to and strengthens sustainable development as an objective and which at the same time codifies the principle of sustainable development, and particularly its operative environmental integration dimension.[15]

3 The legal duties deriving from the position of sustainable development in EU law

3.1 The concept of duty

Duty (or obligation)[16] may be understood in at least three different ways. The first and presumably strongest is the legal duty that is enforceable in a court of law. It appears untenable, however, to draw the conclusion that a legal obligation can only be found to exist where, and to the extent that, it is enforceable in a court of law. If we conclude that a certain obligation rests on the EU institutions, the Court of Justice of the European Union will be under the same obligation (or a similar one, as its precise nature will of course vary according to the institutions' tasks) as the other EU institutions. If the Court does not fulfil its duty, this may mean that it becomes de facto impossible to take enforcement action in respect of non-fulfilment by other EU institutions. Similarly, even if the Court fully understands and conscientiously fulfils its duty, there may be general rules or case-specific issues regarding procedure or competence that may prevent the Court from enforcing the duties of other EU institutions. However, neither of these situations should, in themselves, change the nature of the legal obligation's character. The second understanding of duty is therefore the legal duty that, for various reasons, may not be enforceable in a court of law. The third understanding is the ethical duty that comes within the framework of the law, covering both the situation where ethical arguments may act as support for an uncertain or fragile legal basis for stipulating a legal obligation, and the situation where ethical arguments provide a basis for deciding between legally acceptable alternatives.

[15] Sjåfjell, *Towards a Sustainable European Company Law*, sects. 10.5 and 10.7; and *inter alia* L. Krämer, 'The Genesis of EC Environmental Principles', in R. Macrory (ed.), *Principles of European Environmental Law* (Groningen: Europa Law Publishing, 2004), 29–47.

[16] These two terms are used interchangeably in this chapter.

I have previously concluded that the ultimate objectives and notably sustainable development as an EU law concept entails the following obligations for the EU institutions: first, a duty to stay within the framework of the general objectives; second, a duty to seek a balance between the general objectives (with sustainable development as the overarching goal); third, a general duty to act, and fourth a duty to undertake specific action under certain circumstances. This section briefly introduces these four levels of duty.

3.2 *EU's overarching objectives as a framework*

The system of the treaties as well as the case law of the Court of Justice shows that the general objectives function as a framework for EU law, and thereby for the institutions of the EU.[17] This is supported by the wording of notably Articles 1(1), 3(6) and 13(2) TEU,[18] which also embody the recognized principle that all legislative initiatives must have their legal basis in the Treaty.

Clearly we will not find a great variety of practical examples where an EU institution has gone beyond the competence derived from the objectives of the Treaty, as the scope of the objectives is very wide. This does not, however, alter the consequence of the general objectives, which is to establish the boundaries of EU law.

As the framework is very broad, I will not venture further into a discussion of the obligation to stay within the framework of the objectives in our context.

3.3 *The duty to seek a balance between the objectives*

The duty to seek a balance between the objectives is also supported by the wording of the Treaties.[19] Notably, Article 3 TEU does not set out one objective or indicate that a choice can be made from the list of major and minor objectives – and, promoting all of them means that a balance has to be sought.[20] It may further be argued that an obligation to balance

[17] See Sjåfjell, *Towards a Sustainable European Company Law*, sect. 10.1.3.3.

[18] Cp. ex Articles 3, 4 and 5 EC, and ex Art. 5 EU. See also P. J. G. Kapteyn and P. VerLoren van Themaat, *The Law of the European Union and the European Communities* (4th rev. edn., Alphen aan den Rijn: Kluwer Law International, 2008), 110.

[19] E.g. the consistency requirement set out in Art. 13(1) TEU.

[20] See also: M. P. Maduro, *We, the Court: The European Court of Justice and the European Economic Constitution* (Oxford: Hart, 1998), 150–1; E. Grabitz and M. Hilf, *Das Recht der Europäischen Union* (München: Verlag C. H. Beck, 1990– [loose-leaf]), Art. 2 EGV 8.

the various objectives is an intrinsic part of EU law, and at least it should be common ground that such balancing is intrinsic to EU law. EU law is constantly evolving, as demonstrated through case law of the Court of Justice, which has also stated expressly on a number of occasions that a balance must be sought.[21]

Sustainable development as an overarching objective of EU law strengthens the argument that there is a duty to seek a balance between the objectives. It is sufficient to acknowledge that sustainable development is a general objective, without discussing its status in relation to the other objectives.[22] Balance is the essence of sustainable development. Sustainable development as an overarching objective, strengthened by the express reference to it as the goal for the environmental integration required by Article 11 TFEU, also entails obligations in respect of how the balancing is to take place. First, the global natural environment's non-negotiable limits set the boundaries within which the balancing must take place.[23] Second, and in practice, this entails, with reference to the precautionary principle,[24] that environmental protection may have to be given the highest priority in a number of cases, also where it is not immediately obvious that the global natural environment's limits are being tested in the individual case.[25]

3.4 *The duty to actively work to achieve the overarching objectives*

The EU Treaties both as a system and in the specific wording of relevant provisions show that there is a general duty for the EU institutions to act to achieve the overarching objectives of the EU.[26] The case law of the Court of Justice also indicates that there is such a duty, with its repeated references to the legal basis for the general objectives.[27] The possibility of

21 Sjåfjell, *Towards a Sustainable European Company Law*, sect. 10.1.3.4.

22 For such a discussion, see *ibid.*, sect. 10.9.

23 See C. Voigt, *Sustainable Development as a Principle of International Law: Resolving Conflicts between Climate Measures and WTO Law* (Leiden and Boston, MA: Martinus Nijhoff, 2009), ss. 40–1.

24 E.g. J. Scott 'The Precautionary Principle before the European Courts', in Macrory (ed.), *Principles of European Environmental Law*, 51–72.

25 See Sjåfjell, *Towards a Sustainable European Company Law*, sect. 10.9.3.

26 See *inter alia* Art. 1(1) and Art. 3(6) TEU.

27 Then Art. 2 EC (now Art. 3 TEU); see Sjåfjell, *Towards a Sustainable European Company Law*, sect. 10.1.3.5. Support may be found in early academic works on Community law, see H. P. Ipsen, *Europäisches Gemeinschaftsrecht* (Tübingen: J. C. B. Mohr (Paul Siebeck), 1972), 558, as well as in more recent, see H. v. d. Groeben and J. Schwarze, *Kommentar*

bringing an action against an EU institution for the failure to act before the Court of Justice, which may order an institution to act,[28] supports the argument that there is a general duty for the EU institutions to work towards the achievement of the overarching objectives.

Such an obligation to act must obviously be understood within certain practical limits set by for example the financial resources that are available at any given point of time.

On a general level, the obligation can only be discussed in a rather abstract way. This probably contributes to explaining the lack of case law concerning this duty.[29] The obligation can only be discussed on a concrete level within the realm of specific sets of circumstances, and we will therefore move on to the fourth obligation.

3.5 *The duty to take specific action*

This is clearly the most controversial of the four obligations. Nevertheless, it presents itself as a logical and necessary consequence of the legal basis: in a specific set of circumstances, there will be a duty to carry out specific action to achieve the objectives. The specific set of circumstances I have focused on concern the role of companies in society's achievement of a sustainable development. For the regulation of companies, including company law, this requires taking a new and more holistic approach compared to the EU law focus of today. EU company law today is first and foremost a vehicle of market integration, through the removal of obstacles and barriers, the facilitation and enabling of companies and financial markets and the protection of shareholders, creditors and to a limited extent employees.[30] The argument for the holistic approach to company law in a sustainable development perspective may be summarized in three points: first, we are very far from achieving the goal of a sustainable development; second, we need the contribution of companies to have any hopes of achieving the goal; third, neither the voluntary contribution of companies nor the current legal framework regulating companies' environmental impact is sufficient. If we agree on

zum Vertrag über die Europäische Union und zur Gründung der Europäischen Gemeinschaft (6th edn., Baden-Baden: Nomos, 2003), 600–2, with further references; and Grabitz and Hilf, *Das Recht der Europäischen Union*, Art. 2, 2–3.

[28] Art. 265 and 266 TFEU.

[29] See Sjåfjell, *Towards a Sustainable European Company Law*, sect. 10.1.3.5.

[30] See *ibid.*, ch. 9.

those three points, I put forward that we have the basis for the following conclusion: treaty law requires EU institutions first to identify the necessary steps to integrate the objective of contributing to a sustainable development into the decision-making of companies and second, to execute such steps. In other words: a specific duty to act can under certain circumstances be deduced from the overarching objectives and the environmental integration rule.[31]

4 The legal implications for the main institutions of the EU

4.1 For the European Council

The European Council is an important political institution, an institutionalization of the former Summits,[32] which is to 'provide the Union with the necessary impetus for its development and shall define the general political directions and priorities thereof'.[33] The analysis of the legal implications concentrates on the main institutions of the EU[34] and those that, as opposed to the European Council, have the core legal decision-making powers.[35] Suffice it to say therefore that the legal obligations flowing from the overarching objectives and the environmental integration rule apply to the European Council as they do to the other institutions, i.e. within the realm of its competence. And although the European Council has been a driving force for the recognition of sustainable development as an overarching EU objective,[36] the Council can undoubtedly do more to ensure that the overarching objective of a sustainable development is not lost sight of in the day-to-day politics and practice of the EU.[37] The recent conclusions of the European

[31] See *ibid.*, pt. III. [32] See Art. 13(1) and Art. 15 TEU. [33] Art. 15(1) TEU.

[34] The Council, the Commission, the European Parliament and the Court of Justice of the European Union; the European Central Bank and the Court of Auditors (Art. 13(1) TEU), although important, cannot be dealt with here due to constraints of space.

[35] Although the Treaties give the European Council competence in exceptional cases – see Art. 48 TEU and e.g. Art. 48(2) and 82(3) TFEU – the European Council has no general legislative powers (Art. 15(1) TEU).

[36] As early as from the Presidency Conclusions of the European Council, Rhodes, 2–3 December 1988 (DOC/88/10).

[37] That the European Council had to amend its Lisbon Agenda may serve to illustrate its lack of proper focus: in 2001 the European Council stated that sustainable development is a 'fundamental objective under the Treaties', agreed on a strategy for sustainable development and expressly added an environmental dimension to the Lisbon agenda (Presidency Conclusions of the Gothenburg European Council, 15–16 June 2001 (SN 200/1/01 Rev 1), paras. 1 and 19–21).

Council, focusing on the Euro crisis and the new 'Europe 2020 strategy for jobs and growth', relegating mention of the climate crises to a brief mention under 'Other issues', are illustrative.[38]

4.2 *For the Union legislator: the Council, the Commission and the Parliament*

The three main institutions of the EU lawmaker must, as shown above, 'act within the limits of the powers conferred on it in the Treaties, and in conformity with the procedures, conditions and objectives set out in them'.[39] The overarching objectives are however so broad, that they only very rarely will hinder new initiatives from the EU.[40] The converse is of special interest for the environmental dimension of sustainable development: with reference to the environmental protection objective and the environmental integration rule the Court of Justice has found that the EU lawmaker also can adopt secondary law provisions within the area of criminal law, when necessary to ensure an effective environmental protection.[41] The Court has also established that the environmental integration rule has the following implication: environmental protection measures can be validly adopted under any legal basis of the Treaties, as long as the relevant requirements of that basis moreover are fulfilled.[42]

The EU lawmaker also has a duty to actively work to promote the objectives and a balance between them, and under certain circumstances a duty to undertake specific action. The Council has a policy-making and coordinating function in the EU law system, and is given legislative functions,[43] with the aim of advancing EU objectives.[44] The Council has

[38] Where sustainable is used only in the narrow, economic sense, Conclusions of the European Council of 16–17 December 2010 (available at: www.consilium.europa.eu/uedocs/cms_data/docs/pressdata/en/ec/118578.pdf, last visited 15 Jan. 2011).

[39] Art. 13(2) TEU; cp. ex Art. 5 EC. See also Art. 3(6) TEU.

[40] The division of labour in accordance with the principle of subsidiarity may on the other hand affect the competence of the EU institutions to put forward initiatives in certain areas (see Art. 5 TEU). This is not a topic for this chapter.

[41] See: C-176/03 *Commission* v. *Council* [2005] ECR I-7879; C-440/05 *Commission* v. *Council* [2007] ECR I-9097; and in more detail Sjåfjell, *Towards a Sustainable European Company Law*, 209–10.

[42] See: C-62/88 *Greece* v. *Council* (*Chernobyl I*) [1990] ECR I-1527; C-300/89 *Commission* v. *Council* (*Titanium Dioxide*) [1991] ECR I-2867; C-440/05 *Commission* v. *Council* [2007] ECR I-9097; Sjåfjell, *Towards a Sustainable European Company Law*, sect. 10.5.2.

[43] And also budgetary functions, both together with the Parliament.

[44] Art. 16(1) and 13(1)–(2) TEU.

a central position in the legislative process. The Commission normally has the right of proposal, though – the Council can only rarely adopt legislative measures without prior proposals from the Commission.[45] The Commission is thus, with the aim of promoting 'the general interest of the Union' and of ensuring 'the application of the Treaties', to participate in the EU lawmaking process.[46] The EU Parliament has through a remarkable development[47] been given an ever larger role in the EU lawmaking process.[48]

On all the various levels, the duty to seek a balance and promote a sustainable development is relevant. The duty applies to the chosen approach and the scope of the preparatory work in connection with new secondary legislation. To achieve a true integration of the environmental dimension of sustainable development in the secondary legislation, it will be especially important to integrate this right from the very first planning phase. That this is a part of the duty is clear from the wording of Article 11 TFEU: environmental protection requirements are to be integrated into the 'definition and implementation of' policies and initiatives. The environmental integration rule requires action in general for the lawmaking institutions to ensure the integration of environmental protection requirements in legislative processes that are initiated for other reasons. Especially for the Commission, which has direct competence to propose new legislative initiatives,[49] the rule also entails a duty to act specifically to promote a sustainable development – i.e. to take action where action otherwise would not have been taken (and not only to include environmental considerations in legislative initiatives planned for other reasons). The European Parliament is also subject to this rule, within its competence to request that the Commission 'submit any appropriate proposal

[45] See Art. 289 TFEU and the ordinary legislative procedure as set out in Art. 294 TFEU. Note also the Council's competence to 'request the Commission to undertake any studies the Council considers desirable for the attainment of the common objectives, and to submit to it any appropriate proposals' (Art. 241 TFEU).

[46] Art. 17(1) TEU, cp. ex 211 EC. The Commission of course also has a number of other duties (see further, section 5.1 below).

[47] See pre-Lisbon, Kapteyn and van Themaat, *Law of the European Union*, 207.

[48] Through the co-determination procedure in ex Art 251 EC, now the ordinary legislative procedure in Art. 294 TFEU, see also Art. 14(1) TEU. In addition the Parliament has a general competence to discuss any EU-relevant issue, adopt resolutions thereto and ask the Member States to act thereon.

[49] See the ordinary legislative procedure in Art. 294(1) TFEU.

on matters on which it considers that a Union act is required *for the purpose of implementing the Treaties*'.[50]

Although the legal bases set out a competence to act and not a duty to act expressly, the competence interpreted in light of the overarching objectives and particularly the environmental integration rule entails that the institutions must use their competence where necessary: the Parliament must therefore request that new proposals are submitted by the Commission where necessary to promote the overarching aim of a sustainable development, and the Commission must submit such proposals, whether or not it is requested to do so by the Parliament.

It follows logically, then, that the duty to act also will be a specific duty to undertake specific action in certain circumstances. As indicated above, this entails for the regulation of companies that the EU lawmaker must either initiate a process to integrate environmental protection requirements and the goal of contributing to a sustainable development in the legislative framework of European companies, or find an alternative way to achieve the same good. The status quo is not satisfactory – we are not on track to a sustainable development; the Intergovernmental Panel of Climate Change has made clear that *business as usual* is highly unsustainable[51] and continuing on the same track cannot then be in compliance with Article 11 TFEU and the obligation to promote a sustainable development.[52]

Obviously the environmental integration rule applies fully also for the institutions that play a role in the legislative process after a proposal has been put forward, that is the Council, the Parliament, the Commission and the Conciliation Committee, as the case may be.[53] This gives rise to the questions whether the environmental integration duty is procedural or substantive. When the Parliament is to decide whether to approve, reject or suggest amendments in the legislative proposal, a procedural requirement could entail that it was sufficient for the Parliament to check whether environmental concerns had been considered in the making of the proposal. The environmental integration rule's emphasis of the goal of sustainable development combined with the position of sustainable development as an overarching goal,[54] which the institutions

[50] Art. 225 TFEU (emphasis added), ex Art. 192(2).

[51] Core Writing Team, R. K. Pachauri and A. Reisinger (eds.), Climate Change 2007: Synthesis Report. Contribution of Working Groups I, II and III to the Fourth Assessment Report of the Intergovernmental Panel on Climate Change (Geneva: IPCC, 2008).

[52] Other examples may of course be found in other areas.

[53] Art. 294 TFEU.

[54] Art. 3 TEU.

have a duty to act to achieve, indicates a substantive duty to carry out the integration necessary to achieve a sustainable development. The non-negotiable ecological limits which must be respected if sustainable development is to be achieved, supports the argument.

Once a legislative measure is to be formulated, the environmental integration duty is directly relevant for the choice of rules and the formulation of the rules. Good impact assessment systems are necessary. The first external report of EU's Impact Assessment System[55] is not encouraging. The report indicates that it is a 'widespread problem' that impact assessment is carried out 'to justify a policy choice already made at the beginning of the process',[56] and that the quality is 'found to be varying and often unsatisfactory'.[57] Not implemented properly, the principle of sustainable development – instead of making environmental law less marginal – may serve to 'subsume environmental considerations' and 'perpetuate an approach' to economic activities that encourages environmental problems.[58]

Undoubtedly, the situation today is nowhere near a true integration in all sectors.[59] However, there are some positive indications, and generally an increasing focus on sustainable development issues.[60] Lack of true integration does not constitute an argument against the existence of these legal duties set out here, rather it show the necessity of spelling them out clearly and repeating the message until it gets through.

The ethical necessity of achieving sustainable development, instead of carrying on with the unsustainable 'business as usual', further supports the argument that the duties deduced from Art. 3 TEU and Art. 11 TFEU are substantive obligations, which must be followed up on in a different and more comprehensive way than they are today.

This entails that each institution, when carrying out its tasks according to the treaties, has an independent obligation to ensure that

[55] Introduced in 2003 as a follow-up on environmental integration to promote a sustainable development, 'Evaluation of the Commission's Impact Assessment System. Final Report – Executive Summary' (Report submitted to the Secretariat General of the European Commission, Apr. 2007), at: http://ec.europa.eu/governance/impact/key_docs/key_docs_en.htm; last accessed 2 March 2011, 2.

[56] *Ibid.*, 5. [57] *Ibid.*, 6.

[58] P. Sands, *Principles of International Environmental Law* (Cambridge: Cambridge University Press, 2003), 9.

[59] See: L. Krämer, *EC Environmental Law* (6th edn., London: Sweet & Maxwell, 2007), 396–400 and 402–10; N. Dhondt, *Integration of Environmental Protection into other EC Policies: Legal Theory and Practice* (Groningen: Europa Law, 2003), 479–80.

[60] *Ibid.*, and Sjåfjell, *Towards a Sustainable European Company Law*, 227–228.

the environmental integration duty is carried out and that sufficient action is taken to promote a sustainable development. Indubitably this is demanding. In some cases this will entail that the whole idea of a secondary legislative initiative needs to be reassessed.[61] Correctly implemented this integration could prevent more 'path-dependent' results, and maybe – for a while – lead to fewer legislative proposals and more discussions on a higher level, and thereby better preparatory work. Being forced to integrate environmental protection with the aim of achieving a sustainable development would by necessity lead to more comprehensive thinking and deeper analyses.

4.3 For the Court of Justice of the European Union

The Court of Justice is the guardian of EU law.[62] When the Court deals with Treaty infringement cases against a Member State, reviews the legality of legislative acts by the other EU institutions, handles actions against other EU institutions for infringement of the Treaty through passivity and gives preliminary rulings concerning the interpretation of the treaties and of secondary legislation,[63] the Court must itself comply with the environmental integration rule and ensure that the other EU institutions[64] do the same.

The Court has shown in its practice, employing a dynamic, contextual and teleological method, that it takes the objectives of the Treaties seriously. The overarching objectives have proven to form a framework for EU law and the Court has shown that the objectives require balance.[65] As regards environmental protection, the Court has been in the forefront and lifted environmental protection as such up as an EU law objective also before it was included in then Article 2 EC.[66] The environmental integration rule, now in Article 11 TFEU, has been emphasized and accorded significance in a number of cases before the Court, also before the rule was strengthened and moved to the elevated position in then Article 6 of the EC Treaty. The overarching objective of environmental protection and the environmental integration rule have

[61] See *ibid.*, pt. V. [62] Art. 19(1) TEU.

[63] Especially Articles 258–260, 262, 265 and 267 TFEU, see ex Articles 226, 230, 232 and 234 EC.

[64] And the Member States, as far as applicable (see below, section 5).

[65] See the overview of case law in Sjåfjell, *Towards a Sustainable European Company Law*, sect. 10.1.3.4.

[66] Now Art. 3 TEU.

formed an important part of the Court's reasoning in the cases where the Court expanded the framework of EU law (compared to many's perception of the limits, then, of Community law), by finding that the EU law-maker is competent to include requirements of criminal penalties in secondary legislation where necessary to achieve an effective environmental protection.[67] In its quest for a balance between the overarching objectives, the Court has shown a number of times that environmental protection may substantiate restrictions on free movement.[68]

The potential of the environmental integration rule is shown most clearly through the decisions that clarify that any legal basis in the Treaties also is a legal basis for environmental protection.[69]

The Court has also shown that it is willing to assess the issue of whether the other EU institutions have violated their general duty to promote the overarching objectives.[70]

The Court should to a greater extent and also *ex officio* focus on what the objective of sustainable development and the reference thereto in Article 11 TFEU entails with regard to a duty to integrate environmental protection in all EU law areas – also in areas where environmental concerns traditionally have not been even considered. *Concordia Bus* is one of the cases which does give hope for the future direction of the case law of the Court, as the Court here, in a traditionally economic area emphasized the objective of environmental protection with reference to the environmental integration rule, and indirectly initiated a revision of relevant secondary legislation.[71]

If a well-founded case against a legislative act, based on non-compliance with the environmental integration rule, is brought before the Court sufficiently early, the secondary legislation may – and shall, as a matter

[67] See: C-176/03 *Commission* v. *Council* [2005] ECR I-7879; C-440/05 *Commission* v. *Council* [2007] ECR I-9097; F. Jacobs, 'The Role of the European Court of Justice in the Protection of the Environment' *Journal of Environmental Law*, 18(2) (2006), 185–205.

[68] See briefly, below section 5.3.

[69] See: C-62/88 *Greece* v. *Council* (*Chernobyl I*) [1990] ECR I-1527; C-300/89 *Commission* v. *Council* (*Titanium Dioxide*) [1991] ECR I-2867; C-440/05 *Commission* v. *Council* [2007] ECR I-9097; Sjåfjell, *Towards a Sustainable European Company Law*, sect. 10.5.2.

[70] See Sjåfjell, *Towards a Sustainable European Company Law*, sect. 10.1.3.5.

[71] See: C-513/99 *Concordia Bus Finland* [2002] ECR I-7213, and the follow-up in Directive 2004/17/EC coordinating the procurement procedures of entities operating in the water, energy, transport and postal services sectors [2004] OJ 2004 L 134/1–113; Directive 2004/18/EC coordinating procedures for the award of public works contracts, public supply contracts and public service contracts [2004] OJ 2004 L 134/114–240.

of EU Treaty law – be declared void.[72] More specifically, this entails that secondary legislation may be declared void if – which would be the simplest variety – the environmental integration duty has not even been considered,[73] or – and more difficult, except in the obvious cases of violation – where the environmental integration duty has been considered, but where the environmental integration, as a matter of substance, has not been carried out properly.[74] The Takeover Directive provides an example of the EU legislation where the environmental dimension has not been considered, and which, to the extent that the directive has any effect at all, may be assumed to have a negative impact on the environmental protection dimension of the sustainable development goal.[75]

Where the Court cannot or will not declare the secondary legislation to be void (for example because the action is brought too late or the Court finds the integration effort too difficult to assess or within the legislative margin of appreciation), the integration rule and the duty to seek a balance between the relevant objectives are of significance as Treaty-based principles for the interpretation of the secondary legislation, and as guidelines for the discretion exercised by the EU institution or a Member State, as the case may be. This could also be envisioned in cases concerning the Takeover Directive.[76]

The EU institutions that have the competence to bring a case before the Court of Justice obviously have as a part of their mandate to ensure, in this manner, compliance with the environmental integration rule. This brings us to the next section.

4.4 *For the Commission as a supervisory organ*

The Commission has a number of tasks and a wide competence to 'promote the general interest of the Union'.[77] The environmental

[72] Art. 264 TFEU.

[73] As the case is with the Takeover Directive; see Sjåfjell, *Towards a Sustainable European Company Law*, sect. 18.3.2.

[74] Discussed also by: Krämer, *EC Environmental Law*, 22–3; Dhondt, *Integration of Environmental Protection*, 484–5; J. H. Jans, *European Environmental Law* (2nd rev. edn., Groningen: Europa Law, 2000), 21.

[75] See the analysis in Sjåfjell, *Towards a Sustainable European Company Law*, pt. V.

[76] See *ibid.*, sect. 18.3.2.

[77] In addition to the important legislative and control functions, the Commission is to 'execute the budget and manage programmes', have 'coordinating, executive and

integration rule is relevant for the Commission as a legislative body, as discussed above, and of course very much so in the Commission's control function, i.e. its task of overseeing the application of EU law, which it is to carry out to 'ensure the application of the Treaties, and of measures adopted by the institutions pursuant to them'.[78] The Commission is a key player, together with the Court of Justice,[79] in safeguarding the Treaties, ensuring their correct application and moving EU law forward, through its Treaty-given competence and because of its independence in relation to the Member States.[80]

In practice the Commission has often been the applicant bringing cases against Member States before the Court in the cases where the Court of Justice subsequently has ruled in favour of the Member States in determining that the objective of environmental protection, with reference to the environmental protection rule, has justified Member State restrictions of free movement. On the other hand, the Commission has also brought actions against Member States in a number of cases where Member States were in violation of their duty to protect the environment (concerning lack of proper implementation of secondary legislation aiming to protect the environment).[81]

In a proper search for a balance between the overarching objectives, the Commission's focus should to a higher extent be on the environmental dimension of the overarching objective of a sustainable development. As is the case with the Court,[82] the Commission also fails in the *ex officio* application of the environmental integration rule in non-environment cases, i.e. in policy areas where environmental interests traditionally are not considered, and where environmental protection and sustainable development as Treaty-based objectives and the environmental integration rule in Article 11 TFEU actually require integration. In this respect, the Commission fails in its duty to ensure the application of the Treaties.

management functions', represent the Union externally (with the exception especially of the common foreign and security policy), and 'initiate the Union's annual and multi-annual programming with a view to achieving interinstitutional agreements' (see now Art. 17(1) and (2) TEU). Pre-Lisbon, see Kapteyn and van Themaat, *Law of the European Union*, 193ff.

[78] Art. 17(1) TEU.

[79] That is, 'under the control of the Court of Justice of the European Union' (Art. 17(2) TEU).

[80] Art. 17(3) TEU.

[81] See Sjåfjell, *Towards a Sustainable European Company Law*, sect. 10.9.3.3.

[82] Section 4.2, above.

5 The indirect legal implications for the Member States of the EU

5.1 *The starting point*

The Court of Justice has declared that the objectives in then Art. 2 EC,[83] in themselves and seen in isolation, neither impose legal obligations on Member States nor confer rights on individuals.[84] Correspondingly, it is clear that Article 11 TFEU does not directly address the Member States. It should be just as clear however, that the obligations for the EU institutions indirectly may entail both duties and rights for the Member States. The scope of these duties and rights is the topic of this section.

The duty of loyalty and cooperation in Article 4(3) TEU[85] is an important part of the basis for the argument that the Member States have duties that flow from the overarching objectives and the principle-based rules of the Treaties, beyond those duties that follow directly and narrowly from the provisions of the Treaties and the secondary legislation. Already in the 1970s the Court of Justice found that the Member States had duties based on the predecessor of Article 4(3) TEU.[86] Article 4(3) TEU and its predecessors refer to the 'attainment of the Union's objectives' and similar phrases,[87] entailing that the obligations of the Member States have developed and will continue to develop in pace with the scope and the legal significance of the overarching objectives of the European Union, as set out in the Treaties.[88]

The obligations (and the rights) for the Member States apply on all levels and to all their institutions: the legislative bodies, administrative and supervisory authorities and courts, although it will vary from institution to institution which duty (or right) is the most relevant to discuss. A few practical examples will be addressed in the following.

83 Now Art. 3 TEU.

84 See: Case 126/86 *Zaera* [1987] ECR 3697, paras. 10 and 11; C-339/89 *Alsthom Atlantique* [1991] ECR I-107, paras. 8–9; Joined cases C-72/91 and C-73/91 *Firma Sloman Neptun Schiffahrts* [1993] ECR I-887 para. 28; C-293/03 *Gregorio My* v. *Office national des pensions* [2004] ECR I-12013, para. 29.

85 Ex Art. 10(2) EC, before that: Art. 5 EC.

86 Then Art. 5 EC, later: Art. 10(2) EC.

87 Art. 4(3) third paragraph.

88 See Kapteyn and van Themaat, *Law of the European Union*, 153.

5.2 In the interpretation, implementation and application of EU law

This topic may be discussed as an issue concerning implementation of secondary legislation, but it is also significant for the interpretation of the Member States' obligations flowing directly from the Treaties.

My point of departure is that secondary law must be interpreted in light of the Treaties, which are to be understood as a coherent system.[89] This may be seen as one of the most profoundly important constitutional principles of EU law, supported inter alia by (now) Article 4(3) TEU.[90] Research into the significance of the overarching objectives of EU law strengthens this argument.[91]

Member States accordingly have the right and the duty to follow the principle of sustainable development, as codified in the environmental integration rule, in their interpretation, implementation and application of EU law.[92]

Member States should be obligated to comply with the environmental integration rule also when the EU institutions have not expressly fulfilled their duty according to the rule. Each and every institution of the EU and each and every Member State are obligated to do what they can to 'assist each other in carrying out tasks which flow from the Treaties' and refrain from doing anything that may 'jeopardise the attainment of the Union's objectives'.[93] The principle of loyalty requires cooperation, but it also entails that one party's failure cannot be used to justify another party's failure. This has primarily been expressed concerning the relationship between the Member States, but arguably the same must apply between the Member States and the EU institutions. The Court of Justice has used the predecessors of Article 4(3) TEU as a basis to develop a number of constitutional principles and a finely knit web of obligations to act, to cooperate and to be loyal for both the Member States and the EU institutions.[94] Even though the duty of cooperation originally was interpreted in such a way to entail that a Member State has violated EU law if the Member State was under a sufficiently clear and precise

[89] See e.g. the Court's reasoning in *Albany International*, Case C-67/96 [1999] ECR I-5751, and see also Art. 13(1) TEU.

[90] See J. Temple Lang 'The Development by the Court of Justice of the Duties of Cooperation of National Authorities and Community Institutions under Article 10 EC', *Fordham International Law Journal*, 31 (2007–8), 1483–1532, at 1483.

[91] Sjåfjell, *Towards a Sustainable European Company Law.*

[92] See *ibid.*, sect. 18.3.2.

[93] Art. 4(3) TEU.

[94] See Temple Lang 'Development by the Court of Justice'.

obligation to do something and did nothing, this has developed into a more general obligation in pace with the Court of Justice's development of its understanding of (now) Article 4(3) TEU.[95] As is apparent from the wording of the provision itself, the loyalty is not owed to the EU institutions, but to the Treaties and the overarching objectives.

Accordingly, the Member States' institutions must as far as possible, and in all relevant areas, interpret national law in light of the objectives and the wording of secondary legislation, and in general, in a way that is in accordance with EU law requirements.[96] Further, the Treaties themselves require that the Member States' institutions must interpret and apply secondary law in light of the objectives and obligations flowing from the Treaties. This has often been expressed in cases concerning free movement and there is arguably no reason not to apply the same principles on other Treaty obligations meant to promote the same overarching objectives. The Member States therefore have both a duty to implement, interpret and apply EU law rules in light of the Treaty. More specifically, there is a legal foundation for the establishment of a right and a duty to act in accordance with the environmental integration rule as far as possible, within the framework of the treaties and of the secondary legislation.

For national legislators this means that the (other) general Treaty rules and the secondary legislation must be implemented in an as environmentally-friendly way as possible, aiming to promote sustainable development. All Member State institutions (on state and local level) must interpret national law (as far as relevant) in light of the rules flowing from the Treaties themselves. The Treaty rules themselves must be interpreted and understood in light of EU law's own general and constitutional principles, including the principle of sustainable development as codified in Article 11 TFEU – also where the EU institutions have failed to do so in a proper manner. This applies correspondingly to administrative authorities' implementation and application of the law (whether in the form of administrative regulations or administrative decisions) and national supervisory authorities' control in light of EU law rules.

The national courts are, as we know, all – within their areas of competence – EU law courts, with a right and a duty to apply all relevant

[95] K. Lenaerts and P. Van Nuffel, *Constitutional Law of the European Union*, ed. R. Bray (2nd edn., London: Sweet & Maxwell, 2005), 117; Temple Lang, 'Development by the Court of Justice'.

[96] Lenaerts and Van Nuffel, *Constitutional Law*, 119.

EU law rules in each case, regardless of whether these rules have been the subject of arguments presented by the parties in the case.[97] The legal position of the individual is beyond the scope of this paper. Suffice it to say that the environmental integration rule also is of significance in that respect, as the individual may present arguments based on the rule before the Courts.

5.3 *As a justification of restrictions of free movement*

Even before inclusion as such in the Treaties, the European Court of Justice elevated environmental protection from a position of neglect to one of the 'essential objectives' of the European Union.[98] Based on its case law and the position of environmental protection as an objective, the Court in 1988 declared environmental protection to be a mandatory requirement, i.e. an objective that may justify restrictions on free movement.[99]

An important and illustrative case is *PreussenElektra*,[100] a landmark case in its acceptance of discriminatory measures with reference to the environmental integration rule and its significance for priority objectives in accordance with international climate change obligations.

The Lisbon Treaty has not changed the terminology of the setting out of the objective concerning environmental protection, namely that of achieving 'a high level of protection and improvement of the quality of the environment'.[101] Nevertheless, through the enhanced position of sustainable development as a Treaty goal (and the further strengthening of the *principle* of sustainable development), environmental protection as a Treaty goal may be said to have an even stronger position after the amendments following the Lisbon Treaty.

The environmental integration rule, and its links to the overarching objective of the EU as well as to international climate change obligations, may thereby be seen as broadening the Member States' scope of action, compared to the perceived scope if the rule and its possibilities are not

[97] Reflecting the principle of Roman law: *Juva novit curia.* See also Temple Lang, 'Development by the Court of Justice', 1532 and 1507.

[98] Case 240/83 *ADBHU* [1985] ECR 531, para. 13. E.g. Jacobs, 'Role of the European Court of Justice'; Sjåfjell, *Towards a Sustainable European Company Law*, sect. 10.5.

[99] Case 302/86 *Commission* v. *Denmark* [1988] ECR 4607, paras. 8–9; also J. Scott, *EC Environmental Law* (London: Longman, 1998), 67–8; Jans *European Environmental Law*, 247–8 and 258–62; Krämer, *EC Environmental Law*, 105–6.

[100] C-379/98 *PreussenElektra* [2001] ECR I-2099.

[101] Art. 3(3) TEU.

properly considered. The basis for justification also indicates the direction in which the broader scope of action may be applied – it is the objective of the environmental dimension of sustainable development that provides a (perhaps) broader basis for justifying restrictions, and the Member State initiative must therefore contribute to that overarching objective.[102] Member States may on another basis, in national law, EU law or international law (or politically or even morally), be obligated to use this possibility.

This is of significance for the legislator, for the public administration and for the courts of the Member States, and emphasizes the importance of understanding EU law rules in their full context.

5.4 *A duty to act?*

5.4.1 When the EU institutions have violated Article 11 TFEU

What is the case when interpretation of secondary legislation in light of the Treaties, including the environmental integration rule, does not suffice – in other words, where it is not possible for the Member State to repair the lack of environmental integration by the EU legislator through interpretation? Ideally a Member State should then bring action for 'infringement of the Treaties' within the two-month deadline,[103] whereupon the Court of Justice may declare the secondary legislation to be void. Probably stipulating a duty in the strongest sense and on a general basis for Member States to do this would be too strict, as that would make the Member States responsible for their own infringement if they did not realize that the environmental integration rule had been violated before the two months had passed. However, it is arguably a duty, supported by ethical obligations, for a Member State that *is* aware of the violation of the environmental integration rule and its objective of a sustainable development to either bring the case before the Court or at least refuse to implement or apply the relevant secondary legislation or other rule of EU law. Certainly each Member State has a right to do so. That will lead to conflict – to infringement

[102] See B. Sjåfjell, 'Towards a Sustainable Development: Internalising Externalities in Norwegian Company Law', *International and Comparative Corporate Law Journal*, 8(1) (2011), 103–36.

[103] Art. 261 TFEU.

cases being brought before the Court of Justice – but in conflict lies the possibility for a change in a positive direction.

We may also ask whether the Member States are obligated to bring action against an EU institution that does not do enough to promote a sustainable development.[104] Again, certainly the Member States have a right to do so – and may be obligated to do so, based on other legal arguments.

5.4.2 A duty to promote sustainable development?

The discussion above gives rise to the general issue of whether the Member States have a duty to act – at the national level – to promote sustainable development through the integration of environmental protection requirements in all areas, if the EU institutions do not take sufficient action.[105]

The duties that the Court of Justice has established, with the predecessors of Article 4(3) TEU as a point of departure, are of direct interest in this discussion. There is case law going back to the 1980s that indicates that a Member State is obligated to take the initiative to achieve an EU law objective, also in areas where the entire policy area is within the competence of the EU law, when an EU institution fails to do what it should. In such cases, the Member State must act in cooperation with the EU institutions.[106] In the further line of cases the Court emphasized that the Member States have a duty of action in the form of conservation measures where this is in the common interest.[107] The foundation was first that the conservation of the fish stock in question was a clearly accepted EU law objective, and second, that there was 'clear scientific advice' indicating that the measures (stop fishing of a certain type of fish) should be adopted.[108]

This is directly relevant for the situation today where climate gas emissions may jeopardize the EU law objective of a sustainable

104 Art. 263 TFEU.

105 Whether in violation of the Treaties or due to the limits imposed by the principle of subsidiarity.

106 See: Case 13/83 *Parliament* v. *Council* [1985] ECR 1513; Temple Lang,'Development by the Court of Justice'.

107 Lenaerts and Van Nuffel, *Constitutional Law*, 120, with reference to Case 32/79 concerning marine conversation measures, quote from para. 15: 'In such a situation, it was for the Member States, as regards the maritime zones within their jurisdiction, to take the necessary conservation measures *in the common interest* and in accordance with both the substantive and the procedural rules arising from Community law' (emphasis added).

108 *Ibid.*

development. If there is 'clear scientific advice' that a certain measure must be adopted or stopped to achieve the objective – may we then conclude that the Member States individually have a duty to act, based on Articles 3 and 4(3) TEU and Article 11 TFEU? There is no clear-cut answer.

To stipulate a duty in accordance with Article 4(3) TEU, the context must be a strengthening of an already existing Treaty obligation. Article 4(3) TEU has not been perceived as providing a basis for establishing completely new duties where there is no Treaty-based (or secondary law-based) obligation to start with.[109] When the Court of Justice has declared that the general objectives of the EU do not in themselves give duties for the Member States,[110] it is difficult to argue that Article 4(3) gives sufficient basis to declare that the Member States individually must adopt measures to achieve the overarching objectives in accordance with Article 3 TEU. On the other hand, it follows directly from Article 4(3) EU that the Member States must refrain from doing anything that will jeopardize the achievement of the objectives of the EU. This gives rise to the question whether it nevertheless will be an infringement of the Treaties to adopt or allow new national measures that will dramatically increase climate gas emissions. Arguably, this is the case when we include in the equation the environmental integration rule in Article 11 TFEU as a link in the chain between the general objectives of Article 3 TEU and the obligation to act, to cooperate and to be loyal in Article 4(3) TEU. At the end of the day, and especially in terms of an enforceable obligation, the answer will depend on whether the necessary action to promote the objective (or refrain from jeopardizing the achievement of the objective) can be spelled out concretely enough for a court to feel comfortable in calling it an obligation. Going beyond that is moving on to the question of whether there is a coming general principle of sustainable development at the national level.

5.5 A (coming) general principle of sustainable development in the Member States?

A coming general principle of sustainable development at the national level would entail a duty for the Member States to contribute actively towards the objective of sustainable development, through environmental

[109] Temple Lang 'Development by the Court of Justice'. [110] See above section 5.1.

integration in all areas, within and beyond the scope of EU law. This is in part a question of the effect of general and constitutional principles of EU law beyond the scope of EU law as such and in part a question of the significance of other international and national sources. It is beyond the scope of this paper to develop this issue in full. Suffice it to say therefore, that such a (coming) general principle arguably may be found in several Member States. The Norwegian Constitution, for example, has its own, national and more reticent variant of Article 11 TFEU, which, together with the influence of EU law (through the EEA agreement) and national and international sources, provides arguments for such a principle.[111] The influence of EU law and of international law, directly and indirectly through EU law, together with constitutional principles in national law of the Member States, may form the basis for or lead to the development of a general principle of sustainable development on Member State level.

6 EU law as a way forward

Not everything that has been put forward as obligations flowing from Article 11 TFEU in this chapter, can be substantiated, directly or fully, with reference to case law from the Court of Justice (although some of the obligations can). Legal science will not contribute to developing the law, or can only with much difficulty do so, if our perspective is only to be retrospective. If we are to contribute to solving the challenges of today and of the future, we as legal scholars cannot primarily base ourselves on retrospective, static understanding of the law. It is our responsibility to look forward.

EU law methodology is teleological and dynamic. Although much is left to be desired still also on EU law level, it provides a greater opportunity for a way forward than does many a national legal system, through the EU law focus on the overarching objectives and the dynamic interpretation of the legal requirements flowing from them. Through the implementation of EU secondary law and the recognition of the significance of EU Treaty law, the supranational level of EU law may influence national legal method and thereby lead to greater awareness of the significance of overarching international and supranational goals. This may in turn influence the national methodologies of law, leading to a

[111] See notably Voigt, *Sustainable Development.*

greater significance being attached also at the national level to overarching objectives. Many Member States today have the protection of the environment and even the goal of a sustainable development included in their constitutions. Through the influence of EU law methodology, these objectives may be given greater weight. The constitutional objectives of environmental protection and sustainability may be interpreted in the light of the overarching objective of a sustainable development and a high level of environmental protection in the EU Treaties, while the Treaty objectives themselves may be seen as strengthened through the recognition of these objectives being common to the constitutions of many Member States.

Also, supranational legislation is probably a necessary tool to achieve the desired change towards sustainability. Ideas of coordinated action at the national level may be expected to an ever greater extent than EU law to be hampered by the tragedy of the commons. Conversely, the fear of regulatory competition may be dealt with only on a coordinated European level. Putting the interests of future generations and the really long-term perspective first is perhaps not only more easily achievable but also only possible on a coordinated European level.

The supranational level of EU law may on several levels function to make national law disciplines such as company law comply with and work towards the sustainable development objective and the principle of a sustainable development that flow from international treaties, provided that EU law follows up on the requirements within its own system. EU law then has the potential of taking the lead globally and turning the trend of short-term growth mania into a reflective, long-term sustainable development.

13

Conclusion: centrality and marginality in international law

HILARY CHARLESWORTH

The chapters in this book were the product of a meeting of international lawyers held in Oslo in August 2010. Cecilia Bailliet of the University of Oslo, the editor of this book, organised a group of scholars from all parts of the world to discuss the creation of international law in what she termed 'a time of flux': how, she asked, is international law developed in the context of economic crises, conflict, forced migration, international criminal networks and climate change? These are not uncommon concerns in international law, as the sense that we are in a peculiarly unstable era is endemic in our discipline.

What made the Oslo event unusual was the fact that only women were invited to participate. Although I have attended many workshops, seminars and conferences devoted to discussion of feminist approaches to international law, at which the participants were almost always women, I have never before been at a meeting with an apparently general international legal remit at which only women spoke. Cecilia told us that her goal was to create a network of women scholars as a counterweight to the male domination of international law at both national and international levels, in the academy, in tribunals and courts. She wanted to showcase the work that women were doing in international law to inspire women students and fledgling academics, to provide a springboard for research collaborations by women international lawyers, and to strengthen women's ability to influence the creation and the development of international law. Some participants said that they had initially been wary of such an event, and had only attended because there was no expectation that they would address standard feminist topics.

Is there anything, apart from the sex of the authors, that distinguishes the approaches presented in this collection? One common feature of the chapters is their concern with issues traditionally at the margins of the international law canon, in the sense of being topics that are not dealt with in any depth in classic reference works, such as the seven editions of Ian Brownlie's *Principles of Public International Law.*[1] This characteristic is emphasized in the subtitle of this volume, 'From the Margins'. Many of the contributors also identify themselves and their work as outside the mainstream of international law.

Perhaps the most obviously marginal focus in this book is the question of 'gender' in international law. The gender question can be understood in many different ways, and the book offers a valuable range of them. One sense of the term gender as used in international law scholarship is to draw attention to the absence of women in lawmaking institutions. This has been the focus of much of the international endorsement of 'gender mainstreaming' programs. What is striking is how difficult even this straightforward project has been at the international level. For example, of the fifteen permanent judges on the International Court of Justice in 2011, only two are women (Judge Joan Donoghue from the United States and Judge Xue Hanquin from China); and there are two women members of the thirty-four-member International Law Commission (ILC). These numbers have remained almost unaltered over the past decade, suggesting that the principle of equality of participation is meeting tougher and less visible barriers than imagined by its proponents.

Another way that the idea of gender is invoked in international law is to support the design of legal principles that respond to particular harms that women or girls suffer. Catharine MacKinnon's chapter in this book is a good example of this approach. Her study of the way that the concept of gender has shaped and, indeed, transformed, international criminal law celebrates the capacity of international law to effect change in women's lives. Similarly, although arguing for reform of judicial approaches, or even amendment of the Rome Statute, Christine Byron's account of the invisibility of the sexual abuse of girl soldiers and camp followers by their own forces in international law rests on a faith in law to achieve change through ensuring accountability.

Part I of this collection illustrates a pattern found in the gender and international law literature more generally, which is to focus on the situation of women in times of armed conflict. While this is a crucial area, it tends to overshadow less dramatic but more pervasive human

[1] The first edition was published in 1966 and the seventh in 2008 by Oxford University Press.

rights concerns, such as the high rates of illiteracy among women in many areas of the world and the worldwide issue of women's poverty.

Attention to gender can also mean observing the way that understandings of masculinity and femininity shape the discipline. As feminist theorists have pointed out, gender in this sense does not refer to the characteristics of particular men and women but is a set of social constructions, varying over time and place. Common features of these constructions are, first, that masculinity and femininity are defined as opposite to one other and, second, that what is deemed masculine is assigned a greater value than what is defined as feminine.[2] Masculinity and femininity in turn map onto regulatory concepts of public and private, with the former category appearing more susceptible to regulation. This form of gender analysis is more implicit than explicit in this collection.

The book presents close readings of two areas: aspects of feminist projects in international law and normative developments in environmental law, but there is no overt attempt to bridge the two fields through, for example, a feminist reading of environmental law, or an environmental account of feminist politics in international law. The juxtaposition of these apparently disparate subjects however allows some parallels to emerge. For example, Christine Byron's study of the legal regime relating to child soldiers suggests that sexual abuse of children by the army that they are attached to is currently treated as outside the bounds of international legal regulation; this issue is thus 'domesticated' or feminized and left to national jurisdiction. We can see a similar pattern in Rebecca Bratspies's examination of the multiple tensions in the regulation of international trade and environmental protection. She shows how trade regimes are systematically given priority over environmental concerns, despite evidence that free-trade policies reduce environmental protection. A gender analysis may suggest that the principle of free trade has been masculinized by the international legal system, boosted by its contrast with the feminized area of protection of the environment.

This book also engages with a number of modern international law debates. One is that of fragmentation of international law: the idea that its coherence and legitimacy are threatened by the development of many disparate branches of law. This concern is not new; indeed over fifty

[2] See Hilary Charlesworth and Christine Chinkin 'Sex, Gender and September 11', *American Journal of International Law*, 96 (2002), 600.

years ago Wilfred Jenks examined the issue of conflict in substantive law,[3] as well as the complexity of international institutions, arguing for better coordination between them.[4] The ILC launched a study of fragmentation in 2000 under the rubric 'The risks ensuing from the fragmentation of international law', with risks including jurisprudential conflict, the emergence of special regimes and forum shopping.[5] However, the ILC Study Group on Fragmentation of International Law quickly noted positive aspects of fragmentation, including that it was a demonstration of the discipline's vitality, a way to strengthen international law, to address new areas of activity, and to include new voices.[6] The ILC's final report resisted proposing rules of priority between different rule systems in international law on the basis that normative conflicts were part and parcel of international law and should be resolved, not through legal rules, but through the political ('legislative') preferences of international actors, particularly states.[7] The ILC Study noted, however, that legal techniques drawn mainly from treaty law could assist the political, ad hoc, resolution of normative conflicts.[8] It observed that:

> conflicts between specialized regimes may be overcome by law, even as the law may not go much further than require a willingness to listen to others, take their points of view into account and to find a reasoned resolution at the end. Yet this may simply express the very point for which international law has always exi[s]ted. The move from a world fragmented into sovereign States to a world fragmented into specialized 'regimes' may in fact not at all require a fundamental transformation of public international law – though it may call for imaginative uses of its traditional techniques.[9]

The Report of the Study Group warned about pursuing coherence above values such as justice: '[c]oherence is . . . a formal and abstract virtue. For a legal system that is regarded in some respects and unjust and unworkable, no added value is brought by the fact of its being coherently so.'[10]

[3] C. Wilfred Jenks, 'The Conflict of Law-making Treaties', *British Yearbook of International Law*, 30 (1953), 403.

[4] C. Wilfred Jenks, 'Co-ordination in International Organization: An Introductory Survey', *British Yearbook of International Law*, 29 (1951), 30.

[5] ILC Report of its 52nd session, GAOR, 55th session, Supp No. 10, A/55/10 (2000), 726–8 and 729 (5).

[6] A/CN.4/L.628 1 August 2002, para. 7. [7] *Ibid.*, para. 484.

[8] The ILC referred in particular to Articles 30, 31 and 41 of the Vienna Convention on the Law of Treaties, 1969, as techniques for resolving conflicts (*ibid.*, para. 493).

[9] *Ibid.*, para. 487. [10] A/CN.4/L.683 13 April 2006, para. 491.

This collection can be read as a dynamic conversation on this issue. For example Cecilia Bailliet's Introduction endorses harmonization of international law as a goal over that of fragmentation and presents the collection as of a 'post-fragmentation' era. So, too, Fionnuala Ní Aoláin's account of the fate of the United Nations Security Council Resolution 1325 and its progeny identifies fragmentation of norms relating to women as one of its chief weaknesses. She argues that:

> [f]ragmentation may precisely be in the interests of powerful states and even non-state actors because it enables them to maintain their domination of international systems or to move their claims to other fora when they are unable to get the results they desire in a particular legal arena.

Ní Aoláin's fears about the 'ferocious fragmentation' exhibited in the Security Council resolutions may be fuelled to some extent by the fact that the resolutions are forms of 'soft law', rather than 'hard' treaty obligations, although she suggests that her concern is about lawmaking in general. Bailliet's chapter on the international human rights system considers the fragmentation issue in detail through the lens of the debate over universality and specialization, and proposes a communitarian approach to human rights protection as a unifying conceptual framework. Other contributors, however, illustrate some of the benefits of fragmentation and suggest the energy and normative creativity that it can unleash. Thus Catharine MacKinnon reads the history of the influence of ideas of gender on the development of international criminal law as 'a striking trajectory of innovation on the international legal scene'. She interprets this as a distinct form of law being generated directly from the experiences of women. And Beate Sjåfjell's analyses of the way that the European Union's particular elaboration of the principle of sustainable development at the supranational level can propel national jurisdictions into policies of greater environmental protection to counter what she terms 'the trend of short-term growth mania'.

Another international legal debate in which this book makes a lucid series of interventions is that of the nature of international society. Cecilia Bailliet's Introduction situates the book as 'post-Westphalian' in the sense of moving beyond considering states as the primary actors in international law, and contributors provide rich accounts of the work of non-government groups and institutions in deploying and shaping international legal doctrine. These include organizations with a long history of international advocacy, such as Amnesty International (Karima Bennoune) as well as those with a specific local focus, such as the Norwegian-Pakistani women's group, PAKWOM (Anne Hellum). These accounts highlight the differences in the interests and politics of these institutions, each with a commitment to promoting women's rights. A fruitful endeavour in this context is what Sally Engle Merry has described as the 'vernacularization' of human rights.[11] As Hellum's study of PAKWOM's work illustrates, this involves translating international human rights standards into terms that resonate with local social and cultural systems, without losing the core of the standard. The process of vernacularization is a complex one and requires considerable sensitivity to the many power structures that affect women's lives.

The book's many case studies of NGOs in both the human rights and environmental areas also illustrate the complicated relationships non-state actors have with states, cooperative and fractured by turns. Hari Osofsky broadens the canvas of international society still further by drawing our attention to the way that classically domestic governmental entities – cities, states and provinces – have become significant international players. Through a case study of the negotiation of the Copenhagen Accord on climate change, she shows how these sub-state actors can be much more nimble and creative than states in reaching international agreement. This indicates the potential of engaging sub-state actors in issues beyond the environment.

A further staple of current international legal debate that weaves in and out of many chapters is that of the relationship between 'hard' and 'soft' law: what are the characteristics and benefits of each? These terms in themselves invite an analysis based on the gendered categories of masculinity and femininity, although this is not pursued in this collection. Sumudu Atapattu surveys the soft law literature, describing the gradations of softness. She is a defender of the category of soft law, seeing it as complementary to hard law, and often a precursor of legal developments in the environmental arena. This offers a contrast to Fionnuala Ní Aoláin's sobering account of the pitfalls of the soft law generated in the four UN Security Council resolutions dealing with women and conflict adopted over the last decade. She argues that women's lives are generally confined to the province of soft law. The uncertain fate of soft law in the context of sustainable production, described by Rebecca Bratspies, also suggests it can be a porous form of regulation. The value of soft law then may depend not on its quasi legal form but on the politics of its generation.

[11] Sally Engle Merry, *Human Rights and Gender Violence* (Chicago, IL: Chicago University Press 2006).

Should women scholars aim for the margins or the centre of a discipline? The margin is often understood as the place we want to leave behind as we head for the centre, the mainstream, where, it is assumed, all the action and power are. The contributions to this book, however, nicely complicate the idea of marginality in international law. First, they illustrate that the periphery can be an attractive vantage point, offering the sense of adventure, of originality, of solidarity with the (often vaguely defined) oppressed against those with power, and of virtue. Indeed, highlighting one's marginality, one's willingness to swim against the tide, is a useful technique in international law to bolster claims of academic precision.

Second, the chapters make clear that there are many possible margins to consider and that not all map onto the comfortable progressive consensus of left-leaning elites. A fine example of this is Karima Bennoune's exploration of the often troubled relationships between women's human rights NGOs and the mainstream of the human rights movement. She shows that the explanatory power of the category 'NGO' is limited: it tells us little about a group's politics or its location at the center or periphery of international society. Being a *non*-state actor does not mean that NGOs have different politics to those of states.

Third, the contributions to this book suggest the fluidity of the ideas of marginality and centrality and that there are locations at which they meet and even merge. Thus, analysis of the effect of the UN Security Council's adoption of Resolution 1325 in 2000 shows how a marginal international issue, women in armed conflict, was given an appearance of centrality through being debated in the UN Security Council. This carapace of importance and priority crumbled over the ensuing decade through lack of oversight and implementation. We can also observe that the idea of marginality is influenced by the idea of geographical space that international lawyers deploy to describe their spheres of influence – local, national, international and supranational. Edda Kristjánsdóttir illustrates this in her study of the regime for victims' reparations in the Rome Statute of the International Criminal Court (ICC). Reparations have a marginal and tenuous presence at the international level, but Kristjánsdóttir invokes the concept of 'positive complementarity', by which they could be moved to the centre of national judicial systems. Positive complementarity in this context means that the ICC would support national and local bodies to devise systems for reparations for victims of international crimes.

This collection unsettles some conventions of international law scholarship. It is a forum for women's writing and yet it avoids many of the topics typically associated with women's lives. This book provides a subtle and complex account of the value of the international sphere, offering a variety of approaches to an investment in law. International law has regularly been portrayed as a safety net for women, who often face discrimination in national legal systems. Catharine MacKinnon puts this point pithily in this volume when she notes that 'the further away from home that women go, the experience has been, the more rights they get . . . making it more likely that women's violations will be recognized as real'. Perhaps the most striking contrast is between MacKinnon's optimistic account of the development of gender norms in international criminal law and Fionnuala Ní Aoláin's doubts about the value of creating new principles promoting attention to gender.

The authors leave us with some intriguing questions that provide a research agenda for future explorations in international law. One was first articulated in the eighteenth century by French feminist Olympe de Gouges: are women's rights best protected through general norms and institutions or through specific norms and institutions applicable only to women?[12] Others include: how do sex and gender affect scholarship? Why is gender analysis in international law largely restricted to international criminal law? How can we broaden this focus to questions of illiteracy and poverty? How do concepts of masculinity and femininity shape international legal discourse? How could the concept of vernacularization work in areas other than human rights? Are the categories of hard and soft law useful? What actors are most likely to influence the generation of international law? Is international law a productive site for feminist politics? Could it be better, as the British criminologist Carol Smart once remarked, to be a feminist journalist than a feminist lawyer?

This book reminds us that it is important to understand international law as one thread in a tapestry of effective regulation. It can break if too much weight is placed on it alone and its strength depends on being woven with other types of controls.[13]

[12] Sari Kouvo, *Making Just Rights? Mainstreaming Women's Human Rights and a Gender Perspective* (Uppsala: Iustus, 2004), 104.

[13] John Braithwaite, 'Conclusion: Hope and Humility for Weavers with International Law', in Brett Bowden, Hilary Charlesworth and Jeremy Farrall (eds.), *The Role of International Law in Rebuilding Societies after Conflict* (Cambridge: Cambridge University Press, 2009), 270–88, 276.

INDEX

For EU product safety concerns, contact us at Calle de José Abascal, 56–1°, 28003 Madrid, Spain or eugpsr@cambridge.org.

www.ingramcontent.com/pod-product-compliance
Lightning Source LLC
LaVergne TN
LVHW011526200926
848484LV00001B/164

* 9 7 8 1 1 0 7 0 2 1 8 5 3 *